Integrative CBT for
Anxiety Disorders

Integrative CBT for Anxiety Disorders

An Evidence-Based Approach to Enhancing Cognitive Behavioural Therapy with Mindfulness and Hypnotherapy

Assen Alladin

WILEY Blackwell

KH

Library of Congress Cataloging-in-Publication Data

Alladin, Assen, author.
    Integrative CBT for anxiety disorders : an evidence-based approach to enhancing
Cognitive Behavioural Therapy with mindfulness and hypnotherapy / Assen Alladin.
      pages   cm
    Includes bibliographical references and index.
    ISBN 978-1-118-50992-0 (cloth) – ISBN 978-1-118-50979-1 (pbk.)
  1. Anxiety disorders–Treatment.   2. Cognitive therapy.   I. Title.
    RC531.A43 2016
    616.85'2206–dc23
                                                2015021084

A catalogue record for this book is available from the British Library.

Cover image: alenkadr/ iStock 177263382

Set in 10/12.5pt Galliard by SPi Global, Pondicherry, India
Printed and bound in Malaysia by Vivar Printing Sdn Bhd

1   2016

11/17/16

Contents

About the Author

Dr Assen Alladin is a clinical psychologist and adjunct associate professor in the Department of Psychiatry at the University of Calgary Medical School. He is a fellow of the Royal Society of Medicine, president-elect of the American Society of Clinical Hypnosis and Conference Coordinator and past president (two terms) of the Canadian Federation of Clinical Hypnosis – Alberta Society. He has been practicing and teaching hypnosis, cognitive behavioural therapy (CBT), psychotherapy and clinical psychology for over 30 years, and he is the 2005 recipient of the Best Research Paper from Division 30 of the American Psychological Association.

Dr Alladin has published over 35 chapters and papers on clinical hypnosis and has authored three books – *Handbook of Cognitive-Hypnotherapy for Depression: An Evidence-Based Approach* (2007), *Hypnotherapy Explained* (2008) and *Cognitive Hypnotherapy: An Integrated Approach to the Treatment of Emotional Disorders* (2008). He served as guest editor for special issues in hypnotherapy for the *Journal of Preventive Neurology and Psychiatry* (1992), the *Journal of Cognitive Psychotherapy: An International Quarterly* (1994), the *International Journal of Clinical and Experimental Hypnosis* (April 2007 and July 2007) and the *American Journal of Clinical Hypnosis* (2012). He is also on the Board of Editorial Consultants of the *American Journal of Clinical and Experimental Hypnosis*.

Dr Alladin is internationally recognized as an expert in the field of integrating CBT with hypnosis in the management of emotional disorders. He has presented over 200 papers and workshops nationally and internationally, and he is known to be an excellent and dynamic presenter. He comes from the island of Mauritius, and he completed all his studies in England. He was initially trained as a registered nurse and social worker before pursuing psychology and clinical psychology. Dr Alladin has two adult children, and he lives in Calgary, Alberta, Canada.

Foreword

Millions of people suffer from anxiety, and anxiety disorders are among the most prevalent problems for which individuals seek psychotherapy. Also, anxiety disorders are associated with other psychological disorders such as depression and stress-related symptoms. In *Integrative CBT for Anxiety Disorders: An Evidence-Based Approach to Enhancing Cognitive-Behavioural Therapy with Mindfulness and Hypnotherapy*, Dr Assen Alladin provides an integrative model and understanding of how to identify and provide the most effective therapies for treatment of anxiety disorders.

Every student and clinician who treats patients with anxiety problems will want to have this invaluable text. This book represents a tremendous resource for effectively conceptualizing anxiety disorders and learning effective treatment strategies that are well supported by research. Anxiety disorders can be highly complex with both conscious and unconscious dynamics. Dr Alladin provides an understanding of how cognitive behavioural therapy (CBT) can be enhanced by the skilful use of mindfulness and hypnotherapy techniques. In this regard, this book stands out as highly innovative and clinically useful.

This is a book for clinical practitioners who are on the front lines of treating clients with anxiety disorders. The book includes many clinical case examples and transcripts of actual therapy sessions. A multitude of clinical techniques for relief of anxiety symptoms and for exploration of underlying dynamics are presented. The concept of 'wounded self' is introduced as the theoretical foundation for the understanding of the etiology of anxiety disorders and for an integrative approach to treatment. The concept of self-wounds refers to the interaction between damaging life experiences and the self-defeating cognitive and emotional strategies that clients develop to cope with the associated anxiety. By highlighting *Self-Wounds Model of Anxiety Disorders,* the author explains that anxiety disorders often represent both an implicit (unconscious) fear as well as conscious anticipations. Throughout the book, he illustrates this model through clear case examples and psychotherapy research.

Drawing upon this integrative model, a step-by-step treatment protocol is provided as it relates to specific anxiety disorders. The treatment protocol covers the entire process from case conceptualization to treatment. The initial phase of this integrative approach is on competent clinical assessment, case conceptualization and establishment of a therapeutic relationship. The author illustrates how to use DSM-V diagnostic criteria to identify various anxiety disorders and in treatment planning. The second phase of the protocol is on management of symptoms. Here, the author provides clear guidance on use of relaxation and other cognitive-behavioural methods to reduce symptoms and gain a sense of control. In the third phase, the option of uncovering and healing self-wounds is introduced. In the fourth phase of the treatment protocol, methods are introduced for promoting psychophysiological coherence (PC), acceptance, gratitude and mindfulness.

Psychotherapists will find practical guidance for treatment as well as establishing a therapeutic alliance as the basis for a range of cognitive, behavioural and hypnotherapeutic strategies. The treatment model is both flexible and comprehensive. It emphasizes the integration of theory and empirically based interventions to achieve maximum flexibility and efficacy. The author is the developer of cognitive hypnotherapy (CH), and Chapter 2 describes the latest developments in CH for anxiety disorders at each phase of treatment.

This book is a tremendous resource for treatment of the most commonly encountered anxiety disorders. Treatment of specific phobias, social anxiety disorder (SAD), panic disorder (PD) and agoraphobia have been covered in the clinical chapters. A wealth of precise methods are provided in regard to effective treatment. The author succinctly reviews the relevant empirical research in support of each method. In addition, case examples are used to illustrate interventions. The reader will find a rich resource of transcripts for explaining and delivering interventions. For example, transcripts have been provided for hypnotic suggestions, addressing cognitive distortions, healing the wounded self and mindfulness practice, just to name a few.

Generalized anxiety disorder (GAD) is very well covered in this book. Chapter 7 is highly relevant as GAD is the most prevalent anxiety disorder seen in primary care. It is a disorder that can be chronic. It is not unusual for patients to have experienced anxiety symptoms for more than 10 years before seeking treatment. Medications can reduce symptoms, however, psychotherapy is usually required to identify unconscious issues and to develop coping skills. In this chapter, a wide variety of behavioural, cognitive, hypnotic, unconscious, and acceptance and mindfulness-based strategies have been presented. Methods such as self-monitoring, problem solving and expanding awareness have been covered. Transcripts are provided on techniques such as ego strengthening, learning self-hypnosis, mindfulness and exploring unconscious issues.

Separation anxiety and selective mutism (SM) are covered in the remaining clinical chapters. These are disorders that occur mostly in children but, if untreated, can persist in adolescence or even adulthood. The integrative treatment model provides a comprehensive approach including therapeutic confrontation of unconscious conflicts and emotions that may contribute to maintaining the symptoms. Case examples and transcripts for specific interventions are provided.

This book provides a groundbreaking theoretical model for understanding and treating anxiety disorders. The concept of the wounded self is illustrated throughout the book, and its relationship to the development of anxiety disorders is explained in a way that is clear and useful. Furthermore, it is an essential resource for the most effective psychotherapy methods in treatment of anxiety disorders.

Dr Assen Alladin is a clinician of exceptional talent and knowledge. In this book, he demonstrates the expertise that he has in integrating the best and most effective methods from a variety of theoretical orientations. In addition, he shares his profound knowledge of contemporary psychotherapy research and how it can be applied to effective clinical practice. Although he is the most prolific researcher in the area of CH, he is primarily a clinician, and this book will resonate with most clinicians. With the publication of this book, Dr Assen Alladin, has advanced our understanding of anxiety disorders and provided a model for truly integrative treatment that will serve as an extremely important and useful resource for clinicians for many years to come.

Gary Elkins, PhD, ABPP, ABPH

Professor, Department of Psychology and Neuroscience, Baylor University

Director, Mind-Body Medicine Research Laboratory, Baylor University, Waco, Texas

President, Society of Psychological Hypnosis

President-Elect, Society of Clinical and Experimental Hypnosis

Past-President, American Society of Clinical Hypnosis

Associate Editor, International Journal of Clinical and Experimental Hypnosis

Preface

This project is the product of over 30 years of clinical practice in both in- and outpatient settings. Over these years, there have been some major developments in the classification, understanding and treatment of anxiety disorders. The book incorporates some of these major developments into an integrated perspective on anxiety disorders, known as the Self-Wounds Model of Anxiety Disorders (SMAD). This model of anxiety disorders accesses the best theoretical constructs and the most effective treatment strategies derived from various extant etiological theories and treatment approaches. The focal point of this theoretical integration is Wolfe's (2005, 2006) concept of self-wounds or early unresolved emotional injuries. According to this conceptualization, anxiety represents an unconscious fear of unbearable insult to the wounded self, which is protected by maladaptive conscious strategies such as avoidance, cognitive distortions or emotional constriction. This perspective, which is described in Chapter 1, provides a theoretical basis for blending elements of behavioural, cognitive, psychodynamic, experiential and mindfulness perspectives in the understanding and psychological management of anxiety disorders.

Based on this integrative model, and in recognition of the fact that anxiety disorders do not form a homogeneous group, the book adopts a multi-component approach to treatment. A step-by-step treatment protocol for each anxiety disorder from DSM-V is described in detail in order to provide a practical guide to clinical practice. This book fills an important gap in the literature. It provides a common thread for binding the best extant theoretical constructs and the most effective treatment strategies for anxiety disorders into a comprehensive integrated model. To accomplish this purpose, a number of specific topics are sequentially presented in each chapter. Each chapter begins with a case description, the listing of the DSM-V criteria for each target anxiety disorder, an overview of the prevalence rate, a brief review of the causes and current treatments, followed by detailed description of the treatment protocol.

The treatment protocol itself is subdivided into four separate but over-lapping phases, including (i) assessment, case conceptualization and establishment of therapeutic alliance, (ii) management of symptoms, (iii) uncovering and healing of self-wounds and (iv) promotion of accept-ance, mindfulness, gratitude and PC. The treatment generally consists of 16 weekly sessions, which can be expanded or modified according to patients' clinical needs, areas of concern and severity of symptoms. An additional 10 sessions may be needed for patients who wish to explore and remedy tacit causes of their symptoms. As a rule, uncovering work, which is more dynamic and involves deep hypnotherapy, is introduced later in the therapy.

The first phase of the therapy consisting of assessment, case formulation and therapeutic alliance is not described in detail in each chapter as Chapter 2 covers it in great detail. The second phase of the therapy pri-marily focuses on symptomatic relief, and it comprises a variety of extant behavioural, cognitive and hypnotherapeutic strategies. However, based on research from third-wave cognitive-behavioural therapies, the goal is not on controlling the symptoms but learning to cope with them. Once a patient has overcome his or her symptoms, the therapist has to make a decision about the next stage of intervention. For those patients who have improved and believe that they have met their goals, the therapy is consid-ered complete and is duly terminated. For those patients who wish to explore the roots of their anxiety, they continue with the third phase of therapy, which involves uncovering and healing of tacit self-wounds. The symptom-management phase of the therapy, therefore, for some patients, serves as a preparatory phase for more complex therapy of exploring the roots of the anxiety disorder later in the therapy. Hypnosis and gestalt therapy provides an array of methods for uncovering and healing underly-ing cause of the anxiety disorder.

In the final phase of therapy, acceptance and mindfulness-based strate-gies are applied to anxiety disorders, with the main goal of helping patients learn to observe their symptoms without overly identifying with them or without reacting to them in ways that aggravate their distress. This phase also serves as an evidence-based approach for relapse prevention. Moreover, this phase introduces an innovative and practical approach, breathing with your heart, for integrating mind-body-heart in therapy, which facilitates cultivation of PC. Abundant research evidence suggests that heart-focused positive emotional state synchronizes the entire body system to promote healing, emotional stability and optimal performance.

In summary, each clinical chapter contains a variety of strategies derived from behavioural, cognitive, hypnotic, psychoanalytic and mindfulness strategies from which a clinician can choose the best set of techniques that suits his or her patient. The techniques are described in sufficient details to allow replication and adaptation. For these reasons, the techniques may be repetitive in each chapter. However, each technique is modified according to each target anxiety disorder. For example, the systematic desensitization procedure for agoraphobia and specific phobia may be similar, but the hierarchies and mode of presentation vary. This approach was selected to render each clinical chapter self-sufficient.

The term 'patient' and 'client' are used interchangeably in the book as the author has worked mostly with severe cases and in health settings, where the care-receiver is referred as 'patient'. The usage of the term 'patient' is not to undermine or label the individuals with anxiety disorders.

Assen Alladin
January 2015

Acknowledgements

I would like to thank my wife, Naseem Alladin, for her ongoing support and encouragement— without her help this project would not have been completed.

I would also like to thank all the individuals with anxiety disorders I have worked with. I have learned so much from them, and this book would not have been possible without their presence.

1

An Integrative Approach for Understanding and Treating Anxiety Disorders

Overview

This chapter reviews the concept of wounded self, which provides a common thread for binding the best extant theoretical constructs and the most effective treatment strategies for anxiety disorders into a comprehensive integrated model. The focus of this theoretical integration is the concept of self-wounds or early unresolved emotional injuries. This model offers an integrative perspective on the nature, development, aggravation and maintenance of anxiety disorders. According to this view, anxiety represents an unconscious fear of unbearable insult to the wounded self. This chapter describes SMAD and outlines the theoretical and empirical rationale for integrating CBT, mindfulness and hypnotherapy in the psychological management of anxiety disorders.

Introduction

Although anxiety disorders constitute the most common psychological disorders treated by mental health professionals and family physicians, a coherent etiological theory and a comprehensive integrated treatment for anxiety disorders are lacking. From his review of the literature, Wolfe (2005) found mainstream views of anxiety disorders to be flawed in respect to their conceptualization, etiological theories, treatment approaches, research hypotheses and research methodologies. He noticed that none of the current perspectives on anxiety disorders, including psychoanalytic,

Integrative CBT for Anxiety Disorders: An Evidence-Based Approach to Enhancing Cognitive Behavioural Therapy with Mindfulness and Hypnotherapy, First Edition. Assen Alladin.
© 2016 John Wiley & Sons, Ltd. Published 2016 by John Wiley & Sons, Ltd.

behavioural, cognitive-behavioural, experiential, and biomedical, provide a complete theory or a comprehensive treatment for anxiety disorders, albeit each viewpoint has made some important contribution to our understanding and treatment of the disorders. He also noted that none of the etiological theories upon which the current treatments are based on accentuated the role of interpersonal, family, cultural and ontological factors in the formation, onset and course of anxious symptoms. To rectify these shortcomings, Wolfe has developed an integrated perspective of anxiety disorders that accesses the best theoretical constructs, the most effective treatment strategies and specific evidence-based techniques from various existing etiological theories and treatment approaches. Before discussing the clinical implications of this integrated perspective of anxiety disorders, the main components of Wolfe's model are described and, where relevant, expanded on.

Self-Wounds Model of Anxiety Disorders

To differentiate from other models of anxiety disorders, the integrated perspective described in this book is referred to as the SMAD. The model consists of two interrelated theories: the integrative etiological theory of anxiety disorders and the integrative psychotherapy for anxiety disorders. Both theories represent a synthesis of major extant perspectives of anxiety disorders and their treatments (Wolfe, 2005, 2006). The focus of both the integrated etiological model and the unified treatment is the concept of self-wounds, which in the most general sense can be defined as the patients' chronic struggles with their subjective experiences. The components of SMAD are first discussed before describing the integrated psychotherapy based on the model.

Origin of self-wounds

Self-wounds result from interaction between damaging life experiences and cognitive and emotional strategies that are used to protect oneself from anticipatory catastrophes. Wolfe (2005, 2006) derived the notion of wounded self from his observation of patients with anxiety disorders. He noticed that in most of these patients, the anxious symptoms appeared to represent an implicit (unconscious) fear of unbearable catastrophe to their physical and psychological well-being (exposure of unbearable painful views of the self). Based on this observation, he

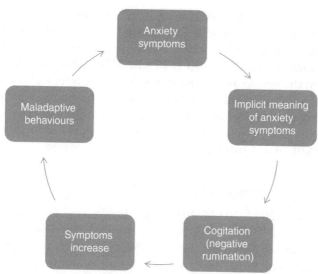

Figure 1.1 Schematic model of an anxiety disorder (adapted from Wolfe, 2005, p. 112).

hypothesized that the experience of severe anxiety in selected situations gives rise to conscious anticipations of impending calamity, which at an unconscious level, represents fear of exposing unbearable painful views of the self. In this sense, the etiological theory of anxiety disorders consists of two layers of information processing – the first layer comprises conscious awareness of anxiety symptoms resulting from anticipatory catastrophes and the second layer entails implicit or unconscious interpretations of what the anxiety symptoms mean to the patient (see Figure 1.1).

Anxious patients believe that exposure of their self-wounds, either to themselves or to others, will produce overwhelming affects, such as humiliation, rage, despair and loss of control, which they desperately want to avoid. These painful views of the self in turn create a feeling and experience that the patient will not be able to cope with the vicissitudes of life. This observation is supported by Kendall and Hollon (1989), who found patients with high levels of anxiety to have automatic thoughts about uncontrollability, threat or danger. Since the rigors and realities of everyday living are unavoidable, anxious individuals develop maladaptive coping strategies such as behavioural avoidance, rumination with cognitive distortions, preoccupation with symptoms and emotional constriction to protect themselves from facing objects and situations that are perceived to produce distressing affect. Unfortunately, these indirect manoeuvres often produce unintended interpersonal consequences (Alden & Taylor, 2004), which reinforce the patient's painful core beliefs about the self (Whisman & Beach, 2010). Moreover, these strategies keep the person away from facing his or her fears and self-wounds head-on, resulting in the perpetuation of the symptoms. Furthermore, in response to the initial anxiety, patients get into the habit of cogitating about being anxious and consequently become anxious for feeling anxious (Goldstein & Chambless, 1978).

Negative self-hypnosis in anxiety disorders

Alladin (1994, 2007, 2013a, 2014a) has depicted the similarities among the concepts of cognitive distortions, cogitation, rumination, worry and negative self-hypnosis (NSH). Although there are some subtle differences among these concepts, there are more similarities. For example, studies by Fresco, Frankel, Mennin, Turk and Heimberg (2002) and Segerstrom, Tsao, Alden and Craske (2000) found repetitive thought to be a common factor in measures of worry and rumination. Moreover, all the five constructs mentioned earlier are typically negative in valence, repetitive, perseverative, self-focused, overgeneralized, and they are all associated with cognitive inflexibility and difficulty in switching attention from negative stimuli. They also lead to performance deficits, difficulties in concentration and attention, poor problem solving, inadequate solution implementation and exacerbation of symptoms (Papageorgiou & Wells, 2004).

Cognitive distortions

Cognitive theorists have always asserted that preoccupation with cognitive distortions – related to threat, danger, loss of control and inability to cope – to be one of the key elements of cognitive theories of anxiety disorders (Beck, 1976, 2005). For example, Barlow (2002, p. 104) defined anxiety as 'a future-oriented emotion, characterized by perceptions of uncontrollability and unpredictability over potentially aversive events and a rapid shift in attention to the focus of potentially dangerous events or one's own affective response to these events'. Similarly, Clark and Beck (2010, p. 5), in their recent volume on anxiety disorders, stated that anxiety is a complex cognitive, affective, physiological and behavioural response system (i.e., threat mode) that is activated when anticipated events or circumstances are deemed to be highly aversive because they are perceived to be unpredictable, uncontrollable events that could potentially threaten the vital interests of an individual.

Cogitation

According to Wolfe, cogitation, or the preoccupation with symptoms, serves anxious patients one of the main defence strategies for protecting themselves from the 'excruciatingly painful view of the self' (p. 117). Rather than exploring the implicit meaning of their anxiety, anxious patients tend to detach from themselves and become absorbed in the imminent catastrophe they expect will occur. This form of catastrophizing is very characteristic of cognitive distortions described by CBT therapists (e.g., Beck, 1976, 2005), rational-emotive behaviour therapists (Ellis, 2005) and cognitive hypnotherapists (Alladin, 2014a).

Rumination

Rumination has also been equated with recurrent negative cognitive style of thinking (Martin & Tesser, 1989, 1996). Rumination can be defined as repetitive negative thinking (Hazlett-Stevens, Pruit, & Collins, 2009) associated with various psychopathologies, including anxiety, binge eating, binge drinking and self-harm (Nolen-Hoeksema et al., 2008; Papageorgiou & Siegle, 2003 for review). Nolen-Hoeksema (1991) has been instrumental in advancing our knowledge of ruminative thinking in depression. She proposed the response styles theory of depression to explain the insidious relationship between rumination and depression. According to her response styles theory, rumination is a mode of responding to distress that involves repetitively and passively focusing on symptoms of distress and on the possible causes and consequences of these symptoms. Rumination does not generate active problem-solving strategies for changing the circumstances surrounding the symptoms, instead it keeps patients fixated on the problems and their feelings. There is strong evidence that rumination exacerbates depression, enhances negative thinking, impairs problem solving, interferes with instrumental behaviour and erodes social support (Nolen-Hoeksema, 1991; Papageorgiou & Wells, 2004). The content of ruminative thought in depressed people is typically negative in valence, similar to the automatic thoughts, schema and negative cognitive styles that have been studied extensively by cognitive theorists (e.g., Beck, 1967, 2005). In addition to depression, there is evidence that rumination is associated with other psychopathologies, including anxiety, binge eating, binge drinking and self-harm (Nolen-Hoeksema et al., 2008).

Pathological worry

Given the high comorbidity between anxiety and depression, rumination is known to increase the risk for anxiety disorders as well as depression (Nolen-Hoeksema et al., 2008). Anxiety disorders, however, involve a different form of perseverative thought pattern from depression that is typically characterized by excessive or pathological worry (Borkovec, 1994; Papp, 2010). Based on empirical literature, Borkovec, Robinson, Pruzinsky and DePree (1983, p.10), define excessive worry as a chain of thoughts and images, negatively affect-laden and relatively uncontrollable. The worry process represents an attempt to engage in mental problem solving on an issue whose outcome is uncertain but contains the possibility of one or more negative outcomes. Consequently, worry relates closely to fear process.

The experimental study of worry began in the 1970s within the context of test anxiety, and by the early 1980s worry was delineated as a common cognitive process associated with states of anxiety (Hazlett-Stevens et al., 2009). This research found worry to be characterized by concerns about the future rather than the present and to be associated with feelings of anxiety, apprehension and general tension. Individuals with high levels of worry were also found to have more uncontrollable cognitive intrusions, poorer ability to focus attention on an experimental task and greater subjective anxiety than 'non-worriers'. In a recent study (Mennin, Heimberg, Turk, & Fresco, 2005), individuals with GAD were noted to have greater tendency to avoid negative experience related to stress, anxiety and emotional responding. Excessive or unrealistic worry is therefore regarded as the central defining feature of GAD (American Psychiatric Association, 2013) and is present in most of the anxiety disorders (Barlow, 2002). Rumination and worry have been found to be significantly correlated with each other (Fresco et al., 2002; Muris, Roelofs, Meesters, & Boomsma, 2004; Segerstrom et al., 2000; Watkins, 2004; Watkins, Moulds, & Mackintosh, 2005), and they share many characteristics (McLaughlin, Sibrava, Behar, & Borkovec, 2006). For example, they are both self-focused, repetitive, perseverative and overgeneralized forms of thinking (Barlow, 2002; Borkovec, Alcaine, & Behar, 2004; Segerstrom et al., 2000; Watkins, Teasdale, & Williams, 2000). Moreover, both are associated with cognitive inflexibility and difficulty in switching attention from negative stimuli (Davis & Nolen-Hoeksema, 2000; Hazlett-Stevens & Borkovec, 2001). These cognitive styles lead to performance deficits, difficulties with concentration and attention, poor problem solving and inadequate solution implementation (Davey, 1994; Lyubomirsky & Nolen-Hoeksema, 1995;

Lyubomirsky et al., 1999; Ward et al., 2003; Watkins & Baracaia, 2002; Watkins et al., 2005). Consequently, both rumination and worry have been found to exacerbate symptoms of anxiety and depression (Abbott & Rapee, 2004; Barlow, 2002; Fresco et al., 2002; Harrington & Blankenship, 2002; Kocovski et al., 2005; Muris et al., 2005; Nolen-Hoeksema, 2000; Nolen-Hoeksema & Morrow, 1991; Schwartz & Koenig, 1996).

Worry, in anxiety disorders, tends to be future-oriented and centres on dangers that might occur but have not yet occurred. Barlow (2002) indicated that even when patients with anxiety disorders worry about something that has happened in the past – such as making a mistake in a social situation – they often worry about the implications of this event for the future (e.g., 'Now everyone will think I am an idiot.'). Moreover, patients with GAD tend to have uncontrollable worry about minor topics more often than non-anxious individuals (Craske, Rapee, Jackel, & Barlow (1989). GAD is thus believed to be maintained by meta-cognitive beliefs about the functions and consequences of worry (Hazlett-Stevens, et al., 2009).

Negative self-hypnosis

There is convergent evidence that patients with anxiety disorders, compared to non-anxious patients, are highly susceptible to suggestions (e.g., to self- and hetero-hypnosis) and have greater capacity to dissociate (Bryant, Guthrie, & Moulds, 2001; Cardena, 2000; Heap & Aravind, 2002; Spiegel, Hunt, & Dondershine, 1988; Stutman, & Bliss, 1985). Clark and Beck (2010) and Taylor (2006) believe dissociative symptoms such as derealization, depersonalization and numbing may be automatic or deliberate cognitive strategies intended to avoid awareness of distressing recollection of the trauma or to suppress hyperarousal symptoms. Dissociative symptoms are also known to impede elaboration of the trauma memory and its integration with other autobiographical memories. Highly socially anxious patients have the tendency to ruminate more (Mellings & Alden, 2000). Abbott and Rapee (2004) found socially phobic patients to engage more in negative rumination. In addition to increasing the level of anxiety, negative ruminations reinforce cogitation or negative self-suggestions. The escalation of such a vicious cycle is readily observed in patients with panic attacks. Once a patient with PD begins to experience bodily sensations, he or she immediately begins to catastrophize about the sensations, and becomes convinced that he or she will lose control, faints, has a heart attack or lose control. Clark (1986, 1997), in his cognitive model of PD, also describes this phenomenon whereby patients with PD becomes stuck in cogitating about their bodily sensation. All these models emphasize that catastrophic rumination adds fuel to anxiety, until it spirals into a panic attack. Likewise, DSM-V (American Psychiatric Association, 2013) describes a panic attack as an abrupt surge of intense fear or intense discomfort that reaches its peak within minutes. DSM-V, however, distinguishes between unexpected and expected panic attacks. Unexpected panic attacks are referred to attacks that occur in the absence of an obvious cue or trigger. In contrast, expected panic attacks are triggered by an obvious cue or trigger, such as elevated heart rate in a patient who has the fear of having a heart attack and dying. This would imply that patients with expected PD have a greater tendency to cogitate with the meanings of their physical symptoms than patients with unexpected panic attacks. Empirical investigation of this hypothesis is likely to provide further information about the nature of these two types of PD proposed by DSM-V.

Another commonality between the phenomenon of hypnosis and Wolfe's perspective on anxiety disorders relates to the experiential nature of anxiety. Wolfe (2005) has clearly asserted that his approach to understanding anxiety disorders represents an experiential model as the syndrome is characterized by 'fear of a future catastrophe that will produce unbearably painful feelings about the self' (Wolfe, p. 51). From this vantage point, anxiety represents a future-oriented emotion that thwarts an individual from focusing on his or her present emotional experience of the world (emotional constriction). This experience of self-endangerment (i.e., the subjective experience of anxiety or panic) emanates from underlying intrapsychic conflicts, negative self-beliefs and a holistic sense of shame about one's value or lovability. All of these forms of self-pathology produce painful self-awareness. In patients with anxiety disorders, this painful and immediate self-awareness is often experienced as dangerous. This sense of danger, coupled with negative cogitation, gradually evolves into a chronic sense of self-endangerment.

Unconscious processing in anxiety disorders

Although behavioural and cognitive theories provide useful explanations of what happens to patients with anxiety disorders once they have had their initial anxiety attack (e.g., panic attack), they do not explain the origin of the initial attack. Moreover, cognitive-behavioural models tend to downplay the significance of implicit meaning of anxiety attacks. Now we have abundant empirical evidence that a great deal of human behaviour arises from unconscious processes (for reviews, Wilson, 2002; Dijksterhuis & Aarts, 2010; Baumeister, Masicampo, Vohs, 2011; van Gaal, de Lange, & Cohen, 2012). Unconscious mental processes have been shown to facilitate goal-directed behaviour (Bargh, Gollwitzer, Lee-Chai, Barndollar, Trotschel, 2001), memory consolidation (Tamminen, Payne, Stickgold, Wamsley, Gaskell, 2010), creativity and insight (Wagner, Gais, Haider, Verleger, & Born, 2004) and decision-making (Creswell, Bursley, & Satpute 2013; Dijksterhuis, Bos, Nordgren, & van Baaren, 2006; Dijksterhuis & Nordgren, 2006; Soon, Brass, Heinze, & Haynes, 2008; Strick, Dijksterhuis, Bos, Sjoerdsma, van Baaren, & Nordgren, 2011). Moreover, Creswell et al. (2013), from a study using blood oxygen level-dependent (BOLD) functional magnetic resonance imaging, found the dorsolateral prefrontal cortex and left intermediate visual cortex to be activated during unconscious thought processing. In the light of these findings, a number of cognitive-behavioural therapists have begun to recognize the existence of internal associative information processing. For example, Barlow (2000) and his colleagues (Bouton, Mineka, & Barlow, 2001) have highlighted the role of unconscious emotional conditioning and early conditioning in the eti-ology of PD. Similarly, Rapee (1991) has argued that conditioning is a subset of cognitive processes, involving implicit information processing. Moreover, cognitive theories undertake that human behaviour and experi-ence are determined by internal processes that are stored in memory in an organized fashion (Mahoney, 1991). These tacit structures are believed to have a powerful influence on how human beings feel, behave and expect to react in certain situations. From this perspective, anxiety is considered to represent the internalization of certain schemas regarding the potential dangerousness of certain situations and the threat they pose, relative to the person's cognitive abilities. The fear schemas are presumed to exert a mostly tacit influence on a patient's perspective towards himself or herself, the world and the future (Beck & Emery, 1985, 2005). Furthermore, the cognitive perspective argues that the functional relationships that are established between certain stimuli and the person's anxiety responses are, in large measure, shaped by tacit psychic structures. Clark and Beck (2010) emphasize that fear schemas 'also represent information about the self in terms of vulnerability to threat as well as specific beliefs about the dangerousness of certain experiences or situations in the external or internal environments' (p. 45). They declare that there is robust experi-mental research (e.g., McLeod, 1999; Wells & Matthews, 1994; Williams, Watts, MacLeod, & Matthews, 1997) in support of unconscious cognitive and attentional processing of fear stimuli, and as such 'the cognitive per-spective on anxiety is misrepresented when cognition is characterized only in terms of conscious appraisal' (p. 27). Foa and Kozak (1986) also emphasize that anxiety is based on either conscious or unconscious fear structures or schemas, which contain stimulus–response associations that do not always reflect an accurate relationships in the world. The recognition of unconscious danger-related schemas in anxiety disorders have encouraged some cognitive-behavioural therapists (e.g., Foa & Kozak, 1986; Leahy, 2003; Young, 1990) to develop new techniques for activating underlying cognitive schemas, predicated on the assumption that therapeutic change is contingent on restructuring of underlying cognitive schemas. This book describes a number of strategies for accessing and restructuring tacit cognitions. The effectiveness of psychodynamic psychotherapy with anxiety disorders provide indirect evidence that restructuring of implicit fear-related schemas reduce anxiety (Alladin, 2014a; Leichsenring, 2005; Milrod et al., 2007; Shedler, 2010).

The implicit processes described earlier are not very different from Freud's (1926/1959) psychodynamic models, which contended that anxiety disorders are developed from unconscious wishes, feelings and fantasies, which are experienced as frightening or intolerable affect (Busch, Milrod, & Shear, 2010). Freud delineated two types of anxiety: traumatic anxiety and signal anxiety. Traumatic anxiety is thought to result when the ego – the psychic apparatus that organizes perception, defences, cognition, anxiety and mood regulation – is overwhelmed by danger. The danger heralds specific psychological meaning to the patient, triggering traumatic anxiety, which may be manifested as an anxiety attack or a panic attack as described in DSM-V (American Psychiatric Association, 2013). Signal anxiety, on the other hand, represents smaller doses of anxiety generated by intrapsychic mechanism, which attempts to alert the ego state about psychologically meaningful dangers. In other words, signal anxiety acts as a stimulus to mobilize defences to prevent the breakthrough of traumatic anxiety from which the ego is overwhelmed and unable to defend itself. Studies of patients with spider phobia clearly demonstrate that these individuals harbour unconscious cognitions related to threat and disgust (Teachman & Woody, 2003). Recently, magnetic resonance imaging (fMRI) study has demonstrated that conversion symptoms are mediated by suppression of adverse life-events (Aybek, Timothy, Zelaya, O'Daly, Craig, David, & Kanaan, 2014).

How does different anxiety disorders develop?

From wounded self perspective, each anxiety disorder consists of two factors: an emotional conflict and the suppression of the re-experiencing of the trauma. While the emotional conflict is believed to be generated from early traumatic events, the inhibition of the re-experiencing of the trauma is determined by the nature of the trauma and the cognitive-emotional coping strategies used by the patient. Although perceived or imagined danger can be internal or external, different anxiety disorders are characterized by the diversity in the contents of threatening self-experience and the experiential processes used to stave off the danger. Although these strategies result in temporary reduction of anxiety, they reinforce the patient's underlying maladaptive self-beliefs. Psychological defences in this model thus serve as self-defeating efforts to protect one's image of the self (see Wolfe, 2005).

According to Wolfe (2005, 2006), external and internal cues that provoke anxiety are developed through one's perception of the relationships between certain life experiences and intense fear. In other words, certain life experiences are perceived as self-endangering. As mentioned before, the cues or events themselves do not provoke anxiety, it is the perceived relationship between certain life experiences and intense fear that creates the sense of self-endangerment. The cues or events often function as a kind of shorthand for unconscious painful memory. Wolfe (2006) provides the example of an agoraphobic woman whose fear of losing control (self-endangerment) is triggered by a feeling of light-headedness (internal cue), which reminds her of the intense fear she first experienced when she panicked at the sight of physically disabled people in a senior's home many years ago. In this case, the anxiety was not related directly to the internal cue (feeling dizzy), but it represented her unconscious fear of becoming physically disabled and confined to a senior's group home (intense fear).

Wolfe (2005) has described the sequential development of an anxiety disorder in the context of self-experiencing and its vicissitudes, which is summarized as follows:

1. The anxiety sequence usually originates from early traumatic experiences, which affects the individual's capacity for immediate self-experiencing. According to Wolfe, most anxiety-related traumas occur in interpersonal context and each trauma leaves the individual feeling helpless, trapped and incapable of warding off the subjective feeling of self-endangerment. Self-endangerment experiences range from a painful self-awareness to extreme trauma, and they seem to be associated with separation, rejection, loss, humiliation, disillusion or self-loss (dissipation of self-experience).

2. Any situation that resembles the trauma generates anxiety. The anxiety is perceived as a signal that something catastrophic is likely to occur.

3. Catastrophic interpretations deflect attention away from direct or immediate experience of the self or the world to reflexive experience of fear and vulnerability. Greenberg, Rice and Elliott (1993)

describe this process as a secondary emotional reaction to the primary experience of anxiety. Secondary emotional reaction shifts attention from immediate experiencing to thinking about one's immediate experience. This shifting of attention from experiencing to thinking increases catastrophizing of first-order anxiety and amplifies the intensity of the anxiety. Goldstein and Chambless (1978) describe this phenomenon as the fear-of-fear response (e.g., feeling anxious for feeling anxious, feeling angry for being fearful, etc.).

4. Another phase in the development of anxiety disorder is avoidance behaviour. Anxious patients often associate anxiety attacks with various contexts in which they have experienced anxiety, and, therefore, they tend to avoid these situations. Avoidance, unfortunately, increases the difficulty of re-entering the feared situation, thus maintaining the anxiety.

Lack of acceptance

In the context of mindfulness-based psychotherapy or third-wave cognitive behavioural therapy (CBT) (Baer & Huss, 2008), suppression of re-experiencing of the initial trauma observed in patients with anxiety disorders (Wolfe, 2005, 2006) can be equated with lack of acceptance. The concept of acceptance can be defined as receiving experience without judgement or preference but with curiosity and kindness (Germer, 2005). Acceptance is not merely tolerance, it is the active nonjudgemental embracing of an experience in the here and now, involving undefended exposure to thoughts, feelings and bodily sensations as they occur (Hayes, 2004). Acceptance is utilized in psychotherapy to reduce suffering by helping distressed individuals observe different aspects of a situation, or the relationship between the situation and the discomfort, or by creating a new stimulus that is less distracting or not distressing at all. This is well illustrated by the case of Ted, reported in a previous publications (Alladin, 2007, 2014), who transformed his suffering into creativity. Ted, a child psychologist, was involved in a road accident (hit by a drunken driver while he was biking) from which he sustained a complicated fracture in his left foot. Initially, he was very angry with the driver and constantly ruminated with the beliefs that he might not be able to ride his bike again or play soccer, which exacerbated his pain, anxiety and sense of hopelessness. But once he accepted the accident and the trauma (including surgery) he went through, he felt grateful that he was off work for 4 months, which he decided to devote to complete a paper he was planning to write for a few years. At times, Ted still had thoughts about the drunken driver and the pain he was experiencing, but the pain or the accident was no longer the focal point for his energy and attention. This case provides an example of pure acceptance. His goal *per se* was not to change his distress but to utilize the time away from work to his advantage. Shifting Ted's attention to his writing might not have altered his experience of discomfort and displeasure, but he felt more content and productive, rather than being demoralized.

Acceptance can also be used in psychotherapy to increase decentring and there is empirical evidence that acceptance-based interventions reduce experiential avoidance and facilitate behaviour change (Levitt, Brown, Orsillo, & Barlow, 2004).

Summary

This chapter described in detail the SMAD. It discussed the theoretical and empirical rationales for integrating such concepts as cognitive distortions, rumination, hypnosis, mindfulness, biological vulnerability and unconscious information processing in the etiological understanding of anxiety disorders. The concept of the wounded self provides a common thread for binding these elements together into a comprehensive integrated model of anxiety disorders. This model offers an integrative perspective on the nature, development, aggravation and maintenance of anxiety disorders. Chapter 2 discusses the clinical implication of this model and describes comprehensive treatment strategies based on the model.

2

Integrated Therapy for Anxiety Disorders

Overview

This chapter describes components of an integrated psychological approach for treating anxiety, based on SMAD. Due to its comprehensiveness, this approach is deemed to provide more accuracy, efficacy and sophistication in the formulation and treatment of anxiety disorders. The treatment strategies described in this book are driven largely by two principles: disorder-specific treatment and the understanding of the development and perseverance of the anxiety disorders. A growing body of research and publications had confirmed the clinical utility of using disorder-specific models of psychological treatments for anxiety disorders (Butler, Fennell, & Hackman, 2008). Additionally, experimental investigations of hypothesized underlying processes have delineated a number of factors that influence the development and maintenance of anxiety (Butler et al., 2008; Dudley, Kuyken, & Padesky, 2011). Moreover, Dudley et al. (2011) have emphasized incorporation of client's strengths and resilience in therapy to achieve lasting improvement in symptoms. Integration of these factors in therapy has substantially increased the effect sizes in treatment trials in the past 20 years (Clark, 2004).

Integrated Therapy

SMAD discussed in Chapter 1 underpins the rationale for synthesizing elements of behavioural, cognitive, hypnotic, psychodynamic and mindfulness-based therapies in the psychological management of anxiety

Integrative CBT for Anxiety Disorders: An Evidence-Based Approach to Enhancing Cognitive Behavioural Therapy with Mindfulness and Hypnotherapy, First Edition. Assen Alladin.
© 2016 John Wiley & Sons, Ltd. Published 2016 by John Wiley & Sons, Ltd.

disorders. This integrated therapy approach to anxiety disorders stresses both intermediary and ultimate treatment goals. The core intermediary goal focuses on reducing or eliminating anxiety symptoms, while the main thrust of the ultimate goal is to heal self-wounds. Attainment of intermediary goal in some patients serves as a necessary prelude to the ultimate goal of healing self-wounds, which are hypothesized to generate the anxiety symptoms. In view of the overarching similarities between NSH and cogitation with symptoms, self-wounds and fear-inducing stimuli in anxiety disorders, Alladin (2013b, 2014b) has incorporated hypnotherapy into Wolfe's integrative psychotherapy for anxiety disorders. He argues that such a combination could be very beneficial as hypnotherapy offers a variety of strategies for accessing and restructuring unconscious experience (e.g., Ewin & Eimer, 2006; Hunter & Eimer, 2012), thus providing a powerful set of techniques for eliciting and healing the wounded self. Moreover, as Wolfe's conceptualization of anxiety disorders embodies an experiential model of psychotherapy (Wolfe, 2005, pp. 51–55), hypnotherapy, by virtue of being an experiential form of therapy, serves as a suitable (necessary in some patients) adjunct to psychotherapy of anxiety disorders (Alladin, 2006, 2013a, 2014a; Daitch, 2007, 2011). Hypnotherapy, however, is not a unitary therapy based on a single theory. It consists of a diverse set of strategies and techniques blended with the therapist's preferred model of psychotherapy (e.g., CBT or psychodynamic psychotherapy). CH, which combines hypnotherapy with CBT, is selected for assimilation with Wolfe's psychotherapy as its procedures are clearly delineated and evidence-based (Alladin, 2007, 2008, 2012, 2014a; Alladin & Alishia, 2007; Alladin & Amundson, 2011). With exception of the hypnotherapy component, Wolfe's (2005, 2006) integrated psychotherapy for anxiety disorders encompasses similar therapeutic elements that embodies CH (e.g., relaxation training, exposure to fearful stimuli, cognitive restructuring, guided imagery training and emotional processing).

CH itself represents an integrated form of therapy. Clinical trials (Alladin & Alibhai, 2007; Bryant, Moulds, Gutherie, & Nixon, 2005; Dobbin, Maxwell, & Elton, 2009; Schoenberger, Kirsch, Gearan, Montgomery, & Pastyrnak, 1997), meta-analyses (Kirsch, Montgomery, & Sapirstein, 1995; Shih, Yang, & Koo, 2009) and detailed reviews (Moore & Tasso, 2008; Schoenberger, 2000) have all substantiated the additive (increase in effect size) value of combining hypnotic procedures with CBT with various emotional disorders. CH is found to be particularly effective with chronic pain (Elkins, Johnson, & Fisher, 2012), acute stress disorder (Bryant et al., 2005), anxiety disorders (Alladin, 2014a; Golden, 2012; Schoenberger et al., 1997), depression (Alladin & Alibhai, 2007; Dobbin et al., 2009;

Moore & Tasso, 2008) and bulimia (Barabasz, 2012). CH also meets criteria for assimilative model of integrative psychotherapy (Alladin, 2008, 2012; Alladin & Amundson, 2011), which is considered to be the most recent model of psychotherapy integration, drawing from both theoretical integration and technical eclecticism (Gold & Stricker, 2006). In this mode of psychotherapy integration, the therapist maintains a central theoretical position but incorporates or assimilates techniques from other schools of psychotherapy. Within CH framework, therapy proceeds according to standard CBT guidelines, but methods from hypnotherapy are used when called for, which indirectly advance certain CBT goals (e.g., accessing and restructuring core beliefs) as well as address the target concern effectively (e.g., reduction of anxiety level). Lampropoulos (2001) and Messer (Lazarus & Messer, 1991; Messer, 1989, 1992) claim that when techniques from different theories are incorporated into one's preferred theoretical orientation, both the host theory and the imported technique interact with each other to produce a new assimilative model. Assimilative integration thus represents the best model for integrating both theory and empirical findings to achieve maximum flexibility and effectiveness under a guiding theoretical framework. When CH was first described, it primarily integrated CBT with hypnotherapy (e.g., Alladin, 1994), but recently it has incorporated 'third-wave' therapies (e.g., acceptance, mindfulness) (Alladin, 2006, 2007, 2014a). CH for each of DSM-V anxiety disorders described in this book combines CBT with hypnotherapy and acceptance and mindfulness strategies, and it represents the latest version of CH. To avoid invention of another name for this particular integrative therapy, it is simply referred as CH.

Cognitive Hypnotherapy for Anxiety Disorders

CH for anxiety disorders consists of four separate but interrelated phases (Alladin, 2014a; Wolfe & Sigl, 1998), including (i) assessment, case conceptualization, and establishment of therapeutic alliance, (ii) management of symptoms, (iii) uncovering and healing of self-wounds and (iv) promotion of acceptance, mindfulness and gratitude. CH for anxiety disorders generally consists of 16 weekly sessions, which can be expanded or modified according to patient's clinical needs, areas of concern and severity of symptoms. An additional 10 sessions may be needed for patients who wish to explore and restructure tacit causes of their symptoms. As a rule, uncovering work, which is regarded an advanced treatment procedure in CH, is introduced later in therapy. The four phases of CH are described in detail next.

Phase I: Assessment, case conceptualization and therapeutic alliance

Clinical assessment and case formulation

Before initiating CH, it is important for therapist to take a detailed clinical history to formulate the diagnosis and identify the essential psychological, physiological and social aspects of the patient's anxieties and other difficulties. An efficient way to obtain this information within the context of CH is to take a case formulation approach as described by Alladin (2007, 2008). A case formulation approach allows clinician to tailor a nomothetic (general) treatment protocol derived from randomized clinical trials to the needs of individual (idiographic) patient. In this framework, clinical work becomes systematic and hypothesis-driven, rather than driven by a dogmatic protocol or the whims of the therapist.

CH case conceptualization underlines the role of cognitive distortions, negative self-instructions, irrational automatic thoughts and beliefs, schemas and negative ruminations or NSH in the understanding of patient's anxiety disorder. Evidence suggests that matching of treatment to particular patient characteristics increases outcome (Beutler, Clarkin, & Bongar, 2000). By formulating a case, the clinician develops a working hypothesis on how the patient's problems can be understood in terms of NSH (cogitation), cognitive-behavioural theories, wounded self and lack of acceptance of personal distress. This comprehensive integration of the unique experience of the individual patient with a psychological theory is described as a central process in effective therapy (Dudley et al., 2011).

Persons (1989) has hypothesized that psychological disorders occur at two levels: overt difficulties and underlying psychological mechanisms. Overt difficulties are signs and symptoms presented by patient that can be described in terms of beliefs, behaviours and emotions. But the manifestation and intensity of cognitive, behavioural or emotional symptoms are largely determined by underlying biological and/or psychological dysfunctions. Chapter 1 reviewed in detail the role of underlying self-wounds that in some patients trigger overt symptoms of anxiety. As the focus of this book is on psychological treatment of anxiety disorders, the underlying psychological mechanism of each disorder will be examined in details. This is not meant to imply that biological factors are not important. They can be as important as psychological factors and hence the book adopts a diathesis–stress model of anxiety disorders. Whenever relevant the psychobiological mechanisms of anxiety disorders will be examined.

To identify the factors that underlie patient's problem, the eight-step case formulation derived from the work of Persons et al. (2001), Ledley, Marx and Heimberg, 2005) and Alladin (2007, 2008) can be used.

Table 2.1   Eight-step cognitive hypnotherapy case formulation

---

1. List the major symptoms and problems in functioning
2. Formulate a formal diagnosis
3. Formulate a working hypothesis
4. Identify the precipitants and activating situations
5. Explore the origin of negative self-schemas
6. Summarize the working hypothesis
7. Outline treatment plan
8. Identify strengths and assets and predict obstacles to treatment

---

The eight components are summarized in Table 2.1, and Appendix A provides a generic template for CH case formulation and treatment plan. This template can be utilized with any specific psychobiological disorder the therapist plans to treat with CH. Appendix B represents a completed example of CH case formulation and treatment plan for Mandy, who had a phobia about using the public washroom. Chapter 4 describes some of the CH strategies that were utilized with Mandy.

CH for anxiety disorders generally consists of 16 weekly sessions, which can be extended or shortened according to patient's clinical needs, areas of concern and severity of presenting symptoms. An additional 10 sessions may be needed for patients wishing to explore and restructure tacit causes of their symptoms. CH takes a parsimonious (Alladin, 2008, 2013a) approach to treatment, that is, CH favours simplest techniques initially. More complex strategies are introduced as the needs arise, or when requested by the patient (e.g., to get at the root cause of anxiety). As a rule, uncovering work, which is considered to be an advanced treatment procedure in CH, is utilized later in therapy. This opinion is shared by other experienced therapists. For example, Frederick (2005), within the context of ego state therapy (EST) for depression, recommends using advanced technique such as EST only after patient had some exposure to CBT, as depressed patients often manifest a variety of cognitive distortions. She believes without some prior experience with CBT, the ego states may not engage in effective cognitive restructuring. Similarly, Wolfe (2005, 2006; Wolfe & Sigl, 1998) has underlined that the first goal of treatment for anxiety disorders should be targeted at overt symptoms. Once patients feel that they have acquired some control over their symptoms, they are asked if they would like to proceed with the next phase of treatment, which targets exploring unconscious issues that might be maintaining their anxiety symptoms. It is at the patient's discretion that the next phase of therapy is determined. The uncovering work often produces substantial network of ideas, images and feelings that might be connected to specific self-wounds, which can be very distressing to patients. Without some preparatory work, it may be difficult for patient to deal with uncovered information and affect. This can be illustrated by the case of Mandy, a 28-year-old woman whose progress with CBT and exposure therapy was stymied (see Chapter 4). Uncovering work revealed a connection between her panic attacks and the fear of drowning in the toilet bowl. When she was four years old, she used a dimly lit washroom at an old camping site, which contained a huge toilet bowl without a lid. She panicked at the sight of the big toilet bowl because she became very fearful that she would fall in the bowl and drown. The panic attacks served as a bridge to the initial panic attack she had in the old washroom. Once this connection was established and the initial fearful experience was worked through (i.e., reframed via psycho-education and CBT), exposure therapy became more tolerable and consequently successful.

As CH targets both intermediary and ultimate treatment goals, at least in some patients, the therapy goes beyond standard CBT strategies. For example, when addressing ultimate treatment goals, in addition to focusing on the relationship between events and cognitive distortions, the following psychodynamic processes (Gabbard & Bennett, 2006) are explored in therapy:

- Careful evaluation of the stressor that triggered the anxiety.
- Assessment of whether the stressor produced a feeling of embarrassment, shame, humiliation or loss of control.
- Assessment of whether the stressor reawakened self-wounds.
- Identification of what meaning did the patient attributed to the stressor.

Although there are many standardized instruments (e.g., Di Nardo, Barlow, Cerny, Vermilyea, Vermilyea, Himadi, & Waddell, 1985) for assessing anxiety disorders, the clinical interview remains the primary means of assessment. The clinical interview not only produces a clear description of symptoms, but also offers some clues regarding the underlying determinants of an anxiety disorder. The major diagnostic tool for uncovering implicit meaning of anxiety symptoms is Wolfe's Focusing Technique (WFT). As WFT does not utilize hypnosis, affect bridge is used in CH, as this hypnotic method (described in detail in subsequent chapters) has some similarities with WFT. Like affect bridge, WFT involves a strict attentional focus on anxiety-inducing cue. For different anxiety disorders, however, the focus of attention varies. For example, in patients with PD, the attentional focus is on fearful bodily sensations. In GAD patients, the focus of attention is the disturbing worrying thoughts, while in specific phobia, the image of the feared object or situation represents the focal attention. This approach of delineating specific symptom cluster associated with a given anxiety disorder, and the formulation of the presumed underlying self-wounds, provides a comprehensive description of a patient's anxiety disorder.

Establishment of therapeutic alliance

This component of CH is not a discrete element; it forms part of the ongoing treatment. Therapeutic alliance is vitally important in psychotherapy (Norcross, 2002) as all effective psychotherapy is predicated on the establishment of a safe, secure and solid therapeutic alliance (Wolfe, 2005). Some clinicians, on the other hand, have argued that therapeutic alliance is 'necessary but insufficient' for change (e.g., Beck, Rush, Shaw, & Emery, 1979). Nevertheless, a patient who feels disrespected or uncomfortable with his or her therapist is more likely to discontinue therapy, while a patient with strong therapeutic alliance may persevere with the difficult work of change. As the life histories of patients with anxiety disorders are often replete with experiences of betrayal, empathic failures, insecure attachments and mistreatment (Wolfe, 2005), they may have some trust issues, which may impede therapeutic alliance (Alladin, 2014a). The negotiation of trust thus becomes the first undertaking of psychotherapy for healing the wounded self. By providing a trusting, empathic, genuine, nonjudgemental and collaborative relationship (Castonguay & Beutler, 2006), therapist fosters hope and positive expectations for change in patients (Dobson & Dobson, 2009). The provision of courage from the therapist gives the patient the confidence to begin to face anxiety-provoking situations and learn to endure automatically occurring anxiety. Moreover, the therapist can provide encouragement by reinforcing any small change that the patient produces and by reminding that their efforts will pay off in the long run. Once trust is established, hypnotherapy can be used to consolidate it experientially. The hypnotic experience is known to break (Lynn, Kirsch, & Rhue, 1996) or utilize resistance (Erickson & Rossi, 1979), promote strong therapeutic alliance (Brown & Fromm, 1986) and facilitate rapid transference (Brown & Fromm, 1986).

Phase II: Management of symptoms

The primary focus of this phase of therapy is to help patients with anxiety disorders achieve some measure of control over their symptoms and enhance their sense of self-efficacy. By achieving some control over their anxiety symptoms, patients start to feel more confident and hopeful about overcoming their fears and solving their basic life difficulties. To achieve these goals in CH, hypnotic and cognitive-behavioural strategies are predominantly used.

Hypnotherapy for symptom management

In CH for anxiety disorders, four to six sessions of hypnotherapy are specifically targeted at symptoms management. The hypnotherapy components include (i) relaxation training, (ii) demonstration of the power of mind over the body, (iii) ego strengthening, (iv) expansion of awareness, (v) modulation and regulation of symptoms, (vi) self-hypnosis and (vii) post-hypnotic suggestions (PHS). Hypnotherapy may be reintroduced again later in therapy with patients who elect to pursue with uncovering work. The initial sessions of hypnotherapy, therefore, for some patients, serve as a preparatory phase for more complex therapy of exploring the roots of the anxiety disorder later in the therapy.

Relaxation training

One of the major reasons for combining hypnosis with CBT in the management of anxiety disorders is to cultivate the relaxation response. The relaxation response can be defined as a set of integrated physiological mechanisms and 'adjustments' that are elicited when an individual engages in a repetitive mental or physical activity and passively ignores distracting thoughts (Esch, Fricchione, & Stefano, 2003). Patients with anxiety disorders experience high levels of tension, nervousness and hyperaroused physiological reactions (e.g., Beck & Emery, 1985, 2005; Clark & Beck, 2010). For these reasons, anxious patients derive considerable clinical benefit from learning and practicing relaxation techniques (e.g., Stahl & Moore, 2013). Bourne (2000), in his well-known book, *The Anxiety & Phobia Workbook* (third edition) states:

> The capacity to relax is at the very foundation of any program undertaken to overcome anxiety, phobias, or panic attacks. Many of the other skills described in this book, such as desensitization, visualization, and changing negative self-talk, build on the capacity to achieve deep relaxation.
>
> (p. 73)

Some cognitive-behaviour therapists, on the other hand, have questioned the wisdom and effectiveness of using relaxation therapy in the treatment of anxiety disorders. For example, White and Barlow (2002) argued that any behaviour that minimizes panic symptoms or provides escape or distraction from the symptoms can be considered maladaptive. They believe relaxation training undermines exposure, which is tantamount to teaching anxious patients avoidance as a coping strategy. Clark and Beck (2010) also indicated that relaxation therapy may be contraindicated with anxiety disorders because

> in many respects relaxation training is also incompatible with the objectives of CT for anxiety. Empirical hypothesis testing of faulty appraisals and beliefs depends on exposure to anxiety situations in order to gather disconfirming information. If relaxation was invoked whenever a person felt anxious, then that person would forfeit an opportunity to learn that the anxious concerns were unfounded. In this way relaxation as an anxiety management response would undermine the effectiveness of cognitive therapy.
>
> (p. 258)

Butler et al. (2008) even went on to say that relaxation might be harmful to patients with anxiety disorder. They argued that when anxious patients let go of their tension, it might 'brings distressing feelings with it and leads to increases in tension and anxiety' (p. 141). Clark and Beck (2010) have therefore recommended that relaxation therapy, as an adjunctive intervention, should only be used when 'an individual's anxiety level was so extreme that the client refused to engage in any exposure or refused to tolerate even the slightest amount of anxiety' (p. 259). In such cases, they suggested, relaxation training could be used to lower the anxiety level so that the individual could engage in exposure or other behavioural techniques to modify the faulty beliefs and catastrophic appraisals of the threat.

Even though relaxation training is considered contradictory to the theoretical framework of CBT, there is no evidence that relaxation causes more anxiety or encourages avoidance behaviour in patients with anxiety disorder. There are exceptional circumstances where relaxation response may generate adverse effects, but these effects are not the same (e.g., escape, distraction) as the ones eschewed by the cognitive theorists. It is well documented in the literature that relaxation training could produce relaxation-induced anxiety (RIA) or relaxation-induced panic (RIP) in some patients with anxiety disorder. RIA refers to the gradual increase in behavioural, physiological and psychological components of anxiety during relaxation training (Edinger & Jacobsen, 1982; Heide & Borkovec, 1983). RIP can occur when there is a rapid development of severe anxiety during relaxation training (Adier, Craske, & Barlow, 1987). Given that 'relaxation' is such a broad and general concept, both of these phenomena described are procedurally induced rather than relaxation-induced (Bernstein, Carlson, & Schmidt, 2007). Several mechanisms have been proposed to account for the development of RIA and RIP, including fear of losing control (Bernstein & Borkovec, 1973; Carrington, 1977), fear of relaxation sensations (Borkovec, 1987), interoceptive conditioning (Adier et al., 1987) and low concentration of carbon dioxide in the blood (Ley, 1988). From their review of the adverse effects of relaxation training, Bernstein et al. (2007) conclude that, in general, 'relaxation training does not appear to have significant and frequent adverse effects, but clinicians should be wary of any potential side effects and ready to address them' (p. 102). From this discussion, it is apparent that RIA and RIP do not represent the same caveats (e.g., relaxation interferes with cognitive restructuring) expressed by cognitive-behaviour therapists.

The second concern expressed by cognitive-behavioural therapists that lack of active exposure to fearful thoughts and symptoms maintains anxiety, may also be unfounded, at least within the sphere of third-wave psychotherapies. Third-wave psychotherapists (e.g., Hayes, 2004; Hayes, Luoma, Bond, Masuda, & Lillis, 2006; Linehan, 1993a, 1993b) have recognized the limitation of mind theories (which is discussed more fully later in this chapter) and have thus incorporated the process of mindfulness in their models of psychotherapy and psychopathology. Contemporary third-wave therapies such as acceptance and commitment therapy (ACT; Hayes, Strosahl, & Wilson, 1999), CH (Alladin, 2007), dialectical behaviour therapy (DBT; Linehan, 1993a) and mentalization therapy (psychodynamic therapy that helps patients recognize what is going on in their own heads and what might be going on in other people's heads) (Fonagy, Gergely, Jurist, & Target, 2002) thus encourage patients to decentre from cognitive distortions rather than analysing or disputing with them. Although all these therapies differ in their underlying theoretical rationales, they all share a common goal; contrary to CBT, they all 'teach patients to view their own cognitions as simply mental events and processes, to which they need not attend and on which they need not act' (Butler et al., 2008, p. 72). In other words, all these strategies are designed to facilitate an acceptance-oriented stance rather than a controlled-oriented stance. The popularity of these approaches has increased exponentially in recent years as data supporting their use in psychiatry and medicine continues to emerge. Alladin (2014a) has provided a detailed account of the rationale for incorporating mindfulness with Western psychotherapies, particularly with CBT and hypnotherapy. For these reasons, the therapeutic approaches for anxiety disorders described in this book emphasize coping with the symptoms rather than controlling them.

From the foregoing discussion it would appear relaxation training, despite the conceptual concerns expressed by some cognitive therapists, continues to be advocated as an effective intervention for inhibiting physical symptoms of anxiety (e.g., Bourne, 2000; Craske, Antony, & Barlow, 2006). For example, Brown, O'Leary and Barlow (2001; see Conrad & Roth, 2007, for review of empirical status) found progressive muscle relaxation (PMR) to be an important therapeutic ingredient in CBT protocols for GAD.

There is extensive evidence that relaxation alone or in combination with other therapies is beneficial to both normal and multiple clinical populations, including anxiety disorders (Walsh, 2011). Relaxation training appears to be well suited for the treatment of diffuse anxieties (Borkovec & Weerts, 1976), and it represents one of the most used nonpharmacological approach in anxiety management worldwide (Barrows & Jacobs, 2002), both as a bona fide anxiolytic treatment in itself (Ost, 1987) or as an adjunct to more complex therapies such as systematic desensitization (SD) (Goldfried, 1971) and CBT (Beck & Emery, 1985, 2005; Clark & Beck, 2010). For decades, relaxation training has been shown to attain many of the same benefits as benzodiazepines but without the side-effect profile of medication (Stahl & Moore, 2013).

Although many types of relaxation methods have received scientific attention, they could be defined globally as cognitive and/or behavioural treatment approaches which accentuate the development of a relaxation response to counteract stress response of anxiety (Manzoni, Gagini, Castelnuovo, & Molinari (2008). Many studies have supported the effectiveness of relaxation trainings in reducing clinical anxiety (Manzoni et al., 2008 for review). A review by Kanji and Ernst (2000) and a meta-analysis conducted by Eppley, Abrams and Shear (1989) demonstrated that relaxation training has medium effect on trait anxiety, whereas transcendental meditation has significantly larger effect size. A more recent review and meta-analysis of relaxation training for anxiety disorders spanning over ten years, between 1997 and 2007, found consistent and significant efficacy of relaxation training in reducing anxiety (Manzoni et al., 2008). Applied relaxation has been adopted for uses in treatment of GAD (Arntz, 2003). In two recent studies, applied relaxation has proven to be equally as effective in treating GAD as cognitive therapy, which demands much more of the therapist's time (Arntz, 2003; Ost & Brietholtz, 2000).

Again, Clark and Beck (2010) point out that the 'empirical research indicates that relaxation training has a far more limited role in treatment of anxiety than once envisioned' (p. 259). This conclusion is justified on the ground that anxiety disorders often manifest as complex conditions, requiring multimodal intervention. In this context, any brief and simple therapy may be inadequate. For this reason, most therapists use relaxation training as an adjunct to CBT (e.g., Bourne, 2000; Craske et al., 2006) or part of a comprehensive treatment protocol (e.g., Alladin, 2014a) for anxiety disorders. In this book, relaxation training, mainly assisted by hypnosis, is used as an important component of CH.

While practitioners of CBT generally use non-hypnotic techniques such as PMR or imagery training for engendering relaxation, hypnotherapists exclusively resort to hypnosis. The greatest advantage of using hypnosis over non-hypnotic relaxation training is that the former provides greater leverage to psychological treatment (Alladin, 2006, 2007, 2013b; Alladin & Amundson, 2011; Dengrove, 1973; DePiano & Salzberg, 1986; Yapko, 2003). Additionally, a deep hypnotic state can be easily and quickly induced in patients with anxiety disorders, as these patients tend to be highly suggestible to hypnosis (Bryant, Guthrie, & Moulds, 2001; Cardena, 2000; Heap & Aravind, 2002; Spiegel, Hunt, & Dondershine, 1988; Stutman, & Bliss, 1985). The hypnotic state, apart from producing the relaxation response, can also be utilized to generate profound mental and physical relaxation, and help patient dissociate from anxiety-related objects and situations (Alladin, 2014a). Hypnotic induction of such positive affect provides a very meaningful experience of the relaxation training. One of the meaningful ways to change or modify the anxiety experience is to create a new experience (calm, relaxed and pleasantly detached). Once a patient feels completely relaxed, in control and safe, the trance state can be further deployed to train the patient how to modulate his or her emotional reactions to fearful objects or situations via self-hypnosis.

Various hypnotic induction techniques can be used to produce relaxation response in patients with anxiety disorder. I use *Relaxation with Counting Method* adapted from Gibbons (1979; see Alladin, 2008, pp. 245–249, for the script) for inducing and deepening the hypnotic trance. I have chosen this technique as it can be easily rendered into a self-hypnosis technique. Deep relaxation and a sense of well-being can be created by using a variety of hypnotic suggestions, including feeling detached (Alladin, 2008), floating away to a tranquil (Spiegel & Spiegel, 1990) or peaceful setting (Field, 1990) and feeling distant from tension-producing sensations (Finkelstein, 1990; Stickney, 1990). The majority of patients with anxiety disorder find the relaxation experience empowering and confidence-boosting. It is not uncommon at the end of the hypnotherapy session for a patient to state: 'I have never been able to relax in my entire life. The hypnosis was magic; it calmed me down so much that I switched off completely' (Alladin, 2008, p. 103). This is not surprising to hypnotherapists, who routinely observe such changes in their patients. For example, Yapko (2003, p. 106) proclaims: 'I have worked with many people who actually cried tears of joy or relief in a session for having had an opportunity to experience themselves as relaxed, comfortable, and positive when their usual experience of themselves was one of pain and despair.'

Demonstration of the power of the mind over the body

To further empower patients with anxiety disorders and to ratify credibility of the hypnotic intervention, I routinely induce eye and body catalepsies during the second or third session of hypnotherapy. This procedure, which entails the patient's inability to open his or her eyes and get out of the chair or couch, demonstrates to the patient that the mind is extremely powerful (see Chapter 3 for a therapy transcript, which offers patient an explanation of the cataleptic response). Most patients regard this experience highly empowering as it instils in them the confidence that they can tap on their personal resources to deal with their anxiety symptoms. The case of Bob, described by Alladin (2006), illustrates how his scepticism for psychological treatment was turned into an asset following the cataleptic experience. Bob was a 55-year-old electronic engineer with recurrent major depressive disorder who was successfully treated with CH. Bob was very sceptical of psychological treatment for depression because he believed his illness was caused by a chemical imbalance. The demonstration of the power of mind over body via eye and body catalepsies (in hypnosis he was challenged to open his eyes and get out of the reclining chair, which he was not able to do) not only reduced his scepticism about hypnosis, but he also became a model patient and his therapy turned into 'fascinating sessions' (Alladin, 2006, p.180).

Ego strengthening

The principles behind ego-strengthening are to increase self-esteem, enhance self-efficacy, and gradually restore patient's confidence in his or her ability to manage symptoms of anxiety disorder (Heap & Aravind, 2002). Bandura (1977) has demonstrated self-efficacy, or the expectation and confidence of being able to cope successfully, to be one of the key elements in the effective treatment of anxiety disorders. Individuals with a sense of high self-efficacy tend to perceive themselves as being in control. If patients with anxiety disorder can be helped to view themselves as self-efficacious, they are less likely to avoid anxiety-provoking situations. Hartland (1971) believes patients need to feel confident and strong enough to let go of their symptoms. The ego-strengthening suggestions are specifically crafted to increase patient's confidence, coping abilities, positive self-image and interpersonal skills (see Alladin, 2008, pp. 247–249). It is important for the ego-strengthening suggestions to appear credible and logical to the patients. For example, rather than stating 'every day you will feel calmer and relaxed', it is advisable to suggest: 'as a result of this treatment and as a result of you practicing self-hypnosis every day, you will begin to feel calmer and relaxed.' This set of suggestions not only sounds logical, but also improvement becomes contingent on continuing with the therapy and adhering to the homework of listening to the self-hypnosis CD every day (after the first hypnotherapy session, the patient is given a self-hypnosis CD – see under the section 'Self-hypnosis training').

Expansion of awareness
As patients with anxiety disorders tend to constantly ruminate with catastrophic thoughts and images, their range of emotional and bodily responses is severely constricted. Hypnosis provides a powerful vehicle for inducing, expanding and amplifying a wide range of experience. I find Brown and Fromm's (1990, pp. 322–324) technique of enhancing affective experience and its expression (hereafter referred as expansion of awareness training; EAT) very effective for (i) bringing out underlying emotions into awareness, (ii) promoting awareness of diverse feelings, (iii) enhancing positive affect, (iv) strengthening 'discovered' experience, (v) generating positive moods and (vi) increasing motivation. The objective of EAT is to help patients with anxiety disorders harness, amplify and express a variety of negative and positive feelings and experiences. The ability to generate and expand various experiences fosters confidence in patients that their anxiety symptoms can be alleviated, transformed, or modified. Moreover, this technique can be easily integrated with exposure therapy (Wolpe, 1958; Wolpe & Lazarus, 1966), which is deemed an important component of CH for anxiety disorders (Golden, 2012).

Modulating and controlling symptoms
Hypnosis is a powerful therapeutic tool for producing syncretic cognition (Alladin, 2006, 2007, 2008). Human experience is not simply experienced as an affect or a thought, it involves syncretic cognition or a cascade of reactions and responses. Safer and Leventhal (1977) define syncretic cognition as the fusion of cognitive, somatic, perceptual, physiological, visceral and kinaesthetic changes that form an undifferentiated experiential matrix. Hypnotic induction and modulation of syncretic cognition – while the patient is in trance – offer dramatic proof to anxious patients that they can regulate and modify their distressing feelings and experiences. DePiano and Salzberg (1981) believe the rapid improvement that is often observed in patients receiving hypnotherapy is partly related to positive syncretic cognition produced by the trance experience. By virtue of being an experiential therapy, hypnotherapy provides patients with anxiety disorder an opportunity to observe the syncretic (total) nature of an experience (Alladin, 2006, 2007, 2008). Once the patients are able to appreciate the total nature of an experience, they can be coached to recognize the syncretic nature of

their anxiety symptoms, rather than focusing on one particular sign or symptom. This training helps patients to begin to view their anxiety not simply as an affect, a thought or a behaviour, but a cascade of cognitive, somatic, perceptual, physiological, visceral and kinaesthetic experience.

Interest in the role of inner experience in therapy stems from two major sources: developments in third-wave cognitive-behavioural therapies and research on maintenance factors in anxiety disorders. Third-wave cognitive-behavioural therapists have been routinely training patients to examine and change their relationship with their internal experience (emotions, physical sensations and symptoms) and cognitive processes (worry, rumination, intrusive thoughts, images and memories) rather than controlling the symptoms (Butler et al., 2008). Research on maintenance factors in anxiety disorders have revealed that symptoms of anxiety are maintained by two interrelated factors: persistent misinterpretations of the significance of internal states (e.g., 'fear of fear') (Rachman & Bichard, 1988) and maladaptive behaviours are engendered by these cognitions (e.g., 'safety-seeking behaviours'; Salkovskis, 1991). Although these cognitions and safety-seeking behaviours are used by patients to control their anxiety; in fact, they maintain and exacerbate their symptoms.

Changing the significance patients attach to their own cognitions about maladaptive cognitions (metacognition) have therefore become central to many contemporary approaches to treating anxiety disorders (Butler et al., 2008). For example, some clinicians have started to question and test metacognitive beliefs in the course of classical CBT (Morrison & Westbrrok, 2004; Salkovskis, 1999; Wells, 1995, 1997, 2000; Wells & Matthews, 1994, 1996). Mindfulness-based cognitive therapists, on the other hand, have always integrated elements of CBT with intensive practice of mindfulness meditation (Baer, 2003; Ma & Teasdale, 2004; Segal, Williams, & Teasdale, 2002; Teasdale, 2004; Teasdale, Segal, Williams, Ridgeway, Soulsby, & Lau, 2000). Similarly, the capacity to decentre from unhelpful thinking is viewed as foundational in various other therapies such as ACT (Hayes, Strosahl, & Wilson, 1999), CH (Alladin, 2013a, 2014a), DBT (Linehan, 1993a, 1993b) and mentalization therapy (Bateman & Fonagy, 2004). Although all these therapies differ in their underlying theoretical rationales, they all share a common goal with CBT, that is, they all 'teach patients to view their own cognitions as simply mental events and processes, to which they need not attend and on which they need not act' (Butler et al., 2008, p. 72).

Butler et al. (2008) have described a number of procedures that can be integrated with CBT to promote metacognitive awareness. These include (i) the 'prejudice model' (Padesky, 1993), (ii) 'theory 1, theory 2'

(Salkovskis, 1996), (iii) 'vicious flowers' (Butler et al., 2008), (iv) 'virtuous flowers' (Butler et al., 2008), (v) cognitive maintaining cycle (Fennell, 1999, 2006), (vi) experiments, (vii) metaphors, analogies and images and (viii) stories. Detailed discussion of these techniques is beyond the scope of this book; interested readers are referred to Butler et al. (2008) for more detail.

Self-hypnosis training

One of the main goals of self-hypnosis training is to equip anxiety disorder patients with confidence and skills for dealing with their symptoms outside therapy sessions. Self-hypnosis also serves as a powerful tool for countering catastrophic cogitation or NSH (Alladin, 1994, 2006, 2007; Araoz, 1981, 1985). In order to facilitate self-hypnosis training, at the end of the first hypnotherapy session, the patient is given a CD recording of the session. The patient is encouraged to listen to the CD at least once a day at home. This homework assignment allows continuity of treatment between sessions and offers patients the opportunity to learn self-hypnosis. The ultimate goal of psychotherapy is to help patients with anxiety disorder establish self-reliance and independence. Self-hypnosis is a very useful tool for achieving self-reliance and personal power (Alman 2001) and for developing self-correcting behaviours (Yapko, 2003). Patients are thus trained to induce self-hypnosis rapidly in diverse anxiety-provoking situations by mastering the clenched fist technique (Stein, 1963), which involves clenching the preferred fist as an anchor. An anchor is any stimulus that evokes a consistent response pattern from a person (Lankton, 1980). The clenched fist technique was first described by Stein, and it has been found to be an effective anxiety management technique (Basker, 1979; Stanton, 1997). The fist as an anchor is easily established during hypnotic trance. When the patient is in a deep trance state, he or she is advised to become aware of the profound relaxation as well as the feeling of confidence and self-control. The patient is then instructed to make a fist with the preferred hand, followed by these suggestions:

> From now on, whenever you wish to feel just as you are feeling now, all you have to do it is to clench your preferred fist and anchor your mind to this experience. Moreover, from now on, whenever you feel anxious, you can tame the feeling by clenching your fist and anchoring your mind to this experience ... and with practice you will get better and better at it.

The anchoring technique is bolstered by PHS and experientially reinforced by imaginal rehearsal training. Most patients find the clenched fist technique concrete and 'portable', and easily applied in a variety of anxiety-provoking situations. However, clenching of the fist may not serve as an appropriate anchor for some patients as it may conjure anger or aggression. In such a case, pressing of the thumb against the little finger (in preferred hand) may be more appropriate.

Post-hypnotic suggestions

Before the termination of the hypnotic session, PHS are offered to counter problem behaviours, negative affect and negative rumination (NSH) or negative self-affirmations (Alladin, 2008). Patients with anxiety disorders have the propensity to ruminate with negative self-suggestions such as 'I will not be able to cope', 'I will lose control' and so on. This kind of NSH can be regarded as a form of PHS, which can become part of the avoidance pattern of behaviour in anxiety disorders. It is of paramount importance to counter the NSH in order to offset the negative rumination. Here are some examples of PHS that can be suggested to patients with anxiety disorders to counter NHS:

- 'Whenever you become anxious in a situation, you will become more aware of how to deal with it rather than focusing on your symptoms or what may happen to you.'
- 'When you plan to confront an anxiety-provoking situation, you will feel less need to avoid the situation.'
- 'As you become more relaxed every day as a result of listening to your Self-Hypnosis CD, you will begin to feel motivated to face the situations you have been avoiding.'

Clarke and Jackson (1983) view PHS to be a form of 'higher-order-conditioning', which can function as positive or negative reinforcement to increase or decrease the probability of desired or undesired behaviours. They have successfully utilized PHS to enhance the effect of *in vivo* exposure in agoraphobics.

Hypnotherapy combined with behavioural therapies

As hypnotherapy primarily involves experiential and imaginal therapies in the office, it is important to transfer the learning from this setting to real-life situations. To facilitate this process, the next phase of therapy integrates cognitive-behavioural strategies, namely SD and *in vivo* exposure, with hypnotherapy. SD is found to be a necessary component of therapy for anxiety disorders to achieve positive treatment outcome (Antony & Barlow, 2002). For example, clinical and experimental evidence demonstrate SD to be an effective treatment for reducing, and in some cases eliminating, simple phobias (Antony & Barlow, 2002; Choy, Fyer, & Lipsitz, 2007; McGlynn, 1994; Kirsch, Capafons, Cardena & Amigo, 1999; Smith, 1990).

Hypnosis-aided systematic desensitization
Although exposure therapy has been found to be very effective with specific phobia (Follette & Smith, 2005), some patients feel too anxious to tolerate this treatment. They feel more comfortable and ready to work with SD, which can be used as a preparatory step for *in vivo* exposure therapy. The procedure is based on reciprocal inhibition, which can be defined as anxiety being inhibited by a feeling or response (e.g., relaxation), which is incompatible with the feeling of anxiety (Wolpe, 1958, 1969; Wolpe & Lazarus, 1996). The operating components of SD include (i) relaxation training, (ii) the construction of a hierarchy of anxiety evoking events associated with the target condition being treated and (iii) imaginal exposure to anxiety evoking situations. The fear-evoking events are rank-ordered into a hierarchy of subjective units of distress/discomfort (SUD) from least evoking to most evoking anxiety (see Table 2.1). The SUD represents subjective distress rated on a scale of 0–100, where 0 represents no anxiety, and 100 stands for the worst anxiety. The patient is exposed to the imagery from the hierarchy, one image at a time, under relaxation, until all images have been presented and the patient has tolerated each without reporting anxiety (Iglesias & Iglesias, 2014). When anxiety is experienced during the imaginal exposure, the image is terminated and a relaxed state is induced. With continued exposure to each image, the patient's level of anxiety weakens progressively, until the patient no longer experiences anxiety in response to the fearful stimuli (Wolpe, 1958, 1990).

In CH, the relaxation component of SD is replaced by hypnosis, and hence, this treatment approach is referred to as hypnosis-aided systematic desensitization (HASD) (Iglesias & Iglesias, 2014). A number of reports in the literature support the effectiveness of combining hypnosis with SD in the treatment of specific phobias (Glick, 1970). There are also several added advantages for integrating hypnosis with SD in the treatment of anxiety disorders: (i) hypnosis reduces the duration of therapy (Meyer & Crisp, 1970); (ii) compared to ordinary relaxation techniques, hypnosis produces deeper relaxation and enhances the intensity and involvement of the visualization experience (Glick, 1970); (iii) hypnosis helps patients reframe their negative thinking into more positive expectations from treatment (Alladin, 2013a); (iv) hypnosis facilitates continuous and smooth flow of anxiety-related imagery; (v) visualization under hypnosis allow images to be observed and examined in a fraction of time; (vi) in hypnosis images can be linked in concatenation, like in a movie, rather than presenting one image at a time; (vii) deep hypnotic trance counteracts anxiety and permits presentation of images without the customary interruptions of signalling distress and (viii) all these hypnotic benefits help to build up the patient's psychic coping resources (Iglesias & Iglesias, 2014). HASD has been found to be effective with odontophobia (Moore, 1990), non-accidental driving phobia (Iglesias & Iglesias, 2014), agoraphobia (Surman, 1979), phobia of a laundry product (Deiker & Pollock, 1975) and fear of recurrent distressing dreams (Surman, 1979).

The next section illustrates how the SD procedure was used with Mandy to help her overcome her fear of using public washrooms (case is described in detail in Chapter 4). Table 2.2 represents various situations – ranked from least feared to most feared – related to public washroom in the local shopping mall that caused anxiety for Mandy. The fear is subjectively measured in terms of SUD as mentioned earlier.

While Mandy was feeling very relaxed in deep hypnosis, she was asked to imagine each hierarchy of fear in turn, starting with the lowest item in the hierarchy ('Ask for location of washroom in shopping mall': 20 SUD). She was suggested to focus on the targeted situation until she was able to bring her SUD level down to 0. It is important for the patient to master one hierarchy, that is, being able to imagine the target situation without any anxiety, before moving on to the next item in the hierarchy. Failure to master previous situation may produce resistance to work with the next item in the hierarchy, which is likely to be more anxiety provoking (higher SUD level). Mandy found the SD very helpful in bringing down her level

Table 2.2   Systematic desensitization hierarchy of fear of using public washroom

Item	Fear rating in SUD (0–100)
Ask for location of washroom in shopping mall	20
Looking for the washroom in the mall	30
Looking at the washroom from a distance	40
Standing in front of the washroom	50
Standing at the entrance of the washroom	60
Going inside the washroom but not using it	70
Opening the washroom door and looking inside	80
Going inside the washroom, door open, not using it	85
Sitting in the washroom, door closed, not using it	90
Inside the locked washroom	95
Inside the locked washroom, using it	100

of anxiety during the session. However, she was still fearful of facing the situations in reality. She managed up to 'Standing in front of the washroom' (SUD: 50), but was not able to progress beyond this point in the real situation. As SD is imagination focused, in order to help patients with anxiety disorder face real situations, gradual *in vivo* exposure therapy is introduced at this stage of therapy.

Gradual in vivo *exposure therapy*

Exposure *in vivo* therapy involves repeated confrontation with the feared objects or situations, and it has been found to be efficacious with a variety of anxiety disorders (Follette & Smith, 2005). Based on learning theory, exposure therapy is conceptualized to function as a form of counter-conditioning or extinction. Exposure therapy was initially used with SD by Wolpe (1958). Since this seminal work, exposure therapy for anxiety disorders have continued to evolve and nowadays it comprises a set of techniques designed to help patients confront their feared objects, situations, memories and images in a therapeutic manner.

Albeit its effectiveness, *in vivo* exposure therapy has many disadvantages in terms of compliance, dropouts, symptoms exacerbation and emotional disturbance (Golden, 2012). It is estimated that approximately one in four patients who initiates treatment drops out (Clum, 1989; Fava, Zielezny, & Savron, 1995; Hofmann & Smits, 2008; Marks, 1978). In addition, Follette and Smith (2005) have expressed several other concerns about this therapy approach, including high attrition rate, exacerbation of symptoms, patient's inability to tolerate distress and not addressing associated or additional problems such as cognitive distortions, anger, guilt, shame and dissociation. To address these concerns and to prepare the patient for this treatment, as it happens to be a very effective therapy for anxiety disorders, exposure therapy has been incorporated with CBT (e.g., Meichenbaum, 1974), cognitive processing therapy (Resick & Schnicke, 1992), ACT (Hayes, Strosahl, & Wilson, 1999), eye movement desensitization and reprocessing (EMDR; Shapiro, 1995) and hypnotherapy (e.g., Golden, Dowd, & Friedberg, 1987; Lynn & Kirsch, 2006). In recognition of the previous concerns, Golden (2012) has recommended that *in vivo* therapy be carried out only after successful completion of in-session hypnotic desensitization. Moreover, with some patients, it may also be beneficial to address unhelpful emotion such as anger prior to starting exposure. For example, Jill was so enraged by the teenagers who mugged her in the park (which caused agoraphobia), that she refused to focus on anxiety during exposure therapy. Foa, Riggs, Massie, and Yarczower (1995) empirically demonstrated that severe anger hinders exposure therapy in patients with posttraumatic stress disorder.

To overcome these obstacles to *in vivo* exposure therapy, the general rule in CH is to introduce patients to HASD (Iglesias & Iglesias, 2014), as described earlier, before initiating exposure to real situations. Another hypnotherapy technique for preparing patients for exposure therapy is hypnotic imaginal exposure (HIE). This technique is similar to HASD, except there is no hierarchy involved and the patient is flooded with the worst fear and then coached to deal with the anxiety head-on. HIE is normally introduced after the patient had some experience with HASD, as HIE is more anxiety provoking (as the anxiety is amplified). The author has noted that patients with anxiety disorder are more prepared to face exposure therapy following HIE than HASD.

HIE helped Jenny, who had social anxiety, cope with the anxiety she experienced at work. To help Jenny bring on her anxious experience associated with her workplace, under hypnosis she was suggested: 'When I count from ONE to FIVE … by the time you hear me say FIVE … you will begin to feel whatever emotion is associated with your thoughts about work.' Then Jenny was helped to amplify the affect associated with her work: 'When I count slowly from ONE to FIVE … as I count you will begin to experience the anxious feelings more and more intensely … so that when I reach the count of FIVE … at the count of FIVE you will feel the full reaction as strongly as you can bear it … Now notice what you feel and you will be able to describe it to me.' Jenny was then instructed to utilize self-hypnosis to deal with her anxious and fearful reactions. This type of mental rehearsal, while the patient is in trance, prepares patients to face anxiety-producing objects and situations. Moreover, the technique encourages patients to focus on feelings head-on, rather than catastrophizing or cogitating about the symptoms.

Cognitive behavioural therapy
CBT is used to help patients with anxiety disorder alter the meaning of their fears and symptoms, and to reframe distorted beliefs associated with maladaptive emotions such as guilt, shame, embarrassment and anger. Within CH perspective, CBT is viewed as a conscious strategy for countering NSH in order to circumvent the negative affect or the symptomatic trance state (Yapko, 1992). The CBT component of CH for this purpose can be extended over four to six sessions. However, the actual number of CBT sessions is determined by the needs of the patient and the severity of the presenting symptoms. As CBT protocols and specific treatment strategies for each anxiety disorder are fully described in several excellent books (e.g., Barlow, 1988; Beck, & Emery, 1985, 2005; Bennett-Levy, Butler,

Fennell, Hackman, Mueller, & Westbrook, 2004; Clark & Beck, 2010; Hawton, Salkovskis, Kirk, & Clark, 1989; Leahy & Hollon, 2000; Simos, 2002; Wells, 1997) and a detailed description of the sequential progression of CBT within the CH framework is provided elsewhere (Alladin, 2007, 2008), they are not described in detail here. However, the following CBT transcript adapted from Alladin (2008, p. 107–110; Alladin, in press) illustrates how Roger was guided to reevaluate and change his maladaptive belief of the world ('The world is unsafe') that stemmed from his traumatic experience (saw many innocent people killed and maimed in a war zone).

THERAPIST: Roger, what do you mean by 'The world is unsafe'?
ROGER: You can't go out there, you may get killed.
THERAPIST: What do you mean by 'out there'?
ROGER: Well, you can't go out in the street without getting killed or mugged.
THERAPIST: So, let me get it right what you are saying. You believe that if you go out in the street, you will either get killed or mugged.
ROGER: Certainly.
THERAPIST: How much do you believe in the belief that you will get shot or mugged when you go out in the street?
ROGER: Totally, one hundred percent.
THERAPIST: What kind of a thinking error is this?
ROGER: All-or-nothing thinking, magnification, and I'm overgeneralizing.

[This transcript is from Roger's third session of CBT. From his previous sessions of CBT and homework assignments, Roger was well versed in the types of cognitive distortions anxious people ruminate with, as described by Burns, 1999.]

THERAPIST: So you are aware that your thinking is inaccurate.
ROGER: Yes, but I can't help it. I know I live in a fairly safe neighborhood, but my mind keeps going back to East Europe. I get confused. My mind keeps going back as if I'm still there. It's so crazy.
THERAPIST: Do you see the connection between your thinking and your negative reaction?
ROGER: Yes, it's so dumb. Whenever I think of going out, I think of the dangerous situations we faced in East Europe, people getting shot, arrested and blown up. But this is so dumb, I know I am not going to get attacked or shot going to the store in Canada.
THERAPIST: So your thinking gets confused. When you think of going out to the local store you think you are in East Europe.
ROGER: Yes, but I can't help it.

THERAPIST: Having the thoughts that you are in East Europe and exposed to dangers are not intentional on your part. You don't think this way on purpose. As a result of your traumatic experiences, your mind has developed many associations with the fearful and dangerous situations you were in. Also you learned to think automatically about danger, even in situations where there is no danger. Does this make sense to you?

ROGER: Yes, but how do I get out of this?

THERAPIST: As we talked before, we use disputation or reasoning? Suppose you are thinking of going to the store and the thought cross your mind that you will be mugged or shot, how would you reason with this statement?

ROGER: I can remind myself that I'm not in East Europe, my assignment is over. I am at home now, and this is a safe environment.

THERAPIST: That's excellent. You have to separate 'then' from 'now'. You have to reason that you are in a safe environment now, even if your thinking keeps going back to East Europe.

ROGER: I guess I always knew my thinking was wrong, but the feelings are so real that you begin to go along with your feeling, rather than thinking with your head. Funny, this is what cops are taught to do.

THERAPIST: What kind of a thinking error is this, when you are thinking with your feeling?

ROGER: Emotional reasoning. You are right, I need to use my head more than my feeling.

THERAPIST: That's right, you have to continue to assess the link between your thinking and your feeling. Try to identity the cognitive distortion and then reason with it.

As a result of this session, Roger was able to modify his maladaptive beliefs and, consequently, he started to venture out more often and to different places. However, it should be pointed out that CH therapists, when indicated, go beyond CBT strategies to address the wounded self. In addition to focusing on the relationship between events and cognitive distortions, the implicit meanings of symptoms are explored. This can be achieved by adopting the following practical guidelines proposed by Gabbard and Bennett (2006): (i) careful evaluation of the stressor that triggered the anxiety; (ii) assessment of whether the stressor produced a sense of self-endangerment; (iii) assessment of whether the stressor reawakened early childhood losses, traumas or self-wounds and (iv) identification of what meanings the patient attributed to the stressor.

Phase III: Hypnotherapy for eliciting and healing self-wounds

Once a patient achieves some measure of control over his or her anxiety symptoms from either hypnotherapy or CBT (or a combination of both), the therapist has to make a decision about the next stage of intervention. For those patients who have improved and believe that they had met their goals, the therapy is considered complete and it is duly terminated. For those patients who wish to explore the roots of their anxiety, they continue with the next two phases of therapy. These two phases of therapy involve uncovering and healing of tacit self-wounds. As these two phases overlap and complement each other, they are described simultaneously.

Hypnotherapy provides an array of methods for uncovering unconscious causes or roots of emotional disorders (Alladin, 2013b; Brown & Fromm, 1986; Ewin & Eimer, 2006; Yapko, 2012; Watkins, 1971; Watkins & Barabasz, 2008). For the present purpose, four hypnotic techniques for accessing and healing tacit self-wounds are described. These include (i) direct suggestions, (ii) hypnotic age regression, (iii) affect bridge and (iv) hypnotic exploration. Once the implicit meaning of the fear and the underlying self-wounds are elicited by a particular uncovering technique, the therapy normally segues into healing. To avoid repeated account of the healing procedures following each uncovering technique, they are described in detail under the section 'Hypnotic exploration technique'.

Direct hypnotic suggestions

While the patient is in deep trance, the therapist may suggest: 'You are in such a deep hypnotic trance that you may remember the root cause of your anxiety.' This simple approach, coupled with a solid therapeutic alliance and no resistance from the patient, may be sufficient to elicit tacit meaning of fear and underlying self-wounds. However, this approach may not work with patients whose self-wounds are well defended and suppressed deeply.

Hypnotic age regression

Age regression can be defined as an intensified absorption in and experiential utilization of memory (Yapko, 2012, p. 344). Age regression can be classified into two general categories: revivification and hypermnesia. In revivification, a patient is guided back in time to relive an episode in life as if it is happening in the here-and-now. In hypermnesia, a patient simply remembers an experience as vividly as possible. Age regression is structured deliberately to engage patients with anxiety disorders in some memory that may have relevance to their symptoms. However, it should be noted that not all patients with anxiety disorders may harbour underlying traumas or emotional injuries. Golden (1994) suggests regression is best reserved for patients who request it and expect it to be superior to other methods (Wolpe & Lazarus, 1966). Moreover, he recommends deploying age regression when the patient is in a deep trance.

Affect bridge technique

The affect bridge technique (Watkins, 1971) is a popular hypnotic procedure for tracing the origin of an inappropriate feeling or emotion in the present. The affect bridge technique is 'based on the psychological fact that emotions, feelings or affect can activate, drive and intensify recall', thus 'feelings can bring you back to earlier times when you felt similarly' (Hunter & Eimer, 2012). The concept of state-dependent memory (Rossi & Cheek, 1988) becomes relevant here. This concept states that memories are often more easily retrieved and recalled when a person is in an emotional and physical state similar to the one he or she was in when the memory was first encoded. Therefore, current emotions and feelings can serve as our connections, or bridge, to the past. The utilization of affect bridge technique with anxiety disorders can be divided into three sequential steps:

1. *Elicitation of a negative feeling associated with anxiety*: While the patient is in a deep hypnotic trance, the therapist suggests that the patient feels an emotion or feeling (e.g., fear) that is linked to existing fear or anxiety.
2. *Amplification of that feeling*: The patient is encouraged to intensify the anxiety or fear as the therapist counts from 1 to 10.
3. *Recalling the first time that feeling was experienced*: Then the therapist, by counting 10 to 1, guides the patient back to the first time, or an earlier time, when the patient first felt that fear or feeling.

Once the bridge between anxiety and the underlying self-wounds are elicited, the treatment can segue into healing the self-wounds as described in the next section.

Hypnotic exploration technique

The hypnotic exploration technique (HET) incorporates WFT (Wolfe, 2005, 2006; Wolfe & Sigl, 1998) and Alladin's hypnotic accessing technique (Alladin, 2013b, pp. 11–14). WFT is a form of imaginal exposure, or a type of affect bridge without hypnosis, for uncovering and healing self-wounds. HET combines both exploration (e.g., affect bridge technique) and healing (e.g., split screen technique), and it can be summarized under the following sequential steps:

1. The patient is inducted into a deep hypnotic trance.
2. The experience is ratified by ego-strengthening suggestions (e.g., 'this shows you can relax', 'you can let go, but still being aware of everything').
3. The patient is encouraged to become fully aware of currently experienced whole range of affect, cognition, physiological reaction, sensations and behaviours (syncretic cognition).
4. Then the therapist suggests that the patient recall the latest occurrence of anxiety or other negative affect experienced by the patient.
5. Once the anxiety is recalled, the feeling is amplified as the therapist counts from 1 to 10. However, the patient is guided to focus on the whole experience (syncretic cognition) rather than on a single affect.
6. While experiencing syncretic cognition, the patient is directed to identify the implicit meaning of his or her anxiety or fear, particularly the underlying self-wounds.

Once the implicit meaning of the fear and the underlying self-wounds are established, HET segues into guided-imagery procedures to explore the network of interconnected ideas, feelings, and associations that constitute the implicit meaning of anxiety. Then the patient is guided to (i) differentiate between accurate and inaccurate self-views, (ii) learn to tolerate painful realities, (iii) transform inaccurate self-views and (iv) resolve catastrophic conflicts.

Differentiate between accurate and inaccurate self-views
The patient is guided to differentiate between painful self-views that are based on facts and those that are based on inaccurate opinions. The empty chair dialogue or the split screen technique can be used here. The empty chair technique is a Gestalt therapy role-playing strategy (Perls, Hefferline, & Goodman, 1951; Woldt & Toman, 2005) for reducing intra- or interpersonal conflicts (Nichol & Schwartz, 2008). In this procedure, the patient is directed to talk to another person who is imagined to be sitting in an empty chair beside or across from the patient. The imaginary person can be a family member or any relevant person with whom the patient is afraid of being honest in expressing strongly charged emotions, either negative or positive. By imagining the other person sitting in the empty chair in the safety of the therapy situation, a patient is able to experiment with the experience and expression of various emotions, including anger

(Greenberg, Rice, & Elliott, 1993). Moreover, it helps patients experience and understand their feelings and think more fully.

The split screen technique (Alladin, 2008; Cardena, Maldonado, van der Hart, & Spiegel, 2000; Lynn & Cardena, 2007; Spiegel, 1981) is used to help patients detoxify the meaning of their anxiety. The split screen technique is a hypnotic strategy that makes traumatic or painful memories or experience more bearable. When in a deep hypnotic trance, following ego-strengthening suggestions, the patient is asked to imagine sitting in front of a large TV or cinema screen, which is vertically split in two halves, consisting of a right side and a left side. The patient is first instructed to imagine experiencing symptoms of anxiety on the left side of the screen. Then the patient is directed to focus on the right side of the screen, where he or she imagines coping with the symptoms by using self-hypnosis, self-talk or other procedures that have been learned in therapy. Creating the coping image on the right side of the screen helps patients build confidence that they could deal with the symptoms rather than catastrophizing about them and labelling themselves as weak or incompetent.

Learning to tolerate painful realities
The patient is encouraged to tolerate painful experience and realities rather than avoiding them. Moreover, they are coached to develop a remediation plan to transform liabilities into strengths. These goals can be achieved through behavioural rehearsal, the empty chair dialogue or the split screen technique. Behavioural rehearsal is a technique specifically used in behaviour therapy. It involves rehearsing behavioural patterns, which were initially introduced by the therapist, until they are ready to be practiced in real-life situations. Behavioural rehearsal is usually used in therapy to modify or improve interpersonal skills and social interactions.

Behavioural rehearsal evolves from social learning theory, which began to gain professional attention in the 1940s and 1950s. Other terms used in connection with this procedure include social modelling theory and observational learning. Observational learning involves some behavioural display by a model, followed by a reproduction of this behaviour by the observer under controlled conditions. Behavioural rehearsal is the process of reproducing the modelled behaviour according to explicit and specific guidelines. The underlying principle is that students can effectively acquire novel behaviours through observation, especially if they have the opportunity to try out the target behaviour. The reproduction may be covert (i.e., imagined) or overt (i.e., verbal and or physical). With cognitive or covert enactments, students imagine themselves performing all the observed responses of the model. Verbal rehearsal entails talking out or labeling each step to facilitate future reproduction. Physical behaviour rehearsal requires that the student physically acts out.

Transformation of inaccurate self-views
The patient is coached to begin to transform inaccurate views of the self into adaptive self-views. Behavioural rehearsal, ego-strengthening or PHS are found to be effective here.

Resolution of catastrophic conflicts
The patient is helped to resolve any catastrophic conflicts that might have helped to maintain self-wounds. The two-chair dialogue or behavioural experiments can be used here.

Phase IV: Promoting acceptance, mindfulness and gratitude

Until recently, Western models of psychotherapy had not included such concepts as acceptance, forgiveness, gratitude, spiritual beliefs, equanimity and the heart in therapeutic process, although these precepts represent very fundamental elements in our daily life. Western models of psycho-therapy tend to view the mind central to understanding and treating psy-chological disorders. In this regard, the mind had been conceptualized, depending on the schools of thought, as verbal behaviour, language, thoughts or 'rational, thinking capacity' (Welwood, 1983, p. viii) or a psychological process of the whole individual (Masuda & Wilson, 2009). Within this framework, a logical mind is deemed healthy. Psychotherapy such as CBT therefore had undertaken to train patients to control their cognitive distortions (illogical thinking) or think more logically or ration-ally (e.g., Beck, 2005; Ellis, 2005). As logic does not always equate with psychological well-being, as discerned by integral and third-wave psycho-therapists (e.g., Cortright, 2007; Forman, 2010; Hayes, 2004; Linehan, 1993a, 1993b; Ryan, 2011; Wilber, 2000), this logic-driven model of psychotherapy is deemed parsimonious. Extensive research has docu-mented the difficulty and the paradoxical effect people have when they attempt to control their internal cognitions and experiences (Hayes, Levin, Plumb-Vilardaga, Villatte, & Pistorello, 2013; Wegner, 2011).

This drawback of the mind had been recognized by Eastern traditions and psychotherapies for centuries and as such the mind had been viewed as a paradoxical concept (Welwood, 1983). On one hand, the mind serves a powerful source for regulating our activities; on the other hand, it troubles us, obscures our raw experience and creates illusion (Hayes et al., 1999). Zen states it is our mind that keeps us from being mindful (Suzuki, 1997).

This position is supported by research evidence from relational frame theory (Dymond & Roche, 2013; Hayes, Barnes-Holmes, & Roche, 2001), which provides a detailed account of the nature and origin of our thoughts. As the processing of our language is highly contextualized and invariably generative, it can either enhance our behaviour or constrict our range of experience and produce maladaptive behaviours (Hayes, Strosahl, & Wilson, 2011). According to Zen, raw experience is the unfolding of moment-by-moment reality (e.g., experience, thought, feeling, etc.) without verbal categorization or evaluation. However, when we are unmindful, our mind is dominated by mental chattering (i.e., living inside our head). As our mind is constantly analysing and evaluating events in our lives, our consciousness becomes dull, and we become removed from the here-and-now experience (Cortright, 2007; Hayes et al., 2001, 2011). Moreover, the discursive and convergent (narrow focus) mind can make life rigid and inflexible by constricting our range of experience and mental events. Alladin (2006, 2007, 2014a) describes this process as a form of cogitation or NSH, which is a key characteristic of emotional disorders.

Another problem with the concept of mind is to treat our mind as a thing and to become attached to it, to the extent that we become fused with it and literally believe in what our mind says (e.g., 'I'm a failure', 'I'm useless') (Hayes et al., 2011). Irene, who became depressed because she was not able to skate competitively (Alladin, 2014a) due to fear of falling, literally believed and felt she was a failure—she became *it*. Once we become fused with mental events (e.g., thoughts and words), they have the power to afflict us relentlessly as mental events can take place virtually anytime and anywhere.

Moreover, our approach to problem-solving creates trouble for the mind. As we are culturally trained to fix problems of daily living, we try the same approach with mental events, rather than experiencing them as they are, without reacting to them. The problem with this approach is that our psychological problems are not easy to fix (Hayes et al., 1999). Abundant research evidence suggests that it is not only ineffective to try to intentionally control private events (e.g., Clark, 2005; Wegner, 1994; Wenzlaff, 2005; Wilson, Lindsey, & Schooler, 2000), but also such attempts produce extremely paradoxical responses (e.g., Campbell-Sills, Barlow, Brown, & Hofmann, 2006; Morita, 1998).

In recognition of these limitations of mind theories, third-wave therapists (e.g., Hayes, 2004; Hayes, Luoma, Bond, Masuda, & Lillis, 2006; Linehan, 1993a, 1993b) have incorporated concepts of acceptance and mindfulness in their models of psychopathology and psychotherapy. For example,

Hayes et al. (2006) developed a contextual and behavioural model of psychopathology called psychological inflexibility, which incorporates process of acceptance and mindfulness. According to this model, human psychopathology (human suffering) is viewed as an individual's narrow, rigid and inflexible pattern of activities in the present moment. As mentioned earlier, this is very apparent in emotional disorders, particularly in anxiety and depression. As anxious or depressed clients tend to ruminate constantly about their fears, failures and symptoms, they avoid daily routine activities (Nolen-Hoeksema, 2000). According to psychological inflexibility theory, when we identify and evaluate our private experiences (e.g., thoughts, feelings, bodily sensations) constantly, we become so attached to them that we become oblivious to our raw moment-by-moment experience. However, there is nothing inherently good or bad about an experience itself. It is our automatic mental activity of categorization, comparison and evaluation that determines the nature (negative or positive) of an experience (Hayes et al., 2006). In the case of Irene mentioned earlier, once her sadness or disappointment over not being able to skate competitively was viewed as a problem (labelled depression), or something bad, unbearable and irrepressible, she was caught up in the web of mental brooding that seriously hampered her daily life. Mindfulness and acceptance-based therapies, on the other hand, which teach patients not to counter their ruminations, but to engage in meaningful activities, are found to decrease cogitation and promote positive affect (Baer & Huss, 2008). Some therapists (e.g., Herbert & Forman, 2014; Roemer, Williston, Eustis, & Orsillo, 2013) have explicitly incorporated this approach within CBT for anxiety disorders, which is described next.

Mindfulness and acceptance-based treatments for anxiety disorders

Drawing from their research on acceptance and mindfulness-based therapies (AMBT) for anxiety disorders, Roemer et al. (2013) have conceptualized anxiety disorders to result from three inter-related learned patterns of responding. First, people with anxiety disorders are found to relate to their internal experiences with a lack of clarity, reactivity and self-criticism (Olatunji & Wolitzky-Taylor, 2009), and they tend to see thoughts as self-defining indicators of truth, rather than transient reactions. Secondly, this reactivity leads patients with anxiety disorders to exert habitual and determined efforts to control their experiences, unfortunately without much success. Finally, the patients' habitual reactivity and avoidance inevitably lead to significant constriction in their lives. This occurs either through behavioural avoidance or through inattention to present moment because of their indelible worries and cogitation about the past and the future.

Moreover, accumulating evidence suggests that patients with anxiety disorders have (i) heightened intensity of emotions, (ii) poor understanding of emotions, (iii) negative reactivity to emotions and (iv) habitually using maladaptive regulation patterns such as avoidance and/or substance use to deal with their emotional dysregulation (Cisler & Koster, 2010; Farnsworth & Sewell, 2011; Mennin, Holaway, Fresco, Moore, & Heimberg, 2007). To enhance response to therapy, it would therefore be necessary to target emotional distress, fear of emotions and problematic emotional regulation in the treatment of anxiety disorders. AMBT for anxiety disorders have specifically targeted these areas of concern.

Acceptance and mindfulness-based strategies have been found to help patients with anxiety disorder develop a wise and accepting relationship with their internal cognitive, emotional and physical experience, even during times of intense fear or worry (Greeson & Brantley, 2009). These strategies, through the cultivation of wise responsivity, rather than automatic reactivity, seem to enable patients to establish a radically different relationship with their inner experience and outer events. This was supported by a recent study, which demonstrated that emotional well-being depended less on frequency of negative emotions, but more on how one related to these emotions as they occurred (Sauer-Zavala et al., 2012). These studies clearly indicate that reactivity to emotional experience (fear of emotions and anxiety sensitivity) interferes with emotional regulation, while acceptance (wise responsivity) promotes emotional well-being. Based on these findings, Roemer et al. (2013) have recommended that the treatment of anxiety disorders should be targeted at (1) fear of emotions, (2) problematic emotion regulation pattern and (3) distress, as this approach has been found to enhance treatment outcome.

In the past 20 years, a variety of third-wave psychological therapies such as mindfulness-based stress reduction (MBSR; Kabat-Zinn, 1990), mindfulness-based cognitive therapy (MBCT; Segal, Williams, & Teasdale, 2002) and ACT (Hayes et al., 1999) have been applied to diverse psychosocial problems (Abbey, 2012; Baer, 2003; Brown, Ryan, & Creswell, 2007; Chiesa & Serretti, 2009; Grossman, Niemann, Schmidt, & Walach, 2004; Hayes et al., 2006; Ludwig & Kabat-Zinn, 2008; Marchand, 2012; Vøllestad, Nielsen, & Nielsen, 2012). Because of their overarching similarities, these new approaches to therapy are all categorized under AMBT in this book. Although each treatment varies in terms of its emphasis on formal mindfulness practice, amount of practice included and the inclusion of exposure and other behavioural elements, all of them focus on teaching clients to relate to their internal experiences differently (Roemer & Orsillo, 2013). For example, a patient with social anxiety is trained to respond to fear with acceptance and mindfulness rather than with aversion or avoidance, and encouraged to focus on meaningful activities or actions rather than on controlling specific symptoms.

Although the research is still in its infancy, there is some evidence that AMBT reduce symptoms of anxiety and improve the quality of life. For example, a recent meta-analysis by Hofmann, Sawyer, Witt and Oh (2010) showed AMBT to produce significant reductions in anxiety and depressive symptoms in a wide range of clinical problems. The treatments were particularly effective with SAD, GAD and obsessive-compulsive disorder. AMBT were also found to significantly improve quality of life among patients with GAD (Craigie, Rees, & Marsh, 2008; Roemer & Orsillo, 2007) or SAD (Koszycki, Laurier, & Rector, 2009). Even though no studies have shown AMBT to be more effective than established therapies (e.g., CBT), two recent investigations found AMBT to produce comparable effects to CBT (Arch, Eifert, Davies, Plumb Vilardaga, Rose, & Craske, 2012) and applied relaxation therapy (Hayes-Selton, Roemer, & Orsillo, 2013) with a sample of GAD and mixed anxiety disorder patients. Nevertheless, some studies of AMBT have yielded smaller effects compared to CBT for the same disorders (e.g., Craigie et al., 2008). From these findings, Roemer and Orsillo (2013) concluded that 'treatments are more efficacious when they incorporate elements of cognitive-behavioral treatments' (p. 170). On the other hand, although CBT has been established as being efficacious with a variety of anxiety disorders, not all receiving the treatment respond to it, and the refusal and dropout rates are surprisingly high (Hofmann & Smits, 2008). Based on these reviews and empirical conclusions, and in view of the fact that anxiety disorders often present complex and heterogeneous conditions, this book takes a multimodal approach to the treatment of anxiety disorders.

There is also some evidence that AMBT helps patients relate differently to their internal experiences, resulting in decreased emotional reactivity and reduced experiential and behavioural avoidance (Roemer & Borkovec, 1994; Wegner, 2011; Wolgast, Lundh, & Viborg, 2011). Open trials have shown changes in experiential avoidance to precede symptom changes (Dalrymple & Herbert, 2007; Kocovski, Fleming, & Rector, 2009; Ossman, Wilson, Storaasli, & McNeill, 2006). For example, Treanor, Erisman, Salters-Pedneault, Roemer, & Orsillo (2011), in their study of AMBT for GAD, found treated patients to have significantly greater decreases in distress about emotions than a waitlist control condition. Analyses of weekly reports indicated that increases in acceptance and valued action significantly predicted responder status over and above decreases in weekly reports of worry, among clients with GAD receiving AMBT (Hayes, Orsillo, & Roemer, 2010). These results clearly indicate that values clarification and valued action are important ingredients of effective therapy for anxiety disorders.

When AMBT are applied to anxiety disorders, the main goal is to help the patients learn to observe their symptoms without overly identifying with them or without reacting to them in ways that aggravate their distress (Roemer, Erisman, & Orsillo, 2008). To achieve this goal, Herbert and Forman (2014) have articulated four overlapping groups of AMBT components for the management of anxiety disorders, which include:

1. Techniques that facilitate awareness of one's current perceptual, somatic, cognitive and emotional experience.
2. Techniques that encourage cognitive distancing or defusion from one's thoughts and inner experience.
3. Techniques that promote nonjudgemental acceptance of subjective experience.
4. Techniques that foster clarity of goals and values.

In the context of CH, two additional groups of strategies for reducing distress in anxiety disorders can be added to this list:

5. Techniques that nurture sense of gratitude
6. Techniques that cultivate PC

The integration of these six components of AMBT in the treatment of anxiety disorders is deemed to produce a fundamental shift in perspective (reperceiving), that is, these lead to a re-evaluation of patient's constructed reality. Strategies based on these six treatment components are briefly described next.

Strategies for cultivating awareness
There are many strategies for cultivating increasing awareness of one's ongoing stream of experience. Some of the commonest techniques include (i) mindfulness meditation, (ii) mindful hypnosis, (iii) concentrative meditation, (iv) walking meditation, (v) eating meditation, (vi) attention training, (vii) compassion meditation and (viii) loving kindness meditation. These techniques are described in other publications, for example, Kabat-Zinn (2013) and Segal et al. (2012); for AMBT specific to anxiety disorders, see Orsillo and Roemer (2011).

Strategies for cognitive distancing

Cognitive distancing strategies are used to help patients with anxiety disorder distance away from their worrying and fearful thoughts. Cognitive distancing can be seen as an extension of cognitive self-monitoring routinely practiced in CBT. While in CBT cognitive distortions are recorded on paper or some other means with the goal of identifying and restructuring them, in AMBT cognitive distancing strategies are used with the purpose of recognizing that thoughts are distinct from the self and that they may not be true. Specifically, AMBT train patients to visualize thoughts from a distance, for example, as floating on a leaf going downstream. This training produces cognitive defusion, or the ability to separate thoughts from the self. Cognitive defusion can be achieved through several strategies, including (i) using metaphors, (ii) recognizing bias in thinking, (iii) hearing thoughts (self-talk) and (iv) seeing thoughts (as images).

Strategies for promoting acceptance

One of the core interventions in AMBT relates to fostering an open, accepting, nonjudgemental and welcoming attitude towards the full range of subjective experience. The most common strategies for promoting acceptance include (i) psychoeducation, (ii) acceptance exercise and (iii) exposure exercises. These strategies are described in detail in Chapter 6. For the present purpose, the therapeutic components of the acceptance exercise are listed. The acceptance exercise involves:

- Focusing on here and now.
- Observing emotional experiences and their contexts non-judgementally.
- Separation of secondary emotions from primary emotions (e.g., not to get upset for feeling upset, not to get anxious for feeling anxious and not to feel depressed for feeling depressed).
- Learning to tolerate distress rather than fighting it (flow with it).
- Adopting healthy and adaptive means to deal with anxiety and chronic distress, rather than resorting to short-term reduction measures such as over-medication, alcohol or substance abuse.
- Tolerance of painful experience.
- Tolerance of frustration.
- Re-contextualizing meaning of suffering, for example, from 'this is unbearable' to 'let me focus on what I can do'.
- Exercising radical acceptance – ability to welcome those things in life that are hard, unpleasant or very painful (e.g., accepting a loss).
- Embracing good or bad experience as part of life.

- Willing to experience the reality of the present moment, for example, believing that 'things are as they should be'.
- Purposely allowing experiences (thoughts, emotions, desires, urges, sensations, etc.) to unfold without attempting to block or suppress them.
- Realizing that anxiety is not caused by object or situation itself, but by our perception of it, our coping abilities and our level of spirituality.

Strategies for clarifying values

Clarification and articulation of one's values are considered to be important in AMBT. As values give meaning to one's life, they often establish the direction one chooses to take in therapy. In this sense, values largely determine whether a patient is willing to commit to the behavioural and emotional challenges that he or she may have to face in the course of therapy. Clarification of patient's values thus becomes an essential ingredient in the development and sustenance of motivation for change (Herbert & Forman, 2014). However, values are more general and they may not be attainable. Goals, on the other hand, are more specific, and can be clearly defined and achieved. Nevertheless, values provide a sense of direction (e.g., going to school to become a teacher), while goals provide concrete steps (e.g., going to classes, passing exams) for achieving something that is valued (e.g., being a good teacher). As part of values work, patients are encouraged not to assume that 'treatment would be solely (or even primarily) on the initial presenting problem, but rather casting a wider net and conducting an inquiry of the patient's broader goals, aspirations, and dreams' (Herbert & Forman, 2014).

Exercises for clarifying values include (i) posting existential questions such as 'What do you want your life to stand for?' or (ii) imagining the eulogy one would hear at one's funeral and comparing it with the most honest rendition based on one's life.

Strategies for learning to express gratitude

Sense of gratitude is used as a means to cultivate acceptance in patients with anxiety disorder. Gratitude is a feeling or attitude in acknowledgement of a benefit that one has received or will receive. The experience of gratitude has historically been one of the core components of several world religions (Emmons & Crumpler, 2000) and has been mulled over extensively by moral philosophers such as Adam Smith (1790/1976). Recent studies suggest that people who are grateful have higher levels of subjective well-being, are happier, less depressed, less stressed out, and more satisfied with their lives and social relationships (Kashdan, Uswatte, & Julian, 2006;

Wood, Joseph, & Maltby, 2008; McCullough, Emmons, & Tsang, 2002). Grateful people also have higher levels of control over their environments, personal growth, purpose in life, and self-acceptance (Wood, Joseph, & Maltby, 2009). Moreover, they have more positive ways of coping with difficulties they experience in life, being more likely to seek support from other people, reinterpret and grow from experience, and spend more time planning how to deal with a problem rather than ruminating about it (Wood, Joseph, & Linley, 2007). Furthermore, grateful people have less negative coping strategies, being less likely to try to avoid or deny their problems, blame themselves or cope through maladaptive means such as substance use (Wood et al., 2007). Grateful people sleep better which appears to be related to less indulgence in negative rumination and more involved in positive thoughts just before going to sleep (Wood, Joseph, Lloyd, & Atkins, 2009).

Strategies commonly used in psychotherapy, particularly in CH, to promote expression of gratitude in patients with anxiety disorder include (i) gratitude education, (ii) gratitude training and (iii) gratitude hypnotherapy.

Gratitude education

Gratitude education explores broad generalizations about different cultural values and beliefs, and Western and non-Western expectations of life and achievement. Patients are also encouraged to read the book *The Narcissism Epidemic: Living in the Age of Entitlement* (Twenge & Campbell, 2009). This book provides a clear account of how high expectations, preoccupation with success and sense of entitlement can set us up for failure. The idea behind the education is to help patient with anxiety disorder understand that values are human-made, subjective and culturally determined. This comparative understanding of societal values helped Irene re-examine her own meaning of success and failure and helped her to begin to focus on what she has (gratitude) rather than ruminating with what she did not have (unable to skate competitively).

Gratitude training

Gratitude training involves carrying out several gratitude tasks. The patient is encouraged to do at least one of these tasks each day.

- Writing gratitude letters
- Writing a gratitude journal
- Remembering gratitude moments
- Making gratitude visits to people one is grateful to
- Practicing gratitude self-talk.

Gratitude Hypnotherapy
Sense of gratitude is easily integrated with hypnotherapy. This excerpt adapted from Alladin (2006, p. 303; 2007, p. 197) illustrates how hypnotic suggestions can be crafted to reinforce sense of gratitude in patients with anxiety disorder. These suggestions are offered while the patient is in a deep trance and fully relaxed mentally and physically.

> Just notice feeling calm, peaceful, and a sense of well-being. Feeling calm ... peaceful ... sense of harmony. No tension ... no pressure ... completely relaxed both mentally and physically ... sense of peace ... sense of harmony ... sense of gratitude. Become aware of your heart. Notice how peaceful you feel in your heart ... you feel calm in your heart ... you feel a sense of gratitude in your heart. When you feel good in your heart, you feel good in your mind. All major religions state that when you wake up in the morning, if you have a roof over your head, you have bread to eat, and water to drink, and are in fairly good health, then you have everything. Just become aware of all the things you have ... all the things you are grateful for. It's okay to have goals and ambitions. When we achieve goals and ambitions, they are bonuses and pluses. When we don't achieve our goals and ambitions, it is disappointing, but we have enough resources to live a comfortable life.

Strategies for nurturing psychophysiological coherence
The sixth component of AMBT targets integration of various subsystems in the body. There is abundant research evidence that heart-focused positive emotional state synchronizes the entire body system to produce PC (McCraty, Atkinson, Tomasino, & Bradley, 2009; McCraty & Tomasino, 2006). Guided by these scientific findings, Alladin (2014a) has developed the breathing with your heart technique to help patients with emotional disorders generate coherence (harmony) of the entire system (mind, body, brain, heart and emotion). This technique integrates both Western (complex information centre) and Eastern (big mind) concepts of the heart to produce psychological well-being. A similar technique called Heart Joy was independently developed by Lankton (2008, pp. 45–50) to create a sense of emotional well-being.

Breathing With Your Heart technique consists of two phases: heart education and breathing with your heart training assisted by hypnosis.

Heart education
Patient is given a scientific account of the role of heart and positive emotions in the generation of PC, which promotes healing, emotional stability and optimal performance. The similarities and the differences between Western and Eastern theories of mind and 'heart' are also discussed.

Breathing with your heart training combined with hypnosis

Heart–mind–body training helps patients with anxiety disorders cope with aversive feelings activated by fearful objects or situations, or other stressors. By breathing with the heart, patients with anxiety disorders are able to shift their attention away from their mind to their heart. When a person feels good in his or her heart, the person experiences a sense of comfort and joy because we validate reality by the way we feel and not by the way we think (Fredrickson, 2002; Isen, 1998). As mentioned before, logic does not always equate good affect, but feeling good in one's heart, especially when associated with sense of gratitude, invariably creates positive affect (Welwood, 1983).

The following transcript from a session with Irene (Alladin, 2014a, pp. 298–299) illustrates how the technique can be introduced in therapy. Prior to this session, Irene had several sessions of hypnotherapy; therefore, she already had some training in hypnosis and deep relaxation. It is advisable to introduce this technique later in therapy, when the patient had sufficient training in CBT, hypnosis and AMBT. The script begins with Irene being in a deep hypnotic trance:

THERAPIST: You have now become so deeply relaxed, that you begin to feel a beautiful sensation of peace and relaxation, tranquility and calm flowing throughout your mind and body. Do you feel relaxed both mentally and physically?

IRENE: Irene nods her head up and down. [Ideomotor signals of 'head up and down for YES' and 'shaking your head side to side for NO' were set up prior to starting the Breathing With Your Heart technique.]

THERAPIST: Now I would like you to focus on the center of your heart. [Pause for 30 seconds.] Can you imagine this?

IRENE: Irene nods her head.

THERAPIST: Now I would like you to imagine breathing in and out with your heart. [Pause for 30 seconds.] Can you imagine this?

IRENE Irene nods her head.

THERAPIST: Continue to imagine breathing in and out with your heart. [She was allowed to continue with this exercise for 2 minutes; the therapist repeated at regular intervals 'Just continue to imagine breathing with your heart' as she did the exercise.] Now I would like you to slow down your breathing. Breathe in and out at 7-second intervals. Breathe in with your heart … 1 … 2 … 3 … 4 … 5 … 6 … 7 and now breathe out with your heart … 1 … 2 … 3 … 4 … 5 … 6 … 7. And now as you are breathing in and out with your heart I want you to become aware of something in your life that you feel good about, something that

	you feel grateful for. [Pause for 30 seconds.] Are you able to focus on something that you are grateful for in your life?
IRENE:	Irene nods.
THERAPIST:	Just become aware of that feeling and soon you will feel good in your heart.
IRENE:	Irene nods.
THERAPIST:	Just become aware of this good feeling in your heart. [Pause for 30 seconds.] Now I would like you to become aware of the good feeling in your mind, in your body and in your heart. Do you feel this?
IRENE:	Irene nods.
THERAPIST:	Now you feel good in your mind, in your body and, in your heart. You feel a sense of balance, a sense of harmony. Do you feel this sense of harmony?
IRENE:	Irene nods.
THERAPIST:	From now on, whenever and wherever you are, you can create this good feeling by imagining breathing with your heart and focusing on something that you are grateful for. With practice you will get better and better at it. Now you know what to do to make your heart feel lighter.

Irene found this technique extremely helpful. It reminded her of her achievements, successes and resources that she had rather than focusing on what she did not have or lost. She indicated that the 'heart-breathing' technique, although seeming 'weird' initially, provided a 'neat method' for restoring inner balance.

Summary

Anxiety disorders represent complex problems that are further compounded by comorbidity and socio-cultural factors. As there is no one treatment that fits every patient, there is an urgent need for clinicians to continue to develop more effective and comprehensive treatments for anxiety disorders. The main purpose of this chapter was to integrate some specific Western and Eastern strategies to catalyse healing. Acceptance, mindfulness, gratitude and the 'heart', as well as the wounded self, were combined with CH to broaden the comprehensivesness of the psychological treatment of anxiety disorders. Additionally, innovative techniques for healing the wounded self and promoting PC were described. This comprehensive treatment protocol provides a variety of treatment interventions for anxiety disorders from which a therapist can choose the 'best-fit' strategies for a particular patient. A case formulation approach guides the clinician to select the most effective and efficient treatment strategies for his or her patient. Number of sessions and the sequence of the stages of CH will be determined by the clinical needs of each individual patient. Although most of the techniques described are scientific and evidence-based, there is a need to study the effectiveness of the multifactorial treatment described in this book. Moreover, to refine the treatment package, it will be important to study the relative effectiveness of each of the treatment component described.

3

Social Anxiety Disorder (Social Phobia)

Case of Betty

This case was briefly described in a previous publication (Alladin, 2014a) to illustrate the elicitation and the healing of self-wounds. In this chapter, Betty's therapy is described in detail to highlight the main CH components for social phobia. Betty, a 33-year-old senior psychiatry resident, was treated by the author for social and public speaking anxiety. Since a teenager, Betty had been experiencing anxiety, especially in social situations involving people she knew. The social anxiety got progressively worse from the start of her psychiatry residency programme and the public speaking anxiety became a serious concern for her as she had to present at ward rounds regularly. The anxiety spiralled in her final year of residency as she was required to make a presentation at the psychiatry grand rounds in the presence of faculty and her peers. Over the weekends, especially on Sundays, she experienced a great deal of anticipatory anxiety regarding the weekly ward round as the rounds were held on Mondays. As the ward round anxiety was not improving, she was convinced that she would not be able to present at the psychiatry grand round and would, consequently, fail her residency program. She constantly cogitated with the beliefs that her peers and professors would think she is 'weak', 'incompetent', 'a failure', 'a moron' and 'not worthy of being a psychiatrist'. She imagined this humiliating experience would be so painful, embarrassing, demeaning, and degrading to her that she would 'not be able to stand it'. It was at this desperate point that she sought help from the author, at the recommendation of her psychotherapy preceptor.

Integrative CBT for Anxiety Disorders: An Evidence-Based Approach to Enhancing Cognitive Behavioural Therapy with Mindfulness and Hypnotherapy, First Edition. Assen Alladin.
© 2016 John Wiley & Sons, Ltd. Published 2016 by John Wiley & Sons, Ltd.

Betty comes from a professional and upper middle-class family. Her grandfather was a neurosurgeon and her father is a distinguished heart surgeon, who excelled both in academia and clinical practice. Her mother is a registered nurse, who works part-time in the diabetic clinic. Betty has one sibling, Tara, who is 3 years older than her, a successful gynecologist, and married to a school teacher. Betty gets on well with Tara, but not very close to each other. While Tara is closer to her father, Betty is 'mummy's girl'. The father is extremely proud of Tara, whom he praises to be in 'real medicine'. He is disappointed that Betty, in spite of his strong discouragement, chose psychiatry, which he considers 'unscientific' and 'a bunch of speculations '. Betty's relationship with her father was difficult and challenging. She saw her father as being cold, unemotional and highly opinionated. He openly expressed resentment at Betty, for choosing psychiatry for her residency. He would spend long hours taking to Tara about medicine and surgery. Betty felt very hurt by this and avoided her father, especially when with other people as she felt undermined and embarrassed by him in front of others. Betty also felt uncomfortable with her father because he openly expressed disappointment of not having a son. He accepted Tara as he hoped the second child would be a boy. As it turned out to be a girl, he expressed disappointment. Although these comments were light, Betty felt unwanted and unappreciated.

Diagnostic Criteria for Social Anxiety Disorder (Social Phobia)

The DSM-V (American Psychiatric Association, 2013, pp. 202–203) diagnostic criteria for social phobia, social phobia, include:

1. Marked fear or anxiety about one or more social situations in which the person is exposed to possible scrutiny by others. Examples of fearful social situations constitute social interactions (e.g., having a conversation, meeting unfamiliar people), being observed (e.g., eating or drinking), and performing in front of others (e.g., giving a speech). In children, the anxiety must occur in peer settings, not only in interactions with adults.
2. The person fears that he or she will act in a way or show anxiety symptoms that will be humiliating or embarrassing and offensive to others and will lead to rejection.
3. The social situations almost invariably provoke fear or anxiety. In children, the fear or anxiety may be expressed by crying, tantrums, freezing, clinging, shrinking or failing to speak in social situations.

4. The feared social situations are avoided or endured with intense fear or anxiety.

5. The person recognizes that the fear or anxiety is out of proportion to the actual threat posed by the social situation and to the sociocultural context.

6. The fear, anxiety or avoidance has been persistent for at least six months.

7. The fear, anxiety or avoidance causes clinically significant distress or impairment in social, occupational or other important areas of functioning.

8. The fear, anxiety or avoidance is not due to a medical condition, substance abuse or another mental disorder.

9. If the fear or anxiety is restricted to performance only, that is, speaking or performing in public, it should be specified in the diagnosis (e.g., social phobia, specific to public speaking).

Prevalence of Social Anxiety Disorder

Social phobia has been reported as one of the most common anxiety disorders, yet it is underdiagnosed and undertreated (Schneier, Johnson, Hornig, Leibowitz, & Weissman, 1992. It has a lifetime prevalence of between 3% and 16% and a 12-month prevalence estimate of approximately 7% in the United States and Europe (American Psychiatric Association, 2013; Kariuki & Stein, 2013; Wancata, Fridl, & Friedrich, 2009). However, the 12-month prevalence estimates for the rest of the world is much lower, clustering around 0.5–2.0% (American Psychiatric Association, 2013). The 12-month prevalence rates in children and adolescents are comparable to those in adults. Epidemiological studies suggest a female preponderance (ratios ranging from 1.5 to 2.2) in the general population, but in clinical samples, males and females are equally affected (e.g., Wancata et al., 2009). Typically, symptoms of social phobia begin to appear in middle childhood or early adolescence (Schneier et al., 1992) and they persist into adulthood if untreated (Leibowitz, Gelenberg, & Munjack, 2005). There is strong evidence that children with social phobia may have an underlying trait characterized by habitual pattern of behavioural inhibition and severe shyness (Turner, Beidel, & Wolff, 1996). Social phobia has significant comorbidities with other anxiety disorders, alcohol use disorders, bulimia nervosa, depression, general medical conditions and certain personality disorders (Davidson, 2006; Schneier et al., 1992; Weiller, Bisserbe, Boyer, Lepine, & Lecrubier, 1996).

Causes of Social Anxiety Disorder

Although the pathogenesis of social phobia is not fully understood, over the past decade there has been an explosion of research devoted to delineating the pathophysiology of social phobia. The key clinical points derived from both biological and psychological available research on social phobia summarized by Morreale, Tancer and Uhde (2010) are highlighted as follows:

- There is some indication that multiple genetic variants may be involved in the development of social phobia, but no single gene responsible for the etiology of the disorder has been detected.
- Although patients with social phobia appear to be more sensitive than healthy volunteers to anxiogenic effects of various substances and circumstances, studies using anxiogenic stimuli have failed to provoke all the symptoms typical of social phobia.
- No clear psychoneuroendocrinal differences exist between patients with social phobia and healthy control subjects.
- When exposed to anxiety, social phobics demonstrate increased amygdalar activation, which is reversed both by pharmacological and psychological therapies.
- Neuroimaging studies suggest a dopamine receptor dysfunction in diagnosed social phobics.
- Studies indicate a differential autonomic response in diagnosed generalized versus specific subtype of social phobia.
- Children with behavioural inhibition have an increased risk of developing social phobia.
- Social phobics have negative cognitions, particularly negative perceptions of themselves and their environment.
- Hispanics have significantly lower lifetime prevalence rate of social phobia compared to Caucasians and African Americans.

In summary, the etiology of social phobia is not fully understood. As social phobia represents a heterogeneous disorder, resulting from complex interactions among inherited traits, environment, personal experience (including the wounded self) and neurobiological vulnerability, it is unlikely that a single cause of the disorder will be found. Examination of intersections between major theories, including the important roles of biological vulnerabilities, early experiences, temperament, cultural factors and cognitive processing, holds promise for expanded understanding of the etiology, maintenance and amelioration of social phobia.

Treatment of Social Anxiety Disorder

CBT and pharmacotherapy are considered the two best-established treatments for social phobia (Blanco, Schneier, Vesga-Lopez, & Leibowitz, 2010). A Cochrane review of pharmacotherapy for social phobia concluded that selective serotonin reuptake inhibitors (SSRIs) are the most effective treatment (Bandelow, Seidler-Brandler, Becker, Wedekind, & Ruther, 2007) and selective monoamine oxidase inhibitors (RIMA) to a lesser extent (Allgulander, Mangano, Zhang, Dahl, Lepola, Sjodin, & Emilien, 2004). A response rate of up to 60% has been reported with SSRIs (e.g., Davidson, 2006). There may be some differences in efficacy between SSRIs, but due to lack of direct within-group comparisons between them, at this point a firm conclusion cannot be drawn (Van Ameringen, Lane, Walker, Bowen, Chokka, Gold, & Swinson, 2001). Although many other agents (e.g., selective noradrenaline reuptake inhibitor, monoamine oxidase inhibitor, 5HT1A-agonist, second-generation antipsychotics, anticonvulsant, etc.) have been used to treat social phobia, at present there is limited evidence for their use with social phobia (Stein, Ipser, & van Balkom, 2009). The benefits of pharmacotherapy for social phobia include relatively rapid reduction in symptoms severity and cost effectiveness (Sadock & Sadock, 2003). The disadvantages of medications with social phobia relate to delayed onset of action of some medications, potential side effects and relapse after treatment discontinuation (Kariuki & Stein, 2013).

Behavioural therapies and CBTs are the best-studied and most widely practiced non-pharmacological treatments for social phobia (D. M. Clark, et al., 2003; Sadock & Sadock, 2003). Several studies have shown CBT to be as efficacious as pharmacologic treatment in terms of both short-term and long-term outcome (D. M. Clark et al., 2003; Heimberg, 2002). Although the effect size of CBT with social phobia appears to be moderate in comparison to pharmacotherapy, it is maintained at follow-ups (Hoffmann, 2004). Moreover, the advantages of CBT include better tolerability, greater likelihood of maintaining response after treatment has been terminated and cost-effectiveness in some settings (Sadock & Sadock, 2003; Veale, 2003). The downside of CBT comprises structural barriers to treatment such as language and transportation, lack of access to CBT, long waiting lists, slower response to treatment, and time-consuming nature of the therapy (Kariuki & Stein, 2013).

In summary, both pharmacological and psychological treatments seem to be equally effective with social phobia. If they are all equally effective, including different medication and varied psychological treatments, how can this be so? How can such apparently diverse treatments be equivalent in reducing social phobia? This lack of major difference in therapeutic outcome among various medications and psychotherapies can be attributed to 'common factors' in therapy (Imel & Wampold, 2008), such as empathy, therapeutic alliance, and patient variables or the placebo effect (Moncrieff & Cohen, 2009; Riess, 2010; Stefano, Fricchione, Slingsby, & Benson, 2001; Tallman & Bohart, 1999). In general, it would appear that no matter which treatment is used, the outcome will be positive for some patients. Alladin (2013a) and Humble, Duncan and Miller (1999) have suggested various strategies for utilizing common factors and the placebo effect in pharmacotherapy and psychotherapy to maximize outcome. CH for social phobia includes these elements to enhance the effect of therapy.

Cognitive Hypnotherapy for Social Anxiety Disorder

Hypnotherapy for managing symptoms of social anxiety disorder

Four to six of the initial sessions of CH consist of hypnotherapy, which is specifically targeted at symptoms management. This phase of therapy serves as a preparation for more complex therapy of exploring the roots of the social phobia later in therapy if the need arises. The hypnotherapy components include (i) relaxation training, (ii) demonstration of the power of mind over the body, (iii) ego strengthening, (iv) expansion of awareness, (v) modulation and regulation of symptoms, (vi) self-hypnosis and (vii) PHS. Hypnotherapy is introduced again later in therapy with patients who elect to pursue with uncovering work. The initial sessions of hypnotherapy, therefore, for some patients, serve as a preparatory phase for more complex therapy of exploring the roots of the anxiety disorder later in the therapy.

Relaxation training

As Betty had been experiencing high levels of tension, nervousness and hyperaroused physiological reactions, she found the relaxation induced by hypnosis very calming and soothing. She was highly susceptible to hypnosis and was able to generate profound mental and physical relaxation without much effort. Her hypnotic talent was utilized to help her dissociate from the anxiety-related situations, namely the ward rounds and the anticipatory anxiety related to presenting at the grand round. The relaxation response associated with the experience of feeling calm, relaxed and detached served as an experiential strategy to modify her anticipatory anxiety. The positive trace state was further deployed to teach Betty how to modulate her emotional reactions via self-hypnosis.

Demonstration of the power of the mind over the body
To further empower Betty and to ratify the credibility of the hypnotic intervention, eye and body catalepsies were introduced in the second hypnotherapy session. Betty was very intrigued that she was not able to open her eyes or get out of the reclining chair. The following transcript illustrates the explanation provided by the author for the eye and body catalepsy in terms of self-hypnosis.

THERAPIST: Let me explain to you why you were not able to open your eyes or get out of the chair. But first let me tell you what you achieved, before explaining to you why you can't open your eyes or get out of the chair. What you achieved is called eye catalepsy and body catalepsy. By eye catalepsy, I mean you paralyzed your eyelids, you were not able to open your eyes. By body catalepsy, I mean you literally paralyzed your body, not able to get out of the chair. This shows that your brain is so powerful and we can use the power of your brain to overcome your anxiety.

Now let me explain to you why you were not able to open your eyes or get out of the chair. This has to do with the power of your brain. As you know the brain is very powerful, everyone talks about the brain being very powerful. But as know the brain is also very dumb, because the brain never thinks for itself, it does what your mind tells it to do. Your brain is like a horse, very powerful, but as you know it's controlled or driven by the rider. In the same way your brain is very powerful, but what drives your brain is your thinking or your imagination, what we call the mind.

Since you have been thinking and imagining that your eyelids are heavy and stuck, your brain made it happen. And when you have been thinking and imagining that your body is heavy and stuck in the chair, your brain made it happen and you were not able to get out of the chair. Since your brain is so powerful, it's a double-edged sword. If you think positively or imagine good things about yourself, you feel it. If you think negative or imagine bad things about yourself you feel it. Since your brain is so powerful it makes it happen, whether it's good or bad. Your brain does not think whether it's true or false, its job is to react as fast as possible, this has to do with our survival. In your case, based on your life experience, you have been focusing on negative and fearful thoughts. In other words, you have been hypnotizing yourself with the wrong suggestions. Does this make sense to you?

PATIENT: Yes.

THERAPIST: Now that we know that you have been hypnotizing yourself
             with the negative suggestions, we can help you change those
             self-suggestions.

At the end of the session, Betty indicated to the therapist that she always
knew that she had been hypnotizing herself with the wrong suggestions,
but she did not know how to change them. The therapist reassured her
and explained that in the future sessions of hypnotherapy and CBT she
would be taught various techniques to counter negative self-hypnosis.
Betty found this session extremely powerful as it instilled in her the hope
and confidence that she can tap on her own personal resources to control
her social and public speaking anxiety. In addition, this session consolidated Betty's sense of positive expectancy and it further strengthened the
therapeutic alliance.

Ego strengthening

Ego-strengthening suggestions were offered to Betty to increase her
self-esteem, enhance her self-efficacy and gradually restore her confidence in her ability to manage her symptoms of social phobia. While in
deep hypnotic trance, Betty visualized herself as being self-efficacious
and dealing with the anxious situations head-on, rather than avoiding
them. Betty commented that the relaxation response and the ego-
strengthening suggestions made her feel strong and confident to deal
with her symptoms. She felt the hypnotherapy sessions increased her
confidence, coping abilities, positive self-image and interpersonal skills.
She found the ego-strengthening suggestion: 'Every day you will feel
calmer and more relaxed as a result of this treatment and as a result of
you practicing self-hypnosis every day' very reassuring and motivated her
to listen to her self-hypnosis CD every day (after the first hypnotherapy
session, Betty was given a self-hypnosis CD – see under the section 'Self-
hypnosis training').

Expansion of awareness

Although the level of her anxiety varied, Betty reported feeling constantly
anxious, unable to experience different emotions, particularly good feeling. This was largely due to her constant rumination with catastrophic
thoughts and images, and associated bodily responses, related to social
situations and public speaking. To expand her range of emotions, during
hypnosis Betty was directed to focus on the relaxation response and
experience a variety of emotions and feelings. This was achieved by using

EAT as described in Chapter 2. While Betty was in deep hypnotic trance, she was directed to focus on the relaxation response:

> You have now become so deeply relaxed and you are in such a deep hypnotic state that your mind and body feel completely relaxed, totally relaxed. You begin to feel a beautiful sensation of peace and tranquility, relaxation and calm, flowing all over your mind and body, giving you such a pleasant, and such a soothing sensation all over your mind and body, that you feel completely relaxed, totally relaxed both mentally and physically, and yet you are aware of everything, you are aware of all the sound and noise around you, you are aware of your thoughts and imagination, and yet you feel so relaxed, so calm and so peaceful. This shows that you have the ability to relax, to let go, and to put everything on hold. This shows that you have lots of control, because you are aware of everything, you can hear all the sounds and noise around you, you are aware of your thoughts and imagination, you are aware that I am sitting beside you and talking to you, yet you are able to put everything on hold and relax completely. This shows you have lots of control.
>
> Now you can become aware of all the good feelings you are feelings. You feel calm, peaceful, relaxed and very, very comfortable. You may also become aware of feeling heavy, light, or detached, or distancing away from everything, becoming more and more detached, distancing away from everything, drifting into a deep, deep hypnotic state.

With EAT, Betty discovered the ability to relax and feel different feelings and sensations. She was surprised that she could put things on hold, that is, although aware of her anxiety, fears and concerns, she was able to detach from her worries and let go. With practice she was able to relax and experience different contextual feelings, although aware of her concerns and worries. Betty's ability to produce, amplify and express a variety of positive feelings and experiences gave her the confidence that she could modify or control her anxiety symptoms. To gain further control over her social phobia, Betty was introduced to imaginal exposure therapy (Wolpe, 1958; Wolpe & Lazarus, 1966), which is considered to be an important component of CH for social phobia (Golden, 2012). While in deep hypnosis, Betty was directed to bring on her anxious experience associated with ward round and the presentation at the grand round. Then she was suggested to utilize self-hypnosis to control her anxious and fearful reaction.

> When I count from ONE to FIVE, by the time you hear me say FIVE, you will begin to feel whatever emotion or reaction that is associated with your thoughts about Monday ward rounds. [Betty was then helped to amplify the affect associated with the ward round.] When I count slowly from ONE to FIVE, as I count you will begin to experience the anxious feelings more and

more intensely, so that when I reach the count of FIVE, at the count of FIVE you will feel the full reaction as strongly as you can bear it. ONE ... TWO ... THREE ... FOUR ... FIVE. Now notice what you feel and you can describe it to me.

[Betty was then instructed to utilize self-hypnosis to cope with the anxious and fearful reactions.]

Now imagine using your self-hypnosis to control the anxiety feeling. Since you have the ability to relax and put things on hold, you can let go and calm down.

After several repetition of this set of suggestions, Betty was able to relax completely, while imagining participating in the ward round. This mental rehearsal in trance, prepared Betty to face the ward round. Moreover, this technique encouraged her to focus on her anxious feelings head-on, rather than catastrophizing or cogitating about her symptoms. The imaginal exposure technique was also used to prepare Betty to deal with anxiety related to the presentation at the grand round. As Betty was already attending ward rounds, although with difficulty initially, there was no need to utilize exposure *in vivo* therapy. As her turn to present at the grand round was not due yet, she was encouraged to attend the grand rounds regularly:

Imagine you are the presenter and doing a good job. You realize that the audience is not there to monitor or scrutinize your behavior, but to listen to the content of your talk. As you have been preparing for months, and you are presenting on your favorite topic, you know what to say. So focus on the content of your talk and not on how you feel.

To increase her confidence further, Betty was encouraged to participate in exposure therapy. This involved *in vivo* exposure to a mock grand round, where Betty gave her presentation.

Modulating and controlling symptoms
As hypnosis is an experiential approach to therapy, Betty was advised to perceive her anxiety symptoms as a syncretic experience (Alladin, 2006, 2007, 2008; Safer & Leventhal, 1977). She was encouraged to view her anxiety not simply as an affect, thought or behaviour, but as a cascade of cognitive, somatic, perceptual, physiological, visceral and kinaesthetic changes. Hypnotic induction, amplification and modification of positive syncretic cognition offered Betty dramatic proof that she can change and regulate anxious and distressing experience. DePiano and Salzberg (1981) believe the rapid improvement that is often observed in patients receiving hypnotherapy is partly related to the positive syncretic cognition produced by the trance experience.

Self-hypnosis training

To generalize her relaxation response and her ability to 'let go' to real situations, Betty was coached in self-hypnosis. To facilitate self-hypnosis training, at the end of the first hypnotherapy session, Betty was given a CD recording of the session. She was encouraged to listen to the CD at least once a day at home. This homework assignment allowed continuity of treatment between sessions and offered her the opportunity to practice self-hypnosis. Betty commented that the training in self-hypnosis provided her the most practical and powerful skill for controlling her anxiety symptoms outside the therapy sessions. The self-hypnosis also served as a powerful tool for countering her catastrophic cogitation (NSH). The ultimate goal of psychotherapy is to help patients with anxiety disorder establish self-reliance and independence. Self-hypnosis is considered a very useful tool for achieving self-reliance and personal power (Alman 2001), and for developing self-correcting behaviours (Yapko, 2003).

Once Betty had built some confidence in self-hypnosis, the generalization of the skill to real situations was consolidated by teaching her the clenched fist technique (Stein, 1963). As discussed in Chapter 2, the clenching of the dominant fist serves as an anchor for the elicitation of the relaxation response. Betty was trained to induce self-hypnosis rapidly in diverse anxiety-provoking situations by mastering the clenched fist technique. (Stein, 1963), which involves clenching the preferred fist as an anchor. An anchor is any stimulus that evokes a consistent response pattern from a person (Lankton, 1980). The dominant fist as an anchor is easily established during deep hypnotic trance. The following transcript illustrates how the clenched fist technique was introduced to Betty while she was in a deep hypnotic trance.

> You have now become so deeply relaxed, that you feel this beautiful sensation of peace and relaxation, tranquility and calm, flowing all over your mind and your body, giving you such a pleasant, such a soothing sensation, all over your mind and your body that you feel completely relaxed, totally relaxed, drifting into a deeper and deeper hypnotic state. This shows that you have the ability to relax, the ability to let go, and the ability to put things on hold. This shows that you have lots of control, because you know what's happening around you, yet you are able to relax your mind and body completely. Since you are able to relax here, you may also be anble to relax in any situation. In order facilitate your ability to relax in the real situations I am going to introduce you to the clenched fist technique [which was discussed prior to the induction of the hypnosis].
>
> Now if you may clench your right fist [it was established that she is right-handed]. As you clench your fist become aware of how very relaxed you are.

You feel completely relaxed, both mentally and physically, and yet you are aware of everything. Also notice that you are in complete control, knowing what to do and knowing what's going on around you. If you slightly tighten your fist you become even more aware of the good feelings, you feel completely relaxed and in complete control.

As you have made an association between your right fist and the ability to relax, from now on, whenever you want to feel this good feeling, you can bring on this feeling by clenching your right fist and anchoring your mind to this session, that is, reminding yourself of this session, that you can relax and let go completely. And from now on, wherever you are, whatever you are doing, if you feel tense, anxious, upset, or stressed out, you can counter these feelings by clenching you right fist and anchoring your mind to this experience. With practice you will get better and better at it.

The anchoring technique is experientially ratified by hypnotic imaginal rehearsal training and reinforced by PHS.

Just undo your fist. Now we are going to practice the clenching fist technique. Imagine from now on whenever you get upset, anxious, or stressed out, utilizing your clenched fist technique to counter the bad feelings. So just continue to imagine, from now on whenever you get anxious, upset or stressed out you are able counter these feelings by clenching you fist and anchoring your mind to this experience. And with practice you will get better and better at it. As a result of this you begin to have more control over your negative feelings.

Betty found the clenched fist technique very useful, in the sense that it was very concrete and very portable. Hence it was easily applied in a variety of anxiety-provoking situations.

Post-hypnotic suggestions

Before the termination of the hypnotic session, Betty was offered a variety of PHS to counter her anxiety, avoidance behaviour and negative rumination. Betty was constantly cogitating with the following negative self-suggestions:

- 'I will not be able to cope.'
- 'I will lose control.'
- 'I can't handle the ward round.'
- 'What if I am not able to answer a question at the ward round? It will be so humiliating and embarrassing.'
- 'I will fail my residency, I am too anxious to be able to present at the grand round. I won't have a job.'

Rumination with these suggestions not only can induce a negative trance, but also serves as powerful self-affirmation or PHS, which can become part of the avoidance pattern of behaviour. To offset the negative rumination, Betty was offered various PHS.

- 'Whenever you become anxious in a situation, you will become more aware of how to deal with it rather than focusing on your symptoms or what may happen to you.'
- 'When you plan to confront an anxiety-provoking situation, you will feel less need to avoid the situation.'
- 'As you become more relaxed every day as a result of listening to your Self-Hypnosis CD, you will begin to feel motivated to face the situations you have been avoiding.'

Clarke and Jackson (1983) regard PHS to be a form of 'higher-order-conditioning', which can function as positive or negative reinforcement to increase or decrease the probability of desired or undesired behaviours. They successfully utilized PHS to enhance the effect of *in vivo* exposure among agoraphobics.

Cognitive behavioural therapy

Patients with social phobia tend to (i) overestimate the danger involved in social situations, (ii) underestimate their ability to cope in such situations, (iii) personalize others' social responses and (iv) undermine their talents despite their ability to perform (Stahl & Moore, 2013). Betty had all these dysfunctional cognitions related to the ward round and public speaking (grand round presentation). CBT helped Betty identify and restructure her negative cognitions. It provided her with a practical strategy to alter the meaning of her anxiety symptoms and the associated maladaptive emotions, namely guilt, shame, embarrassment and anger. With some patients, it may also be beneficial to address unhelpful emotion such as anger prior to starting exposure. As CBT techniques are fully described in several excellent books (e.g., Beck, & Emery, 1985, 2005; Clark & Beck, 2010), and a detailed description of the sequential progression of CBT within the CH framework is provided elsewhere (Alladin, 2007, 2008), they are not described in detail here. For a therapy transcript, see Alladin (2008, p. 107–110), which illustrates how Roger, who was fearful of going to the local grocery store, was guided by the therapist to reevaluate and change his maladaptive belief that 'The world is unsafe '. As a result of this session, Roger was able to modify his maladaptive beliefs and, consequently, his unrealistic fears about the world.

Healing self-wounds

After 10 sessions of CBT and hypnotherapy, Betty made some significant progress. She felt less anxious in the ward rounds and had less anticipatory anxiety about the grand round. As her symptoms were not eliminated completely, and she was still experiencing fear, she was interested to explore the root causes of her social phobia. This segment of therapy thus involved in-depth hypnotherapy and consisted of eliciting self-wounds, detoxifying the meaning of her anxiety and defending the choice of her career, albeit her father's disapproval.

Elicitation of self-wounds

To access Betty's self-wounds, the affect bridge technique was used. The feeling of anxiety that she experienced during the ward round was used as a bridge to elicit her first anxiety attack. While experiencing intense anxiety, she became aware of being 'a fake' and 'a fraud', and she became very fearful that her colleagues and the physicians would find out that she is phony, not a real doctor, but someone who is 'dim-witted' and not deserving to be a physician. Then she remembered her first anxiety attack that occurred five years ago while she was having dinner with her own family and a neighbouring family. The invited family consisted of Phil, who is a heart surgeon and good friend of Betty's father, Phil's wife, a homemaker, and her two sons, Peter and Jack, both at the local university studying electrical engineering and physics, respectively. During dinner, Betty's father expressed his disappointment with Betty's decision to do a psychiatry residency and wondered if Phil could persuade her to change her mind. Phil, who also happened to have a skewed view of psychiatry, stated that psychiatry is an unwise choice as this speciality is represented by 'failed physicians'. Betty felt very angry with her father and offended by Phil's comments, which made her feel dizzy. Before she could recover, Jack commented that 'Freud was a dirty old man, preoccupied with sex and addicted to opium'. Betty felt embarrassed and humiliated and she felt she was going to pass out, whence she left the dinner table and went to her room. As her head was spinning, it occurred to her that if everyone thinks psychiatry is dumb, it must be, and that she must be really 'dim' to have chosen this field.

During her psychiatry residency, Betty was extremely fearful that her patients would find out her real identity and would question her competence, which would be unbearably embarrassing and humiliating to her. From the affect bridge probing, it became evident that she strongly believed she is unworthy of being a physician and her anxiety served as a defence against this painful self-view of herself. Moreover, she was torn between the wish to project to others that she was a competent doctor worthy of approval and the need to hide from others and herself her self-view of inadequacy and incompetence. The implicit meaning of Betty's anxiety attacks were thus related to her deep beliefs that she is not smart; she is a substandard physician, and a fraud to call herself a doctor and treat patients. She also discerned that since she was not able to control her anxiety, it was solid proof to her that she was inadequate and ineffectual. Furthermore, these beliefs represented to her the reasons why her father preferred a son over her. It would appear from these data how Betty's generalized self-wound developed, which swayed her to perceive herself as 'dim-witted', 'incompetent', 'weak', 'a fraud' and 'not deserving to be a doctor'. From the emergence of these information, it was formulated that Betty needed to resolve two main experiential conflicts: (i) to detoxify the meaning of her anxiety and (ii) to convey to her father that psychiatry is a respected medical speciality and that her choice of psychiatry was based on genuine interest, not lack of intellect.

Detoxification of meaning of anxiety
The split screen technique (Alladin, 2008; Cardena et al., 2000; Lynn & Cardena, 2007; Spiegel, 1981) was used to help Betty detoxify the meaning of her anxiety. This is a hypnotic strategy that utilizes the 'adult ego state' to help the 'weak ego state' deal with anxiety-provoking situations. It also facilitates the 'two' ego states to work together as a team, rather than splitting from each other, when the self is threatened or stressed out. The therapy transcript presented here illustrates how the split screen technique was used with Betty to help her deal with the toxic meaning of her anxiety. The transcript begins while Betty was in a deep trance, bolstered by ego-strengthening suggestions.

> THERAPIST: Now I would like you to imagine sitting in front of a large TV or cinema screen, which is vertically split in two halves, consisting of a right side and a left side. Can you imagine this?

> [Betty raised her 'YES' finger. Ideomotor signals were already set up – 'YES' represented raising of her right index finger and 'NO' was represented by raising of her left index finger.]

> THERAPIST: Imagine the right side of the screen is lighting up as if it's ready to project an image. Imagine yourself being projected on the right side of the screen, just as you are now. Feeling very relaxed, very comfortable, in complete control, and aware of everything. And now become aware of the things you have achieved, things that you are proud of. Do you feel these good feelings?

[Betty raised her 'YES' finger.]

THERAPIST: That's very good. Do you feel the sense of achievement?

[Betty raised her 'YES' finger.]

THERAPIST: Are you thinking about your achievement related to having made it to med school? [It is advisable to check out the fact rather than making assumption. In this case, the assumption was made by the therapist as Betty had disclosed to the therapist that she feels very proud of having made it to medical school, which she considers to be a great achievement for her as most people don't make it to medical school. So whenever she thinks of achievement or success, the thoughts about her admission to medical school cross her mind, which usually creates a good feeling inside her.]

[Betty raised her 'YES' finger.]

THERAPIST: Just focus on the good feelings and become aware that you made it to med school in spite of many obstacles and difficulties. This proves to you that you have a strong side, a successful side, a side that can rescue you from difficulties and help you succeed. We are going to call this part of you the 'adult side' or your 'adult ego state'. Is that acceptable to you?

[Betty raised her 'YES' finger.]

THERAPIST: Now leave this side of yourself on the right side of the screen and imagine yourself being projected on the left side of the screen feeling anxious, as if you are in a situation that causes anxiety for you. Imagine you are in a situation that causes anxiety for you and become aware of feeling anxious. Can you imagine this?

[Betty raised her 'YES' finger.]

THERAPIST: Now become aware of all the feelings that you are experiencing. Don't be afraid to let all the anxious feelings come over you, because soon we will show you how to deal with them. Become aware of all the physical sensations you feel. Become aware of all the thoughts that are going through your mind and become aware of your behaviours. Can you feel these?

[Betty raised her 'YES' finger.]

THERAPIST: So just become aware of the whole experience and we are going to call this part of you the 'weak part of you' or the 'child ego state' as we discussed before. Is this acceptable to you? [In a previous therapy session, Betty and the therapist had discussed about the different parts of our selves, which are metaphorically referred as ego states. Betty readily identified that very often she experiences a split of her self – at times she feels strong and confident and at other times, especially when stressed out or feeling anxious, she feels helpless like a child – not knowing what to do.]

[Betty raised her 'YES' finger.]

THERAPIST: Now imagine, your adult ego state stepping out from the right side into the left side of the screen. Can you imagine this?

[Betty raised her 'YES' finger.]

THERAPIST: Imagine your adult ego state is reassuring your child ego state. She is telling your child ego state not to be afraid because she is there to help her out and guide her how to deal with her fear. From now on, the child part of you don't have to handle difficulties on her own, she can work as a team with the strong part of you. Imagine the adult part of you telling the weak part of you that in therapy you she had learned many strategies for dealing with symptoms of anxiety and, therefore, she can teach you these strategies. Imagine she is demonstrating the weak part how to relax, how to let go, and how to reason with fearful thoughts. Continue to imagine this until you feel the weak part of you feel reassured and now she knows what to do when feeling anxious. Imagine your weak part feels protected and empowered knowing she can get help from the adult ego state whenever the needs arise. The weak part also realizes that the strong part is part of your self as well. They both belong to your self. So from now on there is not need to feel separated from the adult ego state.

The split screen technique was repeated over several sessions, with main focus on ward and grand rounds. Betty commented that the strategy created various coping and self-efficacious images for her, which gave her the confidence that she could deal with her symptoms of social anxiety rather than catastrophizing about them and, consequently, she stopped labelling herself as being weak or incompetent. The split screen technique also made her realize that she is an intelligent and proficient person and that there was no need for her to convince others of her competence. Furthermore, she felt safe talking about her symptoms and discomfort rather than having to hide them. Moreover, she started to shift her belief that her colleagues were overly critical to her, instead she began to perceive them as supportive and sympathetic. In addition, she viewed patients expressing relief that their doctor, because of her own personal experience with anxiety, has a better understanding of their problems, which they find reassuring. Most importantly, Betty began to realize that there was no need for her to project an inauthentic image of a doctor and this realization significantly reduced her anticipatory anxiety about the ward round and the ultimate grand round.

Defending her choices

The undermining, disapproval and rejection of Betty by her father not only contributed to her self-wounds, they were also maintaining her social anxiety. The next major component of the experiential hypnotherapy thus consisted of helping Betty to convey to her father that (i) psychiatry is a respected medical speciality, (ii) her choice of psychiatry was based on intrinsic interest, sound professional judgement and personal achievement and (iii) the fact that she was born a girl was not a problem for her but something that her father needed to resolve for himself. As her father is 'very narrow-minded and stubborn', Betty did not feel comfortable facing her father without some preparatory work. The therapist recommended working with the empty chair technique, which is a Gestalt therapy role-playing strategy (Perls, Hefferline, & Goodman, 1951; Woldt & Toman, 2005) for reducing intra- or interpersonal conflicts (Nichol & Schwartz, 2008). In this procedure, while in deep hypnosis, Betty was directed to talk to her father, whom she imagined sitting in an empty chair in the therapist's office, across from her. By imagining her father sitting in the empty chair in the safety of the therapy situation, Betty was able to express various strong feelings about her father she had been harbouring inside her for some time.

By engaging in the empty chair work, and with the support and direction from the therapist, Betty was able to express her strong negative feelings towards her father and reframe her anger into sympathy. She was also able to defend her intellectual and professional integrity for choosing psychiatry as her speciality. By remembering her academic achievements at high school (e.g., being top in classes, winning several prizes, including the scholarship to one of the top universities in the country) and during her undergraduate studies (e.g., very high GPA and very high MCAT score), she recognized her high intellectual functioning. The fact that she made it to medical school proved that she is a very bright person. She also recognized that she had surpassed her father and sister in terms of having an integrative and broader view of medicine. From her training in psychiatry, she was shocked to discover that her father and her sister have very reductionist view of medicine (a view not shared by her mother), while she is able to appreciate the biopsychosocial nature of human suffering. She chose psychiatry not because she is not bright, she chose it because this is what she wanted to do. In fact, she had the opportunity to go into neurology but chose psychiatry because she was genuinely interested in the interaction between the mind and the body.

The empty chair technique also helped Betty to fully understand and experience her feelings for her father. She realized that her father's disappointment of not having a son is not her problem, but an issue that her father had to deal with it himself and not blame her or her mother for it. The empty chair conversation helped her reframe the hurt feeling (caused by her father's preference for a boy) into sympathy for her father.

Betty showed very good response to CH. The therapy helped her identify the explicit and the implicit nature of her anxiety, as well as the roots of her wounded self. While behavioural and cognitive strategies helped her symptomatically, the hypnotherapy, by virtue of its phenomenological nature, made the therapy experiential and thus more meaningful. She found the HET very helpful in accessing and healing her self-wounds. The empty chair and the split screen techniques permitted her to practice future confrontation with her father. As therapy progressed, Betty was able to engage in regular conversations with her father. She started to express her opinions more regularly and began to view her father's disagreements as his opinions rather than undermining her, and she was able to prevent herself from brooding over what he said.

Promoting acceptance and gratitude

As discussed in Chapter 1, patients with anxiety disorders tend to suppress re-experiencing of their initial trauma as it causes extreme distress (Wolfe, 2005, 2006). Such avoidance or intolerance of inner suffering can be regarded as lack of acceptance within the context of third-wave CBT (Baer & Huss, 2008). Although Betty's suppression of her self-wounds warded off her distressing experience temporarily, unfortunately it maintained her symptoms. For this reason, it was important to help Betty accept her emotional distress. However, acceptance is not merely tolerance of inner hurt; it is the active and nonjudgemental embracing of painful experience in the here and now, involving undefended exposure to thoughts, feelings and bodily sensations as they occur (Hayes, 2004). Betty was helped to reduce her suffering by helping her to (i) observe different aspects of a social situation; (ii) establish the relationship between a social situation and her discomfort; (iii) create a new stimulus (e.g., relaxation response) that was less distracting or not distressing at all (Hayes, 2004) and (iv) decentre from distressing thoughts, negative feelings, and unpleasant body sensations (Segal, Williams, & Teasdale, 2002). Levitt, Brown, Orsillo and Barlow (2004) have provided empirical evidence for the effectiveness of acceptance-based interventions in the management of anxiety disorders. Several techniques, including (i) gratitude education, (ii) gratitude training, (iii) acceptance training, (iv) acceptance and gratitude hypnotherapy and (v) mind–body–heart integration were used to help Betty cultivate acceptance. These techniques are described next.

Gratitude education and training

Sense of gratitude is used as a means to cultivate acceptance in patients with social phobia. Gratitude is a feeling or attitude in acknowledgement of a benefit that one has received or will receive. Studies suggest that people who are grateful have higher levels of subjective well-being, have higher levels of control of their environments, have more positive ways of coping with the difficulties they experience in life, spend more time planning how to deal with the problem, are less likely to try to avoid or deny their problems, and they sleep better (for review and references, see Chapter 2).

Gratitude education

Gratitude education focuses on drawing broad generalizations about different cultural values and beliefs, and comparing Western and non-Western expectations of life and achievement. Betty was also encouraged to read the book, *The Narcissism Epidemic: Living in the Age of Entitlement* (Twenge & Campbell, 2009). This book provides a clear account of how high expectations and preoccupation with success, and sense of entitlement can set us up for failure. The gratitude education helped Betty recognize that values are human-made, subjective and culturally determined. This comparative understanding of societal values helped her re-examine her own meaning of success and failure and helped her to begin to focus on what she has (gratitude) rather than ruminating with what she did not have (unable to skate competitively).

Acceptance training

As Betty was so centred on her suffering, she was not mindful of acceptance and gratitude. To increase awareness of her sense of acceptance, she was encouraged to carry out a series of exercises, some of which are listed as follows:

- Focusing on here and now.
- Observing emotional experiences and their contexts non-judgementally.
- Separation of secondary emotions from primary emotions (e.g., not to get upset for feeling upset, or feeling depressed for feeling depressed).

- Learning to tolerate distress rather than fighting it (flow with it).
- Adopting healthy and adaptive means to deal with chronic distress, rather than resorting to short-term reduction (e.g., over-medication or substance abuse).
- Toleration of painful experience.
- Recontextualizing meaning of suffering, for example, from 'this is awful' to 'let me focus on what I can do'.
- Exercising radical acceptance – ability to welcome those things in life that are hard, unpleasant, or very painful.
- Embracing good or bad experience as part of life.
- Willing to experience the reality of the present moment, for example, believing that 'things are as they should be'.
- Purposely allowing experience (thoughts, emotions, desires, urges, sensations, etc.) to occur without attempting to block or suppress them.
- Realizing that depression is not caused by the loss itself, but by our perception of it, our coping abilities, and our level of spirituality.

Gratitude training

Gratitude training involves doing various gratitude tasks. Betty was assigned a list of gratitude tasks as listed here, and she was advised to do at least one of the tasks daily.

- To write gratitude letters.
- To write a gratitude journal.
- To remember gratitude moments.
- To make gratitude visits to people one is grateful to.
- To practice gratitude self-talk.

Acceptance and gratitude hypnotherapy

To make acceptance-based therapy more experiential, it is integrated with hypnotherapy (Alladin, 2006). While Betty was in a deep hypnotic trance she was offered the following suggestions, adapted from Alladin (2006, p. 303; 2007, p. 197), to strengthen her sense of gratitude.

THERAPIST: Just continue to experience this beautiful sensation of peace and relaxation, tranquillity and calm flowing all over your mind and body. Just notice feeling calm, peaceful, and a sense of well-being. Feeling calm, peaceful, and in total harmony. No tension, no pressure, completely relaxed both mentally and physically. Feeling happy that you can relax so deeply, that you can let go, and calm down completely. You feel pleased and grateful that you can let go completely. Now become aware of your heart. Notice how peaceful you feel in your heart, how calm you feel in your heart, and you feel a sense of gratitude in your heart. When you feel good in your heart, you feel good in your mind and in your body. Do you feel good in your heart?

[Betty raised her 'YES' finger.]

THERAPIST: Do you feel good in your mind, body, and heart?

[Betty raised her 'YES' finger.]

THERAPIST: Very good! You have the ability to feel good in your mind, body and heart. All the major religions state that when you wake up in the morning, if you have a roof over your head, you have bread to eat, and water to drink, and are in fairly good health, then you have everything. Just become aware of all the things you have and all the things you are grateful for. When living in the modern world, it's okay to have goals and ambitions. When we achieve them, they can be seen as bonuses and pluses as we have lots of other resources. When we don't achieve our goals and ambitions, it is disappointing, but we have enough resources to live a comfortable life. Do you agree with these comments and observation?

[Betty raised her 'YES' finger.]

It is important that the acceptance-based hypnotherapy is carried out after the acceptance and gratitude training. In the absence of this training, a patient may not appreciate the therapeutic meaning of acceptance and gratitude, and may reject the hypnotic suggestions. Betty found both the acceptance-based training and hypnotherapy very helpful. They gave her a new perspective on success and failure, and they made her become more aware of the many things she is grateful for. Most importantly, she felt less preoccupied and fearful about 'failure '.

Mind–Body–Heart integration

This component of acceptance-based hypnotherapy focuses on the integration of various subsystems in the body. As discussed in Chapter 2, heart-focused positive emotional state engenders synchronization of the entire body system to produce PC (McCraty et al., 2009). Based on these scientific findings, Alladin (2012) has developed the breathing with your heart technique to generate coherence (harmony) of the entire system (mind, body, brain, heart, and emotion). This technique integrates both

Western (heart viewed as a complex information centre) and Eastern (heart regarded as the big mind) concepts of the heart to produce psychological well-being. A similar technique called Heart Joy was independently developed by Lankton (2008, pp. 45–50) to create a sense of emotional well-being.

Heart education

Betty was given a scientific account of the combined role of the heart and positive emotions in the generation of PC, which promotes healing, emotional stability and optimal performance. The similarities and the differences between the Western and Eastern theories of the mind and 'heart' are also discussed. Betty found the Eastern view of the heart – viewed as the big mind – very intriguing but empowering, as now she knows what to do to feel good in her heart.

Heart–mind training combined with hypnotherapy

Heart–mind training helps patients with social phobia cope with negative feelings (heavy heart) triggered by social situations. By breathing with the heart, anxious patients are able to shift their attention away from their mind to their heart. Moreover, when a person feels good in his or her heart, the person experiences a sense of comfort and joy because we validate reality by the way we feel and not by the way we think (Fredrickson, 2002; Isen, 1998). As discussed in Chapter 2, logic does not always equate good affect, but feeling good in one's heart (e.g., by thinking about something one is grateful for) always creates a positive affect (Welwood, 1983).

Breathing with your heart technique

This transcript from a session with Betty illustrates how the technique is introduced in therapy. The script begins with Betty being in a deep hypnotic trance:

THERAPIST: Just continue to experience this beautiful sensation of peace and relaxation, tranquility and calm flowing throughout your mind and body, giving you such a pleasant feeling, such a soothing sensation, that you feel completely relaxed both mentally and physically. Do you feel relaxed both mentally and physically?

[Betty raised her 'YES' finger.]

THERAPIST: Now I would like you to focus on the centre of your heart (pause for 30 seconds). Can you imagine this?

[Betty raised her 'YES' finger.]

THERAPIST: Now I would like you to imagine breathing in and out with your heart (pause For 30 seconds). Can you imagine this?

[Betty raised her 'YES' finger.]

THERAPIST: Continue to imagine breathing in and out of your heart (she was allowed to continue with this exercise for 2 minutes; the therapist repeated at regular intervals: 'Just continue to imagine breathing with your heart' as she did the exercise). Now I would like you to slow down your breathing. Breathe in and out at 7-second intervals. Breathe in with your heart ... 1 ... 2 ... 3 ... 4 ... 5 ... 6 ... 7 and now breathe out with your heart ... 1 ... 2 ... 3 ... 4 ... 5 ... 6 ... 7. And now as you are breathing in and out with your heart I want you to become aware of something in your life that you feel good about, something that you feel grateful for (pause for 30 seconds). Are you able to focus on something that you are grateful for in your life?

[Betty raised her 'YES' finger.]

THERAPIST: Just become aware of that feeling and soon you will feel good in your heart. [After 10 seconds] Do you feel it?

[Betty raised her 'YES' finger.]

THERAPIST: Just become aware of this good feeling in your heart. [Pause for 30 seconds.] Now I would like you to become aware of the good feeling in your mind, in your body, and in your heart. Do you feel this?

[Betty raised her 'YES' finger.]

THERAPIST: Now that you feel good in your mind, in your body, and in your heart, you feel a sense of balance, a sense of harmony. Do you feel this sense of harmony?

[Betty raised her 'YES' finger.]

THERAPIST: From now on, whenever and wherever you are, you can create this good feeling by imagining breathing with your heart and focusing on something that you are grateful for. With practice you will get better and better at it. Now you know what to do to make your heart feel lighter.

Summary

As social phobia is a complex condition, there is no one-size-fits-all treatment for social phobia. Part of the complexity of the problem is the tacit self-wounds that patients carry inside them that leads to avoidance behaviours, thus maintaining the symptoms. This chapter provided a wide array of behavioural, cognitive, hypnotic, unconscious and acceptance-based strategies for treating social phobia, from which a therapist can choose the best techniques that may suit their patients. The case of Betty clearly illustrated that symptom-focused treatment is necessary but not sufficient for treating underlying determinants of an anxiety disorder. A comprehensive and durable treatment requires therapeutic confrontation of unconscious conflicts that harbour painful emotions (Wolfe, 2006).

Although the integrative psychotherapy for social phobia described in this chapter appears heuristic and theoretically sound – currently, beyond clinical observation – there is no empirical data to support the efficacy of treating the wounded self in patients with social phobia. The efficacy of psychodynamic therapy with anxiety disorders (Leichsenring, 2005; Milrod et al., 2007; Shedler, 2010) provides indirect support that resolution of unconscious conflicts (which may be caused by the wounded self) decrease anxiety. To encourage wider application of this integrated perspective to treatment, it will be important to validate this approach empirically. Nevertheless, this book represents a preliminary, but timely, attempt to assimilate the concept of self-wounds in the management of anxiety disorders. As discussed in Chapter 1, cognitive behaviour therapists are beginning to take serious interest in the implicit nature of anxiety disorders and are starting to develop new techniques for activating and restructuring underlying cognitive schemas. This movement is likely to spark empirical studies of the concept of the wounded self in the future, both in the understanding and treatment of anxiety disorders. It is enlightening that hypnotherapy can be part of this movement.

4

Specific Phobia

Case of Mandy

This case of specific phobia (fear of public washroom) highlights the importance of case reformulation and the need for working with resistance in the psychological treatment of anxiety disorder. Mandy, a 28-year-old paralegal assistant was referred to the author by her family physician for treatment of public washroom phobia. Mandy had this problem since childhood. She became fearful of using public washroom following a scary experience at a camp site when she was 8 years old. The camp site was an old barrack, which was once used by the armed forces for field training and as a shooting range. Once the location was abandoned by the army, it became a public camp site for camping during summer, but not very well known to the public because of its remote location in the middle of the forest. The camp consisted of several independent huts built in a circle in the middle of a field, surrounded by forest. In the middle of the circle, there was a large detached hut which consisted of a communal shower and toilet. Mandy was very scared the first time she used the washroom. It was dark, not very well-lighted, the toilet bowl was huge, and it made a loud noise when she flushed the toilet, which involved pulling down a chain from above her head. While sitting on the toilet she felt trapped and panicky. Following this experience, she did not want to use the washroom any more, but was forced by her mother to use it. Since then she has become phobic of using public washrooms. She had no problem using the washroom at home or at her relatives' house. At school it caused some anxiety, but she managed by using the toilet only when she really needed it. She

Integrative CBT for Anxiety Disorders: An Evidence-Based Approach to Enhancing Cognitive Behavioural Therapy with Mindfulness and Hypnotherapy, First Edition. Assen Alladin.
© 2016 John Wiley & Sons, Ltd. Published 2016 by John Wiley & Sons, Ltd.

could not use public washrooms, especially in crowded and unfamiliar public places, and in aeroplanes. She sought help because it was restricting her travel and taking her 4-year-old son to various public places.

Diagnostic Criteria for Specific Phobia

The diagnostic criteria for specific phobia listed in the fifth edition of the *Diagnostic and Statistical Manual of Mental Disorders* (*DSM-V*; American Psychiatric Association, 2013, pp. 187–198) include:

1. Intense fear or anxiety about a specific object or situation such as flying, heights, animals, receiving an injection, seeing blood, and so on.
2. The phobic object or situation almost always induces immediate fear or anxiety.
3. The phobic object or situation is actively avoided or endured with intense fear or anxiety.
4. The person recognizes that the fear or anxiety is out of proportion to the actual danger posed by the specific object or situation and to the socio-cultural context.
5. The fear, anxiety or avoidance has been persistent for at least six months.
6. The fear, anxiety or avoidance causes clinically significant distress or impairment in social, occupational or other important areas of functioning.
7. The fear or anxiety is not due to another mental disorder.

DSM-V (American Psychiatric Association, 2013, p. 198) subdivides specific phobias according to the following five phobic stimuli:

*   Animal (e.g., spiders, insects, dogs)
*   Natural environment (e.g., heights, storms, water)
*   Blood-injection-injury (e.g., needles, invasive medical procedures)
*   Situational (e.g., aeroplanes, elevators, enclosed places)
*   Other (e.g., situations that may lead to choking or vomiting; in children, for example, loud sounds or costumed characters)

Prevalence of Specific Phobia

Specific phobias affect an estimated 19.2 million adult Americans (Kessler, Chiu, Demler, & Walters (2005). The lifetime prevalence rates of specific phobia vary according to the subtype of the phobia. A recent review reported the following lifetime prevalence estimates: animal phobia (3.3–7.0%), natural environment phobia (8.9–11.6%), situational phobia (5.2–8.4%) and blood-injection-injury phobia (3.2–4.5%) (LeBeau et al., 2010). Females are more frequently affected than males, at a rate of approximately 2:1, although the rates vary across different phobic stimuli (American Psychiatric Association, 2013). The prevalence rates are lower in older individuals (about 3–5%), in Asian, African and Latin American countries (2–4%), and in children (5%) compared to teenagers (13- to 17-year-olds: 16%) (American Psychiatric Association, 2013).

Causes of Specific Phobia

As specific phobias form a heterogeneous group of disorders, they do not have a common etiology and pathogenesis. Most specific phobias develop in childhood and adolescence. However, it is possible for a specific phobia to develop at any age, resulting from a traumatic experience. For example, a choking phobia can result from a near-choking event at any age (American Psychiatric Association, 2013). Freud (1909) was the first to attempt to account systematically for the development of specific phobias. According to Freud, phobias represented a defence against the anxiety produced by repressed id impulses. In other words, anxiety is displaced from the feared id impulse and moved on to an object or situation that has some symbolic connection to it. These objects or situations – for example, dogs, elevators, closed spaces – then become the phobic stimuli. By avoiding them, the person is able to circumvent dealing with the repressed conflicts. The phobia is the ego's way of warding off a confrontation with the real problem, a repressed childhood conflict. In his famous case study of Little Hans, a 10-year-old boy with a specific phobia of horses, Freud believed Little Hans had not successfully resolved his Oedipal conflict and as a result his intense fear of his father was displaced onto horses and he became phobic of leaving his home. Arieti (1979) revised this theory and went on to state that the repression does not stem from an id impulse, but from a particular interpersonal problem of childhood. As the psychoanalytic theorizing of specific phobias are derived from clinical case reports, firm scientific conclusions cannot be drawn from these reports. Moreover, psychodynamic therapies for phobias have not been found to be very effective, suggesting that insight into unconscious anxieties is not sufficient to treat phobias. This book adopts the position that none of the monotherapies for anxiety disorders, particularly with complex and comorbid conditions, is likely to be highly effective, although it may serve as an important component of a multimodal therapy. For example, the case of Mandy described in this chapter showed moderate response to CBT and hypnotherapy, but they were not sufficient to overcome her phobia, she needed exploration and healing of her self-wounds.

In contrast to psychodynamic theories, the behavioural models have been very successful in explaining specific phobias. The behavioural theories have demonstrated that phobias can be acquired from different kinds of learning, including avoidance conditioning (involving classical and operant conditioning), modelling (vicarious learning) and prepared learning (some neutral stimuli, for example, heights and snakes, are more likely to be conditioned). Although the behavioural theories explain why some people becomes phobic, it does not explain why many people with phobia do not report either direct exposure to a traumatic event or exposure to fearful models (Merckelbach, de Ruiter, van den Hout, & Hoekstra, 1989). To compensate for this shortcoming, the cognitive behavioural theories of phobias were proposed. These theories focus on how people's cognitions serve both as a diathesis (predisposition) and a maintenance factor in specific phobias. According to these theories, a specific phobia is due to (i) a bias towards negative stimuli, (ii) interpretation of ambiguous information as threatening and (iii) the belief that negative events are more likely than positive ones to occur in the future (Mathews & MacLeod, 1994). For example, research suggests that spider phobia involves automatic thought processes and implicit cognitive associations involving themes of disgust and threat that occur without conscious introspection or awareness (Teachman & Woody, 2003). Although cognitive behavioural theories provide a more comprehensive understanding of the etiology of phobias, the question still remains: why do some people acquire phobias while others do not, given similar learning opportunities? The biological theories of phobias have addressed this question. They proposed that those who are adversely affected by stress may have a biological malfunction (a diathesis) that somehow predisposes them to develop a phobia following a particular stressful event. Studies of the autonomic nervous system and genetic factors have provided some promising data. Gray (1987) observed that people with autonomic lability seem to be readily aroused by a wide range of stimuli and thus prone to conditioning to fearful stimuli. This vulnerability suggests some people are to some degree genetically predisposed to develop phobias (Gabbay, 1992). For example, it is well known that individuals with blood-injection-injury phobia have a unique propensity to vasovagal syncope (fainting) in the presence of the phobic stimulus, and genetic research indicates this phobia to be strongly familial (Öst, 1992). However, data with other phobias do not implicate genetic factors and therefore it is not clear to what extent heredity contributes to the etiology of specific phobias. DSM-V (American Psychiatric Association, 2013) also lists temperamental and environmental factors as risks for specific phobias. Temperamental risk factor incorporates negative affectivity (neuroticism) or behavioural inhibition, whereas environmental risk factors include parental over-protectiveness, parental loss and separation, and physical and sexual abuse. All these indicate the likelihood of multiple factors involved in the etiology and course of specific phobias.

In summary, none of the theories discussed provide a complete explanation of the etiology of specific phobias, although they have contributed a great deal to our understanding and treatment of phobias. This conclusion is not surprising considering specific phobias represent a heterogeneous set of conditions. The concept of wounded self described in this book expands on the extant theories of specific phobias. In particular, it broadens Arieti's (1979) observation that repression of phobic anxiety does not stem from an id impulse, but from a particular interpersonal problem of childhood, possibly fueled by self-wounds (Wolfe, 2005, 2006). Moreover, the self-wounds model incorporates Teachman and Woody's (2003) research findings that individuals with specific phobias are involved in automatic thought processes and implicit cognitive associations involving themes of disgust and threat that occur without conscious introspection or awareness.

Treatment of Specific Phobia

Medications (e.g., antidepressants, anxiolytics, beta-blockers) are often used to treat specific phobias, but reviews of pharmacologic monotherapy for specific phobias have been discouraging (Fyer, 1987; Gros & Anthony, 2006; Shearer, Harmon, Younger, & Brown, 2013). Craske et al. (2006, p. 13) state that 'it is widely believed that medication is not necessary to treat clients with specific phobias', although benzodiazepines may have some utility in the acute treatment of specific phobias (Choy et al., 2007). Similarly, there is no research evidence to suggest that the use of medication in combination with psychological treatment is indicated in uncomplicated cases of specific phobias (Shearer et al., 2013). In contrast to medications, psychological therapies, namely behavioural therapies and CBT, have been found to be highly effective with specific phobias (Choy et al., 2007; Wolitzky-Taylor, Horowitz, Powers, Telch, 2008). Shearer et al. (2013, p. 249) pointed out that the 'effectiveness of exposure-based treatments is so well established that there is very little disagreement among experts regarding best practices for treatment; most agree exposure is both necessary and sufficient to achieve a positive outcome (Antony & Barlow, 2002)'. However, exposure therapy for specific phobias has a major downside – the dropout rates are high, owing to the uncomfortable nature of the treatment (Choy et al., 2007). The behavioural and cognitive treatments are described in detail under the next section.

Cognitive Hypnotherapy for Specific Phobia

Hypnotherapy for managing symptoms of specific phobia

The initial part of the therapy, which consisted of approximately six sessions of hypnotherapy, is targeted at symptoms management. This phase of therapy may be sufficient for some patients with simple phobia. For patients with complex phobia the initial phase of therapy serves as a preparation for more complicated therapy of exploring the roots of the phobia. The initial hypnotherapy components include (i) relaxation training, (ii) demonstration of the power of mind over the body, (iii) ego-strengthening, (iv) expansion of awareness, (v) imaginal exposure, (vi) self-hypnosis, (vii) modulation and regulation of symptoms, (viii) PHS and (ix) hypnotherapy combined with behavioural therapies. Hypnotherapy may be introduced again later in therapy with patients who elect to pursue with uncovering work.

Relaxation training

Relaxation training for the treatment of specific phobia targets physiological arousal in the context of gradual exposure to anxiety-provoking stimuli. Öst, Johansson and Jerremalm (1982) found relaxation training to be as effective as *in vivo* exposure therapy and superior to delayed treatment for claustrophobia. It should be pointed out that traditional relaxation therapy, which promotes parasympathetic response, may be contraindicated with blood-injection-injury phobia. Targeting sympathetic arousal in individuals with blood-injection-injury fear is recommended as these phobics manifest parasympathetic arousal in terms of dilation of blood vessels, drop in blood pressure, slowed heart rate and constricted airways (Magee, Erwin, & Heimberg, 2009; Öst, 1992). Applied relaxation (systematic tension and relaxation of various muscle groups) or applied tension is specifically designed to treat patients with blood-injection-injury phobia. Applied tension requires patients to tense their muscles in the presence of phobic stimuli in order to elevate blood pressure and thus contains an exposure component. Studies by Öst and his colleagues (Öst, Sterner, & Fellenius, 1989; Öst, Fellenius, & Sterner, 1991) found applied relaxation, applied tension and *in vivo* exposure therapy to be equally effective with individuals with phobias for blood, wounds and injuries. However, the treatment gains at one-year follow-up for both applied tension and tension only were superior to *in vivo* exposure. A dismantling study designed to parse out the effects of applied tension and tension only from those of exposure component, found applied muscle tension and tension only to be superior to *in vivo* exposure (Hellstrøm, Fellenius, & Öst, 1996). Moreover, the beneficial effects of applied tension and tension only were achieved in one session (Hellstrøm, & Öst, 1996).

Mandy found the hypnotic relaxation very helpful in reducing her feeling of nervousness and inner tension. As she was highly susceptible to hypnosis, to her surprise, she was able to generate profound mental and physical relaxation without much effort. Her hypnotic talent was utilized to train her to dissociate from the anxiety related to using public washroom. The relaxation response associated with the experience of feeling calm, relaxed and detached served as an experiential strategy to help her modify her anticipatory anxiety. However, when inducing hypnotic dissociation as a technique for countering anxiety, the therapist should be aware that patients with anxiety disorder often dissociate from anxiety-related situations or objects as a form of avoidance behaviour. When dissociation is used therapeutically, the therapist needs to explain to the patient that it is used as a coping strategy and not as a maladaptive avoidance behaviour. The positive trance state was further deployed to teach Mandy how to modulate her emotional reactions via self-hypnosis (further discussed under the section 'Self-hypnosis training').

Demonstration of the power of the mind over the body
As discussed in Chapter 3, eye and body catalepsy is induced in the second hypnotherapy session to empower the patient, to ratify the credibility of hypnotherapy and to enhance positive expectancy (e.g., Alladin, 2013a). Mandy was intrigued that she could not open her eyes or get out of the chair, and this made her feel optimistic and hopeful about the therapy. Moreover, she was able to recognize that it was her constant rumination with NSH that was maintaining and exacerbating her anxiety, and she felt empowered knowing that she has within her the capacity to change them. To further mobilize her positive expectancy, she was explained that in future sessions of hypnotherapy and CBT she would be taught various techniques to counter NSH.

Ego strengthening

In addition to the mind-over-body experience, ego-strengthening suggestions were offered to Mandy to increase her self-esteem, enhance her sense self-efficacy and gradually restore confidence in her ability to control her fear of using public washroom. While in deep hypnotic trance, Mandy was encouraged to visualize coping with her anxiety head-on rather than avoiding it. She found the hypnotherapy sessions, particularly the relaxation response coupled with ego-strengthening suggestions, very relaxing and reassuring. She felt motivated to learn self-hypnosis. At the end of the first hypnotherapy session, she was given a CD recording of the session and advised to listen to it every day.

Expansion of awareness

As described in Chapter 2, Expansion of Awareness Training (EAT) is used to expand the range of subjective experience in patients with anxiety disorder. Mandy reported that, although her anxiety level varied from day to day, she constantly felt a sense of inner tension, which inhibited her ability to experience different emotions, particularly good feeling. This feeling of inner tension was largely due to her constant cogitation with syncretic cognition (constellation of thoughts, images, and bodily responses) concerning using public washrooms. To expand her range of emotions, during hypnosis Mandy was guided to focus on the relaxation response and various emotions and feelings. This was achieved by using EAT as described in Chapter 2. The following transcript, which begins while Mandy was in a deep trance, exemplifies the suggestions used for bolstering her emotional awareness.

> You have now become so deeply relaxed and you are in such a deep hypnotic trance that your mind and your body feel completely relaxed, totally relaxed.
> You begin to feel a beautiful sensation of peace and relaxation, tranquility and calm, flowing all over your mind and your body; giving you such a pleasant and such a soothing sensation all over your mind and body, that you feel completely relaxed, totally relaxed, both mentally and physically. Notice that you are aware of everything, you are aware of all the sound and noise around you, you are aware of your thoughts and imagination, and yet you feel so relaxed, so calm and so comfortable. This shows that you have the ability to relax, the ability to let go, and the ability to put everything on hold. This shows that you have lots of control, because you are aware of everything. You can hear all the sounds and noise around you, you are aware of your thoughts and imagination. You are aware that I am sitting beside you and talking to you. Yet you are able to put everything on hold and relax your mind and body completely. This shows that you have lots of control.

Now you can become aware of all the good feelings you are feeling right now. You feel calm, you feel peaceful, you feel relaxed and you feel very, very comfortable both mentally and physically. You may also become aware of feeling heavy, light, or detached, or distancing away from everything, becoming more and more detached, distancing away from everything, drifting into a deep, deep hypnotic trance. You feel happy and pleased knowing that you can relax, you can let go. You feel delighted and satisfied knowing that you can put things on hold and yet be aware of everything. You feel good and encouraged knowing that you have so much control.

EAT helped Mandy discover that she had the capacity and the talent to relax, to let go, and experience different positive feelings, emotions and sensations. She was surprised that she could put things on hold and detach from her concerns and worries, although she was conscious of her fear and anxiety. With practice Mandy was also able to generate on her own a variety of positive emotions and feelings appropriate to the context. Her ability to produce, amplify and express a variety of positive feelings and experiences gave her the confidence to begin to work with her anxious experience, which is described next.

Imaginal exposure
The expansion of awareness technique is usually segued into imaginal exposure training to help patients with specific phobia tolerate fearful experience. While in deep hypnosis, Mandy was directed to bring on her anxious experience associated with using public washroom. Once she was able to elicit the fearful experience, she was coached to utilize self-hypnosis to control her anxiety.

When I count from ONE to FIVE, by the time you hear me say FIVE, you will begin to feel whatever emotion or reaction that you experience whenever you think of visiting a public washroom.

Mandy was then instructed to amplify the affect associated with the thoughts of using a public washroom.

When I count slowly from ONE to FIVE, as I count, you will begin to experience the anxious feeling more and more intensely, so that when I reach the count of FIVE, at the count of FIVE, you will feel the full reaction as strongly as you can bear it. ONE … TWO … THREE … FOUR … FIVE. Now notice what you feel and can you describe it to me?

Mandy was then instructed to use her self-hypnosis skill to modulate and control the anxious and fearful reactions.

> Now imagine using your self-hypnosis skill to control the anxiety feeling. Since you have the ability to relax and put things on hold, you can let go now and allow yourself to calm down.

After several repetitions of this set of suggestions, Mandy was able to relax completely while imagining using a public washroom in the local mall. This mental rehearsal in trance, prepared Mandy to visit the public washroom in the local mall where she often shops. This technique also encouraged her to focus on her anxious feelings head-on, rather than cogitating with the symptoms. This technique also prepared Mandy for SD, which is a more structured form of imaginal exposure (see Chapter 2).

Self-hypnosis training
To generalize her relaxation response to real situations, Mandy was taught self-hypnosis. At the end of the first hypnotherapy session, she was given a CD recording of the session and encouraged to listen to it at least once a day at home. This homework assignment allowed continuity of treatment between sessions and offered her the opportunity to practice self-hypnosis outside the therapy sessions. Once she had built sufficient confidence in self-hypnosis, generalization of the skill was strengthend by the clenched fist technique (Stein, 1963). As discussed in Chapter 2, the clenching of the dominant fist serves as an anchor for eliciting relaxation response in real situations. The following transcript exemplifies how the clenched fist technique was introduced to Mandy while she was in a deep hypnotic trance.

> You have now become so deeply relaxed, that you feel a beautiful sensation of peace and relaxation, tranquility and calm, flowing all over your mind and your body; giving you such a pleasant, such a soothing sensation, all over your mind and your body that you feel completely relaxed, totally relaxed, drifting into a deeper and deeper hypnotic trance. This shows that you have the ability to relax, the ability to let go and the ability to put things on hold. This shows that you have lots of control because you are aware of what is going on around you, yet you are able to relax completely. Since you have the ability to relax, just as you have the ability to speak, you will be able to relax in any situation, just as you are able to speak in any situation. To facilitate your ability to relax in real situations, I am going to introduce you to the clenched fist technique [which was discussed with Mandy prior to the hypnotic induction].

> Now if you may clench your right fist [it was established that she is right-handed]. As you clench your fist, become aware of how very relaxed you are. You feel completely relaxed both mentally and physically and yet you are aware of everything. Also notice that you are in complete control, knowing what to do and knowing what's going on around you. As you tighten your fist slightly you become even more aware of the good feelings, you feel completely relaxed and in complete control.

Now that you have made an association between your right fist and the ability to relax, from now on, whenever you want to feel this good feeling, you can bring it on by clenching your right fist and anchoring your mind to this session, that is, reminding yourself of this session, that you can relax and let go completely. And from now on, wherever you are, whatever you are doing, if you feel tense, anxious, upset, or stressed out, you can counter these feelings by clenching you right fist and anchoring your mind to this experience. With practice you will get better and better at it, and become more confident controlling negative feelings and emotions.

The clenched fist technique was ratified experientially with imaginal rehearsal and bolstered by PHS.

Just undo your fist. Now we are going to practice the clenching fist technique. From now on, whenever you get upset, anxious, or stressed out, imagine using your clenched fist technique to counter the bad feelings. Just continue to envision, from now on, whenever you get anxious, upset or stressed out, you are able counter these feelings by clenching your right fist and anchoring your mind to the present experience. And with practice you will get better and better at it. As a result of this you begin to have more control over unhelpful feelings, emotions and reactions.

Mandy found the clenched fist technique very reassuring in the therapist's office, but she doubted whether the technique would work for her while she is in a public washroom. Based on this feedback, the next couple of sessions were devoted to further training in affect modulation.

Modulating and controlling symptoms
By virtue of being an experiential therapy, hypnotherapy provided Mandy the opportunity to understand the syncretic (total) nature of her anxious experience (Alladin, 2006, 2007, 2008; Safer & Leventhal, 1977). Once she was able to recognize the total nature of her experience, Mandy was coached to identify the syncretic nature of her anxiety symptoms rather than focusing on one particular sign or symptom. This training encouraged her to begin to view her anxiety not simply as an affect, thought or behaviour, but a cascade of cognitive, somatic, perceptual, physiological, visceral and kinaesthetic experience. This approach to therapy, as discussed in Chapter 2, was influenced by recent trends in third-wave CBTs, whereby clinicians have been teaching their patients to examine and change their relationship with their internal experience and their cognitive activities (Butler et al., 2008). Internal experience, in this context, refers to emotions, physical sensations and symptoms, while cognitive activities comprise worries, ruminations, intrusive thoughts, images and memories.

Interest in inner experience stems from research findings that symptoms of anxiety disorders are maintained by persistent misinterpretations of the significance of internal states (e.g., 'fear of fear'; Rachman & Bichard, 1988) and by the maladaptive behaviours engendered by these internal misinterpretations (e.g., 'safety-seeking behaviours'; Salkovskis, 1991). Although these maladaptive cognitions and safety-seeking behaviours are used by patients to control their anxiety; in fact, they maintain and exacerbate the symptoms. Therefore, changing the significance patients attach to their own cognitions about maladaptive cognitions (metacognition) have become central to many contemporary approaches to treating anxiety disorders (Butler et al., 2008). For example, some clinicians have started to question and test metacognitive beliefs in the course of classical CBT (Morrison & Westbrrok, 2004; Salkovskis, 1999; Wells, 1995, 1997, 2000; Wells & Matthews, 1994, 1996). Mindfulness-based cognitive therapists, on the other hand, have always integrated elements of CBT with intensive practice of mindfulness meditation (Baer, 2003; Ma & Teasdale, 2004; Segal, Williams, & Teasdale, 2002; Teasdale, 2004; Teasdale, Segal, Williams, Ridgeway, Soulsby, & Lau, 2000). Similarly, the capacity to decentre from unhelpful thinking forms the basis for various other therapies such as acceptance and commitment therapy (ACT; Hayes et al., 1999), CH (Alladin, 2013a, 2014a), dialectical behaviour therapy (DBT; Linehan, 1993a, 1993b) and mentalization therapy (Bateman & Fonagy, 2004). Although all these therapies differ in their underlying theoretical rationale, they all share a common goal with CBT, that is, they all 'teach patients to view their own cognitions as simply mental events and processes, to which they need not attend and on which they need not act' (Butler et al., 2008, p. 72).

Hypnotic induction and amplification of positive syncretic cognition provided dramatic proof to Mandy that she could modulate and regulate her inner anxious experience. DePiano and Salzberg (1981) believe the rapid improvement often observed in patients receiving hypnotherapy is partly due to the positive syncretic experience produced by the hypnotic trance.

Post-hypnotic suggestions
Before the termination of the hypnotic trance, Mandy was offered a variety of PHS to counter her anxiety, avoidance behaviour and negative rumination. Whenever Mandy thought about leaving her house, travelling or shopping, she would become preoccupied with the following negative self-suggestions:

- 'I can't use the public washroom.'
- 'It's too terrifying, I can't handle it.'
- 'What if I get this urgent need to use the bathroom?'
- 'It will be so embarrassing if I wet or soil myself.'

Rumination with these self-suggestions not only can induce a negative trance, but also serves as powerful self-affirmation or PHS, which can become part of the avoidance pattern of behaviour. To offset negative rumination, Mandy was offered various PHS.

- 'Whenever you feel anxious, when thinking of using a public bathroom, you will become more aware of how to deal with it rather than focusing on your symptoms or what may happen to you.'
- 'When you plan to visit the public washroom, you will feel less need to avoid the situation.'
- 'As you become more relaxed every day as a result of listening to your Self-Hypnosis CD, you will begin to feel motivated to try using a public washroom.'

Clarke and Jackson (1983) regard PHS as a form of 'higher-order-conditioning', which can function either as positive or negative reinforcement to increase or decrease the probability of desired or undesired behaviours. They found PHS to augment the effect of *in vivo* exposure among agoraphobics.

Hypnotherapy combined with behavioural therapies
As hypnotherapy primarily involves experiential and imaginal therapies in the office, it is important to transfer the learning from this setting to real-life situations. To assist in this process, the next phase of therapy for specific phobia integrates hypnotherapy with behavioural strategies, namely SD and exposure *in vivo*. These behavioural techniques are fully described and their effectiveness reviewed in Chapter 2. SD is found to be a necessary component of therapy for specific phobia, and it is found to be effective for reducing, and in some cases eliminating, simple phobias (Antony & Barlow, 2002; Choy et al., 2007; McGlynn, 1994; Kirsch et al., 1999; Smith, 1990).

Hypnosis-aided systematic desensitization

Although exposure therapy has been found to be necessary for treating specific phobia (Follette & Smith, 2005), Mandy was too anxious to tolerate this treatment. She felt more comfortable and ready to work with SD.

Table 4.1   Systematic desensitization hierarchy of fear of using public washroom

Item	Fear rating in SUD (0–100)
Ask for location of washroom in shopping mall	20
Looking for the washroom in the mall	30
Looking at the washroom from a distance	40
Standing in front of the washroom	50
Standing at the entrance of the washroom	60
Going inside the washroom but not using it	70
Opening the washroom door and looking inside	80
Going inside the washroom, door open, not using it	85
Sitting in the washroom, door closed, not using it	90
Inside the locked washroom	95
Inside the locked washroom, using it	100

SD is an effective evidence-based behavioural method for treating anxiety disorders, specifically phobias (see Chapter 2). Within the framework of CH, the relaxation component of SD is replaced by hypnosis, and hence, this treatment approach is referred to as HASD (Iglesias & Iglesias, 2014). A number of reports in the literature support the effectiveness of combining hypnosis with SD in the treatment of specific phobias (Glick, 1970). Table 4.1 shows the hierarchy of anxiety, which was formulated to help Mandy overcome her public bathroom phobia. The hierarchy represents various situations – ranked from least feared to most feared – related to the public washroom in the local shopping mall that causes anxiety for her. The fear is subjectively measured in terms of SUD, rated on a 0–100 scale; 0 representing no fear and 100 standing for the worst/maximum fear.

While Mandy was feeling very relaxed in deep hypnosis, she was asked to imagine each hierarchy of fear in turn, starting with the lowest item in the hierarchy ('Ask for location of washroom in shopping mall': 20 SUD). She was instructed to focus on the target situation until she was able to bring her SUD level down to 0. It is important for the patient to master one hierarchy, that is, able imagine the target situation without any anxiety, before moving on to the next item in the hierarchy. Failure to master the previous situation may produce resistance to work with the next item in the hierarchy, which is likely to be more anxiety-provoking (higher SUD level). Mandy found the SD very helpful in bringing down her level of anxiety during the session. However, she was still fearful of facing the situations in reality. She managed up to 'Standing in front of the washroom' (SUD: 50), but was not able to progress beyond this point in reality. To help Mandy face the real situations, the next stage of therapy progressed on to gradual *in vivo* exposure.

Gradual in vivo *exposure therapy*

Exposure therapy has been found to be efficacious with a variety of anxiety disorders (Follette & Smith, 2005). Based on learning theory, exposure therapy is conceptualized to function as a form of counterconditioning or extinction (see Chapter 2 for description and review). It is designed to help patients confront their feared objects, situations, memories and images in a therapeutic manner. Exposure *in vivo* therapy involves repeated confrontation with the feared objects or situations. As Mandy did not show good response to imaginal exposure (SD), she was encouraged to participate in exposure *in vivo* therapy. The same hierarchy of fear from SD (see Table 4.1) was used for the *in vivo* therapy. Unfortunately, Mandy made little progress with this therapy – she was able to move on to the next hierarchy of anxiety ('Standing at the entrance of the washroom': 60 SUD), but she was not able to go beyond this. She indicated that the exposure was too anxiety provoking for her and she did not feel she would be able to handle the discomfort. She decided to discontinue with the procedure, although she was encouraged by the therapist to continue with it.

Refusal to participate in exposure therapy is well documented in the literature (e.g., Golden, 2012). It is estimated that approximately one in four patients who initiates treatment drops out (Clum, 1989; Fava et al., 1995; Hofmann & Smits, 2009; Marks, 1978). In addition, Follette and Smith (2005) have expressed several other concerns about this therapy approach, including high attrition rate, exacerbation of symptoms, patient's inability to tolerate distress and not addressing associated or additional problems such as cognitive distortions, anger, guilt, shame and dissociation. To address these concerns and to prepare the patient for this treatment, as it happens to be a very effective therapy for specific phobia, exposure therapy has been incorporated with CBT (e.g., Meichenbaum, 1974), cognitive processing therapy (Resick & Schnicke, 1992), acceptance and commitment therapy (Hayes et al., 1999), eye movement desensitization and reprocessing (Shapiro, 1995) and hypnotherapy (e.g., Golden, Dowd, & Friedberg, 1987; Lynn & Kirsch, 2006).

Cognitive behavioural therapy

The next stage of the therapy concentrated on identifying and restructuring Mandy's maladaptive cognitions, in regards to both her phobia and the refusal to participate in exposure therapy. Patients with specific phobia are known (i) to attend more to negative stimuli, (ii) to interpret ambiguous information as threatening and (iii) to believe that negative events are more likely than positive ones to occur in the future (Mathews & MacLeod, 1994).

CBT helped Mandy identify and restructure some of her negative cognitions, but she still felt fearful using public washroom and her avoidance behaviour persisted. For example, she realized that her belief 'I can't use the public washroom' is irrational and she was able to reason that 'If millions of people can use it, I can use it too, and this prove it's safe, but I feel fearful using it'. She explained that she could reason with her thoughts, but it was not the thoughts that were getting in her way, it was the fearful ('horrible feeling of dread') inner feeling that was holding her back. Since this feeling was so strong and uncomfortable she did not want to take any risk to make it worse. At this point, it was apparent that therapy had reached an impasse and it was evident that Mandy's phobia was more complicated than it appeared on the surface. It was thus decided to explore the implicit nature of her phobia.

Healing self-wounds
As her fear of public washroom still persisted, Mandy requested hypnotic exploration of the deeper meaning of her fear. On a couple of occasions, she hinted that her fear could have been due to some childhood trauma that she did not remember. She mentioned that her neighbour had a 'needle phobia' for many years which was successfully treated by hypnotherapy by discovering the link between her (neighbour) fear and a childhood trauma. It was thus hypothesized that Mandy's fear of public washroom could be due to implicit cognitive associations engendered by self-wounds. Studies of patients with spider phobia clearly demonstrate that there is an association between unconscious cognitions related to threat and disgust and fear of spiders (Teachman & Woody, 2003). As discussed in Chapter 1, it is widely accepted that a great deal of human behaviour arises from unconscious processes. A more recent functional magnetic resonance imaging (fMRI) study demonstrated that conversion symptoms are mediated by suppression of adverse life events (Aybek et al., 2014). The next segment of therapy therefore involved in-depth hypnotherapy to explore any potential connection between Mandy's phobia and implicit cognitive processes.

Elicitation of self-wounds
The affect bridge technique was used to explore the existence of any underlying self-wound that might be connected to Mandy's phobia. The feeling of anxiety that she experienced, whenever she thought about using a public washroom, was used as a bridge to elicit her first anxiety attack. This technique is very similar to imaginal exposure in the sense that both techniques elicit and intensify the anxiety related to the fearful object or situation. Once the anxiety is amplified, both techniques guide patient

to use relaxation or cognitive (or both) strategies to modulate the affect. The main difference between the two techniques is that, in affect bridge, the patient is regressed back to the original anxiety experience and a link between the anxiety and any potential trauma is established, while in imaginal exposure the focus is on the current anxiety (see p. 34). The following is a transcript of the affect bridge technique used, while Mandy was in a deep hypnotic trance, to elicit her original fear of using a public washroom.

Regression

It was a great discovery to her that her phobia is related to control. Once she got this insight, it made sense to her. When she was in 8 years old, she remembered a pupil having measles at school, and she was forced to have an injection by her parents. She felt angry and became oppositional, which made her parents shout at her and she was grounded. It hurt. It was a double hurt. Since then she decided no one was going to control her, and she would never allow anyone to control her. Whenever she perceives loss of control, she becomes a 'child', throws a temper tantrum and gets away with it, or she is forced into doing things, for example, her dad had to hold her to get the needle. She felt she was controlled throughout her whole life. Her existence has been a battle between losing control and maintaining control.

THERAPIST: I would like you to become aware of the feeling you experience whenever you think of visiting a public bathroom.

[Mandy raised her YES finger. Ideomotor signals were already set up – 'YES' represented raising of her right index finger and 'NO' was represented by raising of her left index finger.]

THERAPIST: Now I would like you to think of the most recent incident when you felt anxious while you were thinking of visiting a public washroom. [Pause.] When you feel the anxiety let me know by raising your YES finger.

[Mandy raised her YES finger. She was then instructed to amplify the affect associated with the thoughts of using a public washroom.]

THERAPIST: In a moment when I count slowly from ONE to TEN, as I count, you will begin to experience the anxious feeling more and more intensely, so that when I reach the count of TEN, at the count of TEN, you will feel the full reaction as strongly as you can bear it. ONE ... TWO ... THREE ... FOUR ... FIVE ... SIX ... SEVEN ... EIGHT ... NINE ... TEN. Notice all the feelings and reactions you are experiencing.

[Then the therapist, by counting TEN to ONE, guided Mandy back to the first time she felt that fearful feeling.]

THERAPIST: Now I would like you to use the feeling you are feeling as a bridge to remember the first time you felt that feeling. When I count TEN to ONE, when I reach One, you will be able to remember the first time, or an earlier time when you felt that feeling. TEN ... NINE ... EIGHT ... SEVEN ... SIX ... FIVE ... FOUR ... THREE ... TWO ... ONE. Remember the first time you experienced that feeling. If you remember it, let me know by raising your YES finger.

[Mandy raised her YES finger. Then she started to breathe rapidly and began to twist her body as if she was trying to wrestle out of the reclining chair.]

THERAPIST: Please tell me what is happening. You can speak but you will still be in a deep trance. I am here with you and you are safe in my office.

MANDY: I am scared, I don't want to drown.

THERAPIST: Where are you?

MANDY: In the washroom.

THERAPIST: Where?

MANDY: In the middle of the woods where we are camping.

THERAPIST: How old are you?

MANDY: I am 8 years old.

THERAPIST: Who are you with?

MANDY: I am on my own. I am scared.

THERAPIST: Where's your parents?

MANDY: They are in the hut. I wanted to use the washroom.

THERAPIST: Why are you scared of the washroom?

MANDY: I am afraid I may fall in the toilet bowl and drown. The bowl is so huge. [She started to cry.]

THERAPIST: Anything else you don't like about the bathroom?

MANDY: I hate the noise. When you flush the toilet it makes so much noise. Everyone knows I am in the toilet. I feel everyone is looking at me. I hate it. It's so unfair. I hate it.

THERAPIST: What's unfair?

MANDY: My mother [the crying got more intense]. She forced me to use the toilet [now she started to get angry]. She did not believe me I was scared. She forced me to use the toilet [more angry].

THERAPIST: Can you explain why your mother forced you to use the toilet.

MANY: She said I will be sick if I don't use the toilet. She forced me to use the toilet. She closed the door so I could not get out. I had to finish using the toilet to get out. It was so unfair.

THERAPIST: You were scared you will fall in the toilet bowl and drown and your mother forced you to use the bathroom, how did you feel?

MANDY: I was scared and very angry and I decided I would not allow my mother or anyone to control me.

THERAPIST: What do you mean?

MANDY: My parents always telling me what to do and not to do, just as they forced me to use the bathroom. I made my mind up. I'm not going to let anyone control me. No one is going to control me. I am in charge.

From the affect bridge several new information emerged: (i) Mandy's public bathroom phobia was linked to fear of drowning in the toilet bowl, (ii) when using a public bathroom she felt exposed and embarrassed, (iii) she felt controlled by people and had thus pledged not to allow anyone to control her and (iv) these self-wounds had been subserving implicit cognitive processes, maintaining her phobia. It also became apparent that Mandy was sabotaging therapy, namely exposure *in vivo*, because she resented being told what to do by the therapist. Based on the uncovered information, the case was reformulated and the therapeutic strategies consequently revised. It was hypothesized that (i) Mandy's phobia was caused by implicit fear of drowning and (ii) she was resisting change because she perceived change, especially when ordered by others, as loss of control. Reformulation of the case provided new therapeutic goals, namely the resolution of childhood trauma (fear of drowning) and the removal of resistance to change. Treatment approaches for dealing with these two issues are discussed next.

Reframing the meaning of anxiety
One of the ways of resolving childhood trauma is to reframe or alter the meaning of the traumatic experience. The split screen technique (Alladin, 2008; Cardena et al., 2000; Lynn & Cardena, 2007; Spiegel, 1981) was used with Mandy to reframe her initial fear of public washroom. The split screen technique is a hypnotic strategy which utilizes the 'adult ego state' to help the 'weak ego state' deal with anxiety-provoking situations or objects. It also facilitates the 'two' ego states to work together as a team rather than splitting from each other when the self is threatened or strained. The following therapy transcript exemplifies how the split screen technique was used with Mandy to help her reframe her fear of drowning in the public washroom. The transcript begins while Mandy was in a deep trance, bolstered by ego-strengthening suggestions.

THERAPIST: Now I would like you to imagine sitting in front of a large TV or cinema screen which is vertically split in two halves, consisting of a right side and a left side. Can you imagine this?

[Mandy raised her YES finger.]

THERAPIST: Imagine the right side of the screen is lighting up as if it's ready to project an image. Imagine yourself being projected on the right side of the screen just as you are now. Feeling very relaxed, very comfortable, in complete control, and aware of everything that's going on around you. And now become aware of the things you have achieved and the things that you are proud of. Do you feel these good feelings?

[Mandy raised her YES finger.]

THERAPIST: That's very good. Do you feel a sense of achievement?

[Mandy raised her YES finger.]

THERAPIST: Are you thinking about your achievement related to your job? [It is advisable to check out the fact rather than making assumption. In this instance, the assumption was made by the therapist as Mandy had disclosed to the therapist that she felt very proud working as a paralegal assistant for a very successful law firm.]

[Mandy raised her YES finger.]

THERAPIST: Just focus on the good feelings and become aware that you feel so proud working for such a prestigious firm, working with such well-known lawyers. This proves to you that you have a strong side of you, a successful side of you, a side which can rescue you from difficulties and help you navigate the right path. We are going to call this part of you the 'adult side' or your 'adult ego state'. Is that acceptable to you?

[Mandy raised her YES finger.]

THERAPIST: Now leave this side of yourself on the right side of the screen and imagine yourself being projected on the left side of the screen as an 8-year-old girl, feeling frightened. It is the first time you used the bathroom while you were camping with your parents at the old barrack in the woods. Remember all the feeling you experienced when you were using the bathroom. Remember all the thoughts that went through your mind and remember all the physical sensations you felt. [She felt agitated and started to cry.] Don't be afraid to allow all the thoughts and feelings to come over you, because in a moment we will show you how to deal with them. [She continued to sob.] Let all the fear of drowning come over you.

MANDY: [She started to scream.] I don't want to drown! I don't want to drown!

THERAPIST: Now imagine the adult side of you, your adult ego state, come over to the left side from the right side of the screen to rescue you, to help you out. Can you imagine it?

[Mandy raised her YES finger.]

THERAPIST: Imagine the adult side of you giving you a hug and telling you that she is there to help you. Since she is an adult she has lots of experience and she knows how to help you. She is not going to leave you. She is going to stay with you and protect you. She is not going to let you drown. She is an adult, she is strong, and she will rescue you. I want you to continue to focus on this imagine until you feel reassured.

When you feel reassured that the adult side of you is there to protect you, let me know by raising your YES finger.

[She paused for approximately 20 seconds, and then raised her YES finger.]

THERAPIST: Imagine the right side of you telling you that you have grown up. You are now 28 years old, you are married, you have a 4-year-old son, and you enjoy working as a paralegal assistant. Can you imagine this?

[Mandy raised her YES finger.]

THERAPIST: Tell me what you feel. You can speak up but you will still feel you are in a deep trance.

MANDY: I feel I am 28 and I feel good that I enjoy my work.

THERAPIST: Now imagine the right side of you telling you that you don't need to be afraid of drowning when you are using the washroom because you have grown up and you are an adult. Do you believe that?

MANDY: Yes [without any hesitation and with confidence]. How silly of me? I am an adult, I will not fit in, even if the toilet bowl is big. How silly?

THERAPIST: From now on, the child part of you does not have to handle her fear on her own. She can work as a team with the strong part of you. The strong part of you is there to remind you that you are an adult, strong and resourceful. The weak part also realizes that the strong part is a part of yourself. Both parts belong to yourself. So from now on there is no need to feel separated from the adult ego state. Both of you can work as a team. Is this acceptable to you?

MANDY: Yes.

THERAPIST: From now on whenever you feel fearful of using a public washroom, you will become aware that you are 28 years old, an adult, strong, and too big to fall into the toilet bowl or drown in it. Is this acceptable to you?

MANDY: Yes.

THERAPIST: You will also realize that the public toilets these days do not make so much noise when you flush them and you don't have to pull a chain from above your head to flush them. Would you like to make any comment about this?

MANDY: I don't have to feel embarrassed using the toilet. No one will be watching me.

THERAPIST: Do you feel comfortable using a public washroom now?

MANDY: I feel more confident to try it. I feel safe knowing that I am too big to drown inside a toilet bowl. How silly of me to think that? But I still have the fearful image of the old toilet in my mind. How do I deal with this?

THERAPIST: I am glad you asked. There two things we can do here. First, we can separate the past from the present and second, we can change the fearful image of that old toilet in your mind. Is that acceptable to you? [Since Mandy does not like to be controlled, it is important to introduce any change strategy collaboratively.]

MANDY: Yes.

THERAPIST: Let's focus on the first strategy. Whenever you think of a public washroom, if the fearful thoughts come over your mind, you can remind yourself that the fearful experience relates to a past incident, but right now you are in the present. Do you think you can separate the past from the present?

MANDY: I kind of already knew about it but never tried it. Now that I know the origin of my fear I can separate myself from the scared little girl. Now I am grown so I need to think like a grown up.

THERAPIST: I am very impressed by your answer.

MANDY: Guess what? Now I have my adult ego state with me. This feels good. That's the way I think at my office. Lawyers like facts, not impressions.

THERAPIST: Again I am very impressed by your very mature reasoning. Now let's focus on the second strategy. You can transform the image of the toilet. You can make it less fearful and acceptable to you. If you can go back in time to when you first visited that old toilet, and if you had all the means to change it, how would have liked to see that toilet so that it was not scary to you? [This technique is to help her rewrite the description of the toilet.]

MANDY: I could have done several things. First, I would have positioned the toilet in the back of the huts, not in the middle. Second, I would have made it smaller but big enough to have separate rooms for the toilet, the shower, and the powder room. Third, I would have painted it white inside and well-lighted. Fourth, I would have installed a small toilet bowl but big enough for comfort. Fifth, I would have installed a toilet that makes very little noise when you flush it.

THERAPIST: Good job Mandy! Now would you like to have the image of this new toilet in your mind. Just picture it and become aware of all the details you have included. (Pause for 30 seconds). Are you able to picture it vividly?

MANDY: Yes.

THERAPIST: From now on whenever the thought of the old toilet comes into your mind you will have a choice either to focus on the old one or the new one. Which one would you like to choose?

MANDY: [Without any hesitation.] I prefer my toilet, the new one.

THERAPIST: As you have chosen, from now on whenever the old toilet comes into your mind, you will be able to picture the new one and as a result you will no longer have the fearful reaction.

The split screen technique was repeated over three sessions, with main focus on separating the past from the future and transforming the image of the old toilet into a new one. These sessions dramatically reduced her fear and she started to work diligently with the exposure *in vivo*. She managed to use the public washroom in the shopping mall without any difficulty on two occasions. However, after a couple of weeks later she refused to go to the park downtown for the afternoon with her son and her husband for fear of having to use the public washroom. The idea of going to the park for the whole afternoon came from her husband. As Mandy was less concerned about her phobia, the husband thought it would be very therapeutic for her to go to the park and if the needs arise to use the public washroom. He thought this would provide Mandy the opportunity to increase her confidence using public washroom. Mandy indicated that she did not feel confident enough to visit the park in case she needed to use the public washroom. Her husband tried to persuade her, with the good intention of trying to motivate her. Mandy perceived this as 'he was trying to force me into something I am not ready for'. She became very angry as it reminded her of her mother trying to force her to use the 'creepy' washroom and consequently she refused to go to the park or visit other public washroom.

Defending her autonomy

Fortunately, Mandy's clash with her husband coincided with her next stage of the therapy, which was going to focus on anger and loss of control. Two strategies were used to help Mandy resolve her anger issues: (i) the affect bridge and (ii) the empty chair technique. As she was already familiar with it, the split screen technique was used to work with her fear of loss of control.

The affect bridge technique was used to regress Mandy back to the camping holiday when she was 8 years old to uncover the reasons why her mother forced her to use the toilet, albeit her fear. The regression revealed that (i) her mother forced Mandy to use the toilet because she was constipated for not using the toilet for 2 days; (ii) her mother would not let her get out of the toilet until she had used it; (iii) Mandy perceived her mother's intention as cruel and controlling; (iv) she was very angry with her mum and to punish her she became defiant and oppositional towards her and (v) she became determined not to allow anyone to control her or force her to do anything.

The empty chair technique – a Gestalt therapy role-playing strategy (Perls, Hefferline, & Goodman, 1951; Woldt & Toman, 2005) for reducing intra- or interpersonal conflicts (Nichol & Schwartz, 2008) – was used to help Mandy ventilate her hurt and anger towards her mother. While in deep hypnosis, Mandy was directed to talk to her mother, whom she imagined sitting in an empty chair in the therapist's office across from her. By imagining her mother sitting in the empty chair in the safety of the therapy situation, Mandy was able to express all the strong feelings about her mother she had been harbouring inside her since she was 8 years old.

After having ventilated her strong feelings towards her mother, Mandy was guided to reverse role, that is, she spoke for her mother, explaining why she forced Mandy to use the washroom although she was scared to do so. Mandy accepted the explanation that (i) her mother was concerned about her health, (ii) she sincerely believed that by forcing her to use the toilet she was assisting her to overcome her fear and (iii) she waited in the washroom until Mandy used it not for punishment but to lessen her fear.

As Mandy had some experience with the split screen technique, it was used to assist her differentiate between control and loss of control. While she regressed to her childhood experience of being controlled by her mother (accessed her 'weak ego state' on the left side of the screen), her 'adult ego state' guided her to reframe the experience. After two sessions of the split screen technique, specifically devoted to the 'control issue', Mandy came up with following understanding: (i) her mother persuaded her to use the washroom because she was concerned about her – she was not trying to control her; (ii) there is a difference between control and encouragement/persuasion; (iii) her conclusion that she is controlled by everyone is faulty; (iv) the pledge that she would never allow anyone to control her, since this is based on her faulty belief that everyone is trying to control her, was maladaptive; (v) her anger towards her mother was based on the wrong assumption (i.e., she was trying to control her); (vi) whenever anyone, especially her husband, asked her to do anything, she was reacting with anger because implicitly she was displacing her anger towards her mother onto that person and (vii) she was not differentiating the past from the present.

After the two sessions of split screen technique, Mandy became very compliant to therapy and she significantly improved. She overcame her fear of using public washroom and she was planning to go on a holiday. She was given a follow-up appointment to be seen by the therapist after a month. On the eve of the appointment, she called the therapist's office to cancel her appointment as she felt fully recovered. She was duly discharged.

Summary

Specific phobia can be either simple or complex. From this, it is apparent that specific phobia is not a homogenous disorder. A therapy, particularly if it is symptom-based, that works for one patient may not work for another individual. For a person with simple phobia, monotherapy such as exposure *in vivo* may be sufficient for a positive outcome. A combined or comprehensive therapy may be superfluous for such a patient. A person with complex phobia (as the one described in this chapter), on the other hand, may not respond to a solitary therapy but derive positive benefits from a combined therapy. This chapter described an array of therapies which can be applied to a wide range of patients with specific phobias. To decide on the right course of therapy, each individual patient needs to be thoroughly assessed and the case formulated carefully. The initial case formulation, however, should not be considered the final product. The case may need to be reformulated if the therapy hits an impasse as illustrated by the case of Mandy described in this chapter. Mandy was inadvertently resisting change by protecting her sense of autonomy. The uncovering of her implicit fears (fear of drowning and fear of being controlled by others) guided the therapist to reformulate the case and consequently match the treatment to meet her individual needs.

Although the integrative psychotherapy for specific phobia described in this chapter appears heuristic and theoretically sound – currently, beyond clinical observation – there is no empirical data to support the efficacy of treating the wounded self in patients with specific phobia. The efficacy of psychodynamic therapy with anxiety disorders (Leichsenring, 2005; Milrod et al., 2007; Shedler, 2010) provides indirect support that resolution of unconscious conflicts (which may be caused by the wounded self) decrease anxiety. To encourage wider application of this integrated perspective to treatment, it will be important to validate this approach empirically. Nevertheless, this book represents a preliminary, but timely, attempt to assimilate the concept of self-wounds in the management of anxiety disorders. As discussed in Chapter 1, cognitive behaviour therapists are beginning to take serious interest in the implicit nature of anxiety disorders and are starting to develop new techniques for activating and restructuring underlying cognitive schemas. This movement is likely to spark empirical studies of the concept of the wounded self in the future, both in the understanding and treatment of anxiety disorders.

5

Panic Disorder

Case of Harry

Due to his panic attacks, Harry was unable to have a head MRI done at his local hospital over a span of two months. Since it was important for him to get the MRI done, he sought help from the author.

Harry was 56 years old when he was first seen. He was a bank manager, married for 28 years, with three grown up children (age ranging from 19 to 26 years old). Harry had a history of panic attacks, which waxed and waned since he was 22 years old, but they did not affect him much until recently. The frequency and the intensity of his panic attacks significantly increased since the Copiap mining accident in Chile on 5 August 2010. Thirty-three miners were trapped 700 metres (2,300 ft) underground and about 5 kilometres (3 miles) from the entrance of the copper-gold mine's entrance. Because of previous notorious history of the mine (previous accidents and deaths), it was originally thought that the workers had probably not survived the collapse or would have starved to death before they could be found, if ever. After 69 days of being trapped deep underground, all 33 men were brought safely to the surface on 13 October 2010 by a winching operation that lasted nearly 24 hours. The rescue operation was watched by more than 1 billion TV viewers around the world.

Every time Harry watched the news about the trapped miners on national TV, he would experience an abrupt surge of intense fear that reached a peak within minutes and he would sweat, feel dizzy and light-headed, and would become overwhelmed with the fear of dying. On

Integrative CBT for Anxiety Disorders: An Evidence-Based Approach to Enhancing Cognitive Behavioural Therapy with Mindfulness and Hypnotherapy, First Edition. Assen Alladin.
© 2016 John Wiley & Sons, Ltd. Published 2016 by John Wiley & Sons, Ltd.

several occasions, Harry ended up in emergency room and each time he was diagnosed having panic attacks.

Diagnostic Criteria for Panic Disorder

PD, as defined by the DSM-V (American Psychiatric Association, 2013, pp. 208–209), consists of four criteria (A–D), which assess the frequency, impact, characteristics and cause of the panic attacks.

A.   Presence of recurrent unexpected panic attacks. A panic attack is defined as an abrupt surge of intense fear or discomfort that reaches a peak within minutes, and during which time at least four of the following symptoms occur:
1. Palpitations, pounding heart, or accelerated hear rate.
2. Sweating.
3. Trembling or shaking.
4. Sensations of shortness of breath or smothering.
5. Feelings of choking.
6. Chest pain or discomfort.
7. Nausea or abdominal distress.
8. Feeling dizzy, unsteady, light-hearted, or faint.
9. Chills or heat sensations.
10. Paresthesias (numbness or tingling sensations).
11. Derealization (feelings of unreality) or depersonalization (being detached from onseself).
12. Fear of losing control or 'going crazy'.
13. Fear of dying.
B.   At least one of the attacks has been followed by 1 month (or more) of one or both of the following difficulties:
1.   Persistent concern or worry about additional panic attacks or their consequences, such as losing control, having a heart attack, 'going crazy', and so on.
2.   Adoption of significant maladaptive behaviour after the attacks, such as avoidance of exercise or venturing to unfamiliar situations.
C.   The panic attacks are not directly due to substance use or a general medical condition.
D.   The panic attacks are not accounted for by any other mental disorder.

DSM-V (American Psychiatric Association, 2013) distinguishes two types of panic attacks – unexpected and expected. An unexpected panic attack is referred to an attack which occurs without any obvious cue or trigger – that is, the attack appears to occur out of the blue, such as when a person is relaxing or emerging from sleep (nocturnal panic attack). In contrast, an expected panic attack occurs in response to an obvious cue or trigger, such as a situation in which the panic attacks typically occur (e.g., going to the hospital). Many patients with PD report constant or intermittent feelings of anxiety, mainly due to worries about health or mental illness concerns. Moreover, PD disorder is comorbid with other psychopathologies such as other anxiety disorders, major depression, bipolar disorder and mild alcohol use disorder. It is also comorbid with numerous general medical symptoms and conditions, including dizziness, cardiac arrhythmias, hyperthyroidism, asthma, chronic obstructive pulmonary disease and irritable bowel syndrome (American Psychiatric Association, 2013).

Prevalence of Panic Disorder

The National Comorbidity Survey-Replication (SCS-R), which surveyed 9,282 US adults across a wide range of age groups, reported lifetime and 12-month prevalence of PD disorder with or without agoraphobia, based on DSM-IV-TR diagnosis, to be 4.7% and 2.8%, respectively (Kessler et al., 2006). In contrast, the lifetime and 12-month prevalence of having a panic attack was found to be 28.3% and 11.2%, respectively. The prevalence rate for women had been consistently found to be higher than for men at a rate of 2:1 (Kessler et al., 2006). Studies suggest that prevalence rate for DSM-IV defined PD disorder differ across cultures, and it is higher in United States compared to other countries (Lewis-Fernandez et al., 2009) such as Asia, Africa, and Latin America (American Psychiatric Association, 2013).

Causes of Panic Disorder

No single cause for PD has been delineated. Many writers and clinicians have attempted to integrate multiple factors to explain the etiology of PD. For example, White and Barlow (2002) had proposed the 'triple vulnerability' model to explain how biological, psychological and social factors contribute to the development and maintenance of anxiety to an initial unexpected panic attack.

Biological contributions to PD disorder include the role of genetics and neurotransmitters. Reviews of family history and twin studies (e.g., Craske & Waters, 2005; Hettema, Neale, & Kendler, 2001) suggest that a biological vulnerability to PD, or to a chronic diffuse anxiety that predisposes one to PD, may be transmitted at least in part through genes. Neurotransmitter studies have proposed that norepinephrine may be poorly regulated in people with PD, especially in area of the brain stem called the locus coeruleus (Coplan et al., 1997). There is also evidence that serotonin (Lesch et al., 1992) and gamma-aminobutyric acid (Nutt, Glue, Lawson, & Wilson, 1990) may be involved in the pathogenesis of PD. The role of hyperventilation (Brown et al., 2003) and the impairment of frontal-limbic coordination in the modulation of panic attacks (Hasler et al., 2008) have also been implicated in the etiology of PD. To some extent, all these biological factors may be involved in the pathogenesis of PD, but it is not clear whether the presence of these predisposition factors is necessary for all panic attacks and all cases of PD (Starcevic, 2010).

Although biological vulnerability may predispose an individual for PD, psychological factors appear to determine who will develop the disorder. Cognitive theorists have described the concept of catastrophic misinterpretation to explain the escalation of a panic attack (Clark, 1986). They suggest that people who are prone to panic attacks tend to (i) pay very close attention to their bodily sensations, (ii) misinterpret bodily sensations in a negative way and (iii) engage in snowballing catastrophic thinking and exaggerate their symptoms and the consequences of the symptoms (e.g., Clark, 1988; Craske & Barlow, 2001). The belief that symptoms of anxiety have harmful consequences has been labeled anxiety sensitivity (McNally, 1999; Taylor, 1999). Individuals with high score on the Anxiety Sensitivity Index (ASI) have been shown to (i) have had PD already, (ii) have more frequent panic attacks and (iii) develop panic attacks over time compared with individuals who score low on the ASI (Hayward, Killen, Kraemer, & Taylor, 2000; Shipherd, Beck, & Ohtake, 2001). People prone to panic attacks also seem to have increased interoceptive awareness, that is, a heightened awareness of bodily cues that a panic attack may soon happen (Bouton et al., 2001). The role of psychological factors in the determination of PD had been confirmed in several studies (Craske & Waters, 2005).

Psychodynamic theory views panic attacks as the expression of an intense unconscious conflict that serves a specific psychological purpose (Busch, Milrod, & Singer, 1999). It is believed that individuals with PD struggle with a core conflict of dependency and inadequacy during childhood. This conflict is supposed to arise from an inborn fear of unfamiliar situations, which is amplified by traumatic developmental experiences such as frightening or over-controlling parents (Shear, Cooper, Klerman, Busch, & Shapiro, 1993). The perception of inadequate protection from a caregiver results in feelings of anger in the child. This anger, in turn, elicits fear that the expression of anger may result in further abandonment by and separation from the caregiver. The ego uses multiple immature and neurotic defences to protect against anxiety and awareness of internal conflicts (Kipper et al., 2005). During adulthood, this underlying conflict becomes activated when the individual experiences a life stressor that symbolizes a disruption in attachments (Busch et al., 1999). This explanation does not seem to be too different from the concept of the wounded self described in Chapter 1.

The biological and the psychological theories have been integrated to formulate the vulnerability-stress model of PD (Craske & Barlow, 2001; Craske & Waters, 2005). This integrated theory argues that individuals prone to PD have a biological vulnerability to a hypersensitive fight-or-flight response. Because of this vulnerability, even with a mild stimulus, their heart rate goes up, their breathing becomes more rapid and their palms begin to sweat. However, the physiological arousal on its own does not lead to a panic attack or a PD, unless they cogitate with their symptoms. The catastrophic cognitions increase the intensity of their initial mild symptoms to the point of a panic attack. Consequently, they become hypervigilant for signs of another attack, which constantly maintains a certain level of anxiety. This anxiety level increases the probability of experiencing a panic attack and the cycle continues (Beck & Clark, 1997). The treatment approach for PD described in this chapter is based on this integrated vulnerability-stress model of the disorder.

Treatments for Panic Disorder

A number of biological and psychological treatments have been developed for treating PD, which are briefly reviewed.

Pharmacological treatment

The effectiveness of pharmacotherapy for PD is well established, and comprehensive available data indicate three lines of treatment (see Bandelow & Baldwin, 2010). The first-line treatment includes SSRIs such as citalopram, fluoxetine, fluvoxamine and sertraline. Venlafaxine, a selective serotonin-norepinephrine reuptake inhibitor (SNRI), is also included in the first-line treatment. The second-line medication consists of tricyclic antidepressants (TCAs) such as clomipramine and lofepramine. The third-line treatment comprises of benzodiazepines such as alprazolam, clonazepam, diazepam and lorazepam. Pharmacotherapy, particularly benzodiazepines, provides a rapidly efficacious treatment for PD, and it is less time-consuming for both patients and clinicians. The downside is that about 20%–40% of patients with

PD do not respond to standard pharmacological treatment (Bandelow, Behnke, Lenoir, Hendriks, Alkin, Goebel, & Clary, 2004; Black, Wesner, Bowers, & Gabel, 1993). Moreover, the side effects of pharmacological agents – ranging from minor ones such as dry mouth to more severe ones such as sedation – often interfere with the treatment and may prolong the overall treatment (Charney, Kredlow, Bui, & Simon, 2013). Fortunately, a number of treatment options exist for these patients, in particular CBT, which has been well established as a first-line psychological treatment for PD (McHugh, Smits, & Otto, 2009).

Psychological treatment

CBT has been shown to be at least as effective as pharmacotherapy in elimi-nating PD and more effective in maintaining treatment gains over time and preventing relapse following treatment (Barlow et al., 2000; Clark, Salkovskis, Hackman, Middleton, Anastasiades, & Gelder, 1999; Kenardy et al., 2003; Ost, Thulin, & Ramnero, 2004; Telch et al., 1993). Although the effective-ness of CBT is widely reported, there is a small body of literature providing evidence for the effectiveness of psychodynamic psychotherapy with PD. For example, Milrod et al. (2007) found a 12-week manualized therapy that focused on psychodynamic conflicts to be superior (73% response) to applied relaxation training (39% response rate). Overall, a large body of evidence provides support for the use of evidence-based psychotherapy for treating PD. CBT has been shown to be more cost-effective than pharmaco-therapy and the combination of pharmacological and psychological therapies for PD (McHugh et al., 2009). The disadvantages of psychotherapy include (i) availability of clinicians trained in evidence-based therapy; (ii) it is less accessible than medication; (iii) it is not evenly disseminated across the mental health field and (iv) patient-related factors such as work, childcare, transportation, language and so on, which may prevent weekly engagement of therapy. The behavioural and cognitive treatments for PD are described in detail under the next section.

Cognitive Hypnotherapy for Panic Disorder

Hypnotherapy for managing symptoms of panic disorder

As stated in other treatment chapters, the initial part of the intervention normally consists of approximately six sessions of hypnotherapy, which is targeted at symptoms management. For some patients with simple PD, this phase of therapy may be sufficient. For patients with complex PD, the initial phase of therapy serves as a preparation for more complicated therapy of exploring the roots of the disorder. Delmonte (1995) and Stafrace (1994) have provided evidence for the effectiveness of hypnotherapy with PD. The components of initial hypnotherapy include (i) relaxation training, (ii) demonstration of the power of mind over the body, (iii) ego-strengthening, (iv) expansion of awareness, (v) modulation and regulation of symptoms, (vi) self-hypnosis and (vii) PHS. Hypnotherapy is introduced again later in therapy with patients who elect to pursue with uncovering work. The initial sessions of hypnotherapy, therefore, for some patients, serve as a preparatory phase for more complex therapy of exploring the roots of the PD later in therapy.

Relaxation training
Physiological arousal is one of the five interacting systems involved in the pathogenesis of PD – the other four systems being affect, cognition, behaviour and self-wounds in some patients. It is therefore logical for the treatment of PD to include intervention targeted at physiological arousal. Relaxation therapy is known to neutralize autonomic arousal and provide patients with some sense of control, especially when exposed to situations in which anxiety symptoms are anticipated (Starcevic, 2010, p. 89). However, the effect of relaxation therapy on PD has been variable. Some investigators (e.g., Öst, 1987a, 1987b, 1988) found applied relaxation training to be as effective as standard *in vivo* exposure therapy or CBT in patients with PD with agoraphobia. Other studies have found more mixed results with applied relaxation (e.g., Barlow, Craske, Cerny, & Klosko, 1989; Clark, Salkovskis, Hackman, Middleton, Anastasiades, & Gelder, 1994). This variable effect of relaxation therapy on PD is not surprising considering the complexity and the heterogeneity of PD, and the involvement of multiple interacting systems in the pathogenesis of PD. From this perspective, it is not unreasonable to assume that some patients with PD, especially those with simple PD, are likely to show good response to relaxation therapy or any other mono-therapy, whereas patients with complex PD may not respond to such a single intervention as relaxation; they may require a more comprehensive approach to treatment. Based on this understanding, most CBT-oriented treatment protocols for anxiety disorders incorporate relaxation therapy as an adjunct but an important one. Relaxation therapy is generally used (i) to reduce physiological correlates of anxiety and fear; (ii) broaden the focus of attention; (iii) break perseverating pattern of thinking and (iv) equip patients with coping strategy (Huppert & Sanderson, 2010). As discussed in Chapter 2, contrary to the caution

expressed by some cognitive therapists about the adverse role of relaxation response in CBT, neither hypnosis nor relaxation encourages avoidance behaviour in patients with anxiety disorder. On the contrary, by expanding attention (i.e., by inducing the relaxation response), the patient feels more efficacious dealing with the anxiety-provoking situations rather than avoiding them.

Harry found the relaxation response induced by hypnosis very calming and comforting as it decreased his sense of hyperalertness. In fact, he was very surprised that he was able to 'unwind completely' considering that he was keyed up for such a long time. As he was highly susceptible to hypnosis, his hypnotic talent was utilized to help him decentre from the fear and symptoms he experienced while feeling panicky. However, during the hypnotic experience he was fully aware of his surroundings and conceptual reality. In other words, he was fully aware of his fearful thoughts but not involved with the content or meanings of his cognitions. Harry's positive trance experience and hypnotic talent were also used to teach him how to modulate his emotional reactions to his fears and symptoms via self-hypnosis (further discussed under the section 'Self-hypnosis training').

Demonstration of the power of the mind over the body

As described in other chapters, to ratify the credibility of the hypnotic intervention and to further empower Harry, eye and body catalepsies were introduced in the second hypnotherapy session. Harry was very surprised that he could not open his eyes or get out of the reclining chair. The cataleptic experience confirmed to him that hypnotherapy could be a very powerful treatment and, as a result, he felt hopeful about overcoming his panic attacks. Chapter 3 provides a transcript for inducing eye and body catalepsies, and it offers an explanation of the cataleptic effects in terms of self-hypnosis.

Ego strengthening

Ego-strengthening suggestions were offered to Harry to promote confidence and self-efficacy. While in deep hypnotic trance, he was encouraged to visualize developing skills of 'letting go' whenever he felt anxious and panicky. Harry found the following ego-strengthening suggestions very helpful and reassuring:

- 'Every day as a result of this treatment and as a result of you listening to your self-hypnosis CD every day, you will be begin feel calmer and much more relaxed.'

- 'Although you may be aware of your anxiety and your concerns, you will be able to put everything on hold just as you did in the session. This will show you that you can relax and let go even if you are aware of everything. You don't need to empty your mind to be able to relax.'

After the first hypnotherapy session, Harry was given a self-hypnosis CD to listen to at home (see under the section 'Self-hypnosis training' for further details). As he was able to relax easily and enjoyed the 'time out', he felt motivated to listen to the self-hypnosis CD regularly. Like other patients described in this book, he commented that the relaxation response and the ego-strengthening suggestions made him feel strong and confident to deal with his anxiety and fears. Harry also felt the hypnotherapy sessions increased his self-confidence, coping abilities and positive self-image, and as a result he cogitated less with his PD.

Expansion of awareness

Harry reported feeling anxious and hyperalert most of the time, which constricted his range of emotional experience, resulting in feeling miserable and tense most of the time. To expand his range of affect, while in hypnosis, Harry was directed to focus on the relaxation response and on any feeling or emotion that unfolded. This was achieved by using EAT as described in Chapter 2. From EAT, Harry discovered that he had the ability to relax and experience different feelings and sensations. He was surprised that he could put things on hold, that is, although he was aware of his anxiety and fears, he was able to disengage from them. The ability to experience different feelings and disengage from catastrophic thoughts gave Harry the confidence that he could deal with his panic attacks.

To help Harry consolidate his ability to disengage from his fears and anxiety symptoms, he was introduced to exposure therapy, which is considered to be a critical treatment component for PD (Norton & Price, 2007). Exposure therapy is designed to disconfirm misappraisal of bodily sensations and to extinguish conditioned emotional responses to external situations and internal bodily sensations (Craske & Barlow, 2014).

Two types of exposures are used in CBT for PD: (i) interoceptive exposure and (ii) *in vivo* exposure. In CH for PD, interoceptive exposure involves two sequential phases. In Phase I, while in deep hypnosis and fully relaxed, Harry was directed to focus on his symptoms. Then he was instructed to utilize self-hypnosis to relax and calm down whenever he experienced any anxiety associated with his panic attacks. In other words, the goal was not on controlling his symptoms, the focus was on tolerating his distress.

> When I count from ONE to FIVE, by the time you hear me say FIVE, you will begin to feel whatever emotion or reaction that is associated with your panic attacks.

Once the anxiety occurred, Harry was instructed to amplify the affect associated with his panic attacks. Facing the panic attack can be quite emotionally evocative for PD patients. It is thus important for therapists to gently encourage patient to continue to face their fears and the symptoms as this will help them learn to tolerate the distress associated with their PD. Moreover, by 'staying' with the symptoms, patients learn to generate strategies for coping with their distress.

> When I count slowly from ONE to FIVE, as I count you will begin to experience the anxious feelings and fears associated with your panic attacks more and more intensely, so that when I reach the count of FIVE, at the count of FIVE you will feel the full reaction as strongly as you can bear it. ONE ... TWO ... THREE ... FOUR ... FIVE. Now notice what you feel and you can describe it to me.

Harry was then advised to utilize his self-hypnosis skills to surf over anxious feeling and fearful reactions.

> Now imagine using your self-hypnosis skill to deal with the anxious reaction. Since you have the ability to relax and put things on hold, you can let go and calm down even if the fearful and anxious thoughts cross your mind. You don't have to control your anxiety, just try to calm down and disengage from your thoughts.

After several repetition of this set of suggestions, Harry was able to relax completely, yet he was completely aware of his fearful thoughts. As discussed later in the context of AMBT, the focus of exposure therapy was not to control the symptoms of PD, but to teach Harry techniques to deal with his anxiety, or learn to surf over it (see Chapter 2 for details). Recent research findings indicate fears and anxiety disorders are partly generated by overly rigid attempts to avoid the emotional experience of fear and anxiety. The toleration of fear and anxiety is therefore considered a critical component in the psychological treatment of anxiety disorders. Hence the goal of exposure therapy should not be on immediate reduction of fear and anxiety but on learning to tolerate distress and discomfort.

The mental rehearsal in trance provided Harry an opportunity to learn how to face the symptoms of his panic attacks head-on, rather than catastrophizing or cogitating about them. He indicated that he learned to tolerate his fear of the panic attacks and discovered that 'staying with the anxiety was not as bad' as he thought.

Modulating and controlling symptoms

As hypnosis is an experiential approach to therapy, Harry was advised to perceive his anxiety symptoms as a syncretic experience (Alladin, 2006, 2007, 2008; Safer & Leventhal, 1977). He was encouraged to view his anxiety not simply as an affect, thought or behaviour, but as a cascade of cognitive, somatic, perceptual, physiological, visceral and kinaesthetic changes. The repetition of hypnotic experience and the amplification of positive syncretic cognition in the office offered Harry dramatic proof that he could regulate his anxious and distressing experience, or he could flow with them. The rapid improvement often observed in hypnotherapy is believed to emanate from the positive syncretic cognition experienced during the trance (e.g., DePiano & Salzberg, 1981).

Self-hypnosis training

To generalize his relaxation skill to real situations, Harry was taught self-hypnosis. At the end of the first hypnotherapy session, Harry was given a CD recording of the session, with the instruction of listening to it at least once a day at home. This homework assignment allowed Harry continuity of treatment between sessions and offered him the opportunity to practice self-hypnosis outside the therapy sessions. Harry commented that the training in self-hypnosis provided him the most practical and powerful skill for dealing with his panic attacks. It provided him with a tool that he could easily use in 'real panicky situations'. The self-hypnosis also served as a powerful tool for surfing over catastrophic cogitation (NSH).

To further consolidate his skill of generalizing self-hypnosis to real-life situations, Harry was introduced the clenched fist technique (Stein, 1963). As discussed in Chapter 3, the clenching of the dominant fist serves as an anchor for the elicitation of the relaxation response. Harry was trained to induce self-hypnosis rapidly whenever he worried about a panic attack by clenching his dominant fist, which acted as an anchor. Lankton (1980) defines an anchor as any stimulus that evokes a consistent response pattern from a person (see Chapter 3 for a full transcript of setting up the dominant fist as an anchor). Harry's anchoring training was experientially ratified by two sessions of hypnotherapy, during which he imagined (rehearsed) dealing with a panic attack.

> Now we are going to practice the clenching fist technique. From now on whenever you get upset, anxious, stressed out, or worry about having a panic attack, imagine utilizing your clenched fist technique to deal with it.

Just continue to imagine, from now on whenever you get anxious, upset, stressed out, or worry about having a panic attack, you are able cope with these feelings by clenching you fist and anchoring your mind to this experience. And with practice, you will get better and better with this technique. As a result of this you will begin to disengage from your anxiety although you will be aware of everything around you.

Because of its concreteness and portability, Harry found the clenched fist technique very easy to practice. He was able to apply it easily whenever he worried excessively or catastrophized about a panic attack. As the ultimate goal of psychotherapy is to help patients with anxiety disorder establish independence, self-hypnosis serves a powerful tool for achieving self-reliance, self-efficacy, self-correcting behaviours and personal power (Alladin, 2014a; Alman, 2001; Yapko, 2003).

Post-hypnotic suggestions
In hypnotherapy, it is common practice to provide PHS before the termination of a treatment session. Harry was offered a variety of PHS to help him face his anxiety about having a panic attack.

- 'Because I worry about having a panic attack, it does not mean I will have one.'
- 'Because I worry about losing control, it does not mean I will lose control.'
- 'When I feel anxious I can handle it by not trying to stop or control it, but by surfing over it. I have several techniques for dealing with my anxiety. Nothing bad has happened to me so far, so why should anything bad happen now?'

As the treatment progressed, Harry started to recognize that, to a large extent, his anxiety about having a panic attack was due to his negative rumination. At this point in therapy, Harry was ready to move on to CBT, which is described next.

Cognitive behavioural therapy

CBT for PD is based on the assumption that panic attacks are precipitated by catastrophic appraisals or misinterpretation of benign physical sensations and symptoms. The goals of CBT are to normalize appraisals of physical sensations and symptoms and to decrease the fear of anxiety symptoms and panic attacks. To achieve these goals, CBT guides patients with PD examine and question their underlying beliefs about the dangerousness of anxiety and panic. However, the emphasis in CBT is not to control or eliminate the anxiety, panic and its symptoms, but to appraise the anxiety and panic in a nonthreatening manner and thereby cope with them more effectively (Starcevic, 2010). As mentioned before, CBT is considered a first-line treatment for PD (e.g., see McCabe & Gifford, 2009). Several evidence-based CBT packages are available for the treatment of PD (e.g., Craske & Barlow, 2007; Clark et al., 1999). Although subtle differences exist between these packages, they all contain some common elements, including psychoeducation, cognitive restructuring, interoceptive exposure, *in vivo* exposure and relaxation-based strategies. Each of these CBT techniques, except for relaxation (which is already covered), is briefly described here.

Psychoeducation
Research has shown psychoeducation to be a beneficial component of CBT for PD; it leads to a decrease in negative affect and anticipatory anxiety (Rees, Richards, & Smith, 1999). In the psychoeducational session, the therapist provides information about (i) the nature of anxiety and fear, (ii) the nature of PD and its symptoms, (iii) the CBT model of PD, (iv) the treatment components of CBT, (v) the factors that maintain the symptoms and (vi) the importance of the patient's collaboration in therapy.

Self-monitoring
Self-monitoring is an important component of CBT for PD. It is used both as a treatment technique and as an assessment procedure for identifying catastrophic cognitions that the patient has about specific anxiety symptoms and panic. Different formats exist for recording cognitive distortions and its consequences. Table 5.1 represents a standard form used by Harry to monitor the events that triggered his cognitive distortions and the emotional consequences he experienced. Each time a patient feels anxious, fearful or panicky, he or she is encouraged to record it on the CAB form (see Table 5.1). By monitoring the context and content of their thoughts, patients become aware of their patterns of dysfunctional thinking. In addition to using the CAB form, catastrophic cognitions about anxiety and panic can also be assessed by directly asking patients what they believe would happen as a consequence of their symptoms (e.g., 'What is the worst that will happen to you if your heart rate increases?'). It is recommended that the automatic thoughts are not challenged initially, that is, when recording the CAB form. The goal of the monitoring phase is to bring dysfunctional thoughts into awareness. By recording the CAB form,

Table 5.1 Example of CAB form for monitoring the trigger, cognitive distortions and emotional consequences

Date	C = Emotions	A = Facts or events	B = Automatic thoughts about A
	1. Specify sad/ anxious/angry, and so on 2. Rate degree of emotion 0–100	Describe actual event, stream of thoughts, daydream, and so on, leading to worry and anxiety	Write automatic thoughts and images that came in your mind. Rate beliefs or images 0–100%
15 January 2010	*Anxious (90)* *Fearful (90)* *Panicky (50)*	*Thinking of going to hospital tomorrow for head MRI*	1. *I will feel trapped (100)* 2. *I can't cope with it (100)* 3. *I will freak out (90)* 4. *It will be so embarrassing (90)* 5. *I will fail again (100)*

the patient is able to recognize the relationship between cognition and anxiety. Once the automatic thoughts related to anxiety and panic had been recorded for at least a week, the patient is ready for the cognitive restructuring phase of CBT.

Cognitive restructuring
The next step is to challenge or dispute the catastrophic cognitions that were identified from recording the CAB form. Several procedures are involved in challenging cognitive distortions, including (i) completing the Cognitive Restructuring Form (CRF); (ii) looking for evidence to prove the inaccuracy of catastrophic cognitions; (iii) proposal of alternative explanations; (iv) examining pros and cons for catastrophic cognitions; (v) behavioural experiments and (vi) replacing catastrophic cognitions with realistic thinking (Starcevic, 2010).

Completing cognitive restructuring form
Table 5.2 provides an example from Harry, who used CRF to monitor and challenge his catastrophic thinking about having an MRI head scan. Patients become more efficient completing the CRF as they progress through the cognitive restructuring procedures described further.

Table 5.2 Completed cognitive restructuring form for PD

Date	A Activating event	B Irrational beliefs	C Consequences	D Disputation	E Effect of disputation
	Describe actual event, stream of thoughts, daydream, and so on leading to unpleasant feelings.	Write automatic thoughts and images that came in your mind. Rate beliefs or images 0–100%	1. *Emotion:* specify sad, anxious or angry. Rate feelings 1–100% 2. *Physiological:* Palpitations, pain, dizzy, sweat, and so on 3. *Behavioural:* Avoidance, in bed 4. *Conclusion:* Reaching conclusions	Challenge the automatic thoughts and images. Rate belief in rational response/image 0–100%	1. *Emotion:* Re-rate your feeling 1–100% 2. *Physiological:* Changes in bodily reactions (i.e., less shaking, less tense, etc.) 3. *Behavioural:* Action taken after disputation 4. *Conclusion:* Reappraise your conclusion and initial decision. Future beliefs in similar situation.

Date	Situation	Negative automatic thoughts	Emotions	Rational response	Outcome
22 January 2010	Thinking of going to hospital tomorrow for head MRI.	1. I will feel trapped (100) 2. I can't cope with it (100) 3. I will freak out (90) 4. It will be so embarrassing (90) 5. I will fail again (100)	1. Anxious (90), fearful (90), panicky (50) 2. Dizzy, sweaty, heart pounding 3. Restless 4. I can't handle it	1. I may feel anxious, but not trapped. I can always get out of the chamber if I become too anxious. The technician reassured me that he will stop the procedure and roll me out of the chamber whenever I feel too anxious (90) 2. I may feel anxious, but I can cope with it. Nothing bad will happen to me (100) 3. I may feel anxious or uncomfortable but will not lose control. I have never lost control (100). 4. If I can't go with the procedure the technician will understand and make another appointment for me. He is used to see people get anxious, so I don't need to feel embarrassed (80). 5. If I can't follow it through it does not mean I failed (80).	1. Less anxious (20), less fearful (20), not panicking (0) 2. No longer dizzy, sweaty or heart pounding 3. No longer restless, feeling calmer 4. I may feel uncomfortable but will be able to go through the procedure as I have done before

Looking for evidence to prove inaccuracy of catastrophic cognitions
This procedure involves asking direct questions such as:

- 'How do you know that you will lose control if you feel nervous?'
- 'How do you know that you will pass out if you feel dizzy?'

The listing of different reasons for the fear or anxiety helps the patients recognize that their catastrophic appraisals are incorrect. For example, Harry believed he would freak out (lose control) if he felt anxious during the head scan. Questioning from the therapist made him realize that he might feel anxious but not lose control. Another questioning strategy involves the downward arrow technique (Burns, 1999; Dobson & Dobson, 2009), which helps patient identify what the person is really afraid of in a situation. Here's an example of the downward arrow questioning adapted from Craske and Barlow (2007, pp. 99–100):

PATIENT: I am afraid of feeling panicky.
THERAPIST: What would happen if you felt panicky in that situation?
PATIENT: It would be terrible.
THERAPIST: What do you imagine happening that would be so terrible?
PATIENT: I would lose control.
THERAPIST: What would it mean if you lost control? What do you picture happening?
PATIENT: I would collapse.
THERAPIST: And if you collapsed, then what would happen?
PATIENT: I would never recover, and I would be hospitalized forever.

Proposing alternative explanations
In this procedure, the therapist helps patients generate alternative explanations for the target physical sensations and symptoms. The implementation of this technique is considered crucial in CBT for PD as it introduces a normal interpretation of the overall panic experience. This technique helped Harry recognize that his anxiety about having a head scan while being confined inside a chamber is a normal reaction, and because he had this fear it did not mean he would not be able to tolerate it or lose control (see Table 5.2). Starcevic (2010) points out that the success of this technique depends very much on the psychoeducation phase during which the patient is given a clear understanding of the basic physiological processes involved in the anxiety response. For example, a patient can be explained that there is no direct relationship between increase in heart rate and fainting: 'When we are anxious our heart rate increases because of the high arousal state, which produces catastrophic thoughts of fainting and in turn

we get more anxious and our heart rate goes even higher, but it is impossible to faint when your blood pressure increases; normally it is low blood pressure that leads to fainting.'

Examining pros and cons of catastrophic cognitions
Once PD patients are able to generate alternative or normalizing explanations of their symptoms, they are encouraged to weigh the pros and cons of their particular appraisals. In CBT, pros and cons are arguments for or against a particular belief. Pros are arguments that aim to promote a belief, while cons represent arguments against a belief. The same earlier example about the relationship between increased heart rate and fainting can be used to illustrate the pros and cons procedure. This is clearly described by Starcevic (2010, p. 85):

> [P]atients who think that they will faint and collapse when they feel dizzy may try to support their appraisal of dizziness by asserting that because of their usually low blood pressure, they will faint and collapse. This line of reasoning should be contrasted with information, provided by the therapist, that blood pressure usually rises during panic attacks, which makes it rather unlikely for patients to faint and collapse, despite feeling dizzy.

By practicing the pros and cons technique, and with the encouragement from the therapist, patients are able to replace their catastrophic appraisals with normalizing and realistic cognitions.

Behavioural experiments
Behavioural experiments are an essential component of CBT for PD. Behavioural experiments are designed to validate the alternative thoughts that the patients were encouraged to adopt as a consequence of the reappraisal of their symptoms and panics. The behavioural experiments often take the form of deliberate exposure to anxiety-provoking situations in order to induce fearful symptoms and their outcome. Clark and Beck (2010, pp. 318–319) write:

> Behavior experiments play a particularly important role in treatment of panic. They often take the form of deliberate exposure to anxiety-provoking situations in order to induce fearful symptoms and their outcome. The outcome of the experiment is observed and provides a test of the catastrophic versus the alternative explanation of bodily sensations.

The outcome of the experiment is observed and provides a test of the catastrophic versus the alternative explanation for bodily sensations. Clark and Salkovskis (1986) describe various behavioural experiments that can be used in the treatment of PD. A number of behavioural experiments were used to test Helen's catastrophic interpretations and beliefs. In one homework assignment she was asked to hold her breath whenever she felt breathless sensations in order to amplify the sensations. After a few seconds of breath holding, she was told to breathe normally and note differences between breath holding and breathing. 'Was there any evidence that she was exaggerating the sense of breathlessness prior to breath holding?' 'Was she able to breathe normally after holding her breath?' From these experiences, Helen found evidence that indeed she was exaggerating breathlessness and her breathing was much more normal than she thought. In another behavioural experiment, Helen was encouraged to induce physical sensations while in fear situations by increasing her physical activity level. These experiments provided evidence that physical sensations themselves do not automatically lead to anxiety or panic (e.g., 'Even when anxious, increasing my heart rate by running up stairs does not increase my anxiety level'). Instead, she discovered that how she interprets the symptoms determines whether anxiety escalates into panic (e.g., 'When I know my heart is pounding fast because of exercise I don't feel anxious').

Replacing catastrophic cognitions with realistic thinking
Cognitive restructuring does not occur simply at one particular stage of therapy, it takes place throughout the entire treatment of PD. Therefore, the replacement of catastrophic cognitions occurs throughout the treatment, both as a treatment goal and as a mechanism of change. The homework involving the completion of the CRF (see Table 5.2), which is carried out throughout the whole treatment period serves as a powerful tool for refuting and replacing catastrophic cognitions by more adaptive thinking outside the therapy sessions.

As a result of the CBT, Harry was able to modify his catastrophic cogitations about his symptoms and panic attacks, and consequently he managed to have the head scan done, although he was still fearful of lying inside the MRI scan chamber.

Healing self-wounds
After 10 sessions of CBT and hypnotherapy, Harry noticed significant improvement in his anxiety and panicky feeling, and he managed to have his head scan done. But he still continued to be fearful of being confined to a small space and reported having been claustrophobic for many years. He was therefore interested in knowing why he felt panicky about being 'trapped'. The next segment of therapy thus involved in-depth hypnotherapy and consisted of accessing and healing any underlying fears.

Elicitation of self-wounds

All modern psychodynamic theories of PD share the view that panic attacks are not spontaneous or unexpected, but triggered by events that have a unique and unconscious meaning for the person (Hoffmann, Rief, & Spiegel, 2010; Starcevic, 2009). This explanation is similar to self-wounds theory of anxiety disorders described in Chapter 1. Moreover, psychodynamic psychotherapies have been found to be efficacious for PD (e.g., see Busch et al., 2010). To explore any underlying self-wounds that might have been connected to Harry's panic attacks, the affect bridge technique (Hunter & Eimer, 2012; Watkins, 1971) was used. The feeling of anxiety that he experienced while he was having the head scan was used as a bridge to elicit his first anxiety attack. While feeling very anxious, he remembered the first panic attack he had when he was 24 years old. It was while he was having a bath in the subbasement of the house he was living in. While Harry was a student in London, England, he rented a bed-sitter (one bedroom) on the second floor of an old semi-detached (town house) house. The bathroom was in the subbasement, which was shared by other tenants. The bathroom consisted of a bath, it was dimly lit, had no windows, and with poor ventilation. The bath water was heated by a gas heater connected to a water tank, which was coin-operated. There was no shower – one had to fill the bath with hot water before having a bath. Harry remembered that he passed out for a brief period while he was washing his hair in the bath. He believed he passed out because of the poor ventilation and the heat from the water tank, which was on full blast. He could hear the emission and the burning of the gas under the water tank. Harry was shaken by the experience and it occurred to him that he could have died in the bathroom and no one could have rescued him because the bath was down in the sub-basement and locked from inside. Since then he became claustrophobic and fearful of being trapped, because being trapped meant dying with suffocation.

Immediately after recalling this traumatic event, Harry became very emotional as he remembered another disturbing incident occurring that precipitated the fear of being buried alive. Few months after the bathroom incident, Harry was reading a book on archeological diggings and findings. The book described an incident when a coffin was opened up, they found scratches on the sides of the coffin's interior, from which the writer deduced the victim might have been buried alive accidently or intentionally. Harry was horrified by this account and he could not help internalizing how terrifying it must have been for the person to be trapped inside a sealed coffin and not being able to escape. Then it dawned on him that this could happen to him or to another person and his heart started to pound and he felt dizzy and lightheaded, and had a full blown panic attack. Although Harry tried to reason that this could not happen to him in Canada, he was not totally reassured; he still believed that this could happen to him. As it is inevitable that he is going to die one day and he would be buried (his family are against cremation), he had the horrifying fear that this could happen to him. So whenever he was confined to, or imagined being confined to a small space, he got anxious and dizzy, which could produce a full-blown panic attack. The news of the Copiap mining accident recapitulated his terrifying fear of being buried alive.

From the information that surfaced from the affect bridge, it was formulated that (i) Harry developed a conditioned fear of being trapped following the fainting experience he had in the sub-basement; (ii) he developed fear of being buried alive (taphephobia) from reading the 'archeological' book and (iii) his anxiety symptoms triggered by events such as confined to a small space, news of people being trapped, or imagination of being trapped, produced panic attacks. It was therefore necessary to help Harry detoxify the meaning of his anxiety and panic attacks. Although Harry presented fear of being buried alive, he did not meet criteria for taphephobia, that is, fear of graveyard (including buried alive). Harry did not avoid graveyards or funerals, his fear was specific to being buried alive accidently, and therefore, his fear was seen as part of the PD.

Detoxification of meaning of anxiety
The split screen technique (Alladin, 2008; Cardena et al., 2000; Lynn & Cardena, 2007; Spiegel, 1981) was used to help Harry detoxify the meaning of his anxiety and panic. This hypnotic strategy utilizes the 'strong ego state' to assist the 'weak ego state' or 'fearful ego state' deal with anxiety-provoking situations. It also facilitates the 'two' ego states to work together as a team whenever the self is threatened, rather than splitting from each other when exposed to stressful situations. The therapy transcript presented subsequently illustrates how the split screen technique was used with Harry to help him deal with the toxic meaning of his symptoms. As his fears were complex and overwhelming, the split screen technique focused on one salient fear at a time in the following sequence: (i) fear of fainting, (ii) fear of premature burial and (iii) fear triggers. The transcript begins while Harry was in a deep trance. The first segment of the split screen technique deals with the fear of fainting.

THERAPIST: Now I would like you to imagine sitting in front of a large TV or cinema screen, which is vertically split in two halves, consisting of a right side and a left side. Can you imagine this?

[Harry raised his 'YES' finger. Ideomotor signals were already set up – 'YES' represented raising his right index finger and 'NO' corresponded with raising his left index finger.]

THERAPIST: Imagine the right side of the screen is lighting up as if it's ready to project an image. Imagine yourself being projected on the right side of the screen, just as you are now. Feeling very relaxed, very comfortable, in complete control, and aware of everything. And now become aware of the things you have achieved, things that you are proud of. Do you feel these good feelings?

[After a moment, Harry raised his 'YES' finger.]

THERAPIST: That's very good. Do you feel the sense of achievement?

[Harry raised his 'YES' finger.]

THERAPIST: Are you thinking about your achievement related to having been promoted manager?

[Harry raised his 'YES' finger.]

THERAPIST: Just focus on the good feelings and become aware that you made it to this high position despite your fears and anxiety. This proves to you that you have a strong side, a successful side, a side that can rescue you from difficulties and help you succeed. We are going to call this part of you the 'strong part' of you. Is that acceptable to you?

[Harry raised his 'YES' finger.]

THERAPIST: Leave this part of yourself on the right side of the screen. Now imagine yourself being projected on the left side of the screen, feeling anxious, as if you are in a situation that triggers fear of fainting. Can you imagine this?

[Harry raised his 'YES' finger.]

THERAPIST: Allow yourself to feel all the feelings that you are experiencing. Don't be afraid to let all the fear and anxiety come over you, because soon we will show you how to deal with them. Become aware of all the physical sensations you feel. Become aware of all the fearful thoughts that are going through your head and become aware of your behaviors. Can you feel these?

[Harry raised his 'YES' finger.]

THERAPIST: Are you feeling all the feelings you experience when you become fearful of fainting?

[Harry raised his 'YES' finger.]

THERAPIST: Just become aware of the whole experience and we are going to call this part of you the 'weak or fearful part of you' as you have difficulties coping with the fear of fainting. Is this acceptable to you?

[Harry raised his 'YES' finger.]

THERAPIST: Now imagine, your strong part is stepping out from the right side to the left side of the screen to help you cope with the fear of fainting. Can you imagine this?

[Harry raised his 'YES' finger.]

THERAPIST: Imagine your strong part is reassuring your weak part. He is telling your weak part not to be afraid because he is there to help him out and guide him how to deal with his fear of fainting. From now on, the weak part of you don't have to handle difficulties on his own, he can work as a team with the strong part of you.

Imagine the strong part of you is telling the weak part of you that in therapy you have learned many strategies for dealing with anxiety, fears and panic, and therefore he can walk you through the strategies. Imagine he is demonstrating the weak part of you how to relax, how to let go, and how to reason with anxious and fearful thoughts. Continue to imagine this until you feel the weak part of you feel reassured and now he knows what to do when he feels fearful of fainting. Imagine your weak part feels protected and empowered knowing he is not alone, he can get help from the strong part of you whenever the needs arise. The weak part also realizes that the strong part is of part of your Self just as the weak part is part of your Self. So from now on you can both work as a team. Is this acceptable to you?

[Harry raised his 'YES' finger.]

Harry had a positive experience with the split screen technique working on his fear of fainting. He indicated the 'strong part' coached him how to relax and 'flow' while he was feeling anxious and helped him to lessen his fear of fainting by reminding his 'weak part' that thoughts are not facts and a person cannot faint while feeling anxious because of the concomitant high blood pressure. The second segment of the split screen technique targeted Harry's fear of premature burial.

THERAPIST: Once again allow your 'strong part' to be projected on the right side of the screen. Can you imagine this?

[Harry raised his 'YES' finger.]

THERAPIST: Allow yourself to relax completely, feeling very relaxed and comfortable, and in complete control, and aware of everything. And now become aware of the things you have achieved, things that you are proud of. Do you feel these good feelings?

[After a moment, Harry raised his 'YES' finger.]

THERAPIST: That's very good. Do you feel the sense of achievement?

[Harry raised his 'YES' finger.]

THERAPIST: Just focus on the good feelings and become aware of your achievements despite your anxiety and fears. This proves to you that you have a strong side, a successful side, a side that can rescue you from difficulties and help you succeed.Again we are going to call this part of you the 'strong part' of you. Is that acceptable to you?

[Harry raised his 'YES' finger.]

THERAPIST: Leave this part of yourself on the right side of the screen. Now imagine yourself being projected on the left side of the screen, feeling anxious, as thoughts of being buried prematurely cross your mind. Can you imagine this?

[Harry raised his 'YES' finger.]

THERAPIST: Allow yourself to feel all the feelings that you are experiencing. Don't be afraid to let all the fear and anxiety come over you, because soon we will show you how to deal with them. Become aware of all the physical sensations you feel. Become aware of all the fearful thoughts that are going through your head and become aware of your behaviors. Can you feel these?

[Harry raised his 'YES' finger.]

THERAPIST: Are you feeling all the feelings you experience when you think of being buried prematurely?

[Harry raised his 'YES' finger.]

THERAPIST: Just become aware of the whole experience and we are going to call this part of you the 'fearful part of you' as you have difficulties dealing with thoughts of premature burial. Is this acceptable to you?

[Harry raised his 'YES' finger.]

THERAPIST: Now imagine, your strong part is stepping out from the right side to the left side of the screen to help your 'weak part' cope with the fear of premature burial. Can you imagine this?

[Harry raised his 'YES' finger.]

THERAPIST: Imagine your 'strong part' is reassuring your weak part. He is telling your 'fearful part' not to be afraid because he is there to help him out and guide him to deal with his fear. From now on, the 'fearful part' of you don't have to handle difficulties on his own, he can work as a team with the 'strong part' of you.

Imagine the 'strong part' of you is telling the 'weak part' of you that in therapy you have learned many strategies for dealing with anxiety, fears and panic, and therefore he can walk you through the strategies. Imagine he is demonstrating the 'weak part' of you how to relax, how to let go, and how to reason with anxious and fearful thoughts. Continue to imagine this until you feel the 'weak part' of you feel reassured and now he knows what to do when he has thoughts of premature burial. Imagine your 'weak part' feels protected and empowered, knowing that he is not alone, he can get help from the 'strong part' of you whenever the need arises. The 'weak part' also realizes that the 'strong part' is of part of your Self just as the 'weak part' is part of your Self. So from now on both of you work as a team. Is this acceptable to you?

[Harry raised his 'YES' finger.]

THERAPIST: Imagine the 'strong part' of you reminding the 'fearful part' of you what you discovered from your research on the internet. You discovered that fear of being buried alive is one of the most wide-spread human fears. Hans Christian Anderson, Frederic Chopin and George Washington were known to have this fear. You also found out that Washington instructed his attendants to bury his body three days after his death. You also decided to instruct your family not to bury you before three days. Do you remember this?

HARRY   I do and I feel greatly relieved by this plan, which is agreeable to my family.

THERAPIST: You also discovered that in the event of your death, your body will be embalmed at the funeral home and if you were still alive, it is more than likely that they will find this out. Do you believe this?

[Harry raised his 'YES' finger.]

THERAPIST: Are these facts helpful to you?

[Harry raised his 'YES' finger.]

THERAPIST: Does this information help you cope with your fear?

[Harry raised his 'YES' finger.]

Harry found the split screen technique very helpful in reinforcing his 'rational mind'. The 'strong part' reinforced his rational belief that it was unlikely for him to be buried prematurely as (i) his body would be examined by a physician before issuing a death certificate; (ii) in the event of his death, his body will be embalmed at the funeral home and (iii) he would be buried after three days of his death. Following five sessions of split screen technique and his research on the internet, Harry was able to reappraise his thoughts and beliefs about premature burial. As a result of these interventions, Harry became less preoccupied with the thoughts of premature burial. Moreover, he became less fearful of fainting and confined spaces as he recognized his main fear and panic was related to premature burial. Harry had more sessions (five) of split screen technique than usual as there was less focus on healing 'self-wounds' (further discussed under the section 'Differentiating between accurate and inaccurate self-views').

The last segment of the split screen technique addressed situational and cognitive factors that triggered his fear and panic. This segment excludes description of the initial part of the procedure as it was similar to the two segments described earlier. The transcript begins with Harry imagining his 'fearful part' feeling anxious while he was watching the news on TV about the trapped miners at Copiap in Chile.

THERAPIST: Now imagine yourself being projected on the left side of the screen, feeling anxious, as you watch the news about the trapped miners in Chile. Can you imagine this?

[Harry raised his 'YES' finger.]

THERAPIST: Allow yourself to feel all the feelings that you are experiencing. Don't be afraid to let all the fear and anxiety come over you, because soon we will show you how to deal with them. Become aware of all the physical sensations you feel. Become aware of all the fearful thoughts that are going through your head and become aware of your behaviors. Can you feel these?

[Harry raised his 'YES' finger.]

THERAPIST: Are you feeling all the feelings you experience when you think of being buried prematurely?

[Harry raised his 'YES' finger.]

THERAPIST: Just become aware of the whole experience and we are going to call this part of you the 'weak part' of you as you have difficulties dealing with thoughts of premature burial. Is this acceptable to you?

[Harry raised his 'YES' finger.]

THERAPIST: Now imagine, your 'strong part' is stepping out from the right side to the left side of the screen to help your 'weak part' cope with the fear of being trapped in your grave. Can you imagine this?

[Harry raised his 'YES' finger.]

THERAPIST: Imagine your 'strong part' is reassuring your weak part. He is telling your 'weak part' not to be afraid because he is there to help him out and guide him how to deal with his fear of being trapped in your grave. From now on, the 'weak part' of you don't have to handle difficulties on his own, he can work as a team with the 'strong part' of you.

Imagine the 'strong part' of you is telling the 'weak part' of you that in therapy you have learned many strategies for dealing with anxiety, fears and panic, and therefore he can walk you through these strategies. Imagine he is demonstrating to the 'weak part' of you how to relax, how to let go, and how to reason with anxious and fearful thoughts. He is reminding the 'weak part' that thoughts are not facts and because you feel fearful about something it does not mean it will happen. He is also reminding the 'weak part' to stick to the 'rational' thinking and the discoveries you made from research on the internet.

Continue to imagine this until you feel the 'weak part' of you feel reassured, and now he knows what to do when he is exposed to information, or thoughts that produce fearful thoughts of being trapped in your grave. Imagine your 'weak part' feels protected and empowered knowing that he is not alone, he can get help from the 'strong part' of you whenever the need arises. The 'weak part' also realizes that the 'strong part' is of part of your Self just as the 'weak part' is part of your Self. So from now on, both of you will work as a team. Is this acceptable to you?

[Harry raised his 'YES' finger.]

THERAPIST: The 'strong side' is also telling the 'fearful part' not to confuse yourself with the miners. Although it is distressing to watch the trapped miners, it is not helpful to internalize their fears. Is this acceptable to you?

[Harry raised his 'YES' finger.]

After this split screen sessions, although his anxiety still persisted, Harry felt less anxious when the thoughts about being trapped in his grave crossed his mind or whenever he was exposed to any information about people being trapped.

Differentiating between accurate and inaccurate self-views
Harry was guided to differentiate between his self-views that were based on facts and those that were based on inaccurate opinions. Harry was never undermined or put down by his parents or other adults. He did not have a history of trauma, except for the scary experiences he had in the washroom in the sub-basement and when he read the 'archeological' book. Fortunately, Harry did not have notable painful self-views (negative views of himself as a person). On the contrary, except for his fears, he was confident, assertive and ambitious to do well in life. For these reasons, it was decided to refrain from 'healing self-wounds' work and instead to focus more on the split screen technique and CBT, particularly cognitive restructuring, interoceptive exposure and relaxation-based hypnotherapy. The uncovering work was, nevertheless, fundamental in uncovering his

primary fear, and the split screen technique provided an experiential approach to CBT. The introduction of acceptance and mindfulness-based strategies, described next, further consolidated the treatment gains.

Promoting acceptance and gratitude

As discussed in Chapters 1 and 2, patients with anxiety disorders tend to suppress re-experiencing of their initial trauma as it causes extreme distress (Wolfe, 2005, 2006). Greeson and Brantley (2009) found AMBT to help these patients develop a wise and accepting relationship with their internal cognitive, emotional and physical experience, even during times of intense fear and anxiety, rather than avoiding their fears. In regard to PD, studies suggest a link between acceptance and nonjudgemental attitude and fewer panic symptoms (Eiffert & Heffner, 2003; Levitt, Brown, Orsillo, & Barlow, 2004). Moreover, Kim et al. (2009) have demonstrated MBCT to be more effective than an anxiety disorder programme in the management of PD. When AMBT are applied to PD, the main goal is to help patients learn to observe their symptoms without overly identifying with them, or without reacting to them in ways that aggravate their distress (Roemer, Erisman, & Orsillo, 2008). To achieve this goal with PD, several mindfulness and acceptance strategies are used, which include:

1. Techniques to facilitate awareness of one's current perceptual, somatic, cognitive and emotional experience.
2. Techniques to promote cognitive distancing or defusion from one's thoughts and inner experience.
3. Techniques to assist nonjudgemental acceptance of subjective experience.
4. Techniques to foster clarity of goals and values.
5. Techniques to boost sense of gratitude
6. Techniques to cultivate PC.

Integration of these six set of techniques in therapy engenders a fundamental shift in perspective (reperceiving), that is, they encourage PD patients to re-evaluate their constructed reality (Alladin, 2014a). Treatment strategies based on each set of techniques as applied to PD, are briefly described next.

Strategies for cultivating awareness
Chapter 2 proposed eight common AMBT strategies for cultivating increasing awareness of one's ongoing stream of experience, including (i) mindfulness meditation, (ii) mindful hypnosis, (iii) concentrative

meditation, (iv) walking meditation, (v) eating meditation, (vi) attention training, (vii) compassion meditation and (viii) loving kindness meditation. Harry opted for mindful hypnosis technique, which is described here. For further details about the other techniques, the interested reader can refer to Chapter 2 and several books (e.g., Kabat-Zinn, 2013; Orsillo & Roemer, 2011; Segal et al., 2013).

Mindful hypnosis involves the ability to relax completely and yet being aware of everything. The following transcript, which begins while Harry was in a deep trance, exemplifies the suggestions used for bolstering one's awareness of thoughts, feelings, body sensations and surroundings.

> You have now become so deeply relaxed and you are in such a deep hypnotic trance that your mind and your body feel completely relaxed, totally relaxed.
>
> You begin to feel a beautiful sensation of peace and tranquility, relaxation and calm, flowing all over your mind and your body; giving you such a pleasant and such a soothing sensation all over your mind and your body, that you feel completely relaxed, totally relaxed, both mentally and physically.
>
> At the same time, you may notice that you are aware of everything, you are aware of all the sound and noise around you, you are aware of your thoughts and your imagination, and yet you feel so relaxed, so calm and so peaceful. This shows that you have the ability to relax, the ability to let go, and the ability to put everything on hold. This also demonstrates that you have lots of control, because you are aware of everything. You can hear all the sounds and noise around you, you are aware of your thoughts and imagination. You are aware that I am sitting beside you and talking to you. Yet you are able to put everything on hold and relax your mind and body completely.
>
> Now you can become aware of all the good feelings you are feeling right now. You feel calm, you feel peaceful, you feel relaxed and you feel very, very comfortable both mentally and physically. You may also become aware of feeling heavy, light, or detached, or distancing away from everything, becoming more and more detached, distancing away from everything, drifting into a deep, deep hypnotic trance. Yet you are aware of all the sounds and noise around you. You are aware that you are sitting on this comfortable chair, noticing your back resting on the chair. Your neck and your shoulders and your head are resting against the chair. You are aware of everything, yet being fully relaxed. You are aware of your breathing, breathing in and out, feeling completely relaxed. You feel happy and pleased knowing that you can relax, you can let go. You feel thrilled and satisfied knowing that you can put things on hold and yet be aware of everything. You feel kind of curious that you can relax and yet be aware of everything.

The mindful hypnosis training helped Harry discover he had the capacity and the talent to relax, to let go and to experience different positive feelings, emotions and sensations. He was surprised that he could put things on hold and distance away from his his fears and anxiety, yet being fully conscious of his fearful and anxious thoughts.

With practice Harry was able to generate and experience a variety of positive and negative emotions and feelings appropriate to the context. He was also able to maintain a sense of calm while being aware of anxious thoughts. The mindful hypnosis training helped Harry feel less anxious when the thoughts about being trapped in his grave crossed his mind, or whenever he was exposed to any information about people being trapped.

Strategies for cognitive distancing

Cognitive distancing strategies were used to help Harry further bolster his discovered ability to distance away from his anxious thoughts and fear of being trapped. These strategies helped Harry recognize that his thoughts were distinct from his self and that they were not necessarily true (i.e., thoughts were not facts). AMBT utilize a variety of techniques to train patients with PD decentre from their thoughts, including (i) gazing at thoughts from a distance (e.g., visualizing a thought floating downstream on a leaf); (ii) recognizing bias in thinking (cognitive distortions); (iii) hearing thoughts (self-talk) and (iv) seeing thoughts as images (e.g., as clouds). This training produces cognitive defusion, or the ability to separate thoughts from the self. Harry found 'seeing thoughts as images' very helpful as the thoughts of being trapped or buried alive were always associated with the vivid image of seeing himself waking up in his grave. As mentioned before, from his research on the Internet, he discovered that George Washington had a similar fear and he instructed his attendants not to bury him in less than three days after his death. Harry disclosed his fears to his family and came up with similar arrangement, which was acceptable to his family. Since then he changed the images of premature burial. Whenever the image or thought of being trapped in his grave crossed his mind, he imagined his body, following his death, lying at the funeral home for at least three days, and if he happened to be alive he would be bound to wake up. Changing the image was extremely beneficial to Harry. As a result of this technique, his relationship with his thoughts and images of being trapped transformed and, consequently, he felt less anxious or preoccupied with the thought of being trapped. In other words, he became less fused with the fearful thoughts and images.

Strategies for promoting acceptance

One of the core interventions in AMBT relates to fostering an open, accepting, nonjudgemental and welcoming attitude towards the full range of one's subjective experience. The most common strategies for promoting acceptance in PD patients include (i) psychoeducation, (ii) acceptance exercise and (iii) exposure exercises.

Psychoeducation
This involves defining the meaning of acceptance and understanding the relationship between anxiety and upset. In the context of CH, acceptance is defined as 'being open to experience or willing to experience the reality of the present moment'. The definition is similar to mindfulness in the sense that the patient is trained to be nonjudgemental and purposely allowing experience (thoughts, emotions, desires, urges, sensations, etc.) to occur without attempting to block or suppress them. Acceptance encourages increased contact with previously avoided events and experience.

Patients with PD are also educated to understand the relationship between anxiety and upset. As learned during CBT, patients are reminded that it is not the situations that cause anxiety and panic but the cognitions (usually cognitive distortions) that are triggered by the events. Hence, patients can learn to cope with the anxiety and panic either by changing the cognitive distortions or accepting (decentring or defusion) them. Moreover, patients with anxiety disorder tend to get 'upset for feeling anxious', or get 'anxious for feeling anxious', or feel 'upset for feeling fearful'. The patients with PD are trained to differentiate between 'normal upset' and 'anxiety' and they are encouraged to view feelings of being upset related to 'normal fear' as normal and inevitable. Segal et al. (2002, 2013) have demonstrated that when depressed patients, while in remission, label 'normal' upsets as return of their depressive symptoms, they spiral down into a full-blown depressive episode. However, if they are able to accept their reaction to stress as normal, although upsetting, they are able to prevent relapse. Similarly, patients with PD can learn 'not to feel upset for feeling anxious', 'not to feel anxious for feeling panicky' and 'not to feel anxious for feeling stressed out'.

Acceptance exercise
To consolidate the psychoeducation about acceptance, PD patients are encouraged to carry out a list of exercises:

- Focusing on here and now. If the mind wanders away, the patient accepts it and gently brings it back to the present, becoming mindful of the present activity.
- Observing anxiety and its contexts non-judgementally. The patient becomes aware of the external (e.g., watching the news) or internal (heart rate increasing) reasons for his or her anxiety, rather than blaming oneself for the experience or becomes upset for feeling anxious.

- Separation of secondary emotions from primary emotions (e.g., not to get upset for feeling anxious).
- Learning to tolerate anxiety rather than fighting it (flow with it).
- Adopting healthy and adaptive means of dealing with anxiety rather than resorting to short-term reduction measures such as over-medication, alcohol or substance abuse.
- Toleration of anxiety by adopting healthy adaptive measures as mentioned earlier and reminding oneself of the relatively short duration of the anxiety (e.g., anxiety always subsides after a while).
- Tolerance of frustration by adopting healthy adaptive measures and reminding oneself of the long-term goals (e.g., patient is encouraged to do the acceptance and other mindful exercises on a daily basis, although reduction in anxiety may not be apparent initially, but in the long run they will be beneficial).
- Re-contextualizing the meaning of suffering, for example, from 'this anxiety is unbearable' to 'let me focus on what I can do although I feel anxious'.
- Exercising radical acceptance – ability to welcome those things in life that are hard, unpleasant or very painful (e.g., accepting panic attacks).
- Embracing good or bad experience as part of life.
- Willing to experience the reality of the present moment, for example, believing that 'things are as they should be'.
- Purposely allowing experiences (thoughts, emotions, desires, urges, sensations, etc.) to transpire without attempting to block or suppress them.
- Realizing that anxiety is not caused by object or situation itself, but by our perception of it, our coping abilities and our level of spirituality.

Harry found the concept of acceptance very meaningful to him as he was a devout Catholic. He saw the acceptance exercises as an extension of his faith and an advanced, but practical, form of his CBT training. He indicated the acceptance exercises taught him to 'flow easily' with his symptoms, distress and frustration.

Exposure exercises

As discussed earlier, patients with anxiety disorders avoid painful experience (Michelson, Lee, Orsillo, & Roemer, 2011). Toleration of fear and anxiety is therefore considered an essential component in the psychological treatment of the disorder. Based on this approach, the goal of exposure therapy should not be on immediate reduction of fear and anxiety, but on learning to tolerate distress and discomfort. In this context, AMBT uses exposure exercises to provide training in toleration of distress via acceptance.

Patients with PD are invited to increase their awareness of bodily sensations and fearful images so that they may learn to approach them in a more accepting and compassionate way. These exercises encourage patients to 'go inside' their anxiety and panic rather than trying to fight them. Forsyth and Eifert (2007) believe this approach allows patients to create more space to feel their emotions and to think their thoughts as they are rather than their minds telling them what they are. The following script adapted from Forsyth and Eifert (pp. 196–197) exemplifies an 'acceptance of anxiety' exercise. The exercise is usually performed when the patient is either in a relaxed state or in a light hypnotic trance (a deep trance is avoided to facilitate deeper awareness).

> While you continue to relax, take a few moments to get in touch with the physical sensations in your body, especially the sensations of touch or pressure where your body makes contact with the chair. Notice the gentle rising and falling of your breath in your chest and belly. There's no need for you to control your breathing in any way – simply let the breath breathe itself. Also bring this attitude of kindness and gentleness to the rest of your body experience, without needing it to be other than what it is.
>
> If your mind wanders, this is okay. It's natural for your mind to wander away to thoughts, worries, images, bodily sensations, or feelings. Notice these thoughts and feelings, acknowledge their presence, and stay with them. There's no need to think of something else, make them go away, or resolve anything. As best as you can, allow them to be ... giving yourself space to have whatever you have ... bringing a quality of kindness and compassion to your experience.
>
> Now allow yourself to be present to what you are afraid of. Notice any doubts, reservations, fears, concerns and worries. Just notice them and acknowledge their presence, and don't try to control or influence them in any way. As you do that, allow yourself to be present with your values and commitments. Ask yourself, 'Why am I here?', 'Where do I want to go?', 'What do I want to do?'
>
> When you are ready, gently shift your attention to a thought or situation that has been difficult for you. It could be a troubling thought, a worry, an image, or an intense bodily sensation. Gently, directly, and firmly shift your attention on and into the discomfort, no matter how bad it seems. Notice any strong feelings that may arise in your body, allowing them to be as they are rather than what your mind tells you they are. Simply hold them in awareness. Stay with your discomfort and breathe with it. See if you can gently open up to it and make space for it, accepting and allowing it to be ... while bringing compassionate and focused attention to the discomfort.
>
> If you notice yourself tensing up and resisting, pushing away from the experience, just acknowledge that and see if you can make some space for whatever you are experiencing. Must this feeling or thought be your rival?

Or can you have it, notice it, own it, and let it be? Can you make room for the discomfort, for the tension, for the anxiety? What does it really feel like – moment to moment – to have it all? Is this something you must struggle with, or can you invite the discomfort in, saying to yourself, 'Let me have it; let me feel what there is to be felt because it is my experience right now'?

If the sensations or discomfort grow stronger, acknowledge that, stay with them, breathing with them, and accepting them. Is this discomfort something you must not have, you cannot have? Can you open up a space for the discomfort in your heart? Is there room inside you to feel that, with compassion and kindness toward yourself and your experience?

As you open up and embrace your experience, you may notice thoughts coming along with the physical sensations, and you may see thoughts about your thoughts. When that happens, invite them too … softening and opening to them as you become aware of them. You may also notice your mind coming up with judgmental labels such as 'dangerous' or 'getting worse'. 'If that happens, you can simply thank your mind for the label and return to the present experience as it is, not as your mind says it, noticing thoughts as thoughts, physical sensations as physical sensations, feelings as feelings – nothing more, nothing less.

Stay with your discomfort for as long as it pulls your attention. If and when you sense that the anxiety and other discomfort are no longer pulling for your attention, let them go.

As this practice comes to a close, gradually widen your attention to take in the sounds around you. Take a moment to make the intention to allow this sense of gentleness and self-acceptance continue for the rest of your day. Then, slowly open your eyes.

The combination of CBT, hypnotherapy and the acceptance exposure exercises helped Harry decrease his cogitation about premature burial. He was able to become defused from his fearful thoughts without trying to control them.

Strategies for clarifying values

The importance of clarifying and articulating one's values in AMBT were discussed in Chapter 2. As values give meaning to one's life, they often establish the direction one chooses to take in therapy. In this sense, values largely determine whether a patient is willing to commit to the difficult behavioural challenges and/or accept aversive internal experiences that he or she may have to face in the course of therapy. Clarification of patient's values is therefore an essential ingredient in development and sustaining motivation for change (Herbert & Forman, 2014). Harry was very appreciative of his 'lovely family' and his professional achievement as a bank manager. He decided (established the intention) to 'enjoy' what he had rather than 'giving in' to his fear. This intention motivated him to learn to tolerate his distress and therefore he was 'prepared' to 'go with the punches'.

Strategies for learning to express gratitude
Sense of gratitude is used as a means to cultivate acceptance in patients with anxiety disorder. Recent studies suggest that people who are grateful have higher levels of subjective well-being and have more positive ways of coping with difficulties they experience in life (see Chapter 2 for more details). As Harry was very conscious and appreciative of his strengths and resources, 'gratitude work' was not indicated.

Strategies for nurturing psychophysiological coherence
The sixth component of AMBT targets the integration of various subsystems in the body. Research indicates heart-focused positive emotional state leads to synchronization of the entire body system, producing PC (see Chapter 2 for more detail). As described in other chapters, breathing with your heart technique is used to help patients with anxiety disorders generate coherence (harmony) of the entire system (mind, body, brain, heart and emotion). The technique, consisting of two phases – (i) heart education and (ii) breathing with your heart training assisted by hypnosis – can be easily applied to PD.

Heart education
The patient is given a scientific account of the role of heart and positive emotions in the generation of PC, which promotes healing, emotional stability and optimal performance. The similarities and the differences between Western and Eastern theories of 'mind' and 'heart' are also discussed (Alladin, 2014a), as both 'mind' and 'heart' are incorporated in the breathing with your heart technique.

Breathing with your heart training combined with hypnosis
Heart–mind–body training helps patients with PD deal with panic and symptoms of anxiety. By breathing with the heart, PD patients are able to shift their attention away from their mind to their heart. When a person feels good in his or her heart, the person experiences a sense of comfort and joy because we validate reality by the way we feel and not by the way we think (Alladin, 2014a; Fredrickson, 2002; Isen, 1998). As discussed in Chapter 2, logic does not always correspond with good affect, but feeling good in one's heart, especially when associated with sense of gratitude, invariably creates positive affect (Welwood, 1983).

The following transcript from a session with Harry demonstrates how the technique can be introduced in therapy. The script begins with Harry being in a deep hypnotic trance:

You have now become so deeply relaxed, that you begin to feel a beautiful sensation of peace and relaxation, tranquility and calm flowing throughout your mind and body. Do you feel relaxed both mentally and physically? [Harry nodded his head up and down; ideomotor signals of 'head up and down for YES' and 'shaking your head side to side for NO' were set up prior to starting the breathing with your heart technique.] Now I would like you to focus on the center of your heart. [Pause for 30 seconds.] Can you imagine this? [Harry nodded his head.] Now I would like you to imagine breathing in and out with your heart [Pause for 30 seconds.] Can you imagine this? [Harry nodded his head.] Continue to imagine breathing in and out with your heart. [He was allowed to continue with this exercise for 2 minutes and at regular intervals, the therapist repeated: 'Just continue to imagine breathing with your heart' as he did the exercise.] Now I would like you to slow down your breathing. Breathe in and out at 7-second intervals. Breathe in with your heart ... 1 ... 2 ... 3 ... 4 ... 5 ... 6 ... 7 ... and now breathe out with your heart ... 1 ... 2 ... 3 ... 4 ... 5 ... 6 ... 7 ... And now as you are breathing in and out with your heart I want you to become aware of something in your life that you feel good about, something that you feel grateful for. [Pause for 30 seconds.] Are you able to focus on something that you are grateful for in your life? [Harry] Just become aware of that feeling and soon you will feel good in your heart. [Harry nodded.] Just become aware of this good feeling in your heart. [Pause for 30 seconds.] Now I would like you to become aware of the good feeling in your mind, in your body and in your heart. Do you feel this? [Harry nodded.] Now you feel good in your mind, in your body and, in your heart. You feel a sense of balance, a sense of harmony. Do you feel this sense of harmony? [Harry nodded.] From now on whenever and wherever you are, you can create this good feeling by imagining breathing with your heart and focusing on something that you are grateful for. With practice you will get better and better at it. Now you know what to do to make your heart feel lighter.Also from now on, whenever you feel panicky, you will be able to surf over the feeling by breathing with your heart and focusing on something that you aregrateful for in your life.

Summary

The chapter described a wide variety of behavioural, cognitive, hypnotic, unconscious, and acceptance and mindfulness-based strategies for treating PD. Based on case formulation, a therapist can select the most suitable techniques for each individual patient with PD. The case of Harry illustrated that symptom-focused treatment is necessary but not sufficient for treating underlying determinants of PD. The accessing and healing of his underlying fear of being buried alive produced deeper and more meaningful changes in his symptoms. Moreover, it had a significant impact on the secondary symptoms of being fearful of confined spaces.

6

Generalized Anxiety Disorder

Case of Fred

Fred was referred to the author by his psychiatrist for psychological treatment. He had a long history of chronic 'anxiety' and 'depression', and he had been followed up by a psychiatrist for over 10 years. Fred was a 54-year-old team leader at a highly successful, multinational electronic company. By training Fred is an electric engineer, but for the past five years he had been holding a very senior position as a project manager. The company had invested several millions of dollars on a project for developing the next generation of wireless communication. Fred was very excited to lead the project, but gradually he lost interest in the project and lacked motivation to go to work as he constantly questioned whether he was qualified for the job or whether he would be able to deliver what his boss expected from him. He was also preoccupied with all the negative consequences for himself and his family if he lost his job.

Fred complained of difficulty falling and staying asleep at night. He described himself as a nervous, anxious, restless and at times agitated. He found it very difficult to relax or unwind. He worried excessively and always 'catastrophizing' about the future. For example, he knew that his job was secure, and even if he lost his job, he had sufficient funds to continue with his present standard of life, but he could not stop ruminating with 'what if'. At times he got so anxious, overwhelmed or panicky that he could not cope with his job, hence on two occasions it necessitated short-term admission to the psychiatric unit of the local general hospital. He realized some of the worries were irrational and unjustified but he could

Integrative CBT for Anxiety Disorders: An Evidence-Based Approach to Enhancing Cognitive Behavioural Therapy with Mindfulness and Hypnotherapy, First Edition. Assen Alladin.
© 2016 John Wiley & Sons, Ltd. Published 2016 by John Wiley & Sons, Ltd.

not stop worrying. He constantly worried about being fired from his work and the dire consequences it would have on him and his family, particularly as his daughters who were at the university, fully depended on his income. These worries occupied much of his time and made it difficult for him to concentrate at work and fall asleep at night. He also complained of often waking up in the middle of the night worrying about his numerous obligations and responsibilities. He had been married for over 25 years. His wife, a lawyer by profession, had given up her job to be more supportive to her husband and her two daughters. She was very supportive to Fred and provided the encouragement for her husband to continue with his psychotherapy and his occasional follow-up visits to his psychiatrist. However, at times she got frustrated when Fred 'went on and on with his negative chatter', which at times caused anger and confrontation. Fred interpreted this as lack of understanding from her, and he concluded that his wife believed that he was not making much progress with his therapy as he was not trying hard enough.

Fred was brought up in a 'commercial family'. His father was a successful business man, dominant, charismatic, a 'natural leader' and well respected in the community. Because of his very busy life, Fred's father was detached from the family but not unsupportive. Fred described himself as being the 'total opposite' to his father. He described his mother as being passive, 'an ordinary housewife' and not very knowledgeable about the world. He had two older sisters, who were both married, and living in the same town as his parents.

GAD was established as the main diagnosis; the occasional symptoms of depression appeared to be secondary to his anxiety disorder. However, on two occasions he experienced periods of deep dysphoria that met diagnostic criteria of a major depressive episode. His psychiatrist concurred with the diagnosis and recommended individual psychotherapy as an important adjunct to his pharmacotherapy. There is a positive history of anxiety and depression in the maternal side of his family.

Diagnostic Criteria for Generalized Anxiety Disorder

The diagnostic criteria for GAD listed in the fifth edition of the *Diagnostic and Statistical Manual of Mental Disorders* (DSM-V; American Psychiatric Association, 2013, p. 222) include:

1. Excessive anxiety and worry about a number of events or activities, such as work, relationship, school, and so on. These symptoms should occur on more days than not for at least six months for a diagnosis to be made.

2. The worry is beyond the person's control.
3. The anxiety or worry should be associated with three or more of the following symptoms (one item is required for children):
   (i)   Restlessness or feeling keyed up or on edge
   (ii) Being easily fatigued or exhausted
   (iii) Difficulty concentrating or the mind goes blank
   (iv) Feeling irritable
   (v)   Muscle tension
   (vi) Disturbed sleep, for example, difficulty falling or staying asleep, restless or unsatisfied sleep.
4. The anxiety, worry or physical symptoms cause significant distress or impairment in occupational, social, or other important areas of functioning.
5. The symptoms are not due to substance abuse or a medical condition.
6. The symptoms are not due to another mental illness.

Prevalence of Generalized Anxiety Disorder

GAD occurs in about 5% of the general population in the United States (National Centre for Health Statistics, 1994), and the lifetime prevalence rate is estimated to be approximately 4–7%, while the current prevalence rate ranges from 1.5 to 3% (Blazer, Hughes, George, Swartz, & Boyer, 1991). GAD is often stated as the most common anxiety disorder in primary care with a prevalence rate as high as 8.3% (Katzman, 2009). Women appear to be more affected than men in a 2:1 ratio. The prevalence of the diagnosis seems to peak in middle age and decline across the later years of life (Baldwin, Waldman, & Allgulander, 2011). Individuals of European descent are more frequently diagnosed with GAD than individuals from non-European descent such as Asian, African, Native American and Pacific Islander (American Psychiatric Association, 2013). GAD's impact on social functioning, distress levels and utilization of medical care is equivalent to those of other major psychiatric disorders (Mennin, Heimberg, & Turk, 2004). Moreover, over 90% of patients with GAD also meet criteria for at least one additional anxiety disorder, and they are at risk for developing other mental disorders, particularly major depressive disorder (Bruce, Machan, Dych, & Keller, 2001). In addition, GAD patients use primary care and gastroenterology services more often than those without the disorder (Hoffman, Dukes, & Wittchen, 2008).

Causes of Generalized Anxiety Disorder

Over the past two decades, an abundance of empirical studies have implicated a wide range of cognitive, affective and neurobiological mechanisms in the formation and maintenance of GAD. A synthesis of data on these mechanisms indicates that GAD is a disorder associated with emotional and neurobiological hyperreactivity, and a fear of negative emotional contrasts (Behar, DiMarco, Hekler, Mohlman, & Staples, 2009. The notion of negative emotional contrast stems from Contrast Avoidance Model of GAD, which purports that individuals with GAD engage in chronic worry because they prefer to experience a sustained state of distress as a way to be emotionally prepared for the worst possible outcome to various events (Newman & Llera, 2011). It is believed that these patients choose to maintain a state of chronic negativity because of their emotional sensitivities and vulnerabilities as discussed in Chapter 1. Evidence suggests that individuals with GAD report feeling more distraught than nonanxious controls when experiencing a sharp shift from a euthymic or relaxed state to one that is overwhelmingly negative (Llera & Newman, 2011). This is referred to as a negative emotional contrast experience. It appears individuals with GAD feel compelled to be emotionally braced for negative events at all times to avoid feeling even greater experienced disruption in response to emotional contrasts. Moreover, there is evidence to suggest that worry serves as a compensatory mechanism that creates and prolongs negative emotionality, thereby reducing contrasting emotional experiences (Newman, Llera, Erickson, Przeworski, & Castonguay, 2013). These reviewers propose that the emotional and neurobiological dysregulation observed in patients with GAD are caused or maintained by developmental vulnerabilities (environmental stress, insecure attachment, negative parenting behaviours), temperamental vulnerabilities (behavioural inhibition) and interpersonal processes (sensitivity to social threats and problematic interpersonal behaviours). Many of these factors point to the central role of hyperreactivity and a fear of negative emotional shifts as well as the use of worry to prevent emotional contrasts that are perceived as unmanageable. These explanations complement and support Wolfe's wounded self theory of anxiety disorders. Furthermore, theoretical models of GAD share a common emphasis on the central importance of avoidance of internal experiences (Lee et al., 2010).

Treatment of Generalized Anxiety Disorder

GAD is a chronic disorder, which waxes and wanes, and it is not unusual for patients to have experienced active symptoms for more than 10 years before they seek treatment. Although both psychotropic medications and

CBT have been found to be effective with GAD, pharmacotherapy is the most common treatment (Issakidis, Sanderson, Corry, Andrews, & Lapsley, 2004). Several classes of drugs such as antidepressants, benzodiazepines and anticonvulsants have demonstrated to be effective in placebo-controlled trials. The current consensus across different guidelines consider selective serotonin reuptake inhibitor (SSRI) and SNRI the first line of treatment for GAD (Katzman et al., 2011). Nonetheless, despite some notable benefits, there are also drawbacks and limitations (including adverse side-effects) to medications (Newman et al., 2013), and there is no clear support for an additive effect when combined with CBT (Bond et al., 2002, Crits-Christoph et al., 2011). Moreover, current evidence indicates that pharmacotherapy is effective at reducing symptoms of anxiety, but it does not have a significant impact on worry (Anderson & Palm, 2006), which is the defining characteristic of GAD.

As regards to psychotherapy, CBT had been shown to reduce acute symptoms of GAD compared to pill placebo, no treatment, waiting list and nondirective supportive therapy, and the improvements had been sustained up to two years following treatment (Borkovec & Ruscio, 2001; Gould, Safren, Washington, & Otto, 2004). A recent meta-analysis demonstrated CBT to be highly effective at reducing pathological worry (Covin, Ouimet, Seeds, & Dozois, 2008). However, a meta-analysis of the effectiveness of CBT with GAD by Siev & Chambless, 2007 revealed comparable effects of CBT and relaxation therapy in the treatment of GAD. Moreover, CBT appears to have a positive impact on comorbid symptoms, especially in patients who have been able to reduce their GAD symptoms significantly (Newman et al., 2010). Despite the progress that has been made in creating efficacious therapies for GAD, the accumulation of data on psychotherapy for GAD is lagging behind most other anxiety disorders and depression (Newman, Llera, Erickson, Przeworski, & Castonguay, 2013). For example, most studies of CBT with GAD indicate that fewer than 65% of patients meet criteria for high end-state functioning at posttreatment (Ladouceur et al., 2000; Newman et al., 2011). To enhance the treatment effects of GAD, recent research has refined and expanded our understanding of GAD in an effort to identify causal and maintaining factors to target in therapy and improve its efficacy. Randomized controlled studies based on these models indicate the need to target interpersonal and emotional aspects of GAD (Newman et al., 2011), and the intolerance of uncertainty (Dugas et al., 2010). Driven by some of these findings, Roemer and Orsillo (2009, 2014) have developed an acceptance-based behavioural therapy which explicitly targets reactivity to distress about internal experiences, and experiential and behavioural avoidance. An open trial and a waiting-list RCT revealed significant large effects on GAD severity, self-reported worry, anxiety, depressive symptoms, experiential avoidance and mindfulness (Roemer & Orsillo, 2007; Roemer, Orsillo, & Salters-Pedneault, 2008). All these effects were maintained at 9-month follow-up, and 77% of those treated met criteria for high end-state functioning. Moreover, these studies provided evidence that AMBT works through its proposed mechanisms. For example, session-by-session changes in acceptance of internal experiences and engagement in meaningful activities predicted outcome earlier and beyond change in worry (Hayes et al., 2010).

In summary, it is generally agreed that patients with GAD respond less robustly to psychological treatment compared to patients with other anxiety disorders and this highlights the importance of further research in the understanding and treatment of GAD (Huppert & Sanderson, 2010).

Cognitive Hypnotherapy for Generalized Anxiety Disorder

Hypnotherapy for managing symptoms of generalized anxiety disorder

The initial phase of the therapy, consisting of four to six sessions, is specifically targeted at symptoms management. For some patients this phase of therapy may be sufficient, while for others it serves as a preparation for more complex therapy of exploring the roots of the GAD. The hypnotherapy components focuses on (i) relaxation training, (ii) demonstration of the power of mind over the body, (iii) ego strengthening, (iv) expansion of awareness, (v) modulation and regulation of symptoms, (vi) self-hypnosis and (vii) PHS. Hypnotherapy is introduced again later in therapy with patients who elect to pursue with uncovering work. The initial sessions of hypnotherapy, therefore, for some patients, serve as a preparatory phase for more complex therapy of exploring the roots of the GAD later in the therapy.

Relaxation training

A meta-analysis of the effectiveness of CBT with GAD revealed comparable effects of CBT and relaxation therapy in the treatment of GAD (Siev & Chambless, 2007). As most studies of CBT with GAD indicate that fewer than 65% of treated patients meet criteria for high end-state functioning at posttreatment (Ladouceur et al., 2000; Newman et al., 2011), a multi-component treatment protocol is used to enhance the treatment effects. Relaxation training is one of the components of this comprehensive treatment for GAD. In fact, relaxation training is considered an important component of most CBT-oriented treatments for GAD. Relaxation training is used to reduce physiological correlates of anxiety and worry, broaden the focus of attention, break the perseverating pattern of thinking and equip patients with coping strategy (Huppert & Sanderson, 2010). As discussed in Chapter 2, neither hypnosis nor relaxation response encourages avoidance behaviour in patients with anxiety disorder. On the contrary, by expanding attention, the relaxed state increases patient's ability to consider alternatives in anxiety-provoking situations.

As Fred was experiencing high levels of tension, nervousness, irritation and felt on edge most of the time, he found the relaxation induced by hypnosis very calming and comforting. He was highly susceptible to hypnosis and he was surprised that he could generate profound mental and physical relaxation without much effort. His hypnotic talent was utilized to help him dissociate from anxiety-related worries, namely the negative ruminations regarding supporting to his family and the security of his current job. However, during the dissociative sate he was fully aware of his surroundings and conceptual reality. The relaxation response (feeling calm and fully relaxed) and sense of detachment while he was aware of his worries, but not involved with the content or meanings of his worries, served as an experiential strategy to desensitize his anxiety related to the worries. Fred's hypnotic talent and positive trance experience were further deployed to teach him how to modulate his emotional reactions to worries via self-hypnosis (further discussed under the section 'Self-hypnosis training').

Demonstration of the power of the mind over the body
To further empower Fred and to ratify the credibility of the hypnotic intervention, eye and body catalepsies were introduced in the second hypnotherapy session. Fred was very intrigued that he could not open his eyes or get out of the reclining chair. He confessed that although he responded very well to the first hypnotherapy (that is, he was very relaxed) session, he was sceptical about the power of hypnosis beyond the relaxation response. The catalepsy exercise confirmed to him that hypnotherapy can be a very powerful treatment and he felt hopeful about overcoming his anxiety. Chapter 3 provides a transcript for inducing eye and body catalepsies and it provides an explanation of the cataleptic effects in terms of self-hypnosis.

Ego strengthening
Ego-strengthening suggestions were offered to Fred to promote confidence and self-efficacy. While in deep hypnotic trance, he was encouraged to visualize developing skill of 'letting go' whenever feeling anxious and getting less involved with his worrying thoughts.

Fred found the following ego-strengthening suggestions particularly helpful:

- 'Every day you will feel calmer and more relaxed as a result of this treatment and as a result of you listening to your self-hypnosis CD every day.'
- 'Although you are aware of your concerns and your worries, you will be able to put everything on hold. This shows that you can relax and let go even if you are aware of everything. You don't need to empty your mind to be able to relax.'

After the first hypnotherapy session, Fred was given a self-hypnosis CD to listen to at home (see under the section 'Self-hypnosis training' for further details). As he was able to relax easily and enjoyed the 'break', Fred felt motivated to listen to his self-hypnosis CD regularly. Like other patients, he commented that the relaxation response and the ego-strengthening suggestions made him feel strong and confident to deal with his symptoms. He also felt the hypnotherapy sessions increased his confidence, coping abilities and positive self-image, and as a result he cogitated less with his worries. In fact, Fred started to become more curious about the therapy following the 'mind over the body' experience and felt more flexible and willing to explore 'putting things on hold' despite his uncertainty and recurrent worries about negative possibilities.

Expansion of awareness
Although his level of anxiety varied, Fred reported feeling apprehensive constantly and plagued by worrying thoughts, constricting his range of emotional experience, particularly positive feeling. To expand his range of affect, while in hypnosis, Fred was directed to focus on the relaxation response and on any feeling or emotion that unfolded. This was achieved by using EAT as described in Chapter 2. From EAT, Fred discovered that he had the ability to relax and experience different feelings and sensations. He was surprised that he could put things on hold, that is, although he was aware of his worries, uncertainties and fears, he was able to detach from anticipatory concerns. With practice, he was able to relax and experience different contextual feelings, albeit aware of his concerns and worries.

His discovered ability to produce, amplify and express a variety of positive feelings and experiences gave Fred the confidence that he could deal with his anxiety symptoms.

To become further disengaged from his worries, Fred was introduced imaginal exposure therapy (Wolpe, 1958; Wolpe & Lazarus, 1966), which is considered to be an important component of CH for anxiety disorders (Golden, 2012). While in deep hypnosis, Fred was directed to focus on his worries and uncertainties. He was then instructed to utilize self-hypnosis to relax and calm down whenever he experienced any anxiety associated with recurring worry or uncertainty. In other words, the goal was not on controlling his symptoms; the focus was on tolerating his distress.

> When I count from ONE to FIVE, by the time you hear me say FIVE, you will begin to feel whatever emotion or reaction that is associated with any worrying thought or uncertainty that cross your mind.

Once the anxiety occurred, Fred was instructed to amplify the affect associated with the thought or uncertainty. Facing the worries can be quite emotionally evocative for GAD patients. It is important for the therapist to gently encourage the patient to continue to face the worries as this will help the patient learn to tolerate the distress associated with worries. Moreover, by 'staying' with the worries, the patient will learn to generate strategies for coping with distress.

> When I count slowly from ONE to FIVE, as I count you will begin to experience the anxious feelings more and more intensely, so that when I reach the count of FIVE, at the count of FIVE you will feel the full reaction as strongly as you can bear it. ONE ... TWO ... THREE ... FOUR ... FIVE. Now notice what you feel and you can describe it to me.

Fred was then advised to utilize his self-hypnosis skill to attenuate the anxious feeling or fearful reaction.

> Now imagine using your self-hypnosis skill to deal with the anxious reaction. Since you have the ability to relax and put things on hold, you can let go and calm down even if the worrying thoughts cross your mind. You don't have to control your anxiety, you just try to calm down and distance away from your thoughts.

After several repetition of this set of suggestions, Fred was able to relax completely, while being aware of this worries and uncertainties. As discussed later in the context of AMBT, the focus of the exposure therapy was not to control the symptoms of GAD, but to teach Fred techniques to deal with his anxiety, or learn to surf over it (see Chapter 2 for details). Recent research findings indicate fears and anxiety disorders are partly generated by overly rigid attempts to avoid the emotional experience of fear and anxiety. The toleration of fear and anxiety is therefore considered a critical component in the psychological treatment of anxiety disorders. Hence, the goal of exposure therapy should not be on immediate reduction of fear and anxiety but on learning to tolerate distress and discomfort.

The mental rehearsal in trance provided Fred an opportunity to learn to face his worrying thoughts and associated anxiety head-on, rather than catastrophizing or cogitating about them. He indicated that he learned to tolerate his worrying thoughts and discovered that 'staying with the anxiety was not as bad' as he thought.

Modulating and controlling symptoms

As hypnosis is an experiential approach to therapy, Fred was advised to perceive his anxiety symptoms as a syncretic experience (Alladin, 2006, 2007, 2008; Safer & Leventhal, 1977). He was encouraged to view his anxiety not simply as an affect, thought or behaviour, but as a cascade of cognitive, somatic, perceptual, physiological, visceral and kinaesthetic changes. The repeated hypnotic inductions and the amplification of positive syncretic cognition in the office offered Fred dramatic proof that he can regulate his anxious and distressing experience, or he could flow with them. The rapid improvement often observed in hypnotherapy is believed to be related to the positive trance experience (e.g., DePiano & Salzberg, 1981).

Self-hypnosis training

To generalize his relaxation response to real situations, Fred was taught self-hypnosis. To facilitate the self-hypnosis training, at the end of the first hypnotherapy session, Fred was given a CD recording of the session. He was encouraged to listen to the CD at least once a day at home. This homework assignment allowed Fred continuity of the treatment between sessions and offered him the opportunity to practice self-hypnosis. Fred commented that the training in self-hypnosis provided the most practical and powerful skill for dealing with his anxiety symptoms outside the therapy sessions. The self-hypnosis also served as a powerful tool for surfing over catastrophic cogitation (NSH).

To further consolidate his skill of generalizing self-hypnosis to real-life situations, Fred was introduced to the clenched fist technique (Stein, 1963). As discussed in Chapter 3, the clenching of the dominant fist serves as an anchor for the elicitation of the relaxation response. Fred was trained to induce self-hypnosis rapidly whenever he worried excessively or catastrophized about the future by clenching his dominant fist, which acted as an 'anchor'. Lankton (1980) defines an anchor as any stimulus that evokes a consistent response pattern from a person (see Chapter 3 for a full transcript of setting up the anchor). Fred's anchoring training was experientially ratified by two sessions of hypnotherapy, during which he imagined (rehearsed) dealing with various worrying scenarios.

Now we are going to practice the clenching fist technique. Imagine from now on whenever you get upset, anxious, stressed out, or worry excessively, utilizing your clenched fist technique to deal with the distressing feelings. Just continue to imagine, from now on whenever you get anxious, upset or stressed out, or worrying excessively, you are able cope with these feelings by clenching you fist and anchoring your mind to this experience. And with practice, you will get better and better with this technique. As a result of this you will begin to feel less upset about these feelings, you will become detached from them, yet being aware of them.

Fred found the clenched fist technique very useful as it was very concrete and portable. He was able to apply it easily whenever he worried excessively or catastrophized about the 'ifs'. In fact, Fred came up with an unusual mental image that enhanced the effects of self-hypnosis and the clenching fist technique. Whenever he worried excessively or became preoccupied with the 'ifs', he would imagine travelling on a train and decided to 'jump off the wagon', and now having the freedom to do whatever he chooses to do, while 'still being aware of the train moving'. As the ultimate goal of psychotherapy is to help patients with anxiety disorder establish self-reliance and independence, self-hypnosis serves a powerful tool for achieving self-reliance, self-efficacy, self-correcting behaviours and personal power (Alladin, 2014a; Alman, 2001; Yapko, 2003).

Post-hypnotic suggestions
In hypnotherapy, it is common practice to provide PHS before the termination of the treatment session. Fred was offered a variety of PHS to face his worries, uncertainties and distress head-on.

- 'Because I worry about my job, it does not mean I will lose my job.'
- 'Because I worry about my finance it does not mean I can't survive. In fact, I have enough assets for me and my family to live comfortably even if I lose my job.'
- 'My daughters are very bright and they are likely to graduate from the university.'

- 'We have enough funds and savings to help them through financially even if I lose my job. If the worst happen, they can always get a loan.'

PHS, in conjunction with his self-hypnosis skill, and the 'train imagery', Fred started to recognize that, to a large extent, his anxiety was due to his negative rumination. At this point in therapy, Fred was ready to move on to CBT, which is described next.

Cognitive behavioural therapy

Several evidence-based CBT packages are available for the treatment of GAD (e.g., see Rygh & Sanderson, 2004; Zinbarg, Craske, & Barlow, 2006). Although subtle differences exist between these packages, they all contain some common elements, including psychoeducation, self-monitoring, cognitive restructuring, relaxation, worry exposure, worry behaviour control and problem solving (Huppert & Sanderson, 2010). Each of these CBT techniques, except for relaxation and worry exposure (which are already covered), is briefly described further.

Psychoeducation

Psychoeducation is provided in the initial phase of therapy. Hupert and Sanderson (2010) recommend providing information in a written form first, followed up by a session during which the therapist answers any question the patient may have. Information about GAD can be obtained from the National Institute of Mental Health (http://www.nimh.nih.gov/health/topics/generalized-anxiety-disorder-gad/index.shtml). There are several important reasons for including psychoeducation during the initial part of CBT.

1. Knowledge is power. It provides an important platform to initiate change. Often patients come to therapy with misconceptions about their psychological disorder or uninformed of their diagnosis. Through psychoeducation, the patients get a clearer understanding of their problems and an accurate view of their diagnosis. Such understanding reduces stress and unnecessary worries and prepares the patients for therapy.

2. The therapist gets the opportunity to describe the biopsychosocial model of GAD and within this framework the collaborative role of patient in therapy is discussed. Patients derive considerable reassurance from the scientific explanation of their condition. They also derive great relief knowing the prevalence rate of anxiety disorders.

3. The education session also provides therapist the opportunity to outline treatment strategies to be used and discuss the rationale for using them. Moreover, the therapist is able to clear any misconceptions about therapy, especially about hypnosis. Greater understanding of problems and accurate information about the effectiveness of treatment are known to increase compliance in the patient.

Self-monitoring

Self-monitoring is an important component of CBT. It is used both as an assessment procedure to identify worry and as a treatment technique. Different formats exist for recording worry and its consequences. Table 6.1 represents a standard form used by Fred to monitor the events that triggered his worry, the cognitive distortions that were related to his worry, and the emotional consequences he experienced. Each time a patient feels worried or anxious, he or she is encouraged to record it on the CAB Form (see Table 6.1). By monitoring the context and content of worry, patients become aware of their patterns of dysfunctional thinking and this often leads to a reduction in worry and anxiety. However, with most patients with GAD, cognitive restructuring is required, which is discussed in the next section. However, it is recommended that the automatic thoughts are not challenged initially, that is, when recording the CAB form. The goal of the monitoring phase is to bring dysfunctional thoughts into awareness. By recording the CAB form, the patient is able to recognize the relationship between cognition and anxiety. Once the automatic thoughts related to worries are recorded for the week, the patient is graduated to the cognitive restructuring phase of CBT.

Cognitive restructuring

Research indicates GAD is associated with an automatic attentional bias for threat and, therefore, patients with GAD tend to interpret ambiguous personally relevant information in a threatening manner (Clark & Beck, 2010; MacLeod & Rutherford, 2004). Moreover, patients with GAD overestimate the likelihood of negative events and underestimate their ability to cope with difficult situations. These cognitive distortions 'play a major role in the vicious cycle of anxiety, and they accentuate the patient's feelings of danger and threat' (Huppert & Sanderson, 2010, p. 230). Additionally, worry, which is a core feature of GAD, is predominantly a cognitive process. For these reasons, CBT as discussed earlier under Treatment of GAD section, has been widely used with GAD, and it has been found to be as effective as medication as a first-line treatment. CBT is specifically targeted at the faulty appraisal system and it guides GAD

Table 6.1   Example of CAB form for monitoring worry trigger, irrational beliefs and emotional consequences

Date	C = Emotions	A = Facts or events	B = Automatic thoughts about A
	1. Specify sad/ anxious/angry, and so on 2. Rate degree of emotion 0–100	Describe actual event, stream of thoughts, daydream and so on, leading to worry and anxiety	Write automatic thoughts and images that came in your mind. Rate beliefs or images 0–100%
10 March 2009	*An Example:* *Depressed (75)* *Unhappy (100)* *Miserable (90)*	*Thinking of going to grandson's birthday party tomorrow*	1. *I won't enjoy it (100)* 2. *I can't cope with it (100)* 3. *Everyone will hate me (90)* 4. *I will spoil it for everyone (90)* 5. *I can never be happy again (100)*
15.6.13	*Anxious (90)* *Panicky (75)* *Upset (100)*	*Thinking of my eldest daughter at the university. Became worried about her.*	1. *If I lose my job I will not be able to afford her to be at university.* 2. *She will not graduate.* 3. *I have ruined her life, she will be without a job.* 4. *She will hate me for it.* 5. *I will not be able to handle this.*

patients to recognize and structure their cognitive distortions. Table 6.2 provides an example of using CRF to monitor and restructure catastrophic thinking associated with worry. The concept of cognitive restructuring is introduced in therapy by discussing in detail automatic thoughts, anxious predictions and the maintenance of anxiety through unchallenged negative rumination. As a result of the CBT, Fred was able to modify his maladaptive thoughts and beliefs related to his worries, and consequently he felt less anxious and uncertain about his future.

Table 6.2 Completed cognitive restructuring form

Date	A Activating event	B Irrational beliefs	C Consequences	D Disputation	E Effect of disputation
	Describe actual event, stream of thoughts, daydream and so on, leading to unpleasant feelings	Write automatic thoughts and images that came in your mind. Rate beliefs or images 0–100%	1. *Emotion:* specify sad, anxious or angry. Rate feelings 1–100% 2. *Physiological:* Palpitations, pain, dizzy, sweat and so on 3. *Behavioural:* Avoidance, in bed 4. *Conclusion:* Reaching conclusions	Challenge the automatic thoughts and images. Rate belief in rational response/image 0–100%	1. *Emotion:* Re-rate your feeling 1–100% 2. *Physiological:* Changes in bodily reactions (i.e., less shaking, less tense, etc.) 3. *Behavioural:* Action taken after disputation 4. *Conclusion:* Reappraise your conclusion and initial decision. Future beliefs in similar situation

(*Continued*)

Table 6.2 (Continued)

Date	A Activating event	B Irrational beliefs	C Consequences	D Disputation	E Effect of disputation
15 June 2013	Thinking of my eldest daughter at the university. Became worried about her	1. If I lose my job I will not be able to afford her to be at university (100) 2. She will not graduate (100) 3. I have ruined her life, she will be without a job (75) 4. She will hate me for it (100) 5. I will not be able to handle this (100)	1. Anxious (90), panicky (75), upset (100) 2. Restless, sweaty, tired 3. Pacing up and down, could not concentrate at work 4. I can never do anything right	1. Because I worry about my job, it does not mean I will lose my job (100). My job is fairly secure (90). There is no reason why I can't support her (100). If the worst happen, she can take a loan (100) 2. My daughter is very bright and ambitious and more than likely she will graduate (100) 3. My daughter has not failed yet, I am anticipating the worst scenario. Thoughts are not facts (100) Although it's unlikely, if she does not complete university, it will not be my fault (100). 4. She can't hate me for something I have not done (100). 5. I have always dealt with difficulties, there's no reason why I can't face difficulties in the future (80).	1. Less anxious (20), not panicking (0), less upset (20) 2. No longer restless and sweating. But still feeling tired 3. Not pacing up and down. Able to concentrate at work 4. Most of the time I do the right things. Like anybody else I make mistake sometimes. I am a mixture – not right or wrong all the time. Even if I make a mistake, I am still a mixture. I have got to stick to this belief even when I am feeling anxious.

Worry behaviour control

As discussed before, patients with GAD have a fear of negative emotional contrasts (Behar et al., 2009), that is, these individuals engage in chronic worry because they prefer to experience a sustained state of distress as a way to be emotionally prepared for the worst possible outcome to various aversive events (Newman & Llera, 2011). Therefore, they feel compelled to be emotionally braced for negative events at all times to avoid feeling even greater disruption in response to emotional contrasts. Many of these factors point to the central role of negative emotional shifts as well as the use of worry to prevent emotional contrasts that are perceived as unmanageable. These explanations complement and support Wolfe's wounded self theory of anxiety disorders. Furthermore, the theoretical models of GAD share a common emphasis on the central importance of avoidance of internal experiences (Lee et al., 2010).

Although worry is a negative state, GAD patients continue to worry because it distracts them from negative emotions, which is negatively reinforcing (Borkovec & Newman, 1998). Worry serves several functions: (i) it produces less arousal; (ii) it prevents physiological changes associated with emotions and (iii) it blocks the processing of emotional stimuli. It would thus appear that individuals with GAD are avoiding certain unpleasant images and so their anxiety about these images does not extinguish. There is some evidence that people with GAD report more past trauma involving death, injury or illness (Newman et al., 2013). However, these are not the topics that they worry about. It would thus appear that worry distract them from the distressing images of these past traumas.

GAD patients habitually perform or avoid certain behaviours to keep bad things from happening. For example, Fred will never discuss any issues related to job security or promotion with his boss for fear of being told that he will be laid off. Although this strategy relieved his anxiety initially, it had no power to prevent the prospect of being laid off. Moreover, by avoiding his underlying distress, he was not prepared to cope with his worst fears and uncertainties.

To prevent worry behaviours in GAD patients, Huppert & Sanderson (2010) have suggested the following strategies.

1. The patient is encouraged to carefully monitor what he or she does when he or she notices the onset of worry. This can be recorded by writing down the things the patient does to prevent the disasters the patient worries about from happening. For example, by writing down these details, Fred identified three worry behaviours he used to cope with his fear of being laid down: (i) he avoided contacts with his boss,

except for important scheduled meetings; (ii) whenever he saw his boss, to avoid contact with him, he would avoid the situation and (iii) if he happened to come across his boss by chance (such as walking down the corridor, or meeting him in the parking lot), he would avoid long conversation, except for exchanging greetings.

2. Through careful monitoring, assessment and questioning, the patient is able to detect both subtle and explicit variants of avoidance behaviours. Through his recording, Fred was surprised to discover to what extent he was avoiding his boss. He also realized that his worry behaviours were not helping him.

3. Then the patient is instructed to refrain from these behaviours by utilizing any of the techniques learned so far. Fred found strategies he learned from exposure therapy and CBT helpful in reducing his worry behaviours related to interacting with his boss. In the future (as treatment progressed), Fred was able to integrate these strategies with acceptance and mindfulness-based techniques.

4. If a patient is plagued with too many worry behaviours and he or she is too anxious to give them up, the behaviours can be hierarchically arranged from easier ones to more difficult ones. This allows the patient to start dealing with the easy worry behaviour and then move on to the difficult ones.

5. McKay, Davis & Fanning (2007) also suggest replacing the worry behaviour with a new behaviour. For example, Fred started to make efforts to increase his interaction with his boss and gradually, when appropriate, to begin to explore future developments in his company.

Problem-solving

Problem-solving is an important component of CBT. GAD patients struggle with two major problems: intolerance of uncertainty and catastrophic thinking (Dugas et al., 1998, 2003). As discussed in Chapters 1 and 2, these cogitations and associated anxiety, constrict range of experience and cognitions in patients with anxiety disorder, and thus interfering with the natural ability to problem-solve. In case of GAD, patients become so focused on catastrophic outcome and attempts to avoid anxiety, that they never contemplate a problem-solving approach to resolving their distress. This in turn causes more emotional distress as McKay et al. (2007, p.185) indicate:

> Problems that elude solution result in chronic emotional pain. When your usual coping strategies fail, a growing sense of helplessness makes the search for novel solutions more difficult. The possibility of relief seems to recede, the problem begins to appear insoluble, and anxiety or despair can increase to crippling levels.

Therefore, it is of utmost importance that the problem-solving component should be included in CBT for GAD. The five-step problem-solving strategy devised by D'Zurilla and Goldfried (1971) can be easily applied to GAD patients. The acronym SOLVE includes the five problem-solving steps:

1. State (identify) the problem
2. Outline the goals (goal setting)
3. List (select) alternative solutions
4. View the consequences
5. Evaluate the results.

The goal of introducing these problem-solving steps is not just to solve the identified problems, but also to help GAD patients learn better problem-solving skills and to realize that there are multiple solutions to a problem. As Fred was an electrical engineer, he found the problem-solving approach to dealing with his worry very helpful.

Healing self-wounds

After 10 sessions of CBT and hypnotherapy, Fred noticed significant improvement in his affect; he felt less anxious and worried, and he was less preoccupied with uncertainties of the future. Nevertheless, he still had some anxieties and fear, and felt the need to produce deep changes. He was interested to explore the root cause/s of his fears and worries. He was also interested in knowing why he felt insecure, lacked confidence, and doubted his abilities at work. The next segment of therapy thus involved in-depth hypnotherapy and consisted of accessing and healing the wounded self.

Elicitation of self-wounds

To explore any underlying self-wounds that might be connected with Fred's GAD, the affect bridge technique was used. The feeling of anxiety that he experienced while he was worried about being laid off from his job was used as a bridge to elicit his first anxiety attack. While feeling very anxious, he remembered the first anxiety attack he had when he was 16 years old. It was during his father's 50th birthday party. The party was held at home and most of the guests were his father's close friends and business partners. While Fred was having a casual conversation with one of his father's friend, the person commented: 'You are not like your father. You appear to be very quiet and shy. You should be like your father, look how smart and popular he is.' Fred felt embarrassed, hurt, flustered, confused and so overwhelmed that he had to run out of the house, and he waited for all the guests to leave before he came into the house. Since Fred was about 12 years old, he became aware that he was shy, reserved and lacked confidence. Gradually he became very conscious that he lacked confidence and on several occasions he cried for not being like his father. Subsequently, he concluded that he is weak, inferior and 'not good enough' for anything. The comments from his father's friend confirmed his negative beliefs and severely wounded the self that was already injured. Fred's pathological worry thus serves as a blanket to suppress his feelings of inadequacy and self-doubts.

To compensate for his sense of inadequacy, Fred got involved in sports and academia. He did not do very well in sports, which further reinforced his belief that he is not good enough. He did quite well academically and without much difficulty he graduated with honours in electrical engineering. Because of his good grades and outstanding internship performance, Fred was able to secure a job as an electrical engineer in a large electronic company very easily. He worked diligently and was promoted without having to wait too long. Unfortunately, Fred started to worry about 'everything' and this gradually developed into GAD.

From the emergence of these information it was formulated that Fred needed to detoxify the meaning of his anxiety and worries.

Detoxification of meaning of anxiety and worry

The split screen technique (Alladin, 2008; Cardena et al., 2000; Lynn & Cardena, 2007; Spiegel, 1981) was used to help Fred detoxify the meaning of his anxiety and worry. This hypnotic strategy utilizes the 'adult ego state' to assist the 'weak ego state' deal with anxiety and worry provoking situations. It also facilitates the 'two' ego states to work together as a team when the self is threatened, rather than splitting from each other when stressed out. The therapy transcript presented subsequently illustrates how the split screen technique was used with Fred to help him deal with the toxic meaning of his anxiety and worry. The transcript begins while Fred was in a deep trance.

THERAPIST   Now I would like you to imagine sitting in front of a large TV or cinema screen, which is vertically split in two halves, consisting of a right side and a left side. Can you imagine this?

[Fred raised his 'YES' finger. Ideomotor signals were already set up – 'YES' represented raising his right index finger and 'NO' corresponded with raising his left index finger.]

THERAPIST   Imagine the right side of the screen is lighting up as if it's ready to project an image. Imagine yourself being projected on the right side of the screen, just as you are now. Feeling very relaxed, very comfortable, in complete control, and aware of everything. And now become aware of the things you have achieved, things that you are proud of. Do you feel these good feelings?

[After a moment, Fred raised his 'YES' finger.]

THERAPIST   That's very good. Do you feel the sense of achievement?

[Fred raised his 'YES' finger.]

THERAPIST   Are you thinking about your achievement related to having been promoted to Team Leader in your company?

[Fred raised his 'YES' finger.]

THERAPIST   Just focus on the good feelings and become aware that you made it to this senior position despite your anxiety and worries. This proves to you that you have a strong side, a successful side, a side that can rescue you from difficulties and help you succeed. We are going to call this part of you the 'adult side' or your 'adult ego state'. Is that acceptable to you?

[Fred raised his 'YES' finger.]

THERAPIST   Leave this side of yourself, that is the adult part of you, on the right side of the screen. Now imagine yourself being projected on the left side of the screen, feeling anxious, as if you are in a situation that triggers worry for you. Can you imagine this?

[Fred raised his 'YES' finger.]

THERAPIST   Now become aware of all the feelings that you are experiencing. Don't be afraid to let all the worry and anxious feelings come over you, because soon we will show you how to deal with them. Become aware of all the physical sensations you feel. Become aware of all the thoughts that are going through your mind and become aware of your behaviors. Can you feel these?

[Fred raised his 'YES' finger.]

THERAPIST   So just become aware of the whole experience and we are going to call this part of you the 'weak part of you' or the 'child ego state' as we discussed before. Is this acceptable to you?

[Fred raised his 'YES' finger.]

THERAPIST   Now imagine, your adult ego state stepping out from the right side to the left side of the screen. Can you imagine this?

[Fred raised his 'YES' finger.]

THERAPIST   Imagine your adult ego state is reassuring your child ego state. He is telling your child ego state not to be afraid because he is there to help him out and guide him how to deal with his fears and worries. From now on, the child part of you don't have to handle difficulties on his own, he can work as a team with the strong part of you. Imagine the adult part of you telling the weak part of you that in therapy you have learned many strategies for dealing with anxiety and worries, and, therefore, he can remind you of these strategies. Imagine he is demonstrating the weak part of you how to relax, how to let go, and how to reason with fearful and worrying thoughts. Continue to imagine this until you feel the weak part of you feel reassured and now he knows what to do when feeling anxious or worried. Imagine your weak part feels protected and empowered knowing he is not alone, he can get help from the adult ego state whenever the needs arise. The weak part also realizes that the strong part is of part of your self and so is the strong part of your self. So from now on you can both work as a team.

THERAPIST   Is this acceptable to you?

[Fred raised his 'YES' finger.]

Fred found the split screen technique very helpful. It reminded him of the strategies he learned in therapy, and it serves as a useful mental rehearsal training, 'kind of a preparation for facing the issues in reality'.

Differentiating between accurate and inaccurate self-views

At this stage in therapy, Fred was guided to differentiate between his painful self-views that are based on facts and those that are based on inaccurate opinions. Fred was never undermined or put down by his father. It was Fred who compared himself to his father. Because he did not possess his father's characteristics, Fred concluded he was inferior, inadequate, weak, and not deserving respect from others. These cognitive distortions were confirmed by his father's friend at his father's birthday party. The painful views of his self created a feeling and experience that the he would not be able to cope with the vicissitudes of life. He also came to believe that the exposure of his self-wounds, either to himself or to others, would produce overwhelming embarrassment, shame and humiliation, which he desperately wanted to avoid. Since the rigors and realities of everyday living were unavoidable, Fred developed maladaptive coping strategies such as behavioural avoidance, excessive worries, rumination with cognitive distortions and preoccupation with his symptoms to protect himself from facing situations that were perceived to produce distressing affect. Unfortunately, these indirect strategies did not minimize his distress; they reinforced his painful core beliefs about his self. Moreover, these strategies kept Fred away from facing his fears and self-wounds head-on, resulting in the perpetuation of his symptoms. Furthermore, in response to the initial anxiety, Fred got into the habit of cogitating about being anxious and consequently he became anxious for feeling anxious.

From the uncovering work it emerged that Fred had a major conflict regarding his self. His 'idealized self' was to be like his father; but his 'real self' contrasted his father's attributes and achievements. Not able to achieve his idealized self was unbearable and totally unacceptable to him. He was terrified of exposing his weakness to others. He was thus determined to project his idealized self to others. His 'what ifs' or worries represented self-doubts whether he would be able project and sustain his ideal self in challenging situations. The next component of the experiential hypnotherapy thus consisted of helping Fred acknowledge and accept his real self. The empty chair technique, which is a Gestalt therapy role-playing strategy (Perls, Hefferline, & Goodman, 1951; Woldt & Toman, 2005) for reducing intra- or interpersonal conflicts (Nichol & Schwartz, 2008), was used to help Fred accept his real self. In this procedure, while in deep hypnosis, Fred was directed to talk to his father, whom he imagined sitting in an empty chair in the therapist's office, across from him. By imagining his father sitting in the empty chair in the safety of the therapy situation, Fred was able to express various strong feelings about himself and his father that he had been harbouring inside him since he was a teenager. This procedure consisted of two interrelated parts. During the first part of the procedure, Fred talked to his father, while his father was silent. In the second part, the father spoke to Fred and then they both talked to each other in turn.

By engaging in the empty chair work, and with the support and direction from the therapist, Fred was able to express his strong, both negative and positive, feelings towards his father. He told his father in great details everything he admired and respected about him. He then told his father that he wanted to be like him but was not able to. Fred became very upset and started to cry loudly, could not contain his tears, when he started telling his father how painful it was for him that he could not be strong, charismatic and successful like him. He described how painful it was for him to hear people comment that he was not like his father. Even in sports and at school he was not in the top ten. He expressed in details how embarrassing, humiliating and painful it was for him to hear from people that he was not as good as his father. It was even more painful for him to realize that he will never be like his father nor be successful as him. He saw himself being a failure. He also expressed to his father that he was very hurt and angry because he (father) did not spend much time with him while he was growing up and never got involved in his schooling or sports activities.

In the next segment of the empty chair work, Fred imagined his father talking to him (he talked for his father) after he disclosed his pain, distress and disappointment to him. His 'father' (father in parentheses represents Fred talking for his father) told Fred that he could not be like him as they were both different individuals. 'Father' felt flattered that his son thought so highly of him and wanted to be like him. If his son happened not to be like him, it did not mean he was a failure or a weak person. In fact, 'father' felt relieved that his son was not in the same line of business as him because it is so challenging and demanding, including being less attentive to your family, to be a successful business man. 'Father' expressed envy at his son, that is, his son had the opportunity to go to the university and study to become an electrical engineer, while he never had the opportunity to go to the university; since he graduated from high school he had been working non-stop.

The next part of the therapy session involved both Fred and 'father' talking to each other in turn.

FRED:　　Why you never told me I am a failure?
FATHER:　I did not know you thought you are a failure. I did not know you wanted to be like me.
FRED:　　You should have known because you are my father. You should have looked after me and supported me when I was upset.
FATHER:　I did not know you were upset and how you were thinking.

With prompting from the therapist, 'father' apologized to Fred, who realized that he expected his father to read his mind (cognitive distortion). He realized that it was an unrealistic expectation. Then 'father' described in detail Fred's achievement (which is minimized) in terms of his sports activities and his performance at the university. He emphasized how well Fred did during his internship, which helped him secure a job as an electrical engineer in a very well-known international company. He also pointed out how well Fred did at his job that he was appointed as a team leader. Moreover, 'father' described the positive aspect of his household and family.

In addition to the empty chair technique, as homework, Fred was encouraged to write down a full description of his ideal self in terms personality attributes, education, occupation, achievements and family life. He had to repeat the same with his real self and then to compare the two profiles, highlighting the differences, the similarities and the tenability of the real self in comparison to his ideal self. Finally, he had to decide whether the real self is acceptable to him, although it did not measure up to his ideal self.

The empty chair conversation helped Fred (i) realize that his ideal self was constructed by a set of cognitive distortions; (ii) his father was not responsible for his emotional injury; (iii) not achieving his ideal self did not mean he was a failure; (iv) his father did not perceive him to be a failure; (v) people would not consider him to be failure if he did not reach the ideal self and (vi) he could live a 'normal life' with his real self.

Fred showed very good response to CH. The therapy helped him identify the explicit and the implicit nature of his anxiety, as well as the roots of his wounded self. While behavioural and cognitive strategies helped him symptomatically, the hypnotherapy, by virtue of its phenomenological nature, made the therapy experiential and thus more meaningful. He found the HET very helpful in accessing and healing his self-wounds. The empty chair and the split screen techniques permitted him to accept his real self. As therapy progressed, Fred was less worried about the future and cogitated less about his anxiety. At work he felt more relaxed and worried less about losing his job and no longer avoided speaking to his boss. Generally, he was less plagued by 'what ifs'.

Promoting acceptance and gratitude

As discussed in Chapters 1 and 2, patients with anxiety disorders tend to suppress re-experiencing of their initial trauma as it causes extreme distress (Wolfe, 2005, 2006).

Drawing from their research on AMBT, Roemer et al. (2013) have conceptualized GAD to result from three inter-related learned patterns of responding. First, people with GAD tend to relate to their internal experiences with a lack of clarity, reactivity and self-criticism and they perceive thoughts as self-defining indicators of truth, rather than transient reactions. Second, this reactivity leads GAD patients to exert habitual and determined efforts to control their experiences, unfortunately without much success. Third, their habitual reactivity, avoidance and indelible worries about the past and future cause significant constrictions in their lives. AMBT have been found to help these patients develop a wise and accepting relationship with their internal cognitive, emotional and physical experience, even during times of intense fear or worry (Greeson & Brantley, 2009). Roemer et al. (2013) have therefore suggested that the treatment of GAD, in addition to CBT or other psychotherapy, should be targeted at (i) fear of emotions, (ii) problematic emotion regulation pattern and (iii) distress, as this approach has been found to enhance treatment outcome. When AMBTs are applied to anxiety disorders, the main goal is to help the patients learn to observe their symptoms without overly identifying with them or without reacting to them in ways that aggravate their distress (Roemer, Erisman, & Orsillo, 2008). To achieve this goal with GAD, several mindfulness and acceptance strategies are used, including:

1. Techniques to facilitate awareness of one's current perceptual, somatic, cognitive and emotional experience.
2. Techniques to promote cognitive distancing or defusion from one's thoughts and inner experience.
3. Techniques to assist nonjudgemental acceptance of subjective experience.
4. Techniques to foster clarity of goals and values.
5. Techniques to boost sense of gratitude
6. Techniques to cultivate PC.

Integration of these six techniques in therapy engenders a fundamental shift in perspective (reperceiving), that is, they encourage patients to re-evaluate their constructed reality (Alladin, 2014a). Treatment strategies based on each set of techniques, as applied to GAD, are briefly described next.

Strategies for cultivating awareness
Chapter 2 mentioned eight common techniques for cultivating increasing awareness of one's ongoing stream of experience, including (i) mindfulness meditation, (ii) mindful hypnosis, (iii) concentrative meditation, (iv) walking meditation, (v) eating meditation, (vi) attention training, (vii) compassion meditation and (viii) loving kindness meditation. Fred preferred the mindful hypnosis technique, which is described here. For further details about the other techniques, the interested reader can refer to several books (e.g., Kabat-Zinn, 2013; Orsillo & Roemer, 2011; Segal et al., 2013).

Mindful hypnosis involves the ability to relax completely yet being aware of everything. The following transcript, which begins while Fred was in a deep trance, exemplifies the suggestions used for bolstering one's awareness of thoughts, feelings, body sensations and surroundings.

> You have now become so deeply relaxed and you are in such a deep hypnotic trance that your mind and your body feel completely relaxed, totally relaxed.
> You begin to feel a beautiful sensation of peace and relaxation, tranquility and calm, flowing all over your mind and your body; giving you such a pleasant and such a soothing sensation all over your mind and body, that you feel completely relaxed, totally relaxed, both mentally and physically.

At the same time, notice that you are aware of everything, you are aware of all the sound and noise around you, you are aware of your thoughts and your imagination, and yet you feel so relaxed, so calm and so comfortable. This shows that you have the ability to relax, the ability to let go, and the ability to put everything on hold. This shows that you have lots of control, because you are aware of everything. You can hear all the sounds and noise around you, you are aware of your thoughts and imagination. You are aware that I am sitting beside you and talking to you. Yet you are able to put everything on hold and relax your mind and body completely.

Now you can become aware of all the good feelings you are feeling right now. You feel calm, you feel peaceful, you feel relaxed and you feel very, very comfortable both mentally and physically. You may also become aware of feeling heavy, light, or detached, or distancing away from everything, becoming more and more detached, distancing away from everything, drifting into a deep, deep hypnotic trance. You are aware of the sounds and noise around you. You are aware that you are on this comfortable chair, noticing your back resting on the chair. Your neck and your shoulders and your head are resting against the chair. You are aware of everything, yet being fully relaxed. You are aware of your breathing, breathing in and out, feeling completely relaxed. You feel happy and pleased knowing that you can relax, you can let go. You feel delighted and satisfied knowing that you can put things on hold and yet be aware of everything. You feel curious that you can relax and yet be aware of everything.

Mindful hypnosis helped Fred discover he had the capacity and the talent to relax, to let go, and experience different positive feelings, emotions and sensations. He was surprised that he could put things on hold and distance away from his concerns and worries, yet being fully conscious of his fear, anxiety and worry. With practice, Fred was able to generate and experience a variety of positive and negative emotions and feelings appropriate to the context. His ability to relax, while being aware of everything, gave him the confidence to begin to relate differently (less reactive and controlling) to his anxiety and worry.

Strategies for cognitive distancing

Cognitive distancing strategies were used to help Fred bolster his discovered ability to distance away from his worrying thoughts and fearful ruminations. These strategies helped Fred recognize that his thoughts were distinct from his self and that they were not necessarily true (i.e., thoughts were not facts). AMBT utilize a variety of techniques to train patients with GAD decentre from their thoughts, including (i) gazing at thoughts from a distance (e.g., visualizing a thought floating downstream on a leaf); (ii) recognizing bias in thinking (cognitive distortions); (iii) hearing thoughts (self-talk) and (iv) seeing thoughts as images (e.g., as clouds). This training produces cognitive defusion, or the ability to separate thoughts from the self. Fred found recognizing bias in his thinking extremely useful to him as he considered this technique to be an extension of CBT, which he found very meaningful. From his reading of *Feeling Good: The New Mood Therapy* (Burns, 1999) and from the CBT sessions, Fred memorized the ten cognitive distortions described by Burns. So whenever a distorted thought crossed his mind he would think or repeat to himself: 'This is my distorted thinking, not me.' Whenever he repeated this 'mantra', he felt defused or decentred from the dysfunctional cognition.

Strategies for promoting acceptance

One of the core interventions in AMBT relates to fostering an open, accepting, nonjudgemental and welcoming attitude towards the full range of one's subjective experience. The most common strategies for promoting acceptance include (i) psychoeducation, (ii) acceptance exercise and (iii) exposure exercises.

Psychoeducation

It involves defining the meaning of acceptance and understanding the relationship between stress and upset. In the context of CH, acceptance is defined as 'being open to experience or willing to experience the reality of the present moment'. The definition is similar to mindfulness in the sense that the patient is trained to be nonjudgemental and purposely allowing experience (thoughts, emotions, desires, urges, sensations, etc.) to occur without attempting to block or suppress them. Acceptance encourages increased contact with previously avoided events and experience.

Patients are also educated to understand the relationship between stress and relapse. As learned during CBT, patients are reminded that it is not the stressors that cause anxiety but the cognitions (usually cognitive distortions) triggered by the stressful event. Hence patients can learn to cope with the anxiety either by changing the cognitive distortions or accepting (decentring or defusion) them. Moreover, patients with anxiety or depressive disorder erroneously label feelings of upset as 'return' of their symptoms. The patients are trained to differentiate between 'normal upset' and 'return of symptoms'. Patients with GAD are encouraged to view feelings of upset related to 'normal worry' or stressful events as normal and inevitable. Segal et al. (2002, 2013) have demonstrated that when depressed patients while in remission label 'normal' upsets as return of their depressive symptoms, they spiral down into a full-blown depressive episode. However, if they are able to accept their reaction to stress as normal, although upsetting, they are able to prevent relapse. Within the context of AMBT, GAD patients are trained 'not to feel upset for feeling upset', 'not to feel anxious for feeling anxious' and 'not to worry for worrying'.

Acceptance exercise
To consolidate the psychoeducation about acceptance, the patient is encouraged to carry out a list of exercises:

- Focusing on here and now. If the mind wanders, the patient accept it, and gently bring it back to the present, becoming mindful of the present activity.
- Observing emotional experiences and their contexts non-judgementally. The person becomes aware of the external (e.g., stressed out about overwork) or internal (feeling nervous) reasons for his or her feelings, rather than blaming oneself for the experience or becomes upset for feeling upset.
- Separation of secondary emotions from primary emotions (e.g., not to get upset for feeling upset, not to get anxious for feeling anxious, not to feel depressed for feeling depressed).
- Learning to tolerate distress rather than fighting it (flow with it).
- Adopting healthy and adaptive means to deal with anxiety and chronic distress, rather than resorting to short-term reduction measures such as over-medication, alcohol, or substance abuse.
- Toleration of painful experience by adopting healthy adaptive measures as mentioned earlier and reminding oneself of the relatively short duration of the distress (e.g., anxiety always subsides after a while).
- Tolerance of frustration by adopting healthy adaptive measures and reminding oneself of the long-term goals (e.g., patient is encouraged to do the acceptance and other mindful exercises on a daily basis, although changes may not be apparent initially, in the long run they will be beneficial).
- Re-contextualizing meaning of suffering, for example, from 'this is unbearable' to 'let me focus on what I can do under the circumstances'.
- Exercising radical acceptance – ability to welcome those things in life that are hard, unpleasant, or very painful (e.g., accepting a loss).
- Embracing good or bad experience as part of life.
- Willing to experience the reality of the present moment, for example, believing that 'things are as they should be.'

- Purposely allowing experiences (thoughts, emotions, desires, urges, sensations, etc.) to transpire without attempting to block or suppress them.
- Realizing that anxiety is not caused by object or situation itself, but by our perception of it, our coping abilities and our level of spirituality.

Exposure exercises

As discussed earlier, patients with GAD avoids painful experience (Michelson, Lee, Orsillo, & Roemer, 2011). Toleration of fear and anxiety is therefore considered an essential component in the psychological treatment of the disorder. Moreover, it was suggested that the goal of exposure therapy should not be on immediate reduction of fear and anxiety, but on learning to tolerate distress and discomfort. In the context of AMBT, exposure exercises are used to provide further training in toleration of distress via acceptance. Patients are invited to increase their awareness of bodily sensations and unwanted thoughts, worries and images so that they may learn to approach them in a more accepting and compassionate way. These exercises encourage patients to lean into their anxiety rather than fighting it. Forsyth and Eifert (2007) believe this approach allows patients to create more space to feel their emotions and to think their thoughts as they are rather than their minds telling them what they are. The following script adapted from Forsyth and Eifert (pp. 196–197) exemplifies an 'acceptance of anxiety' exercise. The exercise is usually performed when the patient is either in a relaxed state or in a light hypnotic trance (a deep trance is avoided to facilitate deeper awareness).

> While you continue to relax, take a few moments to get in touch with the physical sensations in your body, especially the sensations of touch or pressure where your body makes contact with the chair. Notice the gentle rising and falling of your breath in your chest and belly. There's no need for you to control your breathing in any way – simply let the breath breathe itself. Also bring this attitude of kindness and gentleness to the rest of your body experience, without needing it to be other than what it is.

> If your mind wanders, this is okay. It's natural for your mind to wander away to thoughts, worries, images, bodily sensations, or feelings. Notice these thoughts and feelings, acknowledge their presence, and stay with them. There's no need to think of something else, make them go away, or resolve anything. As best as you can, allow them to be … giving yourself space to have whatever you have … bringing a quality of kindness and compassion to your experience.

> Now allow yourself to be present to what you are afraid of. Notice any doubts, reservations, fears, concerns and worries. Just notice them and acknowledge their presence, and don't try to control or influence them in any way. As you do that, allow yourself to be present with your values and

commitments. Ask yourself, 'Why am I here?', 'Where do I want to go?', 'What do I want to do?'

When you are ready, gently shift your attention to a thought or situation that has been difficult for you. It could be a troubling thought, a worry, an image, or an intense bodily sensation. Gently, directly, and firmly shift your attention on and into the discomfort, no matter how bad it seems. Notice any strong feelings that may arise in your body, allowing them to be as they are rather than what your mind tells you they are. Simply hold them in awareness. Stay with your discomfort and breathe with it. See if you can gently open up to it and make space for it, accepting and allowing it to be ... while bringing compassionate and focused attention to the discomfort.

If you notice yourself tensing up and resisting, pushing away from the experience, just acknowledge that and see if you can make some space for whatever you are experiencing. Must this feeling or thought be your rival? Or can you have it, notice it, own it, and let it be? Can you make room for the discomfort, for the tension, for the anxiety? What does it really feel like – moment to moment – to have it all? Is this something you must struggle with, or can you invite the discomfort in, saying to yourself, 'Let me have it; let me feel what there is to be felt because it is my experience right now'?

If the sensations or discomfort grow stronger, acknowledge that, stay with them, breathing with them, and accepting them. Is this discomfort something you must not have, you cannot have? Can you open up a space for the discomfort in your heart? Is there room inside you to feel that, with compassion and kindness towards yourself and your experience?

As you open up and embrace your experience, you may notice thoughts coming along with the physical sensations, and you may see thoughts about your thoughts. When that happens, invite them too ... softening and opening to them as you become aware of them. You may also notice your mind coming up with judgmental labels such as 'dangerous' or 'getting worse'. If that happens, you can simply thank your mind for the label and return to the present experience as it is, not as your mind says it, noticing thoughts as thoughts, physical sensations as physical sensations, feelings as feelings – nothing more, nothing less.

Stay with your discomfort for as long as it pulls your attention. If and when you sense that the anxiety and other discomfort are no longer pulling for your attention, let them go.

As this practice comes to a close, gradually widen your attention to take in the sounds around you. Take a moment to make the intention to allow this sense of gentleness and self-acceptance continue for the rest of your day. Then, slowly open your eyes.

The combination of the behavioural (in CBT) and acceptance exposure exercises helped Fred to decrease his rumination about his worries and helped him to feel less anxious at work. He was able increase his interaction with his boss rather than avoiding him.

Strategies for clarifying values

The importance of clarifying and articulating one's values in AMBT were discussed in Chapter 2. As values give meaning to one's life, they often establish the direction one chooses to take in therapy. In this sense, values largely determine whether a patient is willing to commit to difficult behavioural challenges and/or accept aversive internal experiences that he or she may have to face in the course of therapy. Clarification of patient's values is therefore an essential ingredient in development and sustaining motivation for change (Herbert & Forman, 2014). Exercises for clarifying values include (i) posting existential questions such as 'What do you want your life to stand for?' or (ii) imagining the eulogy one would hear at one's funeral and comparing it with the most honest rendition based on one's life.

Here's an example where a patient with OCD was able to surf over her anxiety about contamination by reminding herself of her values as a mother. Dorothy, a 44-year-old social worker and a mother of three children, had been struggling with a fear of contamination by germs for over 10 years. To avoid contamination, Dorothy would not allow her children and her husband to enter the house without washing their hands. Whenever they came in the house, they had to take their shoes off at the front door and walk down the basement where they had to wash their hands thoroughly and then come into the rest of the house. She would also make sure her children wash their hands whenever they play in a public playground before getting in her car.

Dorothy was encouraged to articulate her values as a mother and then to question whether her obsessional behaviour conflicted with her parental values.

THERAPIST	Could you tell me about your values as a mother to your children?
DOROTHY	I want to be a good mother. I want to do everything to make them feel happy and to grow up healthy and well-balanced.
THERAPIST	I see your good values. But how would you reconcile with the fact that you make your children wash their hands whenever they come home or play in the playground?
DOROTHY	Oh My God! I never thought about that. Because of my anxiety I am making them suffer while I should be caring for them.
THERAPIST	It is understandable that your anxiety became the focus of your attention. But now that you are aware about it, would it be possible to change your relationship with your anxiety.
DOROTHY	Although I am anxious I should also be focusing on my values as a mother during the exposure therapy.

The clarification and the articulation of her values helped Dorothy tolerate her anxiety during the exposure *in vivo* therapy. This breakthrough speeded her progress in therapy.

Strategies for learning to express gratitude
Sense of gratitude is used as a means to cultivate acceptance in patients with anxiety disorder. Recent studies suggest that people who are grateful have higher levels of subjective well-being and they have more positive ways of coping with difficulties they experience in life (see Chapter 2 for more details). Strategies commonly used in psychotherapy, particularly in CH, to promote expression of gratitude in patients with GAD disorder include (i) gratitude education, (ii) gratitude training and (iii) gratitude hypnotherapy.

Gratitude education
Gratitude education explores broad generalizations about different cultural definition of success and achievement. Patients are also encouraged to read the book, *The Narcissism Epidemic: Living in the Age of Entitlement* (Twenge & Campbell, 2009). This book provides a clear account of how high expectations, preoccupation with success, and sense of entitlement can set us up for failure. The idea behind the education is to help patient with GAD understand that the definition of success is human-made, subjective and culturally determined. This comparative understanding of success helped Fred feel grateful for what he had achieved rather than focusing on 'what ifs '.

Gratitude training
The goal of the gratitude training is to help GAD patients develop sense of gratitude for what they have rather than focusing on the worry of losing what they have now.

- Writing gratitude letters
- Writing a gratitude journal
- Every day making a list of five things the patient is grateful for
- Remembering gratitude moments
- Making gratitude visits to people the patient is grateful to
- Practicing or repeating gratitude self-talk.

Gratitude hypnotherapy
Suggestions about sense of gratitude is easily integrated with ego-strengthening suggestions that are routinely offered in hypnotherapy. It is advisable to offer gratitude suggestions while the patient is in a deep trance

and fully relaxed mentally and physically. The gratitude hypnotherapy script presented in Chapter 3 illustrates how hypnotic suggestions can be crafted to reinforce sense of gratitude in patients with anxiety disorder. Fred, who was devoutly religious, found the gratitude script 'very meaningful', and it made him become more focused on the present rather than excessively worrying about the future.

Strategies for nurturing psychophysiological coherence
The sixth component of AMBT targets integration of various subsystems in the body. There is abundant research evidence that heart-focused positive emotional state synchronizes the entire body system to produce PC (see Chapter 2 for more detail). Breathing with your heart technique is used to help patients with GAD generate coherence (harmony) of the entire system (mind, body, brain, heart and emotion). This technique integrates both Western (complex information centre) and Eastern (big mind) concepts of the heart to produce psychological well-being. The technique consists of two phases: heart education and breathing with your heart training assisted by hypnosis.

Heart education
The patient is given a scientific account of the role of heart and positive emotions in the generation of PC, which promotes healing, emotional stability and optimal performance. The similarities and the differences between Western and Eastern theories of mind and 'heart' are also discussed (Alladin, 2014a).

Breathing with your heart training combined with hypnosis
Heart–mind–body training helps patients with GAD cope with anxiety, worries and uncertainties. By breathing with the heart, patients are able to shift their attention away from their mind to their heart. When a person feels good in his or her heart, the person experiences a sense of comfort and joy because we validate reality by the way we feel and not by the way we think (Fredrickson, 2002; Isen, 1998). As discussed in Chapter 2, logic does not always equate good affect, but feeling good in one's heart, especially when associated with sense of gratitude, invariably creates positive affect (Welwood, 1983).

The following transcript from a session with Fred illustrates how the technique can be introduced in therapy. The script begins with Fred being in a deep hypnotic trance:

> You have now become so deeply relaxed, that you begin to feel a beautiful sensation of peace and relaxation, tranquility and calm flowing throughout your mind and body. Do you feel relaxed both mentally and physically? [Fred nodded his head up and down; ideomotor signals of 'head up and

down for YES' and 'shaking your head side to side for NO' were set up prior to starting the Breathing With Your Heart technique.] Now I would like you to focus on the center of your heart. [Pause for 30 seconds.] Can you imagine this? [Fred nodded his head.] Now I would like you to imagine breathing in and out with your heart [Pause for 30 seconds.] Can you imagine this? [Fred nodded his head.] Continue to imagine breathing in and out with your heart. [He was allowed to continue with this exercise for 2 minutes; the therapist repeated at regular intervals 'Just continue to imagine breathing with your heart' as he did the exercise.] Now I would like you to slow down your breathing. Breathe in and out at 7-second intervals. Breathe in with your heart ... 1 ... 2 ... 3 ... 4 ... 5 ... 6 ... 7 ... and now breathe out with your heart ... 1 ... 2 ... 3 ... 4 ... 5 ... 6 ... 7 ... And now as you are breathing in and out with your heart I want you to become aware of something in your life that you feel good about, something that you feel grateful for. [Pause for 30 seconds.] Are you able to focus on something that you are grateful for in your life? [Fred nodded.] Just become aware of that feeling and soon you will feel good in your heart [Fred nodded.] Just become aware of this good feeling in your heart. [Pause for 30 seconds.] Now I would like you to become aware of the good feeling in your mind, in your body and in your heart. Do you feel this? [Fred nodded.] Now you feel good in your mind, in your body and, in your heart. You feel a sense of balance, a sense of harmony. Do you feel this sense of harmony? [Fred nodded.] From now on whenever and wherever you are, you can create this good feeling by imagining breathing with your heart and focusing on something that you are grateful for. With practice you will get better and better at it. Now you know what to do to make your heart feel lighter.

Summary

This chapter described a wide variety of behavioural, cognitive, hypnotic, unconscious and acceptance and mindfulness-based strategies for treating GAD. The therapist, based on case formulation, can select the most fitting techniques for each individual patient with GAD. The case of Fred illustrated that symptom-focused treatment is necessary but not sufficient for treating underlying determinants of an anxiety disorder. A comprehensive and durable treatment requires therapeutic confrontation of unconscious conflicts that harbour painful emotions maintaining the symptoms.

7

Agoraphobia

Case of Margaret

Margaret, a 46-year-old housewife, was referred to the author by her psychiatrist for psychological treatment, while she was an inpatient in the psychiatric unit at the local general hospital. Margaret had multiple diagnoses, including migraine headache with aura, severe agoraphobia and recurrent major depressive disorder. She was admitted to the psychiatric unit for an episode of major depressive disorder with suicidal intent. This was her second admission to the hospital for depression. Six years prior to the second episode, she was admitted to the same hospital for her first episode of major depressive disorder. During the second episode, she was in hospital for three months, responded well to pharmacological treatment of her depression but showed little improvement with her migraine and agoraphobia. According to the hospital unit, Margaret showed 'little motivation' to work with her migraine and fear of going out. Nevertheless, she underwent extensive medical tests and examinations to rule out organic causation to her severe migraine. She was diagnosed with a rare presentation of migraine symptomatology, which her neurologist called 'hemiplegic migraine'. The migraine attack was characterized by the right side of her face and lips, and her right arm and hand felt numb and paralysed. The attacks were very frightening to her as she often thought she was having a stroke. The frequency of the attacks varied from one to two attacks per month and each attack lasted for about 4 to 5 hours. Whenever she had an attack, she would stay in bed until it cleared up.

Integrative CBT for Anxiety Disorders: An Evidence-Based Approach to Enhancing Cognitive Behavioural Therapy with Mindfulness and Hypnotherapy, First Edition. Assen Alladin.
© 2016 John Wiley & Sons, Ltd. Published 2016 by John Wiley & Sons, Ltd.

Because of the migraine, Margaret avoided going out for fear of having an attack in public. She was also afraid that if she happened to have an attack in public she might not be able to handle it and it might get worse, and consequently she would lose control. Whenever she thought about going out, or whenever she anticipated someone would ask her to go out, she would experience rapid heartbeat, tightness in her chest, difficulty with breathing, dizziness, sense of unreality and numbness or tingling in her arms and face, often triggering a migraine. For these reasons, she would not go out even if she is accompanied by her family members. She felt safe in her home. Moreover, Margaret avoided visiting people or receiving visitors at home.

Margaret had been married for 20 years. Her husband was a factory worker, who was known to be shy but supportive to Margaret. She had an 18-year son, living at home, who was finishing high school. Before she had her son, Margaret used to work in the same canning factory where her husband worked. Since she had her son, she had not worked.

Diagnostic Criteria for Agoraphobia

In DSM-IV (American Psychiatric Association, 1994), agoraphobia was conceptualized as a condition secondary to PD or sub-clinical panic symptoms. DSM-V (American Psychiatric Association, 2013) classified agoraphobia as a separate disorder from PD and listed the following diagnostic criteria (pp. 217–218):

1. Marked fear or anxiety about two or more of the following situations:
2. Using public transports such as cars, buses, trains, planes, or ships.
3. Being in open spaces such as bridges, marketplaces, parking lots, and so on.
4. Being in enclosed spaces such as shops, cinemas, theatres, and so on.
5. Standing in line or being in a crowd.
6. Being outside of one's home alone.
7. The person is fearful of these situations or avoids them because of the anticipation that he or she may not be able to escape from them, or help may not be available in the event of feeling panicky or experiencing other incapacitating or embarrassing symptoms such as falling, becoming incontinent, and so on.
8. The agoraphobic situations invariably produce anxiety or fear.
9. The agoraphobic situations are actively avoided, or endured with intense fear or anxiety, or require the presence of a companion.

10. The fear or anxiety is out of proportion to the actual danger associated with the agoraphobic situations.
11. The fear, anxiety, or avoidance has been persistent for at least six months.
12. The fear, anxiety, or avoidance causes significant distress or impairment in important areas of functioning (e.g., occupation, socialization, etc.).
13. The fear, anxiety, or avoidance is excessive if another medical condition is present (e.g., inflammatory bowel disease, Parkinson's disease).
14. The fear, anxiety, or avoidance is not due to another psychiatric condition.

In DSM-V, agoraphobia is diagnosed irrespective of the presence of PD. In the case where a person's symptoms meet criteria for agoraphobia and PD, both diagnoses are assigned.

Prevalence of Agoraphobia

It is estimated that approximately 1.7% of adolescents and adults are diagnosed with agoraphobia annually (American Psychiatric Association, 2013), and the overall lifetime prevalence of agoraphobia without PD is 5.6% (Eaton, 1995). Although agoraphobia is approximately 20 times more common among individuals with PD than among those without it (Weissman et al., 1997), large epidemiological surveys in the United States provide strong evidence that agoraphobia is not a consequence of PD (Eaton, 1995). In fact, most individuals with agoraphobia do not have PD (Kessler et al., 1994). Agoraphobia can occur during childhood, but the incidence seems to peak in late adolescence and early adulthood. Agoraphobia with or without PD appears to be about 2 and 1.3 times more likely to occur in women (Kessler et al., 2006). Agoraphobia is a disabling disorder, causing severe functional impairments across many life domains, including interpersonal problems, marital difficulties, unemployment, individual suffering and financially dependent on public assistance programmes (see Hazlett-Stevens, 2006).

Causes of Agoraphobia

The causes of agoraphobia are not known, although several theories have been advanced. In a broader sense, it can be regarded as a prototype of dependent behaviour.

Early theories of agoraphobia, based on Mowrer's (1960) two-factor learning theory, viewed avoidance behaviour as a conditioned fear response maintained by instrumental conditioning (negative reinforcement). According to this view, fear of certain public places occurs when an aversive event takes place in a particular situation (classical conditioning), which the person avoids to escape (negative reinforcement) the conditioned fear response. This theory was supported by a study by Öst and Hugdahl (1983) in which 81% of their agoraphobia sample (N = 91) were able to identify a specific conditioning experience associated with their fear. Subsequent behavioural models of agoraphobia underlined the role of anticipatory anxiety rather than concentrating on the fear of the situation itself. For example, Goldstein and Chambless (1978), in their 'fear of fear' model hypothesized that avoidance in agoraphobics resulted from anticipatory fear of bodily sensations or impending panic. According to this theory, innocuous bodily sensations are classically conditioned to aversive physiological arousal associated fearful experience. In turn, these classically conditioned sensations trigger unwanted anxiety attacks across situations that agoraphobics avoid for fear of inability to cope with an anxiety attack in these situations. The expectation that an attack will be imminent and harmful, and that coping will be ineffective, plays a significant role by influencing and maintaining avoidance behaviour (Taylor & Rachman, 1994).

Recent theories of agoraphobia gave more emphasis to the complex interaction between biological and psychological factors in the development of the disorder. Like all anxiety disorders, agoraphobia is believed to be marked by a general predisposition (Craske, 1999) or 'negative affectivity' (Watson & Clark, 1984). Although the genetic influences for negative affectivity are well established, environmental influences can also make a person vulnerable to experience negative emotional states across situations. For example, early experiences with stressful situations, particularly those in which the individual perceived the event(s) to be unpredictable and difficult to control, have also been found to contribute to negative affectivity (Craske, 1999). Other developmental experiences that can act as 'precursors' to agoraphobia include parental modelling of anxious behaviour, overprotective treatment and parental encouragement of anxious behaviour and avoidance (Goldstein & Chambless, 1978; Vasey & Dadds, 2001). Children growing up with these precursors adopt an avoidant style to problem-solving, thus allowing others to deal with stressors as if they are incapable of handling difficulties on their own. However, the specificity of the link between these features and adulthood agoraphobia is questionable. A link has also been found between separation anxiety and agoraphobia. History of separation anxiety in childhood is found to be consistently more frequent in patients with agoraphobia than in controls (healthy subjects or patients with another psychiatric disorder) (Faravelli, Webb, Ambonetti, Fonnesu, & Sessarego, 1985). However, childhood separation anxiety and separation experiences have also been found among patients with other disorders such as GAD, SAD, specific phobias, OCD, depression and eating disorders. Therefore, childhood separation anxiety may be one of the nonspecific risk factors for developing not only agoraphobia but also a range of other psychiatric conditions in childhood.

Attempts have been made to integrate biological, cognitive and behavioural factors in the understanding of agoraphobia. Two integrated models of etiology, which greatly overlaps, are described here as the therapies for agoraphobia described in this chapter are, to some extent, based on these two models.

The first integrated model is based on the work by Mathews, Gelder and Johnson (1981), which had greatly influenced the clinical practice with agoraphobia in United Kingdom. The model describes two broad, parallel processes – trait anxiety and avoidance coping style – which merge to produce the agoraphobic syndrome. According to the first part of this model, some individuals are born with elevated levels of trait anxiety, which combine with increased 'non-specific' stress to generate high level of general anxiety. The second process entails the development of external locus of control and the learning of avoidant style of coping during childhood. In the presence of these 'childhood precursors', after an acute anxiety attack, which may be triggered by a variety of stimuli, the person begins to avoid various situations. The avoidance behaviours are further reinforced by social reinforcements such as sympathy or adoption of 'sick role', leading to the 'behavioural trap' or avoidance patterns of behaviour.

The second integrated model of agoraphobia was proposed by Chambless and her colleagues (Chambless, 1982; Chambless & Goldstein, 1982), based on research and clinical observation. They argued that a combination of behavioural and psychodynamic processes is needed to understand the nature of agoraphobia. They also posited that agoraphobia should be separated into two syndromes: simple agoraphobia and complex agoraphobia. Simple agoraphobia, which is uncommon, is characterized by several simple phobias of public places, possibly caused by drug experiences or hypoglycaemia, not generalized to other areas of life, and the patients are well-adjusted psychologically. The second type of agoraphobia is described as being more complex and most prevalent, and it is characterized by:

- Fear of fear, which is central to the phobic element.
- Low levels of self-sufficiency due to anxiety and/or lack of problem-solving skills.
- Tendency to misinterpret uncomfortable feelings as disastrous, for example, the anxiety triggered by an interpersonal conflict can be interpreted as fear of being on the street alone.
- Symptoms often occurring in conflicting situations.

Although the model for complex agoraphobia is based on Bowlby's (1973) concepts of vulnerable personality, separation anxiety and fear of abandonment, one of the criticisms levelled against it is the 'explanation of the mechanism of how separation anxiety becomes a fear of public situations' (Gournay, 1989, p. 19). The self-wounds theory of anxiety described in Chapter 1 provides a tentative explanation. According to this theory, agoraphobics have a conflict between being free and being secure. According to Wolfe (2005, p. 200), each 'pole of this conflict possesses both a positive and a negative valence. Freedom connotes autonomy and isolation; security connotes being cared for and being controlled'. The prototypical self-wounds associated with agoraphobia include seeing oneself as inadequate, unlovable, alone and at a loss. Because of these self-wounds and the conflict about freedom and security, agoraphobics feels fearful being in public situations. Moreover, they are horrified with the fear and embarrassment of not being able to cope with their anxiety in public.

Treatment of Agoraphobia

Exposure-based CBT has been the gold standard treatment for agoraphobia for the past 30 years (Chambless, 1985; Hazlett-Stevens, 2006). This approach to therapy has been found to produce at least 50% of improvement in avoidance behaviour in 60–70% of treated agoraphobic patients (Johnson & Öst, 1982). Moreover, the treatment leads to reduction in subjective anxiety, panic attacks and depression associated with the agoraphobia. Although exposure-based CBT is the standard treatment for agoraphobia, several alternative psychological approaches are available for patients seeking treatment, including SD, imaginal flooding, self-observation, participant modelling/guided mastery, self-directed exposure, respiratory training, teletherapy and Internet-based treatments, virtual reality exposure therapy (VRET), interpersonal psychotherapy, acceptance and commitment therapy (see most recent review by Telch, Cobb, & Lancaster, 2014). Other effective psychological therapies include relaxation therapy (Öst, Westling, & Hellstrom, 1993), psychodynamic therapy (Hoffart & Matisen, 1993; Milrod et al., 2001, 2007) and hypnotherapy (Kraft, 2011a, 2011b). Some of these treatment approaches will be further discussed under the section 'Cognitive hypnotherapy for agoraphobia'.

As with other anxiety disorders, pharmacotherapy has been the most accessible treatment for agoraphobia (e.g., Craske & Barlow, 2014; Issakidis et al., 2004). A variety of effective compounds, including SSRIs, SNRIs, TCAs, selective noradrenergic reuptake inhibitors and benzodiazepines, have been used in the pharmacological management of agoraphobia (Perna, Dacco, Menoti, & Caldirola, 2011). However, the role of pharmacotherapy in the management of agoraphobia is not clear as all the studies in the past 25 years had used DSM-IV (American Psychiatric Association, 1994) diagnosis of PD with agoraphobia or without agoraphobia – that is, agoraphobia was considered to be secondary to PD. The DSM-V (American Psychiatric Association, 2013), on the other hand, classifies agoraphobia as a primary diagnosis independent of PD. All studies prior to the publication of DSM-V considered PD and agoraphobia a homogeneous group, without consideration that different symptomatological profiles and pathogenetic mechanisms might have been involved in the development of the two disorders (Perna et al., 2011). Based on their review of 25 randomized, placebo-controlled drug trials for agoraphobia, selected from 235 published studies between 2000 and June 2011, Perna et al. (2011) concluded that much more research is needed before a specific psychopharmacological treatment for agoraphobia can be recommended. This state of affairs has created a tremendous knowledge gap in our understanding of the nature and treatment of agoraphobia.

Another concern relates to the effectiveness of available treatments for agoraphobia. Although a variety of psychological and pharmacological therapies are available for agoraphobia, between 30% and 40% of patients do not achieve significant improvement (van Apeldoorn, van Hout, Mersch, Huisman, & Slaap (2008). Moreover, 25–50% of patients relapse within 6 months after drug discontinuation and up to 40–50% of subjects continue to present residual phobic symptoms, and up to 20–30% still present full-blown disorder after 3–6 years of treatment. Given the tendency for agoraphobia to become chronic and, in severe cases, the symptoms can be debilitating, particularly for the large number of patients who do not respond to current therapies, there is an urgent need to develop more effective therapies for agoraphobia. It also appears that the maintenance of benefit following therapy discontinuation is not related to the duration of treatment, but to the attainment of a complete remission at the end of treatment (American Psychiatric Association, 2009). This underscores the importance of maximizing improvement obtained from initial pharmaco-therapy or psychotherapy.

There is also some concern about the toleration of situational exposure in agoraphobic patients. Although exposure-based CBT is the first-line treat-ment for agoraphobia, it is a good choice for individuals willing to confront their feared situations, but the treatment can be quite difficult for patients with severe agoraphobia (Hazlett-Stevens, 2006). It is therefore important for therapists to assess whether patients can tolerate the distress involved in exposure therapy. Moreover, patients with heightened risk of suicide may need additional intervention before exposure is attempted. One of the reasons for integrating hypnosis in the management of agoraphobia in this chapter is to increase confidence and toleration of discomfort. In fact, both first and second generations (1970s to 1990s) of studies of exposure treat-ments for agoraphobia had indicated the need to combine other therapeutic strategies to augment the effect of exposure therapy. Several studies have demonstrated the additive effect of systematically adding other therapeutic strategies with exposure therapy (Telch, Cobb, & Lancaster, 2014). Because *in vivo* exposure is a cornerstone therapeutic strategy in the treatment of agoraphobia, it makes sense to optimize its efficacy. This chapter provides a variety of techniques, some evidence-based, from which the therapists can choose to enhance the effect of exposure therapy in their individual treat-ment. For example, the addition of hypnosis to CBT has been shown to increase the effect size of CBT with chronic pain and a variety of emotional disorders (see review of this literature in Chapter 2).

From the review of the treatment literature on agoraphobia, it appears (i) about 40% of agoraphobic patients treated do not respond to the available treatment, (ii) almost 50% relapse after discontinuation of treatment, (iii) about 30% of patients treated have full-blown anxiety at follow-ups, (iv) remission of symptoms at the end of treatment predict better outcome at follow-up rather than the number of sessions and (v) although *in vivo* exposure is the key element in the treatment of agoraphobia, many patients, especially the severe agoraphobics, are not able to tolerate the procedure. These findings indicate there is an urgent need to develop a more comprehen-sive and effective therapies for agoraphobia. The treatment protocol described in this chapter attempts to provide a comprehensive and multi-modal treat-ment package for agoraphobia in an attempt to address some of the serious issues that emerged from the critical review of the treatment literature.

Cognitive Hypnotherapy for Agoraphobia

Hypnotherapy for managing symptoms of agoraphobia

The initial phase of the therapy for agoraphobia, consisting of four to six sessions, is specifically targeted at symptoms management. For some patients this phase of therapy may be sufficient, while for others it serves as a preparation for more complex therapy of exploring the roots of the agoraphobia. The hypnotherapy components focuses on (i) relaxation training, (ii) demonstration of the power of mind over the body, (iii) ego strengthening, (iv) expansion of awareness, (v) imaginal exposure, (vi) self-hypnosis, (vii) modulation and regulation of symptoms, (viii) PHS and (ix) hypnotherapy combined with behavioural therapies. Hypnotherapy is introduced again later in therapy with patients who elect to pursue with uncovering work. The initial sessions of hypnotherapy, therefore, for some patients, serve as a preparatory phase for more complex therapy of exploring the roots of the agoraphobia later in the therapy.

Relaxation training

Two studies by Öst (Öst & Westling, 1995; Öst et al., 1993) demonstrated that applied relaxation is as effective as *in vivo* exposure therapy in the treatment of agoraphobia. Beck, Stanley, Baldwin, Deagle and Averill (1994) also found very few differences between CBT and PMR when each treatment was administered without exposure procedures. In contrast, Milrod and her colleagues (Milrod et al., 2001, 2007) found applied relaxation to be ineffective with agoraphobia compared to a 24-session of manualized psychodynamic treatment and the attrition rate for applied relaxation (34%) was significantly higher than in the psychodynamic therapy (7%). How does one make sense of the differential effect of relaxation training with agoraphobia? One of the explanations for the discrepancy can be associated with the severity of the symptoms. It is possible that the study by Beck et al. (1994) and Öst (Öst & Westling, 1995; Öst et al., 1993) might have consisted of a preponderance of simple agoraphobics and hence they showed good response to treatment as Chambless (1985; Chambless & Goldstein, 1982) would have predicted based on the characteristics of simple agoraphobia. On the other hand, it is possible that Milrod's subjects were predominantly complex agoraphobics, and hence they found relaxation training too superficial for their problems, so a significant number of subjects (34%) decided to quit the treatment. The fact that the majority of the subjects (93%) in the psychodynamic group persisted with the treatment indicate they tolerated the treatment approach, possibly because it addressed the complexity of their emotional problem.

For the earlier reasons, this chapter advocates a multi-component treatment protocol for agoraphobia. Relaxation training is deemed one of the components of this comprehensive treatment for agoraphobia. In fact, many therapists (e.g., Huppert & Sanderson, 2010) consider relaxation training to be an important component of most CBT-oriented treatments for anxiety disorders. With agoraphobia, relaxation training is used to reduce physiological correlates of anxiety, broaden focus of attention, break perseverating pattern of thinking and equip patients with coping strategy. As discussed in previous chapters, neither hypnosis nor relaxation response encourages avoidance behaviour in patients with anxiety disorder. On the contrary, by expanding attention, the relaxed state increases patient's ability to consider alternatives in anxiety-provoking situations.

As Margaret was experiencing high levels of tension, nervousness, irritation and frequent attacks of migraine, she found the relaxation induced by hypnosis very calming and comforting. She was highly susceptible to hypnosis and she was surprised that she could generate profound mental and physical relaxation despite her migraine. Her hypnotic talent was utilized to help her decentre from anticipatory and phobic anxieties. However, during the trance state she was fully aware of her surroundings and conceptual reality. The relaxation response (feeling calm and fully relaxed) and sense of detachment, while she was aware of her anxieties, served as an experiential strategy to diminish her anxiety about going out to public places. Margaret's hypnotic talent and positive trance experiences were further deployed to teach her how to modulate her emotional reactions to anticipatory anxiety (further discussed under the section 'Self-hypnosis training').

As Margaret was also concerned with and suffering with her 'hemiplegic migraine', some techniques and sessions were exclusively devoted to working with her migraine. A detailed account of CH for treating migraine is described by Alladin (2008). The treatment sessions did not focus on her depression as it was effectively managed by the medication; and also, Margaret did not feel the need to have psychotherapy for her depression as she viewed her depression secondary to her agoraphobia and migraine. Since the focus of this chapter is on agoraphobia, the migraine treatment is not described here, except for occasional comments about her progress with the treatment.

Demonstration of the power of the mind over the body
To further empower Margaret and to ratify the credibility of the hypnotic intervention, eye and body catalepsies were introduced in the second

hypnotherapy session. Chapter 3 provides a transcript for inducing eye and body catalepsies and it offers an explanation of the cataleptic effects in terms of self-hypnosis. Margaret was very impressed by the power of the hypnosis that she could not open her eyes or get out of the reclining chair. She found this session empowering as it instilled in her the hope and confidence that she could tap on her own personal resources to deal with her anxiety, depression and migraine. Moreover, this session strengthened the therapeutic alliance and consolidated in her a sense of positive expectancy. She indicated that it was for the first time that she felt hopeful about getting better.

As noted earlier, a significant number of agoraphobic patients, particularly those with severe symptoms, are not able to tolerate the anxiety and distress associated with *in vivo* exposure therapy, thus they drop out of therapy. Hypnotherapy provides a powerful vehicle for helping agoraphobic patients build confidence through experiential learning (positive trance experience) and by recognizing the power of their mind over their body (eye and body catalepsy exercise).

Ego strengthening
Ego-strengthening suggestions were offered to Margaret to increase her self-esteem, enhance her self-efficacy and gradually restore her confidence in her ability to tolerate situational anxiety. While in deep hypnotic trance, Margaret was encouraged to visualize herself as being self-efficacious in dealing with her fear and anxiety head-on, rather than avoiding them. Margaret commented that the relaxation response and the ego-strengthening suggestions made her feel strong and confident to deal with her symptoms. She felt the hypnotherapy sessions were having a significant effect on her – she began to feel optimistic and confident that she would get better. She started to interact more actively with her son and husband at home. Prior to the therapy, she used to avoid her husband and son, and would rarely sit down and have a long conversation with them. She found the following ego-strengthening suggestions very helpful and encouraging:

- 'Every day as a result of this treatment and as a result of you listening to your self-hypnosis CD every day, you will begin to feel calmer and more relaxed.'
- 'Although you may be aware of your anxiety and discomfort, you will be able to put everything on hold just as you do in the hypnosis sessions. This will show you that you can relax and let go even if you are aware of everything. You don't need to empty your mind to be able to relax.'

After the first hypnotherapy session, Margaret was given a self-hypnosis CD to listen to everyday (see the section 'Self-hypnosis training' for further details). As she was able to relax easily and enjoyed the sense of calmness, she felt motivated to listen to the self-hypnosis CD regularly. While she was in the hospital, she was encouraged to listen to the CD twice a day.

Expansion of awareness
Because of her long-term disability and isolation, prior to the hypnotherapy, Margaret reported feeling constantly anxious and unable to experience different emotions, particularly good feeling. As she started to feel better, she became afraid of going back to the way she felt before. To capitalize on the change Margaret was experiencing and to safeguard her from 'going back', two sessions of hypnotherapy were targeted at expanding her range of emotions and feelings. While in deep hypnosis Margaret was directed to focus on the relaxation response and to become aware of the various changes in feelings and sensations that she experienced. This was achieved by using EAT as described in Chapter 2. The following script represents a segment of the suggestions she was offered while she was in hypnosis:

> You have now become so deeply relaxed and you are in such a deep hypnotic state that your mind and body feel completely relaxed, totally relaxed. You begin to feel a beautiful sensation of peace and tranquility, relaxation and calm, flowing all over your mind and body, giving you such a pleasant, and such a soothing sensation all over your mind and body, that you feel completely relaxed, totally relaxed both mentally and physically, and yet you are aware of everything, you are aware of all the sound and noise around you, you are aware of your thoughts and imagination, and yet you feel so relaxed, so calm and so peaceful.
>
> This shows that you have the ability to relax, to let go, and to put everything on hold. This shows that you have lots of control, because you are aware of everything, you can hear all the sounds and noise around you, you are aware of your thoughts and imagination, you are aware that I am sitting beside you and talking to you, yet you are able to put everything on hold and relax completely. This shows you have lots of control that you are able to put things on hold.
>
> Now you may become aware of all the good feelings you are feeling. You feel calm, peaceful, relaxed and very, very comfortable. You may also become aware of feeling heavy, light, or detached, or distancing away from everything, becoming more and more detached, distancing away from everything, drifting into a deep, deep hypnotic state. Yet, you are being aware of everything, being aware of different feelings. You may also be aware of feeling light, or heavy; warm or cold. You may also notice the chair you are sitting on, you may be aware of the pressure of the chair wherever your

body is in contact with the chair. You may notice your back resting against the back of the chair; you may notice your head resting against the back of the chair. In fact, you are surprised that you can feel and experience so many things.

With EAT, Margret discovered that she had the ability to relax and the capacity to experience different feelings and sensations. She was surprised that she could put things on hold – that is, she able to relax completely while she was fully aware of her fears, concerns and worries. Margaret's ability to produce, amplify and express a variety of positive feelings and experiences gave her the confidence that she could work with her anxiety feeling, which is described next.

Imaginal exposure

To gain further confidence dealing with her anxious feeling, Margaret was introduced to imaginal exposure (Wolpe, 1958; Wolpe & Lazarus, 1966). Imaginal exposure therapy is considered to be an important component of CH for agoraphobia as it prepares patients for *in vivo* exposure later in therapy (Golden, 2012). In recognition of the large attrition rate in exposure therapy, Golden has recommended that *in vivo* therapy be carried out only after successful completion of in-session hypnotic desensitization or imaginal exposure.

While in deep hypnosis, Margaret was directed to bring on her anxious experience that is associated with going to a public place. She was then suggested to utilize her self-hypnosis skill to cope with her fear and anxiety reaction.

> When I count from ONE to FIVE, by the time you hear me say FIVE, you will begin to feel whatever emotion or reaction that you feel when you think of going to a public place or other anxiety-provoking situation.

Margaret was then encouraged to amplify the affect associated with the public place. There is some evidence that intense exposure to fear-provoking situations lead to large pre-to-post improvements in agoraphobic avoidance, anxiety sensitivity and self-efficacy (Morissette, Spiegel, & Heinrichs, 2006).

> When I count slowly from ONE to FIVE, as I count you will begin to experience the anxious feelings more and more intensely, so that when I reach the count of FIVE, at the count of FIVE you will feel the full reaction as strongly as you can bear it. ONE ... TWO ... THREE ... FOUR ... FIVE. Now notice what you feel and you can describe it to me.

Margaret was then instructed to utilize her self-hypnosis skill to cope and deal with the anxious and fearful reactions.

> Now imagine using your self-hypnosis skill to cope with the anxiety feeling. Since you have the ability to relax and the capacity to put things on hold, you can let go and flow with the feelings.

After several repetition of this set of suggestions, Margaret was able to relax completely, while imagining visiting a public place. This technique encouraged her to begin to focus on her anxious feelings head-on, rather than catastrophizing or cogitating about her symptoms. To increase her confidence further, Margaret was encouraged to participate in exposure therapy. However, at this point in therapy, as her migraine still persisted, it was decided to continue with the hypnotherapy for a few more sessions, to focus specifically on self-hypnosis training and the modulation of her symptoms.

Self-hypnosis training

To generalize her relaxation response and her ability to 'let go' to real situations, Margaret was coached in self-hypnosis. At the end of the first hypnotherapy session, she was given a CD recording of the session to facilitate self-hypnosis training. She was encouraged to listen to the CD twice a day while she was in hospital (at least once a day at home after she was discharged). This homework assignment allowed continuity of treatment between sessions and offered her the opportunity to practice self-hypnosis. Margaret commented that the training in self-hypnosis provided her the most practical and powerful skill for dealing with her anxiety symptoms outside the therapy sessions. The self-hypnosis also served as a powerful tool for countering her catastrophic cogitation (NSH). Once Margaret had built some confidence in self-hypnosis, the generalization of the self-hypnosis skill to real situations was consolidated by teaching her the clenched fist technique (Stein, 1963). As discussed in Chapter 2, the clenching of the dominant fist serves as an anchor for the elicitation of the relaxation response. Margaret was trained to induce self-hypnosis rapidly in diverse anxiety-provoking situations by mastering the clenched fist technique, which involved clenching her preferred fist as an anchor. An anchor is any stimulus that evokes a consistent response pattern from a person (Lankton, 1980). The dominant fist as an anchor is easily established during deep hypnotic trance. The following transcript illustrates how the clenched fist technique was introduced to Margaret while she was in a deep hypnotic trance, feeling completely relaxed.

This shows that you have the ability to relax, the ability to let go, and the ability to put things on hold. This shows that you have lots of control, because you know what's happening around you, yet you are able to relax your mind and body completely.

Since you are able to relax here, you may also be able to relax in any situation. In order facilitate your ability to relax in the real situations, I am going to introduce you to the clenched fist technique [which was discussed prior to the induction of the hypnosis].

Now if you may clench your right fist [it was established that she is right-handed]. As you clench your fist become aware of how very relaxed you are. You feel completely relaxed, both mentally and physically, and yet you are aware of everything around you. Also notice that you are in complete control, knowing what to do and knowing what's going on around you. If you slightly tighten your fist, you become even more aware of the good feelings, you feel completely relaxed and in complete control.

As you have made an association between your right fist and the ability to relax, from now on, whenever you want to feel this good feeling, you can bring on this feeling by clenching your right fist, and anchoring your mind to this session, that is, reminding yourself of this session, that you can relax and let go completely. And from now on, wherever you are, whatever you are doing, if you feel tense, anxious, upset, or stressed out, you can tame these feelings by clenching your right fist, and anchoring your mind to this experience. With practice you will get better and better at it.

The anchoring technique is experientially ratified by hypnotic imaginal rehearsal training and reinforced by PHS.

Just undo your fist. Now we are going to practice the clenching fist technique. Imagine from now on using your anchoring technique whenever you get upset, anxious, or stressed out. Imagine by using your anchoring technique you are able to deal with your anxiety and stress wherever you are, whatever you are doing. And with practice you will get better and better at it. As a result of this you will begin to flow with the anxious feeling.

Although Margaret found the clenched fist technique useful, in the sense that it was very concrete and portable, she was still not ready for *in vivo* exposure. It was therefore decided to devote a couple of hypnotherapy sessions on affect regulation training.

Modulating and coping with symptoms
As hypnosis is an experiential therapeutic approach, Margaret was directed to perceive her anxiety symptoms as a syncretic experience

(Alladin, 2006, 2007, 2008; Safer & Leventhal, 1977). She was encouraged to view her anxiety not simply as an affect, thought or behaviour, but as a cascade of cognitive, somatic, perceptual, physiological, visceral and kinaesthetic changes. The hypnotic induction and the generation and amplification of positive syncretic cognition offered Margaret dramatic proof that she could alter or regulate her anxious and distressing experience. This approach to therapy as discussed in Chapters 2 and 4, is influenced by third-wave CBT. In this approach to treatment, therapists teach their patients to examine and change their relationship with their internal experience and their cognitive activities, rather than trying to control their thoughts or emotions (Butler et al., 2008). This approach is discussed further in section 'Promoting acceptance and gratitude' later in the chapter.

Post-hypnotic suggestions
Before the termination of the hypnotic sessions, Margaret was routinely offered a variety of PHS to deal with her negative cognitions, which in CH, are referred as NSH. Margaret was preoccupied with the following NSH:

- 'I can't go out.'
- 'I'm stuck.'
- 'I can't cope with it.'
- 'I will lose control? It will be so embarrassing.'
- 'I will never get better. I'm doomed.'

Rumination with earlier self-suggestions can not only induce a negative trance, but also serve as powerful self-affirmations or PHS, which can become part of the avoidance pattern of behaviour. To offset the negative rumination, Margaret was offered a range of PHS at the end of each hypnotherapy session. Some of the PHS offered included:

- 'Whenever you feel anxious in a given situation, you will become more aware of how to deal with it rather than focusing on your symptoms or what may happen to you.'
- 'When you plan to approach an anxiety-provoking situation, you will feel less need to avoid the situation.'
- 'As you become more relaxed every day as a result of listening to your Self-Hypnosis CD, you will begin to feel motivated to face the situations you have been avoiding.'

Clarke and Jackson (1983) successfully utilized PHS to enhance the effect of *in vivo* exposure among agoraphobics.

Hypnotherapy combined with behavioural therapies

As hypnotherapy primarily involves experiential and imaginal therapies in the office, it is important to transfer the learning from this setting to real-life situations. To assist in this process, the next phase of therapy for agoraphobia integrates hypnotherapy with behavioural strategies, namely HASD and exposure *in vivo*. These behavioural techniques are fully described and their effectiveness reviewed in Chapter 2. SD is found to be a necessary component of therapy for specific phobia and it is found to be effective for reducing, and in some cases eliminating, simple phobias (Antony & Barlow, 2002; Choy et al., 2007; Kirsch et al., 1999; Smith, 1990).

Hypnosis-aided systematic desensitization

Although imaginal exposure was helpful to Margaret in terms of increasing her confidence to facing her fears in reality, she was too anxious to tolerate *in vivo* exposure. She felt more comfortable and ready to work with SD. SD is an effective evidence-based behavioural method for treating anxiety disorders, specifically phobias (see Chapter 2). Although the effect of SD with agoraphobia has been variable (see Telch et al., 2014), it is introduced to Margaret at her request and to prepare her of *in vivo* exposure therapy. Within the framework of CH, the relaxation component of SD is replaced by hypnosis, and hence, this treatment approach is referred to as HASD (Iglesias & Iglesias, 2014). A number of reports in the literature support the effectiveness of combining hypnosis with SD in the treatment of specific phobias (Glick, 1970). Table 7.1 shows the hierarchy of anxiety, which was formulated to help Margaret overcome her fear of public places. The hierarchy represents various situations – ranked from least feared to most feared – related to visiting the shopping mall downtown on her own. The fear was self- rated in terms of SUD on 0–100 scale; 0 representing no fear and 100 standing for the worst/maximum fear.

While feeling very relaxed in deep hypnosis, Margaret was asked to imagine each hierarchy of fear in turn, starting with the lowest item in the hierarchy ('Standing outside her front door for 15 minutes'; 20 SUD). She was instructed to focus on the target situation until she was able to bring her SUD level down to 0. It is important for patient to master one hierarchy, that is, able to imagine the target situation without any anxiety, before moving on to the next item in the hierarchy. Failure to master previous situation may produce resistance to work with the next item in the hierarchy, which is likely to be more anxiety-provoking (higher SUD

Table 7.1   Systematic desensitization hierarchy of fear of visiting the mall downtown

Item	Fear rating in SUD (0–100)
Standing outside her front door for 15 minutes	20
Walking around the block for 15 minutes	25
Walking around the neighbourhood for 15 minutes	30
Standing at the bus stop for 30 minutes	40
Riding the bus, getting off bus after two stops	50
Riding the bus to the local mall	60
Taking bus to local mall, staying in mall for 30 minutes	70
Taking bus to local mall, staying in mall for 1 hour	85
Taking bus to main mall, downtown	90
Taking bus to mall downtown, staying for 1 hour	100
Taking bus to mall downtown, shopping for 2 hours	100

level). Margaret found the SD very helpful in bringing down her level of anxiety during the session and she felt confident to progress on to gradual *in vivo* exposure.

Gradual in vivo *exposure therapy*
Exposure therapy has been found to be efficacious with a variety of anxiety disorders (Follette & Smith, 2005). As mentioned earlier, exposure-based CBT is the gold standard treatment for agoraphobia (Chambless, 1985; Hazlett-Stevens, 2006) and it has been found to produce at least 50% of improvement in avoidance behaviour in 60–70% of treated agoraphobic patients (Johnson & Öst, 1982). Exposure *in vivo* is designed to help agoraphobic patients confront feared situations, memories, and images in a therapeutic manner. As Margaret's symptoms were severe, she was exposed to the fearful situations in a graded manner. She was already discharged from the hospital – but followed-up by the author as an outpatient in the Department of Psychology at the same hospital she was admitted to – when the exposure therapy started. Margaret was in full agreement with the graded hierarchy and she decided to participate in the exposure therapy unassisted (on her own), one item per day. She made very good progress with the treatment.

Margaret's progress was reviewed five days after she started the graded exposure. In fact, she worked with 'Riding the bus, getting off bus after 2 stops' (50 SUD) item before attending her outpatient appointment with her therapist at the hospital. She was pleased with her progress and she was determined to continue with the rest of the exposure items. When she was seen again after a week, she continued to do well, but 'failed' to handle 'Taking bus to mall downtown, staying for 1 hour' (100 SUD). She managed to go to the mall downtown, but felt too anxious to stay in the mall, so she decided to return home soon after arriving at the mall. She was reassured and advised to repeat the 'failed' situation again and then to proceed to the last item on her hierarchy list. When she was seen a week later, she managed to go to mall and stayed there for one hour, but 'failed' the last item ('Taking bus to mall downtown, shopping for 2 hours'; 100 SUD). She was able to go to the mall, but was not able to go into the stores. She felt so overly conscious of her anxiety that 'it became impossible to focus' on what she was doing, and thus decided not to go in the stores. Again she was reassured and advised to repeat the exposure item. To her surprise, Margaret managed to face the last fearful situation from the hierarchy, although the two hours of shopping appeared to be an 'eternity'. Margaret was encouraged to continue with exposure to other situations she had been avoiding, for example, elevators, train, parks and so on.

Cognitive behavioural therapy

The next stage of therapy concentrated on identifying and restructuring Margaret's maladaptive cognitions related to her fear of public places and other fearful situations. Patients with agoraphobia tend to (i) overestimate the danger of any physical symptoms they experience; (ii) believe prescribed medications will drive them out of control or cause life-threatening side effects; (iii) perceive that other people disapprove of them; (iv) be convinced that their anxiety is apparent to everyone; (v) believe that they act strange when they feel anxious; (vi) believe that their anxiety is pervasive and everlasting; (vii) believe that their anxiety or tension is an abnormal state and (viii) believe that they should always be calm and in control in every situation (Chambless, 1985).

Margaret had all these dysfunctional cognitions. CBT helped her identify and restructure these negative cognitions. It provided her with a practical strategy to alter the meaning of her fear and anxiety, and the associated maladaptive emotions, namely guilt, shame and embarrassment. As CBT techniques are fully described in several excellent books (e.g., Beck, & Emery, 1985, 2005; Clark & Beck, 2010) and a detailed description of the sequential progression of CBT within the CH framework is provided elsewhere (Alladin, 2007, 2008), they are not described in detail here. For a therapy transcript, see Alladin (2008, p. 107–110), which illustrates how Roger, who was fearful of going to the local grocery store, was guided by the therapist to re-evaluate and change his maladaptive belief about 'The world is unsafe'. As a result of this session, Roger was able to modify his maladaptive beliefs and, consequently, his unrealistic fears about the world.

Cognitive restructuring, however, does not occur simply at one particular stage of therapy, it takes place throughout the entire treatment of agoraphobia. Therefore, the replacement of catastrophic cognitions occurs throughout the treatment, both as a treatment goal in itself and as a mechanism of change. The homework involving the completion of CRF (see Table 7.2), which is carried out throughout the whole treatment period serves as a powerful tool for refuting and replacing catastrophic cognitions by more adaptive thinking outside the therapy sessions. Table 7.2 illustrates how she refuted the cognitive distortions that were preventing her from going to the mall shopping.

As a result of the CBT, Margaret was able to modify her catastrophic cogitations about her fears and anxiety, and consequently, she managed to face the many situations she was avoiding. However, it should be mentioned that CBT served as an extra, and not the only, tool to increase Margaret's confidence in facing her fears. The studies of CBT with agoraphobia clearly demonstrate that CBT is a necessary, but not a sufficient, treatment to overcome agoraphobia (see review by Telch et al., 2014).

Healing self-wounds
After 10 sessions of CBT and hypnotherapy, Margaret made significant progress in learning to manage her anxiety. She felt less anxious, less depressed, the frequency and intensity of her migraine decreased, she was able to tolerate exposure *in vivo* therapy, and she was discharged from the hospital (was an inpatient for three months). However, she still continued outpatient therapy with the author and her psychiatrist (once a month, mainly for medication review). As her symptoms were not eliminated completely – she was still experiencing fear and avoiding some situations, and her migraine still persisted – she was interested to explore the root cause(s) of her agoraphobia and migraine attacks. The next segment of therapy described thus involved in-depth hypnotherapy and consisted of eliciting her self-wounds and detoxifying the meaning of her anxiety.

Elicitation of self-wounds
To access Margaret's self-wounds, if present, the affect bridge technique was used. The feeling of anxiety that she experienced during the exposure therapy related to 'Taking bus to mall downtown, shopping for 2 hours' (SUD 100) was used as a bridge to elicit her first anxiety attack. While experiencing intense anxiety, she became aware of starting to lose her hair

Table 7.2 Completed cognitive restructuring form

Date	A Activating event	B Irrational beliefs	C Consequences	D Disputation	E Effect of disputation
	Describe actual event, stream of thoughts, daydream, and so on, leading to unpleasant feelings	Write automatic thoughts and images that came in your mind. Rate beliefs or images 0–100%	1. *Emotion*: specify sad, anxious or angry. Rate feelings 1–100% 2. *Physiological*: Palpitations, pain, dizzy, sweat and so on. 3. *Behavioural*: Avoidance, in bed 4. *Conclusion*: Reaching conclusions	Challenge the automatic thoughts and images. Rate belief in rational response/image 0–100%	1. *Emotion*: Re-rate your feeling 1–100% 2. *Physiological*: Changes in bodily reactions (i.e., less shaking, less tense, etc.) 3. *Behavioural*: Action taken after disputation 4. *Conclusion*: Reappraise your conclusion and initial decision. Future beliefs in similar situation

Date	Situation	Negative thoughts	Symptoms	Rational response	Outcome
10 June 2012	Thinking of going shopping at the mall downtown	1. I will not be able to handle this (100) 2. I will lose control (100) 3. Everyone will look at me; it will be so embarrassing (100) 4. There will be no one to rescue me (100) 5. I will not be able to get home (100)	1. Anxious (90), fearful (90), panicky (80) 2. Dizzy, light-headed, sweating, agitated 3. Restless, don't want to leave home 4. I will not get out of this	1. I am not there yet, how do I know I will not be able to handle it. With all the training I had I may be able to deal with it (75). 2. I have never lost control. There is no reason why I would lose control. I may feel anxious but not lose control (80). 3. People mind their own business, people would not be focusing on me. Even if I feel anxious, this is a private thing, no one knows what goes inside me. I don't have to feel embarrassed if I feel anxious (80). 4. If I feel bad I can call my husband or my son (100). 5. If the worst happen, I can take a cab to home (100).	1. Less anxious (20), less fearful (20), no panic (0) 2. No longer feeling dizzy, light-headed, agitated or sweating. Feeling relaxed 3. No longer restless, wanted to go to the mall to see what happens 4. I managed to travel by the bus on my own and I managed to go to the mall. This proves I am getting better

three months after having her son. She continued to lose her hair and became completely bald after about 6 months. She remembered starting to feel anxious about going out, especially shopping, because she became fearful that people would found out she was bald, although she started wearing a wig. She was terrified that such an experience would be so embarrassing to her that she would 'lose control' and 'go crazy '. Even at home she became extremely conscious of her baldness that she would never take her wig off in front of either her husband or her son. She started having severe anticipatory anxiety about going out and began to experience headaches whenever she had to go anywhere outside her home. She had her first 'hemiplegic migraine' on the eve of going to her good friend's daughter's wedding. This friend whom she met at the factory she was working at had been her good friend for a number of years. She really wanted Margaret to come to the wedding, which took place at the local church and the wedding reception was at a local hotel, where most of the people she knew from the factory was going to be there. Margaret became terrified with the thought that she might feel anxious, lose control, and 'tear off' her wig in front of all those people at the wedding. This anticipatory fear was so horrifying to her that for several nights she did not sleep properly and ended up with a full-blown migraine on the eve of the wedding. She thought she was having a stroke and had to be taken to the Emergency Department of the local hospital by ambulance. Margaret stayed under observation at the hospital for 24 hours and then released with the diagnosis of 'acute migraine attack', and referred to a neurologist. Since then whenever Margaret felt pressurized or stressed out about going out, or whenever she husbands wanted to invite any relative at home, she would have a full-blown hemiplegic migraine and would stay in bed for at least 2 days.

From the affect bridge procedure it was hypothesized that (i) Margaret had a horrifying fear of being discovered that she was completely bald and (ii) the 'hemiplegic migraine', because of its severity and atypical symptomatology, served as a strong defence for not going out to public places. From the surfacing of these information it was formulated that Margaret needed to detoxify the meaning of her anxiety and to build sufficient confidence to deal with the reality of her baldness, rather than using her migraine as an avoidance behaviour.

Detoxification of meaning of anxiety
The split screen technique (Alladin, 2008; Cardena et al., 2000; Lynn & Cardena, 2007; Spiegel, 1981) was used to help Margaret detoxify the meaning of her anxiety and fears. This is a hypnotic strategy that utilizes

the 'adult' or 'strong ego state' to help the 'weak ego state' deal with low self-esteem and anxiety-provoking situations. It also facilitates the 'two' ego states to work together as a team, rather than splitting from each other, when the self is confronted, threatened or stressed out. The therapy transcript presented subsequently illustrates how the split screen technique was used with Margaret to help her deal with the toxic meaning of her anxiety. The transcript begins while Margaret was in a deep hypnotic trance, bolstered by ego-strengthening suggestions.

THERAPIST: Now I would like you to imagine sitting in front of a large TV or cinema screen, which is vertically split in two halves, consisting of a right side and a left side. Can you imagine this?

[Margaret raised her 'YES' finger. Ideomotor signals were already set up – 'YES' represented raising her right index finger and 'NO' was represented by raising her left index finger.]

THERAPIST: Imagine the right side of the screen is lighting up as if it's ready to project an image. Imagine yourself being projected on the right side of the screen, just as you are now. Feeling very relaxed, very comfortable, in complete control, and aware of everything. And now become aware of all the things that you achieved in the past three months. You learned how to relax, you learned to deal with your fears and anxiety, and you managed to go downtown on your own and managed to shop at the mall. Do you feel these good feelings? [Margaret was not able remember many happy memories from her younger years as she was housebound for over 17 years. But she was very proud of the good work she did at the hospital and, therefore, she chose to remember the good things that happened to her in the immediate past 3 months.]

[Margaret raised her 'YES' finger.]

THERAPIST: That's very good. Do you feel the sense of achievement?

[Margaret raised her 'YES' finger.]

THERAPIST: Are you thinking about your achievement related to having made very good progress with your anxiety in the past three months?

[Margaret raised her 'YES' finger.]

THERAPIST: Just focus on the good feelings and become aware that you managed to get discharged from the hospital in three months and managed to go shopping on your own downtown after seventeen years. This is a big achievement. This proves to you that you have a strong side, a successful side, a side that can rescue you from difficulties and help you succeed. We are going to call this part of you the 'adult side', your 'strong part' or your 'adult ego state'. Is that acceptable to you?

[Margaret raised her 'YES' finger.]

THERAPIST: Now leave this side of yourself on the right side of the screen and imagine yourself being projected on the left side of the screen, feeling anxious, as if you are in a situation that causes fear and anxiety for you. Become aware of feeling anxious and fearful. Can you imagine this?

[Margaret raised her 'YES' finger.]

THERAPIST: Now become aware of all the feelings that you are experiencing. Don't be afraid to allow all the anxious feelings to come over you, because soon we will show you how to deal with them. Become aware of all the physical sensations that you are feeling. Become aware of all the thoughts that are going through your mind and become aware of your behaviors. Can you feel these?

[Margaret raised her 'YES' finger.]

THERAPIST: Just become aware of the whole experience and we are going to call this part of you the 'weak part of you' as we discussed before. Is this acceptable to you?

[Margaret raised her 'YES' finger.]

THERAPIST: Now imagine, your 'adult ego state' is stepping out from the right side into the left side of the screen. Can you imagine this?

[Margaret raised her 'YES' finger.]

THERAPIST: Imagine your 'adult ego state' is reassuring your 'weak ego state'. She is telling your 'weak ego state' not to be afraid because she is here to help her out and guide her how to deal with her fear and anxiety. From now on, the 'weak part' of you don't have to handle difficulties on her own, she can work as a team with the 'strong part' of you. Imagine the 'adult part' of you is telling the 'weak part' of you that in therapy she had learned many strategies for dealing with fears and symptoms of anxiety and, therefore, she can teach you these strategies, guiding you what to do. Imagine she is demonstrating to the 'weak part' of you how to relax, how to let go, how to flow, and how to reason with fearful thoughts. Continue to imagine this until you feel the 'weak part' of you feel reassured and now she knows what to do when feeling anxious. Imagine your 'weak part' feels protected and empowered knowing she is not alone, she can get help from the 'adult ego state' whenever the needs arise. The 'weak part' also realizes that the 'strong part' is a part of your self as well. They both belong to your Self. So from now on there is not need to feel separated from the 'adult ego state '.

The split screen technique was repeated over several sessions, with main focus on helping Margaret learn to tolerate the situations she had been avoiding. Margaret found the technique very useful. The self-efficacious images gave her the confidence that she could deal with her symptoms of anxiety, rather than catastrophizing about them and blaming herself of being weak or incompetent.

The split screen technique also focused on helping Margaret come to terms with her baldness and to become less preoccupied with what others might think of her baldness. The 'strong ego state' coached the 'weak part' to come to terms with the baldness just as people come to terms with being overweight, being too tall, being too short and so on. The 'strong ego state' also reminded the 'weak part' that it was a hormonal condition, nothing to do with her personality or self-esteem. The doctor clearly stated that it was a hormonal thing and not a reflection of any form of neglect or incompetence on her part. The doctor believed it could have been triggered by her pregnancy or post-labour. He also reassured her that her hair was not growing because of the hormonal factor and not due to her lack of trying. Margaret saw several specialists and they all reassured her that the main cause was hormonal.

From the split screen technique Margaret also realized that – although it was embarrassing, especially for a woman, to be bald – she did not have to be scared with what others would think of her. She also came up with the revelation that her baldness should not stop her from going out. However, Margaret expressed 'not knowing what to say to people in a conversation' as she had been 'isolated from the world' for such a long time. Margaret was given two sessions of social skills training, which made her feel more confident about having a conversation with people. Following these sessions, Margaret was no longer ruminating about her migraine and she commented: 'I no longer have a migraine. '

Promoting acceptance and gratitude

As discussed in Chapter 1, patients with anxiety disorders tend to suppress re-experiencing of their initial trauma as it causes extreme distress (Wolfe, 2005, 2006). Such avoidance or intolerance of inner suffering can be regarded as lack of acceptance within the context of third-wave CBT

(Baer & Huss, 2008). Although Margaret's suppression and avoidance of her self-wounds warded off her distressing experience temporarily, unfortunately it maintained her symptoms. For this reason, it was important to help Margaret accept her emotional distress related to her baldness, especially as it was considered a permanent condition. However, acceptance is not merely tolerance of inner hurt; it is the active and nonjudgemental embracing of painful experience in the here and now, involving undefended exposure to thoughts, feelings and bodily sensations as they occur (Hayes, 2004). Margaret was helped to reduce her suffering by helping her to (i) observe different thoughts and feelings about her baldness that she experienced; (ii) establish the relationship between her baldness and her avoidance behaviours; (iii) establish the relationship between her baldness and her migraine; (iv) create a new stimulus (e.g., relaxation response) that was less distracting or not distressing at all to focus on (Hayes, 2004) and (v) decentre from distressing thoughts, negative feelings, and unpleasant body sensations (Segal, Williams, & Teasdale, 2002). Levitt, Brown, Orsillo and Barlow (2004) have provided empirical evidence for the effectiveness of acceptance-based interventions in the management of anxiety disorders. Several techniques, including (i) gratitude education, (ii) gratitude training, (iii) acceptance training, (iv) acceptance and gratitude hypnotherapy and (v) mind–body–heart integration were used to help Margaret cultivate acceptance. These techniques are described next.

Gratitude education and training
Sense of gratitude is used as a means to cultivate acceptance in patients with agoraphobia. Gratitude is a feeling or attitude in acknowledgement of a benefit that one has received or will receive. Studies suggest that people who are grateful have higher levels of subjective well-being, have higher levels of control of their environments, have more positive ways of coping with the difficulties they experience in life, spend more time planning how to deal with the problem, are less likely to try to avoid or deny their problems, and they sleep better (for review and references see Chapter 2).

Gratitude education
Gratitude education focuses on drawing broad generalizations about different cultural values and beliefs, and comparing Western and non-Western expectations of life and achievement. The gratitude education helped Margaret recognize that values are human-made, subjective, and culturally determined. This comparative understanding of societal values helped her re-examine her own meaning of success and failure and helped

her to begin to focus on what she has (e.g., home, husband, son, financial security, good physical health, etc.) rather than ruminating with what she did not have (full hair).

Acceptance training
As Margaret was so centred on her baldness, she was not mindful of acceptance and gratitude. To increase awareness of her sense of acceptance, she was encouraged to carry out a series of exercises, some of which are listed as follows:

- Focusing on here and now.
- Observing emotional experiences and their contexts non-judgementally.
- Separation of secondary emotions from primary emotions (e.g., not to get upset for feeling upset; not to feel anxious for feeling anxious; not feeling upset for feeling fearful; not feeling depressed for feeling depressed).
- Learning to tolerate distress rather than fighting it (flow with it).
- Adopting healthy and adaptive means to deal with her anxiety rather than focusing on her migraine.
- Toleration of migraine without going to bed.
- Recontextualizing meaning of anxiety, for example, from 'this will be so embarrassing, I will freak out' to 'it will be somewhat uncomfortable, but I can handle it'.
- Exercising radical acceptance – ability to welcome those things in life that are hard, unpleasant, or very painful.
- Embracing good or bad experience as part of life.
- Purposely allowing experience (thoughts, emotions, desires, urges, sensations, etc.) to occur without attempting to block or suppress them.

Gratitude training
Gratitude training involves doing various gratitude tasks. Margaret was assigned a list of gratitude tasks as listed here, and she was advised to do at least one of the tasks daily. This exercise was very difficult for Margaret as she had been isolated for so long. With encouragement from the therapist, she managed to do the homework.

- Writing gratitude letters
- Writing a gratitude journal
- Remembering gratitude moments
- Making gratitude visits to people she was grateful to
- Practicing gratitude self-talk.

Acceptance and gratitude hypnotherapy
Hypnosis is used to make acceptance-based therapy more experiential (Alladin, 2006). While Margaret was in a deep hypnotic trance, she was offered the following suggestions, adapted from Alladin (2006, p. 303; 2007, p. 197), to strengthen her sense of gratitude.

THERAPIST: Just continue to experience this beautiful sensation of peace and relaxation, tranquillity and calm flowing all over your mind and body. Just notice feeling calm, peaceful, and a sense of well-being. Feeling calm, peaceful, and in total harmony. No tension, no pressure, completely relaxed both mentally and physically. Feeling happy that you can relax so deeply, that you can let go, and calm down completely. You feel pleased and grateful that you can let go completely.

Now become aware of your heart. Notice how peaceful you feel in your heart, how calm you feel in your heart, and you feel a sense of gratitude in your heart. When you feel good in your heart, you feel good in your mind and in your body. Do you feel good in your heart?

[Margaret raised her 'YES' finger.]

THERAPIST: Do you feel good in your mind, body, and heart?

[Margaret raised her 'YES' finger.]

THERAPIST: Very good! You have the ability to feel good in your mind, in your body and in your heart. All the major religions state that when you wake up in the morning, if you have a roof over your head, you have bread to eat, and water to drink, and are in fairly good health, then you have everything. Just become aware of all the things you have and all the things you are grateful for. When living in the modern world, it's okay to have goals and ambitions. When we achieve them, they can be seen as bonuses and pluses as we have lots of other resources. When we don't achieve our goals and ambitions, it is disappointing, but we have enough resources to live a comfortable life. Do you agree with these comments and observation?

[Margaret raised her 'YES' finger.]

It is important that the acceptance-based hypnotherapy is carried out after the acceptance and gratitude training. In the absence of this training a patient may not appreciate the therapeutic meaning of acceptance and gratitude, and may reject the hypnotic suggestions. Margaret found both the acceptance-based training and hypnotherapy very helpful. They gave her a new perspective on success and failure, and they made her become more aware of the many things she is grateful for. Most importantly, she felt less preoccupied and fearful about her baldness.

Mind–body–heart integration
This component of acceptance-based hypnotherapy focuses on the integration of various subsystems in the body. As discussed in Chapter 2, heart-focused positive emotional state engenders synchronization of the entire body system to produce PC (McCraty et al., 2009). Based on these scientific findings, Alladin (2014a) has developed the breathing with your heart technique to generate coherence (harmony) of the entire system (mind, body, brain, heart and emotion). This technique integrates both Western (heart viewed as a complex information centre) and Eastern (heart regarded as the big mind) concepts of the heart to produce psychological well-being. Lankton (2008, pp. 45–50) has also developed a similar technique that he calls *Heart Joy*, which creates a sense of emotional well-being.

Heart education
Margaret was given a scientific account of the joint role of the heart and positive emotions in the generation of PC, which promotes healing, emotional stability and optimal performance. The similarities and the differences between the Western and Eastern theories of the mind and 'heart' are also discussed. Margaret found the Eastern view of the heart – viewed as the big mind – very intriguing but empowering, as now she knew what to do to feel good in her heart.

Heart–mind training combined with hypnotherapy
Heart-mind training helps patients with agoraphobia cope with negative feelings (heavy heart) triggered by public situations. By breathing with the heart, agoraphobic patients are able to shift their attention away from their mind to their heart. Moreover, when a person feels good in his or her heart, the person experiences a sense of comfort and joy because we validate reality by the way we feel and not by the way we think (Fredrickson, 2002; Isen, 1998). As discussed in Chapter 2, logic does not always equate good affect, but feeling good in one's heart (e.g., by thinking about something one is grateful for) always creates a positive affect (Welwood, 1983).

Breathing with your heart technique
This transcript from a session with Margaret illustrates how the technique was introduced into the therapy. The script begins with Margaret being in a deep hypnotic trance:

> THERAPIST: Just continue to experience this beautiful sensation of peace and
> tranquility, relaxation and calm flowing throughout your mind
> and body, giving you such a pleasant feeling, such a soothing

sensation, that you feel completely relaxed both mentally and physically. Do you feel relaxed both mentally and physically?

[Margaret raised her 'YES' finger.]

THERAPIST: Now I would like you to focus on the centre of your heart. [Pause for 30 seconds.] Can you imagine this?

[Margaret raised her 'YES' finger.]

THERAPIST: Now I would like you to imagine breathing in and out with your heart. [Pause for 30 seconds.] Can you imagine this?

[Margaret raised her 'YES' finger.]

THERAPIST: Continue to imagine breathing in and out of your heart. [She was allowed to continue with this exercise for 2 minutes; the therapist repeated at regular intervals: 'Just continue to imagine breathing with your heart' as she did the exercise.] Now I would like you to slow down your breathing. Breathe in and out at 7-second intervals. Breathe in with your heart ... 1 ... 2 ... 3 ... 4 ... 5 ... 6 ... 7 and now breathe out with your heart ... 1 ... 2 ... 3 ... 4 ... 5 ... 6 ... 7. And now as you breathing in and out with your heart I want you to become aware of something in your life that you feel good about, something that you feel grateful for. [Pause for 30 seconds.] Are you able to focus on something that you are grateful for in your life?

[Margaret raised her 'YES' finger.]

THERAPIST: Just become aware of that feeling and soon you will feel good in your heart. [After 10 seconds.] Do you feel it?

[Margaret raised her 'YES' finger.]

THERAPIST: Just become aware of this good feeling in your heart. [Pause for 30 seconds.] Now I would like to become aware of the good feeling in your mind, in your body, and in your heart. Do you feel this?

[Margaret raised her 'YES' finger.]

THERAPIST: Now that you feel good in your mind, in your body, and in your heart, you feel a sense of balance, a sense of harmony. Do you feel this sense of harmony?

[Margaret raised her 'YES' finger.]

THERAPIST: From now on, whenever and wherever you are, you can create this good feeling by imagining breathing with your heart and focusing on something that you are grateful for. With practice you will get better and better at it. Now you know what to do to make your heart feel lighter.

Summary

The chapter described a wide variety of behavioural, cognitive, hypnotic, unconscious, and acceptance and mindfulness-based strategies for treating agoraphobia. The therapist, based on case formulation, can select the most fitting techniques for each individual patient with agoraphobia. The case of Margaret illustrated that symptom-focused treatment is necessary, but not sufficient for treating the underlying determinants of agoraphobia. The case clearly demonstrates that durable treatment outcome requires a multi-component approach to treatment consisting of both conscious and unconscious strategies. Moreover, the chapter focused on different strategies to prepare the patient for exposure *in vivo* therapy, which is the gold standard treatment for agoraphobia. In addition, several techniques were combined to enhance the effect of exposure therapy with agoraphobia.

8

Separation Anxiety Disorder

Case of Andrew

Andrew, a 12-year-old, grade 7 student, was referred to the author for psychological treatment for separation anxiety disorder by his paediatrician. Andrew was experiencing excessive anxiety and fear whenever he had to leave home or be away from his mother. He was terrified to be away from his mother because he feared something bad would happen to her. By being with his mother, he felt a sense of control over the situation, which made him feel less anxious.

Andrew had always been a clingy child and he had been exhibiting separation anxiety in situations where he was separated from his mother. Even when his mother was at home, he felt anxious if she is not in the same room. Although he slept in his own bedroom at night, he wanted his and his parents' bedroom doors to be open, and he would often come into their bedroom in the middle of the night. When going to school he insisted that his mother drove him to and collected him from school, and he insisted that he called his mother 2–3 times a day on his cell phone. The clinging behaviours were more apparent when he started kindergarten, but it gradually improved. Occasionally he refused to go to school, especially on Mondays, because of headaches or stomach cramps. However, his anxiety was not persistent or severe, and he responded well to reassurance from his parents. Although Andrew was close to both of his parents, he had no anxiety about separating from his father.

The fear and anxiety became severe in the past two years, following a motor vehicle accident (MVA). On a Saturday morning while his mother

Integrative CBT for Anxiety Disorders: An Evidence-Based Approach to Enhancing Cognitive Behavioural Therapy with Mindfulness and Hypnotherapy, First Edition. Assen Alladin.
© 2016 John Wiley & Sons, Ltd. Published 2016 by John Wiley & Sons, Ltd.

was driving home from the grocery store, she was involved in a MVA. As she was turning right at a four-way stop junction, a mini-van, coming from the left 't-boned' her vehicle, damaging the front part of her car on the driver's side. The driver indicated that he thought he had the right of way and he thus drove across the junction without realizing that Andrew's mother was turning right. Andrew (was 10 years old) and his sister (was 8 years old) were sitting in the back of their car. Although his mother was not seriously injured – except for minor cuts in her face and left arm sustained from flying glasses from the broken windshield – she was shocked and shaken by the experience. It took a while before she could recover from the shock, and it took a while before she could call her husband at home.

The children did not sustain any injury. However, they were equally shocked by the experience as it happened so suddenly and at a place (in their neighbourhood) where they least expected to have an accident (four-way stop). In addition to being shocked, Andrew became terrified as he thought his mother could have died unexpectedly. Since the accident Andrew became progressively more attached to his mother and felt anxious whenever he had to be away from her. While at home he did not allow his mother to leave. If she went shopping or anywhere, he had to go with her. Gradually, he stopped visiting any friends or leaving home to play sports. He had become dependent on his mother for reassurance and management of his fear and anxiety, thereby losing confidence in his ability to manage situations independently. He was frequently absent from school as he could not tolerate the high distress associated with being away from his mother for the whole day. Consequently, Andrew was not functioning well and it was also very stressful for the family to deal with his sense of insecurity. At this point, the family consulted Andrew's family physician, who referred him to a child psychiatrist. The psychiatrist referred Andrew to the author as he believed he needed psychotherapy rather than medication.

Diagnostic Criteria for Separation Anxiety Disorder

The DSM-V (American Psychiatric Association, 2013, pp. 190–191) diagnostic criteria for SAD include:

A. Excessive anxiety or fear concerning separation from an attached figure, which is deemed developmentally inappropriate, as evidenced by at least three of the following:
   1. Recurrent excessive distress when anticipating or experiencing separation from home or from major attachment figures.

2. Persistent and excessive worry about losing major attachment figures or about possible harm to them, such as illness, injury, disasters, or death.
3. Persistent and excessive worry about experiencing an untoward event (e.g., getting lost, being kidnapped, having an accident, becoming ill) that causes separation from a major attachment figure.
4. Persistent reluctance or refusal to go out, away from home, to school, to work, or elsewhere because of fear of separation.
5. Persistent and excessive fear of or reluctance about being alone or without major attachment figures at home or in other settings.
6. Persistent reluctance or refusal to sleep away from home or go to sleep without being near a major attachment figure.
7. Repeated nightmares involving the theme of separation.
8. Repeated complaints of physical symptoms (e.g., headaches, stomach aches, nausea, vomiting) when separation from major attachment figures occurs or is anticipated.

B. The fear, anxiety, or avoidance is persistent, lasting at least 4 weeks in children and adolescents and typically 6 months or more in adults.
C. The disturbance causes clinically significant distress or impairment in social, academic, occupational, or other important areas of functioning.
D. The disturbance is not due to another psychiatric disorder.

Prevalence of Separation Anxiety Disorder

SAD is one of the most common disorders experienced by children and adolescents in the United States (Doobay, 2008). In children, 6- to 12-month prevalence is estimated to be approximately 4%; in adolescents, the 12-month prevalence is 1.6%; and in adults, the 12-month prevalence is 0.9–1.9% (American Psychiatric Association, 2013). The gender dispersion of the disorder is inconsistent. While clinical samples of children indicate equal prevalence rates in males and females, community samples show the disorder to be more frequent in females (Masi, Mucci, & Millepiedi, 2001). Lower socioeconomic status and lower parental education level have been found to be associated with greater prevalence of SAD (Bird, Gould, Yager, Staghezza & Canino, 1989). Cultural variations have also been observed. European children show lower prevalence rate of anxiety disorders (Orvaschel, 1988), but in New Zealand, SAD is the most frequently diagnosed childhood anxiety disorder (Anderson, Williams, McGee, & Silva, 1987). SD is highly comorbid with other anxiety disorders (American Psychiatric Association, 2013).

Causes of Separation Anxiety Disorder

The etiology of SAD is not fully understood. Several factors have been identified to contribute to the disorder, including (i) environmental change, (ii) genetic link, (iii) biological vulnerability, (iv) quality of attachment, (v) developmental history, (vi) negative rumination and (vii) maladaptive behaviours (*Gale Encyclopedia of Mental Disorders*, pp. 880–884; Kapalka & Peters, 2013).

In addition to the factors listed in Table 8.1, it has been identified that in children in whom the diagnosis of SAD persists over time, there is (i) higher prevalence of ODD, (ii) greater prevalence of depression, (iii) more impairment

Table 8.1   Factors that are known to precipitate SAD

Environmental change	SAD is often precipitated by stress or change in the child's life such as death or illness of a close relative or pet, changing school, or moving home
Genetic link	Research indicates a genetic link between SAD in children and a history of anxiety, PD or depression in their parents
Biological vulnerability	Hyperactivity of the limbic, specifically the pituitary–hypothalamic–adrenal axis, appears to underlie the biological vulnerability of SAD
Quality of attachment	The quality of attachment between children and their parents has been observed to lead to SAD. Children who feel emotionally distant from their parents tend to draw more closely to their parents. Other family factors that are associated with SAD include family conflict, marital discord, frequent negative feedback from parents, and parental restriction
Developmental history	Slower developmental milestones can foster anxiety within a child and thus making separation from the parents more difficult
Negative rumination	Repeated worries with such thoughts as getting lost, parents getting hurt, and so on cause excessive negative affect in the child. Consequently the child is so overwhelmed by anxiety and fears that he or she is not able to think rationally and may develop SAD
Maladaptive behaviours	A child's distressing behaviours such as crying or clinging related to certain situations, people, or places can be easily reinforced by parents. Gradually these behaviours may become the child's mode of expression

associated with ADHD, (iv) high degree of impairment in adulthood and (v) poor response to treatment (Foley et al., 2004; Silove et al., 2010). As SAD appears to represent a heterogeneous disorder, resulting from complex interactions among inherited traits, environment, personal experience and neurobiological vulnerability, it is unlikely that a single cause of the disorder will be found.

Treatment of Separation Anxiety Disorder

As with other anxiety disorders, pharmacological treatment is the most widely used treatment for SAD. A variety of agents including SSRIs, TCAs, benzodiazepines and buspirone have been used with SAD. Of all these medications, SSRIs have been shown to be the most effective pharmacological treatment for decreasing symptoms of anxiety in children (Kapalka & Peters, 2013; Reinblatt & Walkup, 2005). However, the treatment literature recommends that pharmacotherapy should not be used as the primary treatment for SAD but as an adjunct to other treatments in children whose symptoms have failed to respond to previous interventions and who are significantly impaired (American Academy of Child and Adolescent Psychiatry, 1997; Masi, Mucci, & Millepiedi, 2001). Other disadvantages of medications with SAD relate to delayed onset of action of some medications, potential side effects and relapse after treatment discontinuation (Kariuki & Stein, 2013). On the other hand, the benefits of pharmacotherapy for SAD include relatively rapid reduction in symptoms severity, cost effectiveness and wider availability (Sadock & Sadock, 2003).

Because of their demonstrated efficacy, psychosocial interventions, particularly CBT, are considered the first-line treatment for SAD in children and adolescents (Masi et al., 2001; Kapalka & Peters, 2013). CBT for SAD involves psychoeducation about the anxiety and fearful situations, cognitive restructuring of maladaptive patterns of thinking, exposure therapy, learning coping skills, management of somatic symptoms and relapse prevention (Compton et al., 2010). Some therapists have incorporated CBT in comprehensive treatment protocols for SAD that can be used in specialized clinics, in community settings, or in schools. One of the most popular of these protocols is the *Coping Cat Programme* developed by Kendall (Kendall, 1990). The Coping Cat Programme requires a child or adolescent with SAD to attend 12–16 weeks sessions of therapy; each session lasting 60 minutes. The first 6–8 weeks of the programme teach children (i) new skills such as identifying anxious feelings and cognitive distortions, (ii) new coping strategies and actions and (iii) understanding behavioural exposure techniques. The second 8–16 sessions focus on coaching children how to apply the new skills in real situations. To prevent relapse the children are assigned homework tasks. The effectiveness of the Coping Cat Programme with SAD is well documented in the literature (Kendall, 1994; Kendall et al., 1997; Kendall & Southam-Gerow, 1996). It is recognized as the most widely disseminated CBT protocol for childhood anxiety disorders, and it has been used with success in the United States, Australia and Canada (Sacks, et al., 2013).

Although CBT is considered the first-line treatment for SAD and includes better tolerability, greater likelihood of maintaining response after treatment has been terminated, and cost-effectiveness in some settings (Sadock & Sadock, 2003; Veale, 2003), it has limitations. First, it sets structural barriers to treatment such as language and transportation, lack of access to CBT, long waiting lists, slower response to treatment and time-consuming nature of the therapy (Kariuki & Stein, 2013). Second, only about 50% of the children and adolescents diagnosed with SAD show significant clinical response (e.g., Kendal, 1994; Kendal et al., 1997, 2008; Liber et al., 2008). Kapalka and Peters (2013, p. 273) have therefore concluded that the currently available psychological interventions alone are not sufficient or helpful for some patients with SAD. These reviews indicate the urgency of developing more effective psychological treatment for SAD. One of the ways to enhance the effects of psychological treatment for SAD is to make the intervention more comprehensive. CH for SAD described in this chapter attempts to broaden the comprehensiveness of the treatment protocol for SAD.

Cognitive Hypnotherapy for Separation Anxiety Disorder

Hypnotherapy for Managing Symptoms of Separation Anxiety Disorder

As described in other clinical chapters, four to six of the initial sessions of CH consist of hypnotherapy, which is specifically targeted at symptoms management. This phase of therapy serves as a preparation for more complex therapy of exploring the roots of SAD later in therapy if the needs arise. The hypnotherapy components include (i) relaxation training, (ii) demonstration of the power of mind over the body, (iii) ego-strengthening, (iv) expansion of awareness, (v) coping with somatic symptoms, (vi) self-hypnosis and (vii) PHS. Hypnotherapy is introduced again later in therapy with patients who elect to pursue with uncovering work. The initial sessions of hypnotherapy, therefore, for some patients, serve as a preparatory phase for more complex therapy of exploring the roots of the anxiety disorder later in the therapy. These multi-components described in this chapter should be used fluidly and simultaneously throughout treatment to maximize their effects (Velting et al., 2004). Before starting the hypnotherapy, however, it is important to spend a session on psychoeducation when working with children.

Psychoeducation
The first step in the management of SAD, usually involving a few sessions, focus on psychoeducation of the parents and child, as well as treatment planning (Masi et al., 2001; Jurbergs & Ledley, 2005). The psychoeducation involves providing information about the length, frequency, nature and the duration of the treatment. It is emphasized that the treatment for SAD is time-limited, usually about 20 sessions, and it is present- and problem-focused. The interventions concentrate on changing current behaviours and improving functioning rather than delving into the origins of SAD, which may occur if the condition does not improve or there is a need for deeper exploration.

The psychoeducation also includes an explanation of the meaning of the symptoms, their consequences on the child's daily life, the treatment strategies involved and the prognosis of the illness. Such an approach serves as a precursor to a strong therapeutic alliance and good compliance with the treatment. If the therapist elects to use CBT, both the child and the parents should be engaged in discussion about the nature and treatment of his or her difficulties in terms of CBT. The parents and child are informed about the factors that maintain SAD over time, and what will be done during treatment to try to ameliorate the problems. The parents should also understand the relationship between worry and anxiety, and how avoidance behaviour and reassurance-seeking can make the symptoms worse and maintain the disorder (Gosch et al., 2006; Velting et al., 2004). Moreover, by avoiding situations, the child with SAD never gets the chance to learn that the bad things that he or she fears are unlikely to happen. In treatment, the child, the parents and therapist work together, to help the child confront feared situations gradually through specific behavioural strategies. To a large extent, the therapist, in collaboration with the parents, coaches the child to learn new ways of handling anxiety-provoking situations (Heyne, 2006).

When the child is young, and the severity of the symptoms is mild to moderate, parental intervention may suffice. However, for this to occur the therapist should help and educate the parents to (i) encourage their child to face new situations, (ii) refrain from criticizing the child excessively, (iii) help the child to carry out activities despite his or her anxieties and (iv) collaborate with school personnel if the child was avoiding school.

Relaxation training

Relaxation training is one of the major components of Coping Cat programme for SAD. The main purpose of the relaxation training is to teach children with SAD relaxation techniques that could be used to 'alleviate symptoms of anxiety' (Sacks et al., 2013). More specifically, training in relaxation aims to provide children with SAD with an efficient means of managing physiological discomfort in situations associated with anxiety (Heyne, 2014). By learning to identify and manage discomforting feelings, children and adolescents are better placed to confront challenging situations and to employ other skills and strategies in the process of coping while being away from home or attached figures.

As Andrew experienced high levels of anxiety, nervousness and elevated physiological reactions, he found the relaxation induced by hypnosis very calming and soothing. Because of his high susceptibility to hypnosis, he was able to generate profound mental and physical relaxation without much effort. His hypnotic talent was further utilized to help him dissociate from anxiety-related situations such as being away from his mother or being at school (yet being aware of his surroundings). The good feelings associated with the relaxation experience gave Andrew the hope that he could learn to deal with anxious and fearful situations.

Demonstration of the power of the mind over the body

As children with SAD lack confidence, they progressively become more dependent on their parents for managing their fears and anxiety. It is therefore very important to empower these children. To achieve this and to ratify the credibility of the hypnotic intervention, eye and body catalepsies were introduced in the second hypnotherapy session. Chapter 3 provides a transcript for inducing eye and body catalepsies, and it also offers an explanation of the cataleptic effects in terms of self-hypnosis. Andrew was amazed that he could not open his eyes or get out of the reclining chair. He found this session empowering as it instilled in him the hope and confidence that he could tap on his own personal resources to deal with his fears and anxiety. Moreover, the session provided credibility to the hypnotic intervention, which created a sense of positive expectancy and strengthened the therapeutic alliance. Furthermore, Andrew became very interested in hypnosis and its application to healing, and asked the author for titles of books he could read.

In addition, the hypnotherapy sessions prepared Andrew for *in vivo* exposure later in the therapy. As noted in Chapter 7, a significant number of patients with anxiety disorder, particularly those with severe symptoms, are not able to tolerate anxiety and distress associated with *in vivo* exposure therapy and, as a result, they drop out of therapy. As exposure is a very important component of treatment for SAD, hypnotherapy – through experiential learning (catalepsy and positive trance experience) – provides a powerful vehicle for helping patients build confidence to tolerate fearful reaction.

Ego strengthening

Ego-strengthening suggestions were offered to Andrew to increase his confidence in his ability to manage his symptoms of anxiety. While in deep hypnotic trance, Andrew was encouraged to visualize himself coping with anxious situations head-on, rather than avoiding them. Andrew indicated that the relaxation response and the ego-strengthening suggestions made him feel strong and confident dealing with his symptoms. He found the following ego-strengthening suggestion very helpful:

- 'Every day you will feel calmer and more relaxed as a result of this treatment and as a result of you listening to your Self-Hypnosis CD every day.'
- 'As you listen to your CD every day, you will learn how to let go and take it easy. You will learn how to flow.'

At the end of the first hypnotherapy session, Andrew was given a self-hypnosis CD to listen to every day at home (further discussed under the section 'Self-hypnosis training'). To be consistent with AMBT (discussed later in this chapter; also see Chapter 2) and the latest research on 'suppression' (e.g., Wegner, 2011), the words 'control' or 'suppression' are not used, instead the words 'coping' or 'dealing' are used.

Expansion of awareness

As mentioned earlier, children with SAD lack confidence in their problem-solving abilities and therefore they tend to rely on their parents for managing their fears and anxiety. Unfortunately, this process leads to further cogitation with their distorted thinking and associated symptoms, resulting in constriction of emotions and feelings. Andrew reported feeling anxious constantly and unable to experience different affect, particularly happy or positive feelings. It is thus important to help these children broaden their range of thinking and feeling, otherwise they are likely to be stuck in this negative trance, maintaining and aggravating their symptoms. To expand his range of emotions and feelings, Andrew was introduced to EAT as described in Chapter 2. While Andrew was in deep hypnotic trance, he was first directed to focus on the relaxation response:

> You have now become so deeply relaxed and you are in such a deep hypnotic trance that your mind and body feel completely relaxed, totally relaxed. You begin to feel a beautiful sensation of peace and relaxation, tranquility and calm, flowing all over your mind and body. Giving you such a pleasant, and such a soothing sensation all over your mind and body, that you feel completely relaxed, totally relaxed both mentally and physically. And yet you are aware of everything. You are aware of all the sound and noise around you, you are aware of your thoughts and imagination, and yet you feel so relaxed, so calm and so peaceful. This shows that you have the ability to relax, to let go, and to put everything on hold. This shows that you have the ability to flow. You can be aware of everything and yet you can flow with everything around you.

The next set of suggestions were offered to help Andrew experience a variety of emotions and feelings.

> Now you can become aware of all the good feelings you are feelings. You feel calm, peaceful, relaxed and very, very comfortable. You may also become aware of feeling heavy, light, or detached, or distancing away from everything, becoming more and more detached, distancing away from everything, drifting into a deep, deep hypnotic state. You may also feel good knowing that you can relax completely. Feeling happy to know that you have the ability to relax and flow. It feels so good knowing that you can feel and do all these things.

With EAT, Andrew discovered that he had the ability to relax and feel different feelings and sensations. He was surprised that he could put things on hold, that is, although he was aware of his fears, anxiety and concerns, he was able to detach from his problems. He was also surprised that he could 'flow' with what was happening around him. With practice Andrew was able to 'flow' in different situations. Andrew's ability to produce, amplify and express a variety of positive feelings and experiences gave him the confidence that he could learn to cope with his anxiety symptoms.

Hypnosis-assisted imaginal exposure

To gain further control over his anxiety, Andrew was introduced to imaginal exposure (Wolpe, 1958; Wolpe & Lazarus, 1966), which is considered to be an important component of CH for SAD (Golden, 2012). In hypnosis-assisted imaginal exposure, the child uses his imagination to see himself being self-efficacious (successful) in a stressful situation. For example, before heading off to school, a child could imagine himself handling the separation from his mother. Instead of crying, he could see himself calmly saying goodbye to his mother. Use of such positive mental imagery can help the child rehearse separating from an attached figure, which may decrease his or her anxiety when the real separation occurs (King et al., 2001).

While in deep hypnosis, Andrew was directed to bring on his anxious experience associated with separating from his mother. He was encouraged to use his relaxation response or self-hypnosis to 'flow' with his anxious and fearful reactions.

> When I count from ONE to FIVE, by the time you hear me say FIVE, you will begin to feel whatever emotion or reaction that is associated with your thoughts about going to school.

Andrew was then helped to amplify the affect associated with going to school and being away from home.

> When I count slowly from ONE to FIVE, as I count you will begin to experience the anxious feelings more and more intensely, so that when I reach the count of FIVE, at the count of FIVE you will feel the full reaction as strongly as you can bear it. ONE ... TWO ... THREE ... FOUR ... FIVE. Now notice what you feel and you can describe it to me.

Andrew was then instructed to utilize self-hypnosis to 'flow' with his anxious and fearful reactions.

> Now imagine using your self-hypnosis to cope with the anxiety feeling. Since you have the ability to relax and put things on hold, you can let go and calm down.

After several repetition of this set of suggestions, Andrew was able to relax completely, while imagining being at school. This imaginal exposure in trance helped Andrew cope with the anxiety feeling at school. Moreover, this technique encouraged him to focus on his anxious feelings head-on, rather than catastrophizing or cogitating about his symptoms. There is some evidence that intense exposure to fear-provoking situations lead to improvements in avoidance behaviour, anxiety sensitivity and self-efficacy (Morissette, Spiegel, & Heinrichs, 2006).

The imaginal exposure technique was also used to help Andrew deal with other situations where he was away from his mother. To increase his confidence further regarding being away from his mother, Andrew was encouraged to participate in exposure *in vivo* therapy. However, before starting the *in vivo* exposure, Andrew was taught several coping techniques, including dealing with his somatic symptoms, self-hypnosis training, CBT and SD, to ensure compliance and success with the therapy (this issue was discussed in detail in Chapter 7). Moreover, these techniques were consolidated by PHS.

Coping with somatic symptoms
This component of CH helped Andrew recognize and deal with his somatic responses to anxiety. The therapist and Andrew collaboratively reviewed his specific somatic reactions to anxiety (e.g., rapid heartbeat, stomach cramps, nausea, headaches), which he experienced in different fearful situations. Then the therapist helped Andrew to understand that anxiety is not just fear or physical sensations but an experience consisting of several elements, just like hypnosis. As described in previous chapters, the intent of the therapist was to help Andrew, by using age-appropriate language, view his anxiety as a syncretic experience (Alladin, 2006, 2007, 2008; Safer & Leventhal, 1977), not too different from the hypnotic experience (albeit this experience is usually positive). A syncretic experience is a cascade of cognitive, somatic, perceptual, physiological, visceral and kinaesthetic changes. As Andrew was highly susceptible to hypnosis, the hypnotic experience coupled with his cataleptic accomplishment, offered him dramatic proof that he could modulate anxious and distressing experience. This approach to therapy, as discussed in Chapters 2 and 4, is influenced by third-wave CBT. In this approach to treatment, therapists teach their patients to examine and change their relationship with their internal experience and their cognitive activities, rather than trying to control the symptom(s) or the cognitions (Butler et al., 2008).

To cope with his anxious experience, Andrew was introduced to the clenched fist technique (Stein, 1963). As discussed in Chapter 3, the clenching of the dominant fist acts as an anchor for the elicitation of the relaxation response. Andrew was trained to induce self-hypnosis rapidly whenever he felt anxious about being away from his mother by clenching his dominant fist, which acted as an anchor. Lankton (1980) defines an anchor as any stimulus that evokes a consistent response pattern from a person (see Chapter 3 for a full transcript of setting up an anchor). Andrew's anchoring training was experientially ratified by two sessions of hypnotherapy, during which he imagined (rehearsed) being away from his mother.

Now we are going to practice the Clenching Fist Technique. From now on whenever you feel anxious or fearful about being away from your mother, imagine using your Clenched Fist Technique to deal with the stressful experience. Just continue to imagine, from now on whenever you get anxious or fearful about being away from your mother, you are able cope with the experience by clenching your fist and anchoring your mind to this experience. With practice you will get better and better with this technique. As a result of this you will begin to feel less upset about these feelings and you will be able to 'flow' with them, yet you will be aware of them.

Andrew found the clenched fist technique very useful as it was very concrete and portable. He was able to apply it easily whenever he catastrophized about being away from his mother.

Self-hypnosis training

To generalize his relaxation response and his ability to 'flow' in real situations, Andrew was taught self-hypnosis. To facilitate self-hypnosis training, at the end of the first hypnotherapy session, Andrew was given a CD recording of the session. He was encouraged to listen to the CD at least once a day at home. This homework assignment allowed continuity of treatment between sessions and offered him the opportunity to practice self-hypnosis. On several occasions, Andrew commented that the training in self-hypnosis and the clenched fist technique were practical and powerful skills that he could use outside the therapy sessions, especially at school, to deal with his anxiety. The self-hypnosis also helped him to 'move away' from the fearful thoughts.

Post-hypnotic suggestions

Before the termination of the hypnotic sessions, Andrew was routinely offered a variety of PHS to deal with fears and anxiety reactions. Andrew tended to cogitate with the following negative self-suggestions:

- 'I will not be able to cope being away from my mom.'
- 'I will not be able to handle it if something bad happens to her.'
- 'I will freak out; it will be so embarrassing.'
- 'I can never be independent.'
- 'I will never be able to do anything on my own.'

Rumination with these suggestions can not only induce a negative trance, but also serve as powerful self-affirmation or PHS, which can become part of the avoidance pattern of behaviour. To offset the negative rumination, Andrew was offered a range of PHS at the end of each hypnotherapy session. Here is a sample of PHS that was offered:

- 'Whenever you feel anxious in a given situation, you will become more aware of how to deal with it rather than focusing on your symptoms or your thoughts.'
- 'When you plan to be away from home, you will feel less inclined to stay in.'
- 'As you become more relaxed every day as a result of listening to your Self-Hypnosis CD, you will begin to feel motivated to spend more time away from your home doing your own things.'
- 'When you are at school you will become so absorbed in your school work that you will think very little about home.'

Clarke and Jackson (1983) regard PHS to be a form of 'higher-order-conditioning', which can function as positive or negative reinforcement to increase or decrease the probability of desired or undesired behaviours. They successfully utilized PHS to enhance the effect of *in vivo* exposure among agoraphobics.

Cognitive behavioural therapy

Once Andrew became conscious of his bodily responses, he was taught to become aware of his thoughts, beliefs and images during anxiety-provoking situations. Children with SAD tend to repeatedly worry about what they are afraid of (e.g., my parents will get hurt). This thought pattern is repeated so often in the child's mind that he or she begins to feel his or her emotions are beyond his or her control. The child feels unable to think of anything else, except his or her fears and worries, which contribute to the maintenance of anxiety and irrational behaviours. The main purpose of identifying self-talk during anxiety-provoking situations is to reduce anxiety-provoking self-talk and to replace it by coping self-suggestions. Moreover, by confronting and correcting catastrophic beliefs, a child with SAD becomes less anxious about separation.

One of the ways to reduce these internal symptoms of SAD is to use CBT strategies. CBT has been found to be efficacious and effective in reducing SAD symptoms (Barrett, Dadds, & Rapee, 1996; Doobay, 2008; Gosch, Flannery-Schroeder, Mauro, & Compton, 2006; Kendall et al., 1997; Perwien & Bernstein, 2004). More specifically, CBT has been shown to (i) reduce overall anxiety and internalizing symptoms, (ii) increase coping skills and (iii) provide long-term effect (Perwien & Bernstein, 2004).

Several CBT techniques have been employed for reducing the internal symptoms of SAD (Farris & Jouriles, 1993). Cognitive restructuring is the most common CBT technique that is used for identifying and changing cognitive distortions about separation (Beck et al., 1979; Ellis, 1962, 1994; Farris & Jouriles, 1993; Gosch et al., 2006; Lease & Strauss, 1993). As discussed in Chapters 1 and 2, CBT theory of anxiety disorders is based on the premise that distorted self-statements cause and sustain maladaptive physiological and behavioural responses (Beck et al., 1979; Ellis, 1962, 1994; Farris & Jouriles, 1993). For example, if a child with SAD, while sleeping alone, says to himself or herself, 'If I go to sleep alone, something bad will happen to my parents, and they will be gone when I wake up', is likely to feel worried and anxious (Doobay, 2008). In such a case, the therapist can help the child use the cognitive restructuring technique to (i) identify the cognitive distortions, (ii) pinpoint the maladaptive physiological arousal and behaviours (feeling tense, leaving bed to find parents) associated with the irrational thoughts and (iii) question his irrational thoughts and adopt alternative cognitions, such as

> My parents are sleeping in the next room and they will still be there when I wake up in the morning. I can handle this; I have slept alone before, and I can do it again. (Adapted from Doobay, 2008.)

Such coping statements create a sense of self-efficacy and the child begins to tell himself or herself that I can cope with the situation (Lease & Strauss, 1993). From a hypnosis perspective, the child starts to alter NSH into positive self-hypnosis. Masi et al. (2001) consider the identification and replacement of negative thoughts with adaptive coping self-statements to parallel a plan of action, favouring exposure to fearful situations.

Other cognitive strategies, depending on the age of the child with SAD, can also be used to replace or modify maladaptive thoughts with more helpful cognitions. Some of these techniques include (i) using cartoon bubbles to identify thoughts that reduce stress and thoughts that might induce stress; (ii) modelling and role-playing, involving parents and therapist; (iii) practicing coping self-talk; (iv) detecting possible 'thinking traps' and (v) gradually coping with more anxiety-provoking situations (Sacks et al., 2013).

Controlled studies have shown the efficacy of CBT with anxiety disorders (Kendall, 1994) and specifically with SAD (King et al., 1998; Last, Hansen, & Franco, 1998), thus supporting this approach as the best proven treatment. CBT combines a behavioural approach with cognitive therapy, based on the theory that faulty cognition may be a central determinant of the anxiety.

Hypnosis-aided systematic desensitization

Although imaginal exposure was helpful to Andrew in terms of increasing his confidence about being away from his home or from his mother, he was too anxious to tolerate *in vivo* exposure. He felt more comfortable and ready to work with SD. SD, also known as counter-conditioning, is a common evidence-based behavioural technique based on classical conditioning (Farris & Jouriles, 1993; also see Chapter 2). This technique involves pairing two stimuli that elicit incompatible responses. For example, fear and anxiety are each incompatible with relaxation. In SD, a person with anxiety disorder is gradually exposed to an anxiety-provoking object or situation while learning to be relaxed. In the case of SAD, a child may be told to sleep in his or her own bedroom without the parent, while engaging in an imaginal relaxation exercise. Over time, the child will no longer experience anxiety as this response is incompatible with the relaxation response (Doobay, 2008).

Within the framework of CH, the relaxation component of SD is replaced by hypnosis, and hence, this treatment approach is referred to as HASD (Iglesias & Iglesias, 2014). A number of reports in the literature support the effectiveness of combining hypnosis with SD in the treatment of specific phobias (Glick, 1970). Table 8.2 shows the hierarchy of anxiety, which was formulated to help Andrew overcome his fear of separation. The hierarchy represents various situations – ranked from least feared to most feared – related to being away from his mother. The fears were self-rated in terms of SUD on 0–100 scale, 0 representing no fear and 100 standing for the worst/maximum fear.

While feeling very relaxed in deep hypnosis, Andrew was asked to imagine each hierarchy of fear in turn, starting with the lowest item in the hierarchy ('Staying at home in the evening with babysitter while his mother is away for 1 hour'; SUD = 20). He was instructed to focus on the target situation until he was able to bring his SUD level down to 0. It is important for patient to master one hierarchy, that is, able imagine the target situation without any anxiety, before moving on to the next item in the hierarchy. Failure to master previous situation may produce resistance to work with the next item in the hierarchy, which is likely to be more anxiety-provoking (higher SUD level). Andrew found the SD very helpful in bringing down his level of anxiety during the sessions. After three sessions of SD he felt confident to progress on to gradual exposure *in vivo*.

Gradual in vivo exposure therapy

Exposure *in vivo* is a key component of CBT for SAD (Heyne, 2006). Exposure therapy has also been found to be efficacious with a variety of anxiety disorders (Follette & Smith, 2005), and it is considered to be the gold standard treatment for agoraphobia (Chambless, 1985; Hazlett-Stevens, 2006). Exposure *in vivo* is designed to help SAD patients confront fearful situations, memories and images in a therapeutic manner. As a child with SAD exhibits high levels of anxiety, in conjunction with the involvement of the parents and the preparatory strategies learned so far, a graduated *in vivo* desensitization is designed. This involves a step-by-step approach to conquering the anxiety elicited by the separation from an attached figure. The child draws on his or her relaxation skills, self-hypnosis and cognitive coping strategies to manage the anxiety associated with the successive exposure steps.

The same hierarchy of fear (see Table 8.2) that was used for SD was employed with Andrew for the graded *in vivo* desensitization procedure. Andrew and his parents were in full agreement with the graded hierarchy schedule. Andrew, to his surprise, made very good progress with the treatment, and he was determined to master all the situations listed in the fear hierarchy. He accomplished each of the hierarchy items with the first trial except for 'Making no phone call from school' (SUD = 85) and 'Staying with grandmother for whole weekend' (SD = 100). Although he was not permitted to call his mother from school (except for emergency), he felt so

Table 8.2 Systematic desensitization hierarchy of fear of separation

Item	*Fear rating in SUD (0–100)*
Staying at home in the evening with babysitter while his mother is away for 1 hour	20
Mother away from home shopping for 2 hours	30
Staying at home in the evening with babysitter while his mother is away for 3 hours	30
Mother away from home shopping for 3 hours	40
Visiting friend on his own for 2 hours	45
Visiting friend on his own for 3 hours	50
Making only one phone call to mother when at school	55
Making no phone call to mother when at school	60
Staying with grandmother while parents are away to an evening party until midnight	70
Staying with grandmother for whole night	80
Making no phone call from school	85
Staying with grandmother for whole weekend	100
Staying at friend's house for whole weekend	100

anxious and overwhelmed that he had to call his mother for reassurance. With reassurance and encouragement from his parents, Andrew was able to handle not making calls to his mother from school. He also had difficulty staying with his grandmother over the whole weekend. On the Saturday he felt very anxious and distressed that he pleaded with his mother to take him home. Again the parents were very supportive and the issue was discussed at great length in the next session of therapy. Consequently, he tried the exposure for another weekend and he was able to handle it. Encouraged by his success, gradually Andrew was able face other situations that he had been avoiding. Jurbergs and Ledley (2005) have offered several suggestions to ensure the success of exposure *in vivo* with children with SAD: Tailor treatment to the individual child.

1. Encourage the child to self-monitor the effects SAD has in his or her life. Teach the child to identify the 'triggers' to his or her anxiety and the physiological and behavioural responses.
2. Encourage the child to use somatic strategies such as relaxation, breathing, self-hypnosis to deal with anxiety.
3. Create a hierarchy of feared situations early in treatment as this can provide a road map for treatment. The hierarchy should take into account the age of the child. For younger children, exposure may include the presence of parents.
4. Involve parents in the construction of the feared hierarchy.
5. Both the child and the parents need to have a good grasp of the CBT model and treatment of SAD.
6. Encourage the child to stay in the feared situation until the anxiety subsides completely (i.e., the SUD level should be '0').
7. Concurrent with the exposures, the child should be taught effective coping skills (e.g., doing homework, watching TV). These coping strategies should not be seen as avoidance behaviours, they are replacement for safety behaviours (e.g., repeatedly calling mother to check on her).
8. Homework assignments are given at each session.
9. The child's 'bravery' during exposure is reinforced by providing rewards (e.g., pizza dinner).
10. At the end of treatment review accomplishment and set new goals.

Healing self-wounds

After 15 sessions of CBT and hypnotherapy, Andrew made some significant progress in symptom management. He felt less anxious being away from his mother and the anxiety he experienced at school was 'gone completely'. Andrew also started to interact more often after school, especially during weekends and he signed for outdoor soccer. He also started experimenting with closing his bedroom door at night while in bed. However, Andrew still had some anxiety about being separated from his mother, although he was handling the anxiety better than before and having less impact on his daily activities. For this reason, Andrew wanted to know about the 'real cause' of his fear of being away from his mother. He was also intrigued that his sister was not impacted by the MVA as much as he did. He believed there should be some special reason that he was so traumatized by the accident. The parents were also interested to know the 'real reason' for Andrew to have developed the full-blown symptoms of SAD following the accident, although they were aware that Andrew was always a 'sensitive child '. The next segment of therapy thus involved in-depth hypnotherapy and consisted of eliciting and healing the self-wounds.

Elicitation of self-wounds
To access Andrew's self-wounds, the affect bridge technique was used. The feeling of anxiety that he experienced while he was at his grandmother's house over the weekend was used as a bridge to elicit his first anxiety attack. While experiencing intense anxiety, he became aware of his mother dying in a MVA. Andrew started to scream: 'No', 'No', 'Please don't die'. Then he remembered the nightmares he had about his mother dying in MVA. The first nightmare occurred on the night of the accident (the MVA occurred in the morning). He was shaken by it but reasoned that the nightmare was due to the upset he experienced at the accident and as a result he was not too upset by it. After about a week, he had the same nightmare on three consecutive nights, and he became convinced that something bad was going to happen to his mother. He never told anyone about the nightmare because he felt guilty about having 'such a horrible dream', and he thought this would upset his mother. After those nightmares he became preoccupied with the belief that something 'serious' would happen to his mother and therefore he wanted to be with her all the time as a protection. With some questioning from the therapist, Andrew disclosed that his worst fear was that his mother would die from an accident and he would not be able to deal the loss. The thought is so fearful to him that he blocks it by being preoccupied with providing safety to his mother by being with her. Andrew also disclosed that although he was coping better with his fear of being away from his mother, his 'deep fear' (i.e., inability to cope with the loss of his mother dying) is still intact.

From the uncovering of the earlier information, it was formulated that Andrew needed to resolve two main experiential conflicts: (i) to detoxify the meaning of his anxiety and (ii) to learn to tolerate the fear of loss.

Detoxification of meaning of anxiety

The split screen technique (Alladin, 2008; Cardena et al., 2000; Lynn & Cardena, 2007; Spiegel, 1981) was used to help Andrew detoxify the meaning of his anxiety. This is a hypnotic strategy that utilizes the 'strong ego state' to help the 'weak ego state' deal with anxiety-provoking situations. It also facilitates the 'two' ego states to work together as a team, rather than splitting from each other, when the self is threatened or stressed out. The therapy transcript presented subsequently illustrates how the split screen technique was used with Andrew to help him deal with the toxic meaning of his anxiety. The transcript begins while Andrew was in a deep trance, bolstered by ego-strengthening suggestions.

THERAPIST: Now I would like you to imagine sitting in front of a large TV or cinema screen, that is vertically split in two halves, consisting of a right side and a left side. Can you imagine this?

[Andrew raised his 'YES' finger. Ideomotor signals were already set up – 'YES' represented raising of his right index finger and 'NO' was represented by raising of his left index finger.]

THERAPIST: Imagine the right side of the screen is lighting up as if it's ready to project an image. Imagine yourself being projected on the right side of the screen, just as you are now. Feeling very relaxed, very comfortable, in complete control, and being aware of everything around you. Do you feel these good feelings?

[Andrew raised his 'YES' finger.]

THERAPIST: And now become aware of the things you have done, or places you have been to, that make you feel good. Do you feel these good feelings?

[Andrew raised his 'YES' finger.]

THERAPIST: That's very good. Do you feel the good feelings?

[Andrew raised his 'YES' finger.]

THERAPIST: Are you thinking about the good feelings you had when you went to Disneyland last year? [It is advisable to check out the fact rather than making assumption. In this case, the assumption was made by the therapist based on what Andrew had disclosed to the therapist. He told the therapist that Disneyland had a special meaning to him as he had such a good time there last year. Whenever he thought about it, it made him feel proud and happy that he had been there.]

[Andrew raised his 'YES' finger.]

THERAPIST: Just focus on the good feelings and the sense of pride you feel for having been to Disneyland. This proves to you that you can feel good about yourself even if you have problems or difficulties. We are going to call this part of you the 'strong part' or the 'relaxed part' of you. Is this acceptable to you?

[Andrew raised his 'YES' finger.]

THERAPIST: Now leave this 'strong part' of you on the right side of the screen and imagine the anxious part of you is projected on the left side of the screen. Imagine yourself being in a situation that makes you feel anxious. Become aware of the anxious feeling you are experiencing. Can you imagine this?

[Andrew raised his 'YES' finger.]

THERAPIST: Become aware of all the feelings that you are experiencing. Don't be afraid to let all the anxious feelings come over you, because soon we will show you how to deal with them. Become aware of all the physical sensations you feel. Become aware of all the thoughts that are going through your mind and become aware of your behaviors. Can you feel these?

[Andrew raised his 'YES' finger.]

THERAPIST: Just become aware of the whole experience and we are going to call this part of you the 'anxious part' of you. Is this acceptable to you?

[Andrew raised his 'YES' finger.]

THERAPIST: Now imagine, your 'strong' part is stepping out from the right side into the left side of the screen. Can you imagine this?

[Andrew raised his 'YES' finger.]

THERAPIST: Imagine your 'strong part' is hugging your 'weak part' and telling him that he is here to help out. He is telling your 'anxious part' not to be afraid because he is here to guide you how to deal with the fear. You may or may not know this, the 'strong part' of you had been very attentive to the therapy sessions and he had learned lot of tricks to deal with fear and anxiety. If you want to, he can share this with you? Does your 'anxious part' want to know about this?

[Andrew raised his 'YES' finger.]

THERAPIST: From now on, the 'anxious part' of you don't have to work on his own. The 'strong part' of you can join you. He can show you how to deal with stress and fear. He will show you how to relax, how to calm down, and how to 'flow'. He will also remind you of the Clenched Fist Technique and how to reason with your fearful thoughts. Does your 'anxious part' agree to this?

[Andrew raised his 'YES' finger.]

THERAPIST: From now on, the 'anxious part' of you don't have to handle difficulties on his own, he can work as a team with the 'strong part' of you. Now become aware of the anxious feelings you are feeling on the left side of the screen. Imagine the 'strong part' of you is telling the 'anxious' part of you how to deal with the fearful feelings you are feeling right now. Imagine he is demonstrating the 'anxious part' how to relax, how to let go, how to 'flow', and how to reason with fearful thoughts. Continue to imagine this until you feel the 'anxious part' of you feel good and less fearful. When he feels good and less fearful, let me know by raising your 'YES' finger.

[Andrew raised his 'YES' finger after about 30 seconds.]

THERAPIST: Imagine your 'anxious part' feels protected and he knows what to do now when he feels anxious or fearful. He feels good knowing that he is not on his own; he has the 'strong part' to help him out. The 'anxious part' also realizes that the 'strong part' is part of your Self as well. They both belong to your self. So from now on there is no need to feel separated from the 'strong part' of you. Two is better than one. You are a team now. Do you agree with this?

[Andrew raised his 'YES' finger.]

The split screen technique was repeated over several sessions, with main focus on coping with anxiety related to being away from home and from his mother. Andrew found the strategy 'weird' but very effective. He found it weird because he felt there were different parts of him. He felt both the 'strong part' and the 'anxious part', and it dawned on him that he was a 'mixture of strong and weak'. This discovery had a significant effect on him. Prior to these sessions, Andrew used to think he was 'weak' for feeling anxious and fearful. He came to realize that he was a 'mixture of weak and strong' and as a result he no longer felt 'weak' when he experienced fear or anxiety. He figured out that he felt anxious whenever he was away, or thought about being away, from his mother because he was afraid of losing her. He was even more afraid that he would not be able to deal with it if he lost his mother. The next part of the hypnotherapy therefore focused on helping Andrew (i) separate reality from unreality (nightmares), (ii) reducing guilt about having bad dreams about his mother and (iii) coming to terms with fear of losing his mother. The empty chair technique was used to deal with these conflictual issues.

The empty chair technique

As Andrew did not feel comfortable talking to his parents, particularly his mother, about his nightmares and 'real fears', the therapist recommended working with the empty chair technique. This technique, derived from Gestalt therapy, is a role-playing strategy (Perls, Hefferline, & Goodman, 1951; Woldt & Toman, 2005) for reducing intra- or interpersonal conflicts (Nichol & Schwartz, 2008). In this procedure, while in deep hypnosis, Andrew was encouraged to role-play his 'strong part' having a conversation with his 'weak part'. He imagined each of them sitting in an empty chair facing each other (two-empty-chair technique) right in front of him in the therapist's office. By imagining his 'anxious part' sitting in the empty chair in the safety of the therapy situation and in the presence of his 'strong part', Andrew's 'anxious part' was able to express various strong feelings (fear and guilt) about his mother he had been harbouring inside him for some time. By engaging in the two-empty-chair work, and with the support and direction from the therapist, Andrew's 'anxious part' was able to express his anxiety, guilt and fear related to losing his mother. In turn, his 'strong part' was able to guide him how to deal with these issues. The following transcript which began while Andrew was in a deep trance depicts the therapeutic dialogue between the 'anxious' and the 'strong' parts.

THERAPIST: Andrew, is it okay for your 'anxious part' and your 'strong part' to have a conversation about the fear of losing mother?

[Andrew raised his 'YES' finger.]

THERAPIST: Maybe your 'anxious part' can start by telling the 'strong part' of you about the nightmares.

ANXIOUS PART: I had nightmares after the accident. They were horrible. [Andrew started to cry.] I saw mother died. No God! No! [Still crying.]

STRONG PART: [After about a minute.] I am sorry to hear about the nightmares. You know they were dreams. Mom is still here.

ANXIOUS PART: I guess you are right. But they were so real and I felt guilty for having those bad dreams.

STRONG PART: Still they were dreams and dreams are not caused by you. We dream when we are fast asleep so we have no control about our dreams.

ANXIOUS PART: I guess I knew about that, but they happened several times and I started to think they might be true. I thought they were warnings about mom dying soon.

STRONG PART: I am glad you realized they were dreams. I was worried too, I also thought they might be warnings, but I remember what Dr Alladin told me. He talked about science of dreams and said dreams are made of past stuff and nothing to do with the future. I believe it because when I think too much about something, I dream about it.

ANXIOUS PART: I also remember what Dr Alladin told us, but I was too scared to think about it. Now that you mention it, it makes sense. Mom is still here and I know dream don't tell us about the future, otherwise we would know everything about the future. Now it makes sense why I had those nightmares because I was thinking a lot about the accident. I was so scared that I could not cope if mom dies. It had nothing to do with me wishing something bad happening to her.

STRONG PART: I am glad you figured out dreams are not true. In the same way, thoughts are not truth. Again I remember Dr Alladin telling us that thoughts or beliefs are not facts. What we think do not happen usually. If everything we think do happen, then there will be no control in the world.

ANXIOUS PART: I remember this. I guess I did not believe him because I was too scared I could not cope if bad things happen to mom.

STRONG PART: There is no reason for anything bad to happen to mom. It's true that something bad may happen to her or to anyone else, but because something bad has not happened yet we don't need to worry. But if something bad happen somehow we have to deal with it.

ANXIOUS PART: What if I'm not able to handle it?

STRONG PART: Maybe as Dr Alladin said, we must not focus on 'what if', instead we have to remember thoughts are not facts. 'What ifs' are speculation, not facts. You may remember the story he told us about the lady who had fear of cancer.

ANXIOUS PART: Can you tell me the story again.

STRONG PART: This 30-year-old lady was fearful that when she gets old, maybe 20 years down the road, she may have cancer. So she was very upset and anxious about it, that she became depressed and was not functioning well. Dr Alladin told her that there is a 50% chance she may have cancer in the future, but also she has a 50% chance of not having cancer. If she has cancer down the road, then she has to deal with it. But if she does not have cancer in the future then she suffered all those years for nothing. If you don't have cancer now, you don't have to suffer now, but if you happen to get it in the future then you have to deal with it.

ANXIOUS PART: I get it. I am suffering as if something has already happened to mom. Really nothing has happened to her now so I don't need to worry. If something does happen to her then we have to deal with it. But it's possible nothing may happen to her. Like that lady, I don't have to suffer when I don't have the illness.

The empty chair technique helped Andrew deal with the 'real' reasons for his SAD. Once he was able to uncover and deal with the implicit reasons for his fear, the symptoms of SAD significantly improved. Andrew indicated he felt better prior to the uncovering work due to CBT and hypnotherapy, but 'now I feel good inside'. As a result of the uncovering work, Andrew reported having no anxiety leaving home or being away from mom. At this point he was discharged.

Separation anxiety disorder in adults
When working with children or adolescents with SAD, the components of CH described so far are usually sufficient for producing significant improvement. In case of adult SAD, AMBT may be necessary, especially for relapse prevention. Although most children grow out of SAD, some recent studies found a form of separation anxiety, although no longer directed at parents, to persist in adults or may even begin in adulthood. For example, a national survey found 2% of adult American population to have suffered from separation anxiety in the previous year (Manicavasagar et al., 2000). It was estimated that one third of childhood SAD persisted in late teens or early 20s.

DSM-V recognizes adult SAD to be a distinct diagnosis. However, to meet criteria for adult SAD, the symptoms must persist for over 6 months (in children 4 weeks). Adults with SAD find it difficult to cope with changes in circumstances (e.g., taking a new job, moving, getting married). They are over-concerned about their children and spouses and experience marked discomfort when separated from them. They also experience significant disruption at work or during social interaction as they need to continuously check on the whereabouts of a significant other (American Psychiatric Association, 1993, pp. 192–193).

The treatment for adult SAD is the same as described for Andrew, except for using age-appropriate language, and not involving other adults (although, at times, it may be necessary to involve the partner or the family). Moreover, as mentioned before, AMBT is integrated with CH when treating adults with SAD. Mind–body–heart integration training is also included. Before describing the treatment procedures, an adult case of SAD is briefly described.

Case of Fran

Fran was a 40-year-old insurance broker, referred by her psychiatrist for the treatment of SAD. Fran was overly concerned about her 18-year-old daughter Katie, who worked as a receptionist at a health club. Fran was extremely worried about her daughter, fearing something bad will happen to her. While Katie was at work, she had to call her almost every hour to check whether she was safe. If Katie went out with her friends, she had to call her mother to tell her she arrived. If happened to be late returning home, Katie had to call her mother to let her know otherwise Fran would call. Katie was embarrassed about her mother calling her every hour while she was with her friends. Therefore, the arrangement was for Katie to call her.

Fran had been married for 20 years to a high school teacher, who was very understanding and supportive of Fran's 'obsession'. Katie was the only child, who liked to socialize with her friends and enjoyed going out. However, she was 'traumatized by her boyfriend'. He cheated on her and he was 'very abusive' and 'cruel' when Katie confronted him. According to Fran, Katie was dependent on the boyfriend, although he was abusive to her. Against her parents' advice she continued to cling to him. Gradually, Katie became progressively depressed and attempted suicide by taking an overdose of her antidepressant medication. Fortunately, she was discovered by Fran, who had to call an ambulance. The doctor at emergency room informed Fran that she could have died if she was not discovered by her. Since then Fran became very clingy to her daughter and became over-concerned about her daughter's safety. When her daughter was out at night, Fran could not sleep and whenever she heard any news about an accident she would call Katie to check on her safety. She became so overwhelmed with the anxiety and worries, she had to see her family physician, who referred her to a psychiatrist.

Uncovering work indicated Fran's 'real fear' was related to the anticipation of inability to cope if anything serious happened to her daughter. Fran believed in such an event she would not be able to deal with it and she might have to commit suicide. The split screen and the empty chair techniques helped Fran heal the self-wounds. However, to prevent relapse, it was felt necessary to offer some sessions on AMBT.

Promoting acceptance and gratitude

As discussed in Chapter 1, patients with anxiety disorders tend to suppress re-experiencing of their initial trauma as it causes extreme distress (Wolfe, 2005, 2006). Such avoidance or intolerance of inner suffering can be regarded as lack of acceptance within the context of third-wave CBT (Baer & Huss, 2008). Although Fran's suppression of her self-wounds warded off her distressing experience temporarily, unfortunately it maintained her symptoms. For this reason, it was important to help Fran accept her emotional distress. However, acceptance is not merely tolerance of inner hurt; it is the active and nonjudgemental embracing of painful experience in the here and now, involving undefended exposure to thoughts, feelings and bodily sensations as they occur (Hayes, 2004). Levitt, Brown, Orsillo and Barlow (2004) have provided empirical evidence for the effectiveness of acceptance-based interventions in the management of anxiety disorders. Several techniques, including (i) gratitude education, (ii) gratitude training, (iii) acceptance training, (iv) acceptance and gratitude hypnotherapy and (v) mind–body–heart integration were used to help Fran cultivate acceptance of her fear and anxiety. These techniques are described next.

Gratitude education and training

Sense of gratitude is used as a means to cultivate acceptance in patients with SAD. Gratitude is a feeling or attitude in acknowledgement of a benefit that one has received or will receive. Studies suggest that people who are grateful have higher levels of subjective well-being, have higher levels of control of their environments, have more positive ways of coping with the difficulties they experience in life, spend more time planning how to deal with the problem, are less likely to try to avoid or deny their problems, and they sleep better (for review and references see Chapter 2).

Gratitude education

Gratitude education focuses on drawing broad generalizations about different cultural values and beliefs, and comparing Western and non-Western expectations of life, loss and achievement. The gratitude education helped Fran recognize that values and sense of loss are human-made, subjective and culturally determined. This comparative understanding of societal values helped her re-examine her own meaning of life and loss and encouraged her to begin to focus on what she has (gratitude) rather than ruminating with what may happen in the future.

Acceptance training
As Fran was so centred on her anxiety and what may happen to her daughter, she was not mindful of acceptance and gratitude. To increase awareness of her sense of acceptance, she was encouraged to carry out a series of exercises, some of which are listed as follows.

- Focusing on here and now.
- Observing emotional experiences and their contexts non-judgementally.
- Separation of secondary emotions from primary emotions (e.g., not to get upset for feeling upset, or feeling depressed for feeling depressed).
- Learning to tolerate distress rather than fighting it (flow with it).
- Adopting healthy and adaptive means to deal with chronic distress, rather than resorting to short-term reduction (e.g., calling her daughter excessively).
- Toleration of painful experience.
- Recontextualizing meaning of suffering, for example, from 'this is unbearable' to 'let's see how I can handle this'.
- Exercising radical acceptance – ability to welcome those things in life that are hard, unpleasant or very painful.
- Embracing good or bad experience as part of life.
- Willing to experience the reality of the present moment, for example, believing that 'things are as they should be'.
- Purposely allowing experience (thoughts, emotions, desires, urges, sensations, etc.) to occur without attempting to block or suppress them.
- Realizing that anxiety is not caused by the situation itself, but by our perception of it, our coping abilities and our level of spirituality or acceptance.

Gratitude training
Gratitude training involves doing various gratitude tasks. Fran was assigned a list of gratitude tasks as listed here, and she advised to do at least one of the tasks daily.

- To write gratitude letters
- To write a gratitude journal
- To remember gratitude moments
- To make gratitude visits to people one is grateful to
- To practice gratitude self-talk.

Acceptance and gratitude hypnotherapy
To make acceptance-based therapy more experiential, it is integrated with hypnotherapy (Alladin, 2006). While Fran was in a deep hypnotic trance,

she was offered the following suggestions, adapted from Alladin (2006, p. 303, 2007, p. 197), in order to strengthen her sense of gratitude.

> THERAPIST: Just continue to experience this beautiful sensation of peace and relaxation, tranquillity and calm flowing all over your mind and body. Notice feeling calm and peaceful. Feeling calm and peaceful, and in total harmony. No tension, no pressure, feeling calm and peaceful, and a sense of well-being. Feeling calm, peaceful, and in total harmony. Feeling happy that you can relax so deeply, that you can let go, and calm down completely. You feel pleased and grateful that you can let go completely. Now become aware of your heart. Notice how peaceful you feel in your heart, how calm you feel in your heart, and you feel a sense of in your heart. When you feel good in your heart, you feel good in your mind and in your body. Do you feel good in your heart?

> [Fran raised her 'YES' finger.]

> THERAPIST: Do you feel good in your mind, body, and heart?

> [Fran raised her 'YES' finger.]

> THERAPIST: Very good! You have the ability to feel good in your mind, body and heart. All major religions state that when you wake up in the morning, if you have a roof over your head, you have bread to eat, and water to drink, and are in fairly good health, then you have everything. Just become aware of all the things you have and all the things you are grateful for. When living in the modern world, it's okay to have goals and ambitions. When we achieve them, they can be seen as bonuses and pluses as we have lots of other resources. When we don't achieve our goals and ambitions, it is disappointing, but we have enough resources to live a comfortable life. Do you agree with these comments and observation?

> [Fran raised her 'YES' finger.]

It is important that the acceptance-based hypnotherapy is carried out after the acceptance and gratitude training. In the absence of this training, a patient may not appreciate the therapeutic meaning of acceptance and gratitude, and may reject the hypnotic suggestions. Fran found both the acceptance-based training and hypnotherapy very helpful. They gave her a new perspective on life and loss, and they made her become more aware of the many things she is grateful for in life. Most importantly, she felt less preoccupied and fearful about something bad happening to her daughter.

Mind–body–heart integration
This component of acceptance-based hypnotherapy focuses on the integration of various subsystems in the body. As discussed in Chapter 2, heart-focused positive emotional state engenders synchronization of the entire body system to produce PC (McCraty et al., 2009). Based on these scientific findings, Alladin (2012) has developed the breathing with your heart technique to generate coherence (harmony) of the entire system (mind, body, brain, heart, and emotion). This technique integrates both Western (heart viewed as a complex information centre) and Eastern (heart regarded as the big mind) concepts of the heart to produce psychological well-being.

Heart education
Fran was given a scientific account of the combined role of the heart and positive emotions in the generation of PC, which promotes healing, emotional stability and optimal performance. The similarities and the differences between Western and Eastern theories of mind and 'heart' were also discussed. Fran found the Eastern view of the heart very helpful in understanding her anxiety about her daughter. She was surprised to discover that mind (small mind) is a 'double-edged sword'. As a result of this understanding, Fran shifted her attention to the love she has for her daughter and the joys that she brings, instead of focusing on 'what may happen to my daughter '.

Heart–mind training combined with hypnotherapy
Heart–mind training helps patients with SAD cope with negative feelings (heavy heart) triggered by separation, or anticipation of separation, from an attached figure. By breathing with the heart, anxious patients are able to shift their attention away from their mind to their heart. Moreover, when a person feels good in his or her heart, the person experiences a sense of comfort and joy because we validate reality by the way we feel and not by the way we think (Fredrickson, 2002; Isen, 1998). As discussed in Chapter 2, logic does not always equate good affect, but feeling good in one's heart (e.g., by thinking about something one is grateful for) always creates a positive affect (Welwood, 1983).

Breathing with your heart technique
This transcript from a session with Fran illustrates how the technique is introduced in therapy. The script begins with Fran being in a deep hypnotic trance:

THERAPIST: Just continue to experience this beautiful sensation of peace and relaxation, tranquility and calm flowing throughout your mind and body, giving you such a pleasant feeling, such a soothing sensation, that you feel completely relaxed both mentally and physically. Do you feel relaxed both mentally and physically?

[Fran raised her 'YES' finger.]

THERAPIST: Now I would like you to focus on the centre of your heart. [Pause for 30 seconds.] Can you imagine this?

[Fran raised her 'YES' finger.]

THERAPIST: Now I would like you to imagine breathing in and out with your heart. [Pause for 30 seconds.] Can you imagine this?

[Fran raised her 'YES' finger.]

THERAPIST: Continue to imagine breathing in and out of your heart. [She was allowed to continue with this exercise for 2 minutes; the therapist repeated at regular intervals: 'Just continue to imagine breathing with your heart' as she did the exercise.] Now I would like you to slow down your breathing. Breathe in and out at 7 second intervals. Breathe in with your heart ... 1 ... 2 ... 3 ... 4 ... 5 ... 6 ... 7 and now breathe out with your heart ... 1 ... 2 ... 3 ... 4 ... 5 ... 6 ... 7. And now as you breathing in and out with your heart I want you to become aware of something in your life that you feel good about, something that you feel grateful for. [Pause for 30 seconds.] Are you able to focus on something that you are grateful for in your life?

[Fran raised her 'YES' finger.]

THERAPIST: Just become aware of that feeling and soon you will feel good in your heart. [After 10 seconds.] Do you feel it?

[Fran raised his 'YES' finger.]

THERAPIST: Just become aware of this good feeling in your heart [pause for 30 seconds]. Now I would like to become aware of the good feeling in your mind, in your body, and in your heart. Do you feel this?

[Fran raised his 'YES' finger.]

THERAPIST: Now that you feel good in your mind, in your body, and in your heart, you feel a sense of balance, a sense of harmony. Do you feel this sense of harmony?

[Fran raised his 'YES' finger.]

THERAPIST: From now on, whenever and wherever you are, you can create this good feeling by imagining breathing with your heart and focusing on something that you are grateful for. With practice you will get better and better at it. Now you know what to do to make your heart feels lighter.

Summary

SAD is a disorder that can cause a great deal of distress and impairment. Children with the disorder often miss school, as well as many other important social opportunities such as playing with friends and participating in extracurricular activities. Moreover, if untreated, SAD can lead to numerous negative psychosocial outcomes and may persist in adolescence and adulthood. Although a variety of effective treatments for SAD are available, including CBT and SSRI pharmacotherapy, a large number of patients do not improve significantly. This is not surprising given SAD is a complex condition and part of this complexity relates to tacit self-wounds in some patients, which maintain the symptoms. The chapter provided a wide array of behavioural, cognitive, hypnotic, unconscious and acceptance-based strategies for treating SAD from which a therapists can choose the best techniques that may suit their patients. The case of Andrew clearly illustrated that symptom-focused treatment is necessary but not sufficient for treating underlying determinants of SAD. A comprehensive and durable treatment requires therapeutic confrontation of unconscious conflicts that harbour painful emotions (Wolfe, 2006). The second case (Fran) illustrated the usefulness of combining AMBT with CH in the management of adult SAD.

Andrew showed very good response to CH. The therapy helped him identify the explicit and the implicit nature of his anxiety, as well as the root cause of his irrational fear. While behavioural and cognitive strategies helped him symptomatically, the hypnotherapy, by virtue of its phenomenological nature, made the therapy more experiential and thus more meaningful to him. He found the two-empty-chair and the split screen techniques very helpful in coming to terms with his nightmares and the fear of losing his mother. The case of Fran demonstrated the value of reassessing the meaning of life and loss. Fran's sense of acceptance and gratitude redirected her psychic energy to loving and appreciating her daughter rather than cogitating about something bad happening to her.

Although the integrative psychotherapy for SAD described in this chapter appears heuristic and theoretically sound – currently, beyond clinical observation – there is no empirical data to support the efficacy of treating the wounded self in patients with SAD. As discussed in Chapter 3, the efficacy of psychodynamic therapy with anxiety disorders provides indirect support that resolution of unconscious conflicts (which may be caused by the wounded self) decrease anxiety. To encourage wider application of this integrated perspective to treatment, it will be important to validate this approach empirically. Nevertheless, the book represents a preliminary, but timely, attempt to assimilate the concept of self-wounds in the management of SAD. As discussed in Chapter 1, cognitive behaviour therapists are beginning to take serious interest in the implicit nature of anxiety disorders and are starting to develop new techniques for activating and restructuring underlying cognitive schemas. This movement is likely to spark empirical studies of the concept of the wounded self in the future, both in the understanding and treatment of anxiety disorders. It is enlightening that hypnotherapy can be part of this movement.

9

Selective Mutism

Case of Jessica

Jessica, a 14-year-old, grade 9 student, was referred to the author for psychological treatment for SM by her child psychiatrist. Jessica was able to speak at home and to her close relatives but was not able to initiate speech or verbally respond to her peers at school. In past two years preceding the referral, Jessica had become more anxious attending school. At school, she was having little communication and social interaction with her teachers and peers. She felt too anxious to participate in school activities and, because of her high anxiety, she was frequently absent from school. Her marks had progressively gone down as she was not completing her class assignments and homework. She found it difficult to write essays and understand math concepts (barely passing math exams and tests). Psychological assessment indicated above-average intellectual functioning, and there was no evidence of verbal or nonverbal cognitive deficits or concentration problems. Her parents were concerned about her low academic performance and her not working to full potential. Although the parents were supportive, their concerns caused significant anxiety for Jessica, as she felt pressurized to do well academically.

She was described by her mother as being shy, anxious, clingy and fearful of leaving home when she first started kindergarten. Since primary school Jessica had become timid and withdrawn and, at times, she would appear to freeze when she had to speak to her peers or to her teacher. When she was spoken to she would blush and avoid eye contact 'as if she did not want to speak'. She felt anxious whenever she felt the pressure to speak to

Integrative CBT for Anxiety Disorders: An Evidence-Based Approach to Enhancing Cognitive Behavioural Therapy with Mindfulness and Hypnotherapy, First Edition. Assen Alladin.
© 2016 John Wiley & Sons, Ltd. Published 2016 by John Wiley & Sons, Ltd.

her peers or to her home teacher. Jessica's 'withdrawal' became noticeable to her parents and home teacher in grade 2. The home teacher was very supportive and in collaboration with her parents, she came up with a plan to help Jessica 'come out of her shell'. She encouraged Jessica to sit in front of the class and encouraged her to speak whenever she felt comfortable. The teacher also arranged to meet with Jessica once a week for an hour to talk about her difficulties and once a month to meet with the parents to review progress. As a result of these meetings, Jessica was able to talk to her teacher comfortably. She disclosed to her teacher that she was embarrassed to talk to her peers and teachers because she was conscious of her East European accent, and she did not want to make any mistake in case they laughed at her. Jessica was born in East Europe; she came to Canada when she was four years old. Before leaving her native country, she spoke English but not fluently. While her father was pursuing the formalities to immigrate to Canada, the whole family had private English tuition as a preparation for settling down in Canada. Once she arrived in Canada, Jessica became fluent in English fairly quickly, although her accent was noticeable (as her family spoke their native language at home). Also, for the same reasons, she felt anxious speaking to her peers at the Sunday Bible school, although most of the children were from her native country. She indicated that although these children were from her native country, they were more fluent in English than her and therefore she was afraid they would laugh at her if she made any mistake. However, she gradually felt more comfortable and after a few months she was able to interact normally with her peers at the Sunday school. Moreover, with the help from her home teacher, Jessica overcame her mutism at school, although at times she felt nervous communicating with her schoolmates. Unfortunately, she relapsed in grade 7, and her anxiety about speaking in school got progressively worse, which necessitated seeing a child psychiatrist, who referred her to the author for psychological intervention.

In the first session, because of her severe anxiety, Jessica was seen together with her mother, and her mother did most of the talking. As treatment progressed, she felt more comfortable in the sessions, and her verbal communication transformed into normal conversation. Jessica reported feeling anxious most of the time as if she was 'trapped in a bubble' and she could not get out of it. She perceived herself as being 'weak, ugly, stupid and a failure' and 'an embarrassment' to her family. She indicated that she lost confidence in herself and started to think of herself as being unworthy as a result of being bullied at school over several years. She was afraid to speak in case she made a mistake. She believed if she made an error speaking, her peers would 'yell' at her and use it as an excuse to bully her further. Thus, she 'preferred to be quiet'. She disclosed that her SM in the early grades was more related to her accent and fear of being laughed at. But in the higher grades, her mutism was primarily based on fear of being bullied, which got worse in grade 7 and, consequently, she stopped talking to her teachers and peers at school.

Jessica's father was a petroleum engineer, who worked for a large multinational oil and gas company. Her mother was a homemaker. She had an older sister, who was at the university at the time when Jessica was seen. The family was quite supportive to Jessica. Her mother was shy and reticent and had 'one time seen a therapist for social anxiety'. Her sister was also diagnosed with GAD but overcame it with medication. Jessica was closer to her mother but quite detached from father, who spent a substantial amount of time travelling on business.

Diagnostic Criteria for Selective Mutism

The DSM-V (American Psychiatric Association, 2013, p. 195) diagnostic criteria for SM (hereafter abbreviated as SM) include:

A. Consistent failure to speak in specific social situations such as school, at home, and so on, where speech is expected, despite speaking in other situations.
B. The condition interferes with educational or occupational achievement, or with social communication.
C. The condition must have persisted for at least one month (not limited to the first month in school).
D. The failure to speak in the specific situation is not due to insufficient knowledge of the language.
E. The condition is not accounted for by a language disorder or psychiatric condition.

Prevalence of Selective Mutism

SM is a rare condition and therefore it has not been studied extensively. The estimated prevalence rate of SM ranges between 0.03% and 0.2% in community samples (Bergman, Piacentini, & McCracken, 2002; Elizur & Perednik, 2003). Some research indicate higher prevalence of SM in girls than in boys (e.g., Cunningham, McHolm, Boyle, & Patel, 2004), while the studies by Bergman et al. and Elizur and Perednik suggest that it occurs equally in both sexes. There is a high degree of comorbidity between SM and social phobia (Kristensen, 2000), and similar treatments seem to work for both SM and social phobia (Cohan, Chavira, & Stein, 2006). These findings have led some investigators to believe SM may be a developmental precursor of adult social phobia (Sharkey & McNicholas, 2008).

Causes of Selective Mutism

The etiology of SM is unknown, although several theories have been put forward to explain the development of the disorder. The current conceptualization of the disorder links elective mutism (EM; former name for SM; therefore EM and SM are used interchangeably) to social phobia, (Sharkey & McNicholas, 2008). Children with EM have been observed to be behaviourally inhibited in their early childhood years and 'slow-to-warm-up' in infancy (Black & Uhude, 1995; Dummit, Klein, Tancer, Asche, Martin, & Fairbanks, 1996). In school they feel anxious about being judged, they avoid verbal confrontation and they experience physical symptoms of anxiety in social situations (Standart & Couteur, Vecchio & Kearney, 2005). Up to 97% of children with EM meet criteria for social phobia (e.g., Kristensen, 2000), and a family history of social anxiety and EM has been reported in 70% and 37% of first-degree relatives, respectively (Black & Uhude, 1995). These findings have led to the suggestion that EM should be viewed as a subtype, or an early developmental expression of social phobia, rather than a separate diagnostic entity. EM has also been found to be associated with a wide variety child psychopathology, including enuresis, encoperesis, separation anxiety, obsessive-compulsive trait, somatization and some neuro-developmental delays (Sharkey & McNicholas, 2008).

Some studies have indicated a connection between children with EM and their close relationship with their mothers. For example, Hayden (1980), in his case series of EM, found a strong bond between mother and child, causing difficulties for the child to separate and individuate from mother. Within this context, social phobia Hayden called the speech problem in the children 'symbiotic mutism' and recommended family therapy as the treatment of choice.

The role of trauma or hospitalization during early childhood has also been implicated in the etiology of EM. In one-third of their clinical sample of EM children, Anderson and Thomsen (1998) found the presence of a traumatic event during the critical years of speech development. Despite the clear evidence that some children react to traumatic event(s) by becoming mute, there is little evidence to support the claim that trauma is a common cause of SM per se (e.g., Black & Uhde, 1995; Dummit et al., 1996). Furthermore, there is some evidence that genetics may be involved in the etiology of SM. The high prevalence of communication deficits in families with EM, the close relationship between EM and social phobia and the high rates of developmental delays suggest the role of genetic vulnerability in the development of the disorder (Sharkey & McNicholas, 2008).

However, the role of the aforementioned predisposing and precipitating factors in the development of SM is unclear. In an attempt to integrate these factors, Cohan et al. (2006) have suggested a diathesis–stress model of the developmental trajectory of SM. According to their model, a child who experiences high level of anxiety and behavioural inhibition, either because of high genetic loading for anxiety or an unstable home environment, may develop a heightened sensitivity to verbal interactions with others, especially a child with developmental immaturity, a communication disorder or immigrant status. A child with these biological and psychological predispositions becomes vulnerable to SM, which may be triggered by an environmental stressor (e.g., interpersonal trauma or school entry), leading to a failure to speak in a given setting, despite the ability to do so (Sharkey & McNicholas, 2008). Based on these findings, this chapter, as the rest of the anxiety disorders described in the book, adopts a diathesis–stress model of SM.

Treatment of Selective Mutism

The population of patients with SM form a heterogeneous group (Dow, Sonnies, Scheib, Moss, & Leonard, 1995) and therefore a variety of treatments have been used, including behavioural, psychodynamic, family, pharmacological and multimodal interventions. However, the empirical literature on the treatment of SM is very limited compared to the extensive studies carried out with other anxiety disorders (Garcia, Freeman, Francis, Miller, & Leonard, 2004). The behavioural approaches focus on the modification of the environment, contingency management, shaping, stimulus fading, SD, graded *in vivo* exposure, positive reinforcement, audio/video self-modelling and CBT (see Hung, Spencer, & Dronamraju, 2012). The psychodynamic therapies, which usually involve art and play therapy, focus on the identification and the resolution of the underlying intrapsychic conflicts of the child with SM (Stone, Kratochwill, Sladezcek, & Serlin, 2002). The essence of family therapy is on exploring the disadvantageous family dynamics that might be resulting in and maintaining the child's mute behaviour (Tatem & Delcampo, 1995). Regarding medication, a number of case reports and a few clinical trials have supported the use of medication in children with SM, who not respond to psychosocial intervention (Sharkey & McNicholas, 2008). The best-practice guidelines recommend the use of fluoxetine, but it should be started with a low dose and the child's response should be monitored closely. It is also recommended that medication should not be the only intervention used to treat SM, but it should be combined with psychosocial intervention (Black & Uhde, 1994; Dummit et al., 1996; Hung et al., 2012; Krohn, et al., 1992; Wright et al., 1985). As SM is a multifaceted disorder and presents itself in many different ways, a multimodal approach is the preferred treatment (Cohan et al., 2006). This approach usually involves psychodynamic and behavioural interventions, along with occupational therapy, dance therapy, special education, family participation, school-based intervention and medication if required.

Cohan et al. (2006) critically reviewed the psychosocial treatment literature on SM from 1990 to 2005. From their examination of 23 studies, they concluded that (i) much of the SM treatment literature lacked methodological rigor; (ii) the effectiveness of behavioural and cognitive/behavioural interventions for SM was supported and (iii) multimodal behavioural techniques were more successful than those that relied upon only one technique as the combination of techniques addressed different aspects of the child's mutism. Research also indicates that EM is difficult to treat (Kolvin & Fundudis, 1981; Sluckin, Foreman, & Herbert, 1991) and optimal intervention requires long-term, multimodal and multifaceted therapeutic approaches (Hechtman, 1993).

Multi-method behavioural treatments for SM seek to address the relationships between a child's speech behaviour and environmental conditions and to investigate how the child's mutism may be maintained by the child's environmental surroundings (Anstendig, 1998; Labbe & Williamson, 1984). This chapter adopts a diathesis–stress model of SM and accordingly describes a multimodal approach to treatment. As (i) there is a high degree of comorbidity between SM and social phobia (Kristensen, 2000); (ii) both conditions respond to similar treatments (Cohan et al., 2006) and (iii) SM is considered to be a developmental precursor of adult social phobia (Sharkey & McNicholas, 2008), the CH for SM described in this chapter share some similarities with treatment protocol for SAD.

Cognitive Hypnotherapy for Selective Mutism

CH is a multimodal therapy for SM. It involves four separate but interrelated stages of interventions: (i) anxiety management and confidence building; (ii) initiation and increase of speech in 'muted' situations; (iii) uncovering and healing the root cause of the problem and (iv) if relevant, acceptance and mindfulness-based strategies for preventing relapse.

Phase I: Hypnotherapy for managing symptoms of SM

Four to six of the initial sessions of CH consist of hypnotherapy, which is specifically targeted at anxiety management and promoting self-confidence. At this phase of therapy the mutism is not addressed directly. This stage of intervention serves as a preparation for the next phase of therapy which involves behavioural and cognitive strategies for initiating and increasing speech. The third stage focuses on more complex therapy for exploring the roots of the SM later in therapy if the need arises. The fourth stage, if indicated and determined by the age of the child and the level of functioning, promotes acceptance and mindfulness in order to prevent relapse in the future. Before describing the components of hypnotherapy, the importance of assessment and therapeutic alliance is briefly reviewed.

Case formulation and therapeutic alliance

Before starting therapy, it is good clinical practice for the therapist to take a detailed clinical history to formulate the diagnosis and identify the essential psychological, physiological, and social functioning of the child with SM. It is critical to conduct a comprehensive evaluation in order to (i) rule out other explanations of the mutism, (ii) assess comorbid factors and (iii) plan an individualized treatment plan. The assessment process with a SM child can be challenging as in most cases SM children may not speak to the clinician. Parents' reports become particularly important here. Nevertheless, it is still important to conduct part of the evaluation directly with the child. Furthermore, CH case formulation highlights the importance of understanding the underlying role of cognitive distortions, negative self-instructions, irrational automatic thoughts and beliefs, schemas and negative ruminations or NSH in the understanding of child with SM. An efficient way of obtaining all the salient information within the context of CH is to take a case formulation approach as described by Alladin (2007, 2008). A case formulation approach allows the clinician to tailor nomothetic (general) treatment protocol, derived from randomized clinical trials, to the needs of the individual (idiographic) patient.

Therapeutic alliance is also vitally important in psychotherapy (Norcross, 2002) as all effective psychotherapy is predicated on the establishment of a safe, secure and solid therapeutic alliance (Wolfe, 2005). Some clinicians, on the other hand, have argued that therapeutic alliance is 'necessary but insufficient' for change (e.g., Beck et al., 1979). Although this may be true, a patient who feels disrespected or uncomfortable with his or her therapist is more likely to discontinue therapy, while a patient with strong therapeutic alliance may persevere with the difficult work of change.

Hypnotherapy for reducing anxiety and promoting confidence
The initial phase of hypnotherapy, specifically targeted at anxiety management and promoting self-confidence, consists of (i) relaxation training, (ii) demonstration of the power of mind over the body, (iii) ego-strengthening, (iv) expansion of awareness, (v) modulation and regulation of symptoms, (vi) self-hypnosis and (vii) PHS. Hypnotherapy is re-introduced to patients who elect to move on to the third stage of therapy, which involves exploration of the root cause of MS.

Relaxation training
Large sample studies of SM children, using validated rating scales, have identified anxiety as a hallmark of SM (Vecchio & Kearney, 2005). For this reason, many children continue to be mute in certain situations, largely due to severe anxiety. For example, Steinhausen and Juzi (1996) found 85% of their sample of SM children to be shy and 66% to be anxious. Moreover, as noted earlier, there is a high rate of comorbidity with social phobia and separation anxiety disorder (Cunningham, McHolm, & Boyle, 2006). For these reasons, selectively mute children experience high and pervasive level of physical anxiety. Relaxation training is used to help these children learn to alleviate the symptoms of anxiety. More specifically, training in relaxation aims to provide children with SM an efficient means of managing their physiological discomfort in situations associated with anxiety. By learning to identify and manage discomforting feelings, children with SM are better placed to confront challenging situations and to employ their relaxation skills and strategies to cope with situations where they feel anxious speaking.

As Jessica had been experiencing high levels of tension, nervousness and steep physiological reactivity, she found the relaxation response induced by hypnosis very calming and soothing. An added advantage of using hypnosis with SM children is the experiential nature of hypnotherapy. As hypnosis facilitates greater involvement in expansion of experience and little participation in verbalization, SM children feel secure in the therapy session. Jessica was highly susceptible to hypnosis. She was surprised that she could generate profound mental and physical relaxation without much effort. Her hypnotic talent was utilized to help her dissociate from anxiety-related situations and to become fully absorbed in the feeling of calmness and deep relaxation, and yet being aware of her thoughts and surroundings. At the end of the session, without prompting, Jessica indicated the session was 'cool', 'very relaxing' and for the first time she was able to step out of the anxiety 'bubble' (in the first session she described being stuck in an 'anxious bubble').

Demonstration of the power of mind over the body

To further empower Jessica and to ratify the credibility of the hypnotic intervention, eye and body catalepsies were introduced in the second hypnotherapy session. Jessica was very surprised that she was not able to open her eyes or get out of the reclining chair. The following transcript illustrates how the explanation of induced catalepsy was used to link self-hypnosis with Jessica's symptoms.

THERAPIST:　Let me explain to you why you were not able to open your eyes or get out of the chair. But first let me tell you what you achieved. What you achieved is called eye catalepsy and body catalepsy. By eye catalepsy, I mean you paralyzed your eyelids; you were not able to open your eyes. By body catalepsy, I mean you literally paralyzed your body, not able to get out of the chair. This shows that your brain is so powerful and that you can use the power of your brain to produce dramatic changes in your body.

Now let me explain to you why you were not able to open your eyes or get out of the chair. This has to do with the power of your brain. As you know the brain is very powerful, everyone talks about the brain being very powerful. But as know the brain is also very dumb, because the brain never thinks for itself, it does what your mind tells it to do. Your brain is like a horse, very powerful, but as you know it's the rider or the driver who controls the horse. In the same way your brain is very powerful, but what drives your brain is your thinking or your imagination, what we call the mind.

Since you have been imagining that your eyelids are heavy and stuck, your brain made it happen. And when you have been imagining that your body is heavy and stuck in the chair, your brain made it happen so that you were not able to get out of the chair.

Since your brain is so powerful, it's a double-edged sword. If you think positively or imagine good things about yourself, you feel good about yourself. If you think negative, or imagine bad things about yourself you feel it. Since your brain is so powerful it makes it happen, whether it's good or bad. Your brain does not think whether it's true or false, its job is to react as fast as possible, this has to do with our survival. In your case, based on your life experience, you have been focusing on negative and fearful thoughts. In other words, you have been hypnotizing yourself with the wrong suggestions. Does this make sense to you?

PATIENT:　Yes.

THERAPIST:　Now that we know you have been hypnotizing yourself with the negative suggestions, we can help you change those self-suggestions.

Jessica found this session extremely powerful as it instilled in her the hope and confidence that she could use the 'power' of her brain to overcome her fear of speaking at school. Moreover, this session reinforced in her a sense of positive expectancy; it further consolidated the therapeutic alliance and lowered her inhibition about speaking in the therapy sessions.

Ego strengthening

As it is common practice in hypnotherapy, Jessica was offered a variety of ego-strengthening suggestions to increase her self-esteem, enhance her self-efficacy and restore her confidence in her ability to speak in situations where she had been mute. While in deep hypnotic trance, following ego-strengthening suggestions, Jessica was guided to visualize herself beginning to talk in situations she was avoiding to speak because of her anxiety. She commented that, as a result of the ego-strengthening suggestions and the positive hypnotic experience, she felt motivated to overcome her speaking difficulties. The hypnotic experience also encouraged her to listen to her self-hypnosis CD every day (after the first hypnotherapy session, Jessica was given a self-hypnosis CD).

Expansion of awareness

Although selectively mute, Jessica felt anxious constantly and unable to experience different emotions, particularly good feeling. She described this constricted feeling as being 'trapped inside a bubble'. This was largely due to her constant rumination with the belief that she was a weak and a useless person, who was 'not able to talk normal'. To expand her range of emotions, during hypnosis, she was directed to focus on the relaxation response and then to become aware of different emotions and feelings. This was achieved by using EAT as described in Chapter 2. The following script illustrates the types of hypnotic suggestions that can be used to expand the range of experience:

> You have now become so deeply relaxed and you are in such a deep hypnotic trance that your mind and body feel completely relaxed, totally relaxed. You begin to feel a beautiful sensation of peace and tranquility, relaxation and calm, flowing all over your mind and your body, giving you such a pleasant, and such a soothing sensation all over your mind and body, that you feel completely relaxed.
>
> You feel totally relaxed both mentally and physically, and yet you are aware of everything, you are aware of all the sound and noise around you, you are aware of your thoughts and imagination, and yet you feel so relaxed, so calm and so peaceful. This shows that you have the ability to relax, to let go, and to put everything on hold. This shows that you have lots of control,

because you are aware of everything, you can hear all the sounds and noise around you, you are aware of your thoughts and imagination, you are aware that I am sitting beside you and talking to you, yet you are able to put every-thing on hold and relax completely. This shows you have lots of control.

Now you can become aware of all the good feelings you are experiencing. You feel calm, peaceful, relaxed and very, very comfortable. You may also become aware of feeling heavy, light, or detached, or distancing away from everything, becoming more and more detached, distancing away from everything, drifting into a deep, deep hypnotic trance. Yet you are able to relax and let go.

From EAT, Jessica discovered that she had the ability to relax and the capacity to experience different feelings and sensations. She was surprised that he could put things on hold, that is, although she was aware of her worries and anxieties, she was able to detach from anticipatory concerns. With practice she was able to relax and experience different contextual feelings, albeit aware of her concerns. Her greatest discovery was that she had the talent to produce, amplify and express a variety of positive feelings and experiences. She realized that she could learn to 'flow' with her distress and concerns rather than trying to control them.

Modulating and coping with symptoms

Consistent with the main tenet of AMBT, in CH, patients are not pressed to control their symptoms (e.g., Hayes et al., 2011), instead they are trained to change the relationship with their symptoms. As hypnosis is an experiential therapy, it provides patients with a secure base for expanding and modulating their experience. In hypnosis, Jessica was coached to perceive her anxiety symptoms as a syncretic experience (Alladin, 2006, 2007, 2008; Safer & Leventhal, 1977). In other words, she was encouraged to view her anxiety not simply as an unpleasant reactivity but as a cascade of cognitive, somatic, perceptual, physiological, visceral and kinaesthetic changes. Similarly, she was instructed to view the hypnotic trance state as a syncretic experience. The positive hypnotic experience, therefore, proffers patients the proof that experience, including symptoms, can be amplified or modulated. As mentioned in previous chapters, DePiano and Salzberg (1981) attribute the rapid improvement often observed in patients receiving hypnotherapy to be related to the positive syncretic cognition produced by the trance experience.

Self-hypnosis training

To generalize her relaxation response and her ability to 'let go' in real situations, Jessica was trained in self-hypnosis. At the end of the first hypnotherapy session, she was given a CD recording of the session. She was advised to listen to the CD at least once a day at home. This homework assignment allowed continuity of treatment between sessions and offered her the opportunity to practice self-hypnosis. Jessica commented that the training in self-hypnosis provided her the most practical and powerful skill for dealing with her anxiety symptoms outside the therapy sessions.

Once Jessica had built sufficient confidence in self-hypnosis, the generalization of this skill to real situations was further assisted by teaching her the clenched fist technique (Stein, 1963). As discussed in Chapter 2, the clenching of the dominant fist can act as an anchor for the elicitation of the relaxation response. Jessica was trained to induce self-hypnosis rapidly in anxiety-provoking situations by mastering the clenched fist technique. The following transcript shows how the clenched fist technique was introduced to Jessica while she was in a deep hypnotic trance.

> You have now become so deeply relaxed, that you feel this beautiful sensation of peace and relaxation, tranquility and calm, flowing all over your mind and your body, giving you such a pleasant, such a soothing sensation, all over your mind and your body that you feel completely relaxed, totally relaxed, drifting into a deeper and deeper hypnotic trance. This shows that you have the ability to relax, the ability to let go, and the ability to put things on hold. This shows that you have lots of control, because you are aware of what's happening around you, yet you are able to relax your mind and body completely. Since you are able to relax here, you may also be able to relax in any situation. In order facilitate your ability to relax in real situations I am going to introduce you to the clenched fist technique [which was discussed prior to the induction of the hypnosis].
>
> Now if you may clench your right fist [it was established that she is right-handed]. As you clench your fist become aware of how very relaxed you are. You feel completely relaxed both mentally and physically, and yet you are aware of everything. Also notice that you are in complete control, knowing what to do and knowing what's going on around you. If you slightly tighten your fist you may become even more aware of the good feelings. You feel completely relaxed and in complete control.
>
> As you have made an association between your right fist and the ability to relax, from now on, whenever you want to feel this good feeling, you can bring on this feeling by clenching your right fist and anchoring your mind to this session, that is, reminding yourself of this session, that you can relax and let go completely. And from now on, wherever you are, whatever you are doing, if you feel tense, anxious, upset, or stressed out, you can counter these feelings by clenching you right fist and anchoring your mind to this experience. With practice you will get better and better at it.

The clenched fist technique is bolstered by PHS and experientially ratified by imaginal rehearsal (in hypnosis visualizing using the clenched fist technique in real situations).

> Just undo your fist. Now we are going to practice the clenching fist technique. Imagine from now on using your clenched fist technique whenever you get upset, anxious, or stressed out. Imagine by using the clenched fist technique you are able to cope with bad feelings. Just imagine, from now on whenever you get anxious, upset or stressed out, you are able to cope with the bad feelings by clenching you fist and anchoring your mind to this experience. And with practice you will get better and better at it. As a result of this you will learn to cope better with negative reaction. If the negative reaction persists, you don't have to control them, you don't have to try to get rid of them, just learn to cope with them, or flow with them. As you have learned from the self-hypnosis training, you can be aware of everything but able to let go, able to flow.

Jessica found it reassuring to know that she did not have to control or get rid of her anxiety or distress, rather learning to cope with them by facing them and accepting them. She found the clenched fist technique very concrete, potable and easy to use in real situations. She indicated that these techniques made her feel empowered in the sense that she knew what to do when feeling anxious rather than being reactive.

Post-hypnotic suggestions
PHS are routinely delivered during hypnotherapy to counter problem behaviours, negative emotions, dysfunctional cognitions and NSH. Jessica was offered a variety of PHS to counter her anxiety and her SM. Jessica was constantly cogitating with the following negative self-suggestions:

- 'I will not be able to speak.'
- 'I will make mistake.'
- 'They will laugh at me.'
- 'It will be so embarrassing if I say the wrong word.'

Rumination with these suggestions not only can induce a negative trance but also can become part of the avoidance pattern of behaviour. To offset the negative rumination, Jessica was offered various PHS, including:

- 'Whenever you become anxious in a situation, you will become more aware of how to deal with it rather than focusing on all the things that can go wrong.'

- 'When you plan to face an anxiety provoking situation, you will feel no need to avoid the situation.'
- 'As you become more relaxed every day as a result of listening to your Self-Hypnosis CD, you will begin to think of speaking naturally.'

Clarke and Jackson (1983) found PHS to enhance the effect of *in vivo* exposure among agoraphobics.

Phase II: Behavioural and cognitive therapies for selective mutism

Once the child with SM has learned to relax and built some confidence with hypnotherapy, the treatment is segued into the second phase. The main focus of this stage of therapy is to help the SM child initiate and increase speech in the selectively muted situations. From behavioural perspective, SM is conceptualized as a learned behaviour. Irrespective of the original cause, SM is viewed as a product of a series of conditioning events. In this model, SM is thought to develop either as an escape from anxiety or as a way of gaining attention (secondary gain) from others. Unfortunately, the secondary gain maintains the mutism over time (Labbe & Williamson, 1984). Behavioural interventions, therefore, employ a variety of techniques to increase verbalizations in settings where the child has previously remained mute. Some of the common strategies include imaginal exposure, HASD, gradual exposure *in vivo*, contingency management, shaping, positive reinforcement, audio/video self-modelling and cognitive therapy. Although these techniques are described separately here, in practice they are usually used in conjunction with other strategies.

Imaginal exposure

This technique involves guiding the patient to imagine dealing with the anxiety head-on rather than avoiding it. It serves as a preparation for desensitization, which involves systematic and graded exposure to anxiety-provoking situations. Imaginal exposure therapy (Wolpe, 1958; Wolpe & Lazarus, 1966) is, nevertheless, considered to be an important component of CH for anxiety disorders (Golden, 2012).

While in deep hypnosis, Jessica was directed to bring on her anxious experience associated with speaking at school. She was then suggested to utilize self-hypnosis to cope with the anxiety.

> THERAPIST: When I count from ONE to FIVE, by the time you hear me say FIVE, you will begin to feel whatever emotion or reaction that you feel when you think about talking to your teachers or

your peers at school. ONE ... TWO ... THREE ... FOUR ...
FIVE. [Pause.] Do you feel the feeling you experience when
you think about speaking in school?

[Jessica raised her 'YES' finger.]

[Jessica was then encouraged to amplify the feeling she was experiencing
while she was thinking about speaking to her peers or to her teachers.]

THERAPIST: This time when I count ONE to FIVE, you will begin to experience the anxious feeling even more intensely, so that when I
reach the count of FIVE, at the count of FIVE you will feel the
full reaction as strongly as you can bear it. ONE ... TWO ...
THREE ... FOUR ... FIVE. Can you feel it?

[Jessica raised her 'YES' finger.]

THERAPIST: Now notice what you feel and you can describe it to me. [Jessica
was asked to describe her feeling in order to encourage her to
speak.]

JESSICA: I feel scared I may say the wrong thing. I feel nervous and shaky
and very uncomfortable.

[Jessica was then instructed to utilize her self-hypnosis skill to cope with the
anxious feeling.]

THERAPIST: Now imagine using your self-hypnosis to cope with the anxiety
feeling. Since you have the ability to relax and put things on
hold, you can let go and calm down.

After several repetition of this set of suggestions, Jessica was able to
relax completely, while imagining speaking to her teachers and peers at
school. This mental rehearsal in trance, prepared Jessica to face her fear of
speaking at school. Moreover, this technique encouraged her to focus on
her anxious feelings head-on, rather than catastrophizing or cogitating
about her symptoms. The imaginal exposure technique was also used to
prepare Jessica for systematic desensitization, which is more structured
than imaginal exposure.

Hypnosis-aided systematic desensitization
Although imaginal exposure was helpful to Jessica in terms of increasing
her motivation to speak at school, she was too anxious to tolerate *in vivo*
exposure. She felt more comfortable and ready to work with SD. SD,
also known as counterconditioning or graduated exposure therapy, is a
common evidence-based behavioural technique based on classical conditioning (Farris & Jouriles, 1993; also see Chapter 2). The goal of SD is to
pair mildly anxiety-provoking stimuli with anxiety-incompatible strategies
(e.g., relaxation) in a gradual fashion so that the child's anxiety is reduced

with repeated pairings (Garcia et al., 2004). In SD for SM, the child is gradually exposed to initiating and increasing verbal activities in situations that he or she had been avoiding to speak. This procedure allows the child to learn to cope with and overcome anxiety in small steps, which then allows the child to take greater steps to self-reliance (Cohan et al., 2006). Rye and Ullman (1999) provide an excellent case study of a 13-year-old boy who had been selectively mute for 7 years to demonstrate the effectiveness of SD with SM (see Garcia et al., 2004 and Sharkey & McNicholas, 2008, for reviews of effectiveness of SD with SM).

In CH, relaxation component of SD is replaced by hypnosis, and hence, this treatment approach is referred to as HASD (Iglesias & Iglesias, 2014). With younger children the presence of a familiar and trusted adult can be used as the anxiety-incompatible stimulus. A number of reports in the literature support the effectiveness of combining hypnosis with SD in the treatment of specific phobias (Glick, 1970). Table 9.1 shows the hierarchy of anxiety, which was constructed to help Jessica overcome her fear of speaking at school. The hierarchy represents various verbal activities, ranked from least anxious to most anxious, that Jessica had been avoiding because of her anxiety. The anxiety was self-rated in terms of SUD on 0–100 scale; 0 representing no anxiety and 100 standing for the worst anxiety.

While feeling very relaxed in deep hypnosis, Jessica was asked to imagine each hierarchy of verbal activity in turn, starting with the lowest

Table 9.1   Systematic desensitization hierarchy of anxiety related to speaking at school

Item	Fear rating in SUD (0–100)
Initiation of facial gestures	20
Mouthing answers	25
Whispering	30
Whispering to the parent in front of the therapist	35
Talking in an audible voice to the parent in front of the therapist	40
Answering a question from a teacher	50
Speaking with teacher in a loud voice	60
Answering a question from a peer	65
Speaking in a loud voice to her peers	75
Raising hand to answer a question from the teacher	80
Initiating conversation with teacher	90
Initiating conversation with peers	100

item in the hierarchy ('Initiation of facial gestures'; SUD = 20). She was instructed to focus on the target verbal activity until she was able to bring her SUD level down to 0. It is important for patient to master one hierarchy, that is, able to imagine the target activity without any anxiety, before moving on to the next item in the hierarchy. Failure to master previous activity in the hierarchy may produce resistance to work with the next item, which is likely to be more anxiety-provoking (higher SUD level). Jessica found the desensitization procedure very helpful in bringing down her level of anxiety during the sessions. After five sessions of SD she felt confident to handle gradual *in vivo* exposure.

Gradual in vivo *exposure therapy*

Exposure *in vivo* is an evidence-based key component of CBT for anxiety disorders (e.g., Follette & Smith, 2005), and it is considered to be the gold standard treatment for agoraphobia (Chambless, 1985; Hazlett-Stevens, 2006). Exposure *in vivo* is designed to help children with SM confront fearful situations, memories and images in a therapeutic manner. As a child with SM exhibits high levels of anxiety, a graduated *in vivo* desensitization is designed. This involves a step-by-step approach to conquering the anxiety elicited by the anticipation of speaking in certain situations. The SM child draws on his or her relaxation skills, self-hypnosis and cognitive coping strategies to manage the anxiety associated with the successive exposure steps.

The same hierarchy of anxiety (see Table 9.1) that was constructed for SD was used with Jessica for the graded *in vivo* desensitization procedure. Jessica's and her parents were in full agreement with the graded hierarchy schedule. Jessica was very surprised that she was able to complete the *in vivo* exercises in three weeks. However, she confessed that she was still feeling anxious talking to her teacher and peers, although she managed to speak to them.

Contingency management

Contingency management strategies, based on operant learning principles, have received the most empirical attention in the management of SM (Cunningham, Cataldo, Mallion, & Keyes, 1984). Contingency management interventions involve positive reinforcement of verbal behaviour to increase verbalizations in problematic settings.

In this procedure, a reinforcement menu is first developed in collaboration with the child and reinforcement is provided for approximations of the target verbal behaviour such as mouthing words, whispering, talking on the telephone and later for normal speech (Cohan et al., 2006). Positive and negative consequences are added or taken away to increase the frequency of speech and decrease the frequency of mutism. For example, the SM child who speaks in class is allowed to play video games at home in the evening, but the child who refuses to talk in class loses the privilege of playing games at home. Negative or aversive consequences can also be used to increase the frequency of speech and reduce not speaking. When this behavioural strategy is used, the SM child is informed that he or she could avoid aversive consequences by speaking. So when the child fails to speak, negative consequences such as time-out, response cost (loss of reinforcement previously earned for speaking), punishment (e.g., after school detention) or overcorrection (e.g., repeated writing of a sentence) are administered. The goal of these strategies is to teach the child to speak in order to avoid an aversive consequence. Garcia et al. (2004) have, however, emphasized that for these behavioural strategies to work, they should be part of a comprehensive treatment protocol.

Shaping

In shaping, the SM child is gradually encouraged to first communicate nonverbally, then to make certain sounds, then whisper, and finally speak a word or a sentence. The phrase 'vocalization ladder' has been used as a metaphor to represent the shaping process for working with children with SM (McHolm, Cunningham, & Vanier, 2005; Oon, 2010). Shaping is usually used to increase the length or complexity of spoken communication.

Stimulus fading

The stimulus-fading intervention is capitalized on the success derived from contingency management and shaping by gradually increasing the number of people and places in which speech is rewarded (Cohan et al., 2006). This behavioural strategy is also known as 'sliding-in technique' (Garcia et al., 2004). The stimulus-fading procedure involves bringing the SM child into a controlled environment with someone with whom he or she is comfortable with and with whom he or she can communicate, and then more people are introduced, one at a time. Because the child's mute behaviour is usually manifested at school and speaks normally at home, a parent usually functions as the safe base, and gradually classmates and the teacher are introduced to generalize the child's speaking behaviour. This can be illustrated by using the example cited by Cohan et al. (2006, p. 1091):

> [T]he child may first be rewarded for speaking to a classmate to whom s/he already speaks outside of school. Gradually, other students are introduced into the group until the child is able to speak in the presence of a large

group of peers. Stimulus fading can also be used in problematic situations that occur outside of school (e.g., talking to grandparents, ordering in fast food restaurants).

Positive reinforcement
This strategy involves rewarding the SM child for speaking. Every time the child initiates or increases speech in a 'muted' situation, the child is positively reinforced. The positive reinforcement could be praise, a privilege, an object (money, toys, etc.) or tokens that can be exchanged later for a positive reinforce.

Audio/Video self-modelling
The self-modelling strategy is derived from social learning theory. In this procedure, the SM child exhibits verbal behaviour by watching self- or model-behaviour. Model-behaviour can be displayed by a peer, a sibling, a parent, a teacher, or someone that the child respects. Self-modelling entails the SM child watching a videotape or listening to an audiotape of himself or herself speaking in target situations such as talking to a peer at school, answering the teacher's question, and so on. The videotape modelling usually involves the SM child being videotaped while he or she is talking with a parent and then the tape is edited as if the child is speaking to a teacher. The child then views the tape, watching himself or herself modelling verbal behaviour (Garcia et al., 2004). Case studies have demonstrated the efficacy of using audiotape (Blum et al., 1998) and videotape (e.g., Holmbeck & Lavigne, 1992) self-modelling in the management of SM. Again as emphasized for contingency management training, the behavioural techniques work best as part of a multimodal therapy.

Cognitive therapy
Use of cognitive therapy strategies with SM is based on the premise that anxiety stems from irrational or maladaptive thoughts, beliefs or self-talk. Research has consistently documented that children with anxiety disorders have distortions in information processing, memory biases for distressing events, hypersensitivity to threat cues, and a bias towards interpreting ambiguous situations as threatening (Vasey & Dadds, 2001). Cognitive techniques are therefore designed to identify and modify maladaptive self-talk, which was referred to as NSH in the context of hypnotherapy. Children with SM tend to be preoccupied with such self-talk as 'They will laugh at me if I make a mistake', 'I don't know what to say', 'I may say the wrong thing', 'It will be so embarrassing to say the wrong thing'. A variety

of cognitive techniques have been developed to assist children with SM identify their maladaptive cognitions related to selective mute situations. One of the most common methods is to use the empty 'thought bubble' (Kendall, 2000). In this procedure, children are shown various cartoons in which people's self-talk or thoughts appear in a bubble above their heads. While the children are observing these cartoons, they are asked, 'What's in your self-talk bubble?' Once the children become efficient at identifying their self-talk, they are trained to analyse their thoughts by asking questions such as:

- Is your thought that you would not be able to speak at all true?
- Do you always know what to say at home?
- Has it happened before that you were not able to say a single word?
- What is the worst that will happen to you if you get embarrassed?
- What is the worst that will happen to you if you say the wrong word?
- Is there another way of looking at the situation if you have difficulty talking?

From the analysis of their self-talk, and with coaching from the therapist, children with SM are able to generate coping thoughts to counter their negative self-talk and, consequently, reduce their anxiety about selective situations. This approach may not be appropriate with younger children who do not have the cognitive ability to identify their cognitive distortions. Children of age eight and over are able to handle the empty 'thought bubble' techniques. As Jessica was 14 years old, she participated in more formal cognitive therapy as described in other chapters in the book. Some of Jessica's maladaptive cognitions included:

- I am ugly.
- I am stupid.
- I will hurt their feelings if I say the wrong thing.
- They will yell at me.
- It's safer to be quiet.
- I can't express my feelings.

Jessica had three sessions of CBT. These sessions helped her identify and alter her negative self-talk and as a result she felt more confident participating in exposure therapy. For more detail about the sequential presentation of CBT, see Chapter 4, and for a CBT transcript with anticipatory anxiety, see Alladin (2008, pp. 107–110).

In summary, it would appear that there is extensive preliminary evidence for the effectiveness of cognitive-behavioural strategies for the management of SM. However, for the treatment effect to endure, it is important to use these strategies in the context of a multimodal approach to treatment. This is very well illustrated by Hung et al. (2012), who describe a comprehensive treatment intervention for a preschool child with SM involving the therapist, the family and the school environment in the successful management of mutism at school. Also based on their experience working with SM children, they (Hung et al., 2012, pp. 227–228) have provided the following recommendations for increasing the effectiveness of psychological intervention with SM:

1. Form an intervention team consisting of key workers such as therapist, teacher and family members.
2. Share details of intervention and encourage cooperation and collaboration with team.
3. Develop a home- and school-based intervention plan with the teachers, the family and the child.
4. Allow the child to become familiar with the therapist with minimum stress at or before the first individual session.
5. Arrange for the therapist to initially interact and talk with the child in a place where the child normally speaks.
6. Increase the child's sense of continuity between home and school.
7. Do not allow anyone, especially team or family members, to assign blame for the child's mutism as this may increase the child's stress and worsen the condition.
8. Examine environmental factors to determine possible barriers preventing the child from speaking.
9. Never force the child to speak but gradually encourage different attempts at communication such as head nodding, hand shaking, facial expressions, writing, drawing or whispering.
10. Minimize pressure, and emphasize trust to enable the child to build confidence in his or her attempts at verbal communication.
11. Analyse and manage all the factors that contribute to changes in the child's verbal behaviours.
12. Introduce behavioural techniques appropriately to gradually generalize the child's verbal behaviour.
13. Report progress in a timely manner and share information from school and home with all key workers.
14. Praise or celebrate the child's accomplishments in low-key ways that he or she is able to accept.

Phase III: Healing self-wounds

Once a child with SM has achieved some measure of control over his or her SM from either hypnotherapy or CBT (or a combination of both), the therapist has to make a decision about the next step of intervention. For those patients who have improved and believe that they had met their goals, the therapy is considered complete, and it is duly terminated. For those patients who wish to explore the roots of their mutism, they are enrolled in the third phase of therapy. This phase of intervention involves two separate, but inter-related, procedures: uncovering and healing of tacit self-wounds. The role of trauma during early childhood, delayed grief, parental hostility, stranger anxiety and impaired object relations has been implicated in the etiology of EM. For example, Anderson and Thomsen (1998), in their clinical sample of EM children, found the presence of a traumatic event during the critical years of speech development in one-third of the children. Psychodynamic approaches to treatment thus emphasize the identification and resolution of inner conflicts. Although controlled studies of psychodynamic therapies for SM are lacking, a number of case studies have reported the effectiveness of psychodynamic approaches to treatment (see Cohan et al., 2006).

Although Jessica had significantly decreased her mutism at school after about 4 months of therapy, she still felt anxious talking and at time avoided verbal interaction with her peers. Both Jessica and her parents were interested in knowing why she still continued to feel uncomfortable talking to her peers at school. They were puzzled that she could converse at home and with her relatives but not with her schoolmates. The next segment of therapy thus involved in-depth hypnotherapy and consisted of accessing and healing any underlying fears or conflicts.

Elicitation of self-wounds
To access Jessica's self-wounds, if present, the affect bridge technique was used. The feeling of anxiety that she experienced at school when talking to her peers was used as a bridge to elicit her first anxiety attack. While experiencing intense anxiety, she became aware of being bullied at school. With promptings from the therapist, she described a series of bullying incidents ranging from grade 2 to grade 7 listed as follows:

- Grades 2–4 bullied at school on several occasions.
- She was called ugly, fat, 'gross' and worthless.
- In Grade 7 she was pinned against the wall by a Grade 9 boy. Rather than rescuing her, all her peers laughed at her and called her a 'weak slob'.

As a result of these recurrent traumas, Jessica was convinced that she was fat, ugly and worthless. She lost 'all confidence' and started to believe that was 'unworthy as a human being' and 'not deserving to be happy'. She thus decided not to speak to anyone in school as they 'hurt' her 'so much'. After speaking for a while, Jessica went silent and then she started to cry loudly. With prompting from the therapist Jessica disclosed the main reason for her SM. She indicated that she was gay and was terrified to be found out by her peers at school. Since her school peers were so 'cruel' to her, she was petrified that if they found out she was gay, they would 'destroy' her. To hide her secret, she decided to be selectively mute in situations where she felt threatened, especially the school. Since she was 12 years old, she became aware that she was gay. She had no interest in boys. She was attracted and aroused by girls, and all her sexual and relationship fantasies were with girls. She was 'turned on' by several girls at school, but has not communicated this to anyone, again having this fear that she would be 'roasted' if found out. Jessica had discussed her sexual preference to her parents. Although they were supportive to her, she believed they were supportive to her to be polite rather than 'meaning it'. Jessica felt 'guilty' and hated herself for being gay. She felt she was a 'failure' and 'an embarrassment' to her family. For these reasons, on occasions, she had felt hopeless and 'extremely frustrated', and dealt with her sense of helplessness by scratching her arms. On occasions the thought of suicide crossed her mind, but she never had the intent to die or injure herself seriously.

From the information derived from the affect bridge procedure it was hypothesized that (i) Jessica was terrified to be discovered by her school peers that she was gay; (ii) she was selectively mute, especially at school, as a defence against any form of disclosure about her sexual preference and (iii) the recurrent traumatic experience (being bullied) at school had shaped her negative self-schemas, which was maintaining her anxiety and SM. From these hypotheses it was formulated that Jessica needed to resolve two main experiential conflicts: (i) to detoxify the meaning of her anxiety and (ii) to defend her sexual preference.

Detoxification of meaning of anxiety

The split screen technique (Alladin, 2008; Cardena et al., 2000; Lynn & Cardena, 2007; Spiegel, 1981) was used to help Jessica detoxify the meaning of her SM. This is a hypnotic strategy that utilizes the 'adult ego state' to assist the 'weak ego state' deal with anxiety-provoking situations. It also facilitates the 'two' ego states to work together as a team, rather than splitting from each other, when the self is threatened or stressed out.

The therapy transcript presented here illustrates how the split screen technique was used to help Jessica deal with the toxic meaning of mutism. The transcript begins while Jessica was in a deep trance, bolstered by ego-strengthening suggestions.

THERAPIST: Now I would like you to imagine sitting in front of a large TV or cinema screen, that is vertically split in two halves, consisting of a right side and a left side. Can you imagine this?

[Jessica raised her 'YES' finger. Ideomotor signals were already set up – 'YES' represented raising of his right index finger and 'NO' was represented by raising of his left index finger.]

THERAPIST: Imagine the right side of the screen is lighting up as if it's ready to project an image. Imagine yourself being projected on the right side of the screen, just as you are now. Feeling very relaxed, very comfortable, in complete control, and being aware of everything around you. Do you feel these good feelings?

[Jessica raised her 'YES' finger.]

THERAPIST: And now become aware of the things you have done, or places you have been to, that make you feel good. Do you feel these good feelings?

[Jessica raised her 'YES' finger.]

THERAPIST: That's very good. Do you feel the good feelings?

[Jessica raised her 'YES' finger.]

THERAPIST: Are you thinking about the good feelings you had when you went to Italy with your parents last year? [It is advisable to check out the fact rather than making assumption. In this case, the assumption was made by the therapist based on what Jessica had told the therapist. She related to the therapist the 'wonderful' feelings she had when she visited the Vatican and Venice.]

[Jessica raised her 'YES' finger.]

THERAPIST: Just focus on the good feelings and the sense of pride you feel for having been to Italy. This proves to you that you can feel good about yourself even if you have problems or difficulties. We are going to call this part of you the 'strong part' or the 'relaxed part' of you. Is this acceptable to you?

[Jessica raised her 'YES' finger.]

THERAPIST: Now leave this 'strong part' of you on the right side of the screen and imagine the anxious part of you is projected on the left side of the screen. Imagine yourself being at school and is thinking of speaking to the person who sits next to you in class.

Become aware of the anxious feeling that you are experiencing. Can you imagine this?

[Jessica raised her 'YES' finger.]

THERAPIST: Become aware of all the feelings that you are experiencing. Don't be afraid to let all the anxious feelings come over you, because soon we will show you how to deal with them. Become aware of all the physical sensations you feel. Become aware of all the thoughts that are going through your mind and become aware of your behaviors. Can you feel these?

[Jessica raised her 'YES' finger.]

THERAPIST: Just become aware of the whole experience and we are going to call this part of you the 'anxious part' of you. Is this acceptable to you?

[Jessica raised her 'YES' finger.]

THERAPIST: Now imagine, your 'strong' part is stepping out from the right side into the left side of the screen. Can you imagine this?

[Jessica raised her 'YES' finger.]

THERAPIST: Imagine your 'strong part' is hugging your 'weak part' and telling her that she is here to help out. She is telling your 'anxious part' not to be afraid because she is here to guide you how to deal with the fear. You may or may not know this, the 'strong part' of you had been very attentive to the therapy sessions and she had learned lot of tricks to deal with fear and anxiety. If you want to, she can share this with you? Does your 'anxious part' want to know about this?

[Jessica raised her 'YES' finger.]

THERAPIST: From now on, the 'anxious part' of you don't have to work on her own. The 'strong part' of you can join you. She can show you how to deal with stress and fear. She will show you how to relax, how to calm down, and how to 'flow'. She will also remind you of the Clenched Fist Technique and how to reason with your fearful thoughts. Does your 'anxious part' agree to this?

[Jessica raised her 'YES' finger.]

THERAPIST: From now on, the 'anxious part' of you don't have to handle difficulties on her own, she can work as a team with the 'strong part' of you. Now become aware of the anxious feelings you are feeling on the left side of the screen. Imagine the 'strong part' of you is telling the 'anxious' part of you how to deal with the fearful feelings you are feeling right now. Imagine she is demonstrating the 'anxious part' how to relax, how to let go, how to 'flow', and how to reason with fearful thoughts. Continue to imagine this until you feel the 'anxious part' of you feel good and less fearful. When she feels good and less fearful, let me know by raising your 'YES' finger.

[Jessica raised her 'YES' finger after about 30 seconds.]

THERAPIST: Imagine your 'anxious part' feels protected and she knows what to do now when she feels anxious or fearful. She feels good knowing that she is not on her own; she has the 'strong part' to help her out. The 'anxious part' also realizes that the 'strong part' is part of your self as well. They both belong to your self. So from now on there is no need to feel separated from the 'strong part' of you. Two is better than one. You are a team now. Do you agree with this?

[Jessica raised her 'YES' finger.]

The split screen technique was repeated over several sessions, with main focus on coping with anxiety about speaking at school. Jessica found the strategy 'very helpful'. She indicated that 'a part' of her knew that she could speak at school if she 'really wanted to'. This realization, coupled with the clear understanding that her SM was related to fear of disclosing to her peers that she was gay, had a significant effect on her. Prior to these sessions, Jessica was preoccupied with various toxic self-talk, for example, 'I am weak', 'Don't know what to say', 'I will say the wrong thing', and so on. After the split screen sessions, she was able change these negative cognitions into 'I can talk, but I did not want to talk, because I did not want to tell my peers I am gay; I was afraid if I tell them they would humiliate me '. The next part of the hypnotherapy therefore focused on helping Jessica (i) separate reality from unreality (reframing her self-schemas based on trauma); (ii) reducing guilt for being gay (defending her sexual orientation); and (iii) coming to terms with being gay. The empty chair technique was used to deal with these conflictual issues.

The empty chair technique

As Jessica did not feel comfortable talking to her peers about being bullied at school, the therapist recommended working with the empty chair technique. This technique, derived from Gestalt therapy, is a role-playing strategy (Perls, Hefferline, & Goodman, 1951; Woldt & Toman, 2005) for reducing intra- or interpersonal conflicts (Nichol & Schwartz, 2008). In this procedure, while in deep hypnosis, Jessica was encouraged to role-play her 'strong part' having a conversation with her 'weak part'. She imagined each of them sitting in an empty chair facing each other (two-empty-chair technique) right in front of her in the therapist's office. By imagining her 'anxious part' sitting in the empty chair in the safety of the therapy situation and in the presence of her 'strong part', Jessica's 'anxious part' was able to express various strong feelings (fear, insecurity, lacking confidence, etc.) about her peers she had been harbouring inside her since grade 2. By engaging in the two-empty-chair work, and with the support and direction from the therapist, Jessica's 'anxious part' was able to express her anxiety, feeling of insecurity, hurt feeling, lack of confidence and sense of rejection because of the bullying at school. In turn, her 'strong part' was able to guide her how to deal with these issues. The following transcript which began while Jessica was in a deep trance depicts the therapeutic dialogue between the 'anxious' and the 'strong' parts.

THERAPIST: Jessica, is it okay for your 'anxious part' and your 'strong part' to have a conversation about the hurt that was caused to you by the recurrent bullying at school?

[Jessica raised her 'YES' finger.]

THERAPIST: Maybe your 'anxious part' can start by telling the 'strong part' of you about the bullying.

ANXIOUS PART: I was bullied at school. It started in Grade 2 and carried on until Grade 7. [Jessica started to cry.] It was so unfair. Kids were so cruel.

STRONG PART: [After about a minute] I am sorry to hear about the bullying. They must have been very painful to you.

ANXIOUS PART: It was so unfair. I did not do anyone any wrong. I did not deserve it.

STRONG PART: Tell me how was the experience for you?

ANXIOUS PART: I was traumatized. It was worse when the Grade 9 boy pinned me against the wall and everyone was laughing at me. [Continued to cry and talked for about 5 minutes how 'horrible' the experience was for her.]

STRONG PART: I am sorry to hear that you had to suffer so much. How did it change your thinking?

ANXIOUS PART: I lost confidence. I started to think I am useless, weak and unworthy.

STRONG PART: Is there anything we can do about it now?

ANXIOUS PART: I guess it's over now. Does no good wallowing about it now?

STRONG PART: I am glad you figured it out that wallowing over it does not help. Can you let the past go?

ANXIOUS PART: I guess I have to because it does not help, it brings bad memories. I remember Dr Alladin said we don't have the past, we don't have the future, but we have the present. What we do in the present determine how we feel now.

STRONG PART: I am so happy to hear that you are letting the past go. I also remember Dr Alladin saying 'You can't prevent the birds flying over head, but you can prevent them from building their nests in your hair.'

ANXIOUS PART: I agree with you. I don't have to forget the past, but I can dodge it. Since we did the CBT, I have already started to do this.

STRONG PART: I am really happy that you are in the right track. Now that you have been finding new ways to cope with the bad experience, what do you think about yourself now compared to before?

ANXIOUS PART: I realized that I should not suffer twice. I have already suffered so much because of the bullying and now I don't have to suffer by downing myself. I have started to think of myself who I am rather than thinking I am bad or worthless person. Those kids bullied me not because I had a problem, they bullied me because they are losers. I feel sorry for them. You can't solve your problems by hurting others.

The empty chair technique helped Jessica get out of the victim role. Once she was able to discover that her negative cognitions were maintaining her anxiety, she was able to reframe her self-schemas that emanated from the repeated bullying. She also came up with the realization that the main cause of her mutism at school was not the bullying (although related) but the fear of disclosing that she was gay. The next segment of the hypnotherapy focuses on reducing her guilt about being gay.

Defending her sexual preference

The recurrent bullying at school not only contributed to Jessica's self-wounds and SM, but also contributed to the terror of her peers finding out that she was gay, which maintained her SM. The next major component of the experiential hypnotherapy thus consisted of helping Jessica (i) accept her sexual preference, (ii) reduce her guilt of being gay and (iii) defend her sexual preference with regard to her peers.

Two sessions of split screen technique was used to help Jessica (i) have 'ownership' being gay and (ii) alleviate her guilt for her sexual preference. Her 'strong PART' communicated to the 'weak part' that:

1. It is not abnormal to be gay.
2. Being gay is acceptable in our culture.
3. Some people do not accept gays, but that's their personal beliefs. We should not live our life based on others' beliefs. Once should stick to his or her own belief.

4. Being gay is not a choice one makes, one is biologically programmed to be gay.
5. Her parents are supportive to her.
6. She should not feel guilty for being gay. Being gay does not mean letting your parents down. It is not your fault.
7. One can still be a 'good and loving child' despite being gay.
8. One is not less of a person being gay.
9. Being gay does not stop you live a normal life and be a successful citizen.
10. Being gay may be challenging, but one can only focus in the present and 'play it by ears'.
11. She realized that being gay is not a weakness.

Jessica found the split screen technique very useful. It clarified her thinking and made her become more objective and realistic in her thinking, rather than 'catastrophizing'.

As it was not appropriate for Jessica to confront her school peers about her sexual preference, the empty chair technique was re-visited. However, this time the interaction was between Jessica and her peers. While in deep hypnosis, Jessica was directed to talk to her peers. She imagined several of her peers, particularly those who bullied her, were sitting in several empty chairs in the therapist's office, across from her. By imagining her peers sitting in the empty chairs in the safety of the therapy situation, Jessica was able to express various strong feelings about her peers that she had been harbouring inside her for several years.

By engaging in the empty chair work, and with the support and direction from the therapist, Jessica was able to express her strong negative feelings towards them and then reframed her anger into sympathy. She was also able to defend her sexual preference. She indicated that it was her right to be who she wanted to be, they were not the ones who decide how she should live her life, and if they did like her sexual preference that was their problems, not hers. She felt sorry for them that they projected their frustration and anger onto other people rather than dealing with them. She pointed out to them that she was much stronger than they were because she was able to solve her problems rather than scapegoating. She also indicated that she was no longer going to blame herself for their negative views about gay people. Their negative views and their homophobia did not equate she was weak or worthless. Self-worth had nothing to do with sexual preference.

The empty chair technique helped Jessica vent and release her anger and hurt related to her peers. She showed very good response to hypnotherapy and cognitive-behavioural therapies. They helped her identify the explicit and the implicit nature of her anxiety and SM, as well as the roots of her wounded self. While behavioural and cognitive strategies helped her symptomatically, the hypnotherapy, by virtue of its phenomenological nature, made the therapy experiential and thus more meaningful to her. She found the HET very helpful in accessing and healing her self-wounds. The empty chair and the split screen techniques permitted her to resolve her anger and hurt related to her peers. She was also able to take 'ownership' of her sexual preference and decreased her mutism very significantly. Gradually, she was able to initiate and engage in regular conversations with her teachers and peers. She even managed to disclose to one of her peers from her classroom that she was gay. To her surprise the friend was 'very supportive and friendly' to her. As a result of this experience, she felt motivated to 'experiment' with other peers.

Phase IV: Promoting acceptance and gratitude

Although Jessica responded very well to CH and decreased her SM significantly, she was encouraged to do some relapse prevention work prior to her discharge, to which Jessica and her family agreed. Because of her vulnerable background and the challenges she might have to face for being gay, the therapist was concerned about relapses in the future. The fourth phase of CH for SM promotes acceptance and mindfulness in order to prevent relapse in the future. However, this phase of therapy is determined by the age and needs of the child with SM. The author recommends this phase of therapy primarily to adolescents and adults as children may not be cognitively mature to grapple with the concepts of acceptance and mindfulness.

As discussed in Chapter 1, avoidance or intolerance of inner suffering can be regarded as lack of acceptance within the context of third-wave CBT (Baer & Huss, 2008). Although Jessica's suppression of her self-wounds warded off her distressing experience temporarily, unfortunately it maintained her SM. For this reason, it was important to help Jessica accept her emotional distress. However, acceptance is not merely tolerance of inner hurt; it is the active and nonjudgemental embracing of painful experience in the here and now, involving undefended exposure to thoughts, feelings and bodily sensations as they occur (Hayes, 2004). Levitt, Brown, Orsillo and Barlow (2004) have provided empirical evidence for the effectiveness of acceptance-based interventions in the management of anxiety disorders. Several techniques, including (i) gratitude education, (ii) gratitude training, (iii) acceptance training, (iv) acceptance and gratitude hypnotherapy and (v) mind–body–heart integration were used to help Jessica cultivate acceptance.

Gratitude education and training

Sense of gratitude is used as a means to cultivate acceptance in patients with anxiety disorders. Gratitude is a feeling or attitude in acknowledgement of a benefit that one has received or will receive. Studies suggest that people who are grateful have higher levels of subjective well-being, have higher levels of control of their environments, have more positive ways of coping with the difficulties they experience in life, spend more time planning how to deal with the problem, are less likely to try to avoid or deny their problems, and they sleep better (for review and references see Chapter 2).

Gratitude education

Gratitude education focuses on drawing broad generalizations about different cultural values and beliefs, and comparing Western and non-Western expectations of life and achievement. Jessica was also encouraged to read the book, *The Narcissism Epidemic: Living in the Age of Entitlement* (Twenge & Campbell, 2009). This book provides a clear account of how high expectations and preoccupation with success, and sense of entitlement can set us up for failure. The gratitude education helped Jessica recognize that values are human-made, subjective and culturally determined. This comparative understanding of societal values helped her overcome her guilt about being gay and also facilitated the understanding that different people have different views, and therefore a person should not feel victimized if others do not acquiesce to one's views.

Acceptance training

As Jessica was so centred on her self-wounds, the need for acceptance was not apparent to her. To raise her awareness about acceptance, she was encouraged to carry out a series of exercises, some of which are listed as follows.

- Focusing on here and now.
- Observing emotional experiences and their contexts non-judgementally.
- Separation of secondary emotions from primary emotions (e.g., not to get upset for feeling upset, or feeling depressed for feeling depressed).
- Learning to tolerate distress rather than fighting it (flow with it).
- Toleration of painful experience.

- Embracing good or bad experience as part of life.
- Purposely allowing experience (thoughts, emotions, desires, urges, sensations, etc.) to occur without attempting to block or suppress them.

Gratitude training

Gratitude training involves doing various gratitude tasks. Jessica was assigned a list of gratitude tasks as listed here, and she was advised to do at least one of the tasks daily.

- Writing gratitude letters
- Writing a gratitude journal
- Remembering gratitude moments
- Making gratitude visits to people she was grateful to
- Practicing gratitude self-talk

Acceptance and gratitude hypnotherapy

Acceptance-based therapy can become more experiential and meaningful when it is combined with hypnotherapy (Alladin, 2006). Therefore, to strengthen Jessica's sense of gratitude, she was offered the following suggestions, adapted from Alladin (2006, p. 303, 2007, p. 197), while she was in a deep hypnotic trance.

THERAPIST: Just continue to experience this beautiful sensation of peace and tranquillity, relaxation and calm flowing all over your mind and body. Notice feeling calm, peaceful, and a sense of well-being, and in total harmony. No tension, no pressure, completely relaxed both mentally and physically. Feeling happy that you can relax so deeply, that you can let go, and calm down completely. You feel pleased and grateful that you can let go completely. Now become aware of your heart. Notice how peaceful you feel in your heart, how calm you feel in your heart, and you feel a sense of a sense of gratitude in your heart. When you feel good in your heart, you feel good in your mind and in your body. Do you feel good in your heart?

[Jessica raised her 'YES' finger.]

THERAPIST: Do you feel good in your mind, body, and heart?

[Jessica raised her 'YES' finger.]

THERAPIST: Very good! You have the ability to feel good in your mind, body and heart. There is a saying that when you wake up in the morning, if you have a roof over your head, you have bread to eat, and water to drink, and are in fairly good health, then you have everything. Do you believe this?

[Jessica raised her 'YES' finger.]

THERAPIST: Just become aware of all the things you have and all the things you are grateful for. When living in the modern world, it's okay to have goals and ambitions. When we achieve them, they can be seen as bonuses and pluses as we have lots of other resources. When we don't achieve our goals and ambitions, it is disappointing, but we have enough resources to live a comfortable life. Do you agree with these comments and observation?

[Jessica raised her 'YES' finger.]

It is important that the acceptance-based hypnotherapy is carried out after the acceptance and gratitude training. In the absence of this training, a patient may not appreciate the therapeutic meaning of acceptance and gratitude, and may reject the hypnotic suggestions. Jessica found both the acceptance-based training and hypnotherapy very helpful. They gave her a new perspective on people's attitude, success and failure. Most importantly, she felt less preoccupied and fearful about being gay.

Mind–body–heart integration

This component of acceptance-based hypnotherapy integrates various subsystems in the body. As discussed in Chapter 2, heart-focused positive emotional state engenders synchronization of the entire body system and produce PC (McCraty et al., 2009). Based on these scientific findings, Alladin (2012) has developed the breathing with your heart technique to generate coherence (harmony) of the entire system (mind, body, brain, heart and emotion). This technique involves three sequential steps: (i) heart education, (ii) heart–mind training combined with hypnotherapy and (iii) breathing with your heart technique.

Heart education

Jessica was given a scientific account of the combined role of the heart and positive emotions in the generation of PC, which promotes healing, emotional stability and optimal performance. The similarities and the differences between the Western and Eastern theories of the mind and 'heart' were also discussed.

Heart–mind training combined with hypnotherapy

Heart–mind training helps patients with anxiety disorders cope with negative feelings (heavy heart) triggered by aversive situations. By breathing with the heart, anxious patients are able to shift their attention away from their mind to their heart.

Breathing with your heart technique
This transcript from a session with Jessica illustrates how the Breathing With Your Heart Technique is used to induce PC. The script begins with Jessica being in a deep hypnotic trance:

THERAPIST: Just continue to experience this beautiful sensation of peace and relaxation, tranquility and calm flowing throughout your mind and body, giving you such a pleasant feeling, such a soothing sensation, that you feel completely relaxed both mentally and physically. Do you feel relaxed both mentally and physically?

[Jessica raised her 'YES' finger.]

THERAPIST: Now I would like you to focus on the centre of your heart [pause for 30 seconds]. Can you imagine this?

[Jessica raised her 'YES' finger.]

THERAPIST: Now I would like you to imagine breathing in and out with your heart. [Pause for 30 seconds.] Can you imagine this?

[Jessica raised her 'YES' finger.]

THERAPIST: Continue to imagine breathing in and out with your heart. [She was allowed to continue with this exercise for 2 minutes.] The therapist repeated at regular intervals: 'Just continue to imagine breathing with your heart'. Now I would like you to slow down your breathing. Breathe in and out at 7-second intervals. Breathe in with your heart ... 1 ... 2 ... 3 ... 4 ... 5 ... 6 ... 7 and now breathe out with your heart ... 1 ... 2 ... 3 ... 4 ... 5 ... 6 ... 7 And now as you breathing in and out with your heart I want you to become aware of something in your life that you feel good about, something that you feel grateful for [pause for 30 seconds]. Are you able to focus on something that you are grateful for in your life?

[Jessica raised her 'YES' finger.]

THERAPIST: Just become aware of that feeling and soon you will feel good in your heart. [After 10 seconds] Do you feel it?

[Jessica raised her 'YES' finger.]

THERAPIST: Just become aware of this good feeling in your heart [pause for 30 seconds]. Now I would like to become aware of the good feeling in your mind, in your body, and in your heart. Do you feel this?

[Jessica raised her 'YES' finger.]

THERAPIST: Now that you feel good in your mind, in your body, and in your heart, you feel a sense of balance, a sense of harmony. Do you feel this sense of harmony?

[Jessica raised her 'YES' finger.]

THERAPIST: From now on, whenever and wherever you are, you can create this good feeling by imagining breathing with your heart and focusing on something that you are grateful for. With practice you will get better and better at it. Now you know what to do to make your heart feel lighter.

Although this phase of therapy was targeted for relapse prevention, Jessica found the techniques very helpful in dealing with her anxiety, and as a result, she reported overcoming her mutism and embarrassment of being gay.

Summary

Although the onset of SM is usually between the ages of three and five years, most children with SM are referred for treatment between the ages of 6 and 11, usually when they enter elementary school. As SM can cause long-lasting complications such as socialization and learning problems (Hung et al., 2012), early detection and early intervention is strongly recommended. The chapter provided a wide array of behavioural, cognitive, hypnotic, unconscious and acceptance-based strategies for treating SM, from which therapists can choose the best techniques that may suit their patients. The case of Jessica clearly illustrated that symptom-focused treatment is necessary but not sufficient for treating underlying determinants of an anxiety disorder. A comprehensive and durable treatment requires therapeutic confrontation of unconscious conflicts that harbour painful emotions (Wolfe, 2006). However, for the treatment to be effective, it is important to involve the school and the family in the treatment process. Gortmaker, Warnes and Sheridan (2004) have demonstrated successful treatment outcomes for SM when parents and teachers are included in the intervention process and when clinicians use an approach that is collaborative.

10

Conclusions and Future Directions

This book described SMAD and outlined the theoretical and empirical rationale for integrating CBT, psychodynamic therapy, mindfulness and hypnotherapy in the psychological management of anxiety disorders.

To provide a practical guide to clinical practice, each chapter pertaining to a specific anxiety disorder from DSM-V described in detail a step-by-step treatment protocol. Moreover, each chapter explained a variety of extant strategies derived from behavioural, cognitive, hypnotic, psycho-analytic and mindfulness strategies from which a clinician can choose the best-fit techniques to meet the needs of his or her individual patient. The techniques are described in sufficient details to allow replication and adaptation in different settings. However, the fleshing out of the self-wounds model and the elaboration of CH for anxiety disorders are not seen as a finished product but as an evolving process requiring further refinement if possible.

The main goal of writing this book has been to describe and encourage evidence-based clinical practice and research in hypnotherapy. Hence the book provides therapists a template for assimilating hypnosis with CBT, mindfulness and psychodynamic therapies in the management of anxiety disorders. However, the book goes beyond this. First, it lays down a solid theoretical foundation for combining hypnosis with CBT, mindfulness and psychodynamic therapies in the management of anxiety disorders. Second, the book provides a case formulation approach to clinical practice. This approach to clinical practice allows the assimilation of techniques based on empirical findings rather than using techniques haphazardly in a hit and miss fashion. Evidence suggests that matching of treatment to

Integrative CBT for Anxiety Disorders: An Evidence-Based Approach to Enhancing Cognitive Behavioural Therapy with Mindfulness and Hypnotherapy, First Edition. Assen Alladin.
© 2016 John Wiley & Sons, Ltd. Published 2016 by John Wiley & Sons, Ltd.

particular patient characteristics increases outcome (Beutler et al., 2000). Third, each chapter pertaining to a specific anxiety disorder offers a step-by-step treatment protocol. The treatment protocol, based on latest empirical evidence, provides an additive design for studying the additive effect of hypnosis. An additive design involves a strategy in which the treatment to be tested is added to another treatment to determine whether the treatment added produces an incremental improvement over the first treatment (Allen, Woolfolk, Escobar, Gara, & Hamer, 2006).

Although CH meets criteria for an assimilative model of psychotherapy, it requires further empirical validation. Without empirical validation it is not possible to establish whether the importation of the hypnotic techniques into CBT, mindfulness or psychodynamic therapies positively impact therapy. It is only through empirical validation that ineffective and idiosyncratic assimilation can be avoided. Moreover, empirical validation is important for the re-evaluation of the assimilative model itself. The book offers detailed description of treatment strategies for each anxiety disorder from DSM-V so that they can be easily validated. Once the treatment protocols are validated, they need to be subjected to second-generation studies, that is, studies using dismantling design to evaluate the relative effectiveness of the imported techniques (Alladin & Alibhai, 2007). As CH imports multiple components (e.g., relaxation, ego-strengthening, mindfulness, etc.), without further studies (second-generation studies), there is no way of knowing which techniques are effective and which are superfluous.

Although it is important to empirically evaluate and validate CH, it is also important to bear in mind that the term '*psychotherapy integration* is synonymous with *psychotherapeutic creativity and originality*', that is, 'many advances occur in the consulting room of individual therapists who cannot submit their work to large-scale research investigations' (Gold & Stricker, 2006, p. 13). In other words, these non-publishers, but competent clinicians, have a lot to offer to clinical practice. Often their work can be very creative and innovative, providing several hypotheses that can be tested by investigators. Moreover, beyond the blending of techniques, clinicians should also attempt to integrate patient's insights and feedbacks into their assimilative therapies.

Furthermore, it is important to integrate innovative strategies such as VRET in the management of anxiety disorders. VRET, bolstered by the advancement of technology, is lauded as an alternative to *in vivo* and imaginal exposure (Krijn, Emmelkamp, Olafsson, & Biemond, 2004; Wiederhold & Wiederhold, 2005).

Appendix A

Appendix 1A: Cognitive-Hypnotherapy Case Formulation and Treatment Plan

Identifying Information:

Today's Date:
Name:
Age:
Gender:
Marital Status:
Ethnicity:
Occupational Status:
Living Situation:
Referred by:

1. *Problem List*
   (List all major symptoms and problems in functioning.)

   Psychological/psychiatric symptoms:
   Interpersonal difficulties:
   Occupational problems:
   Medical problems:
   Financial difficulties:
   Housing problems:
   Legal issues:
   Leisure problems:

2. *Diagnosis*

   Axis I:
   Axis II:

Integrative CBT for Anxiety Disorders: An Evidence-Based Approach to Enhancing Cognitive Behavioural Therapy with Mindfulness and Hypnotherapy, First Edition. Assen Alladin.
© 2016 John Wiley & Sons, Ltd. Published 2016 by John Wiley & Sons, Ltd.

Axis III:
Axis IV:
Axis V:

3. *Working Hypothesis*
   (Hypothesize the underlying mechanism producing the listed problems.)

   Assess schemas related to:
   Self:
   Other:
   World:
   Future:
   Recurrent core beliefs
   Rumination/negative self-hypnosis:
   Hypnotic suggestibility:

4. *Precipitant/Activating Situations*
   (List triggers for current problems and establish connection between underlying mechanism and triggers of current problems.)

   Triggers:
   Are triggers congruent with self-schemas/rumination/self-hypnosis:

5. *Origins of core beliefs*
   (Establish origin of core beliefs from childhood's experience.)

   Early adverse negative life events:
   Genetic predisposition:
   History of treatment(include response):

6. *Summary of Working Hypothesis*
   1.
   2.
   3.

7. *Treatment Plan*
   1.
   2.
   3.
   4.

   Modality:
   Frequency:
   Interventions:
   Adjunct Therapies:
   Obstacles:

8. *Strengths and Assets*
   (Based on the formulation, predict obstacles to treatment that may arise.)

Appendix B

Cognitive-Hypnotherapy Case Formulation and Treatment Plan

A Completed Example

Name: Mary
Age: 29 years old
Marital Status: Single
Date: June 15, 2004

Problem List

(List all major symptoms and problems in functioning.)

Psychological/psychiatric symptoms:
Depressed, lacking motivation, unfocused, disturbed sleep, tiredness, lacking energy, and difficult concentrating. At times she feels suicidal, but has no plan. She feels angry and fearful about the world. She always feels a sense of inner tension, and can't unwind or relax.

Interpersonal difficulties:
She is socially isolated, avoids friends and social events. She has good social skills, but she has only a few women friends. She has never dated seriously, but she wants to marry and have children. Her friends from her office have, on several occasions, arranged for her to meet men, but she always declined their offers at the last minute. She believes she will never marry because she feels uncomfortable meeting men.

Occupational problems:
She works as an administrative assistant in a small office consisting of six other women. She does not dislike her job, but she would like to hold a more

Integrative CBT for Anxiety Disorders: An Evidence-Based Approach to Enhancing Cognitive Behavioural Therapy with Mindfulness and Hypnotherapy, First Edition. Assen Alladin.
© 2016 John Wiley & Sons, Ltd. Published 2016 by John Wiley & Sons, Ltd.

responsible job in the future. However, she believes she is not bright enough to go to college for further training.

Medical problems*:*
None

Financial difficulties:
None

Housing problems:
None

Legal issues:
None

Leisure problems:
She avoids going out because she feels unsafe. She spends her leisure time in her apartment reading romantic novels or watching television.

Diagnosis
Axis I: *Major Depressive Disorder, Recurrent, Moderate*
Axis II: *Avoidant personality traits*
Axis III: *None*
Axis IV: *Socially isolated, occupational problems.*
Axis V: *GAF score = 50*

Working Hypothesis
   (Hypothesize the underlying mechanism producing the listed problems.)

Assess schemas related to:

Self:
'I am abnormal and weird because I can't go out and meet people.'
'I am a coward and a freak.'
'I am ugly and unattractive, no one will like me.'

Other:
'You can't depend on others, people are bad and selfish, they always want to hurt you.'

World:
'The world is scary and no one is there to protect you.'
'I hate the world.'

Future:
'The future is uncertain and bleak.' 'I see myself being lonely and isolated for the rest of my life.' 'At times, I feel life is not worth living.'

Recurrent core beliefs:
'I am abnormal, there's something wrong with me and I will never be normal.'

Rumination/negative self-hypnosis:
She ruminates with the belief that she is not normal and often has the image of being isolated and lonely for the rest of her life, and there is no one to care for her. She reports having a good imagination, but she tends to focus more on negative thoughts.

Hypnotic suggestibility:
She scored maximum on the Barer Suggestibility Scale.

Precipitant/Activating Situations
(List triggers for current problems and establish connection between underlying mechanism and triggers of current problems.)

Triggers:
Watching other women dating or getting married. One of the women from her office got engaged and this triggered her depressive episode. Other activating events include attending special social functions such as wedding, Christmas party, or not able to go on a date.

Are triggers congruent with self-schemas/rumination/self-hypnosis:
The triggers activate her self-schema of being abnormal or defective.

Origins of core beliefs
(Establish origin of core beliefs from childhood's experience.)

Early adverse negative life-events:
She was brought up in a very hostile and stressful environment. Her father was a gambler and an alcoholic. On many occasions, she witnessed her father being physically aggressive towards her mother, who never confronted her husband or tied to get out of the relationship or sought help to sort out her domestic problems. He constantly undermined Mary and called her 'stupid' and 'a whore'. Mary was scared and frightened of her father and often used to have nightmares about her father killing her and her mother. The most traumatic experience for Mary was when her father got her out of the shower naked to switch the TV off. Mary left the TV on while she was having a shower. She was 11 years old. Mary learned to be scared of men and she became passive, fragile and unassertive like her mother.

Genetic predisposition:
Mary's mother and grandmother have a history of major depressive disorder. Mary reported that, like her, her mother too has a tendency to think very negatively about everything.

History of treatment (include response):
Followed up by a psychiatrist for 3 years. Tried several antidepressant medications, but none has worked for her. Also seen a mental health therapist in the community for counselling. She derived support from the counselling, but it did not improve her symptoms significantly.

Summary of Working Hypothesis:
Whenever Mary faced a social event, it reminded her of how Judy was faced with taking actions to further her goals, her schemata that she was incapable and damaged were activated. She learned from her mother's passivity and father's abuse that she was damaged and incapable of taking actions.

Strengths and Assets: Stable lifestyle; bright; excellent social skills; has friends

Treatment Plan

Goals (Measures):

1. Reduce depressive symptoms via BDI-II, procrastination via log of activities.
2. Increase ability to prioritize and organize work and at home.
3. Find a more satisfying job (measured directly).
4. Increase time spent with friends (measured via number of contacts).
5. Begin dating in an effort to meet husband (measured via number of dates).
6. Increase assertiveness (measured via log of assertive behaviours).

Modality:
Individual CBT.

Frequency:
Weekly for 10 weeks.

Interventions:

- Teach the formulation (to provide rationale for interventions)
- Activity scheduling (work tasks, socializing, dating, job search)
- Completing Cognitive Restructuring Form (CRF) behavioural experiments

- Assertive training
- Schema change interventions

Adjunct Therapies:
Medication an option if she does not respond to CBT.

Obstacles:
Procrastination, unassertiveness, 'I'm incapable of succeeding.'

References

Abbey, S. E. (2012). Mindfulness and psychiatry. *Canadian Journal of Psychiatry*, *57*, 61–62.

Abbott, M. J., & Rapee, R. M. (2004). Post-event rumination and negative self-appraisal in social phobia before and after treatment. *Journal of Abnormal Psychology*, *113*, 136–144.

Adier, C. M., Craske, M. G., & Barlow, D. H. (1987). Relaxation-induced panic (RIP): When resting isn't peaceful. *Integrative Psychiatry*, *5*, 94–112.

Alden, L. E., & Taylor, C. T. (2004). Interpersonal processes in social phobia. *Clinical Psychology Review*, *24*, 857–882.

Alladin, A. (1994). Cognitive hypnotherapy with depression. *Journal of Cognitive Psychotherapy: An International Quarterly*, *8*:4, 275–288.

Alladin, A. (2006). Cognitive hypnotherapy for treating depression. In R. Chapman (Ed.), *The clinical use of hypnosis with cognitive behavior therapy: A practitioner's casebook* (pp. 139–187). New York, NY: Springer.

Alladin, A. (2007). *Handbook of cognitive hypnotherapy for depression: An evidence-based approach*. Philadelphia: Lippincott Williams & Wilkins.

Alladin, A. (2008). *Cognitive hypnotherapy: An integrated approach to treatment of emotional disorders*. Chichester: John Wiley & Sons, Ltd.

Alladin, A. (2012). Cognitive hypnotherapy for major depressive disorder. *American Journal of Clinical Hypnosis*, *54*, 275–293.

Alladin, A. (2013a). The power of belief and expectancy in understanding and management of depression. *American Journal of Clinical Hypnosis*, *55*, 249–271.

Alladin, A. (2013b). Healing the wounded self: Combining hypnotherapy with ego state therapy. *American Journal of Clinical Hypnosis*, *56*, 3–22.

Alladin, A. (2014a). Mindfulness-based hypnosis: Blending science, beliefs, and wisdoms to catalyze healing. *American Journal of Clinical Hypnosis, 56*(3), 285–302.

Alladin, A. (2014b). The wounded self: A new approach to understanding and treating anxiety disorders. *American Journal of Clinical Hypnosis, 56*(4), 368–388.

Alladin, A., & Alibhai, A. (2007). Cognitive-hypnotherapy for depression: An empirical investigation. *International Journal of Clinical and Experimental Hypnosis, 55*, 147–166.

Alladin, A., & Amundson, J. (2011). Cognitive hypnotherapy as an assimilative model of therapy. *Contemporary Hypnosis & Integrative Therapy, 28*, 17–45.

Allen, L. A., Woolfolk, R. L., Escobar, J. I., Gara, M. A., & Hamer, R. M. (2006). Cognitive-behavioral therapy for somatization: A randomized controlled trial. *Archives of Internal Medicine, 166*, 1512–1518.

Allgulander, C., Mangano, R., Zhang, J., Dahl, A. A., Lepola, U., Sjodin, I., & Emilien, G. (2004). Efficacy of Venlafaxine ER in patients with social anxiety disorder: A double-blind, placebo-controlled, parallel-group comparison with paroxetine. *Human Psychopharmacology: Clinical and Experimental, 19*, 387–396.

Alman, B. (2001). Self-care: Approaches from self-hypnosis for utilizing your unconscious (inner) potentials. In B. Geary & J. Zeig (Eds.), *The handbook of Ericksonian psychotherapy* (pp. 522–540). Phoenix, AZ: The Milton H. Erickson Foundation Press.

American Academy of Child and Adolescent Psychiatry (1997). Practice parameter for the psychiatric assessment of children and adolescents. *Journal of American Academy of Child and Adolescent Psychiatry, 36* (suppl): 4SY20S.

American Psychiatric Association (1994). *Diagnostic and statistical manual of mental disorders* (4th ed.). Washington, DC: American Psychiatric Publishing.

American Psychiatric Association (2009). *Practice guideline for the treatment of patients with panic disorder* (2nd ed.). Washington, DC: American Psychiatric Publishing.

American Psychiatric Association (2013). *Diagnostic and statistical manual of mental disorders* (5th ed.). Washington, DC: American Psychiatric Publishing.

Anderson, I. M., & Palm, M. E. (2006). Pharmacological treatments for worry: focus on generalized anxiety disorder. In: G. C. L. Davey & A. Wells (Eds.), *Worry and its psychological disorders: Theory, assessment and treatment*. West Sussex, England: John Wiley & Sons.

Anderson, C. B., & Thomsen, P. H. (1998). Electively mute children: An analysis of Danish cases. *Nordic Journal of Psychiatry, 52*, 231–238.

Anderson, J. C., Williams, S., McGee, R., & Silva, P. A. (1987). DSM-III disorders in preadolescent children: Prevalence in a large sample from a general population. *Archives of General Psychiatry, 44*, 69–76.

Anstendig, K. (1998). Selective mutism: A review of the treatment literature by modality from 1980–1996. *Psychotherapy, 35*(3), 381–391. doi:10.1037/h0087851

Antony, M. M., & Barlow, D. H. (2002). Specific phobias. In D. H. Barlow (Ed.), *Anxiety and its disorders* (2nd ed., pp. 380–417). New York, NY: Guilford Press.

Araoz, D. L. (1981). Negative self-hypnosis. *Journal of Contemporary Psychotherapy, 12,* 45–52.

Araoz, D. L. (1985). *The new hypnosis.* New York, NY: Brunner/Mazel.

Arch, J.J, Georg H. Eifert, C. Davies, J. Vilardaga, R. D. Rose, M. G., & Craske, M. (2012). Randomized clinical trial of cognitive behavioral therapy (CBT) versus acceptance and commitment therapy (ACT) for mixed anxiety disorders. *Journal of Consulting and Clinical Psychology, 80,* 750–765.

Arieti, S. (1979). New views on the psychodynamics of phobias. *American Journal of Psychotherapy, 33,* 82–95.

Arntz, A. (2003). Cognitive therapy versus applied relaxation as treatment of generalized anxiety disorder. *Behaviour Research and Therapy, 41,* 633–646.

Aybek, S., Timothy, T. R., Zelaya, F., O'Daly, O. G. Craig, T., David, A. S., & Kanaan, R. A. (2014). Neural correlates of recall of life events in conversion disorder. *JAMA Psychiatry, 71*(1), 52–60.

Baer, R. A. (2003). Mindfulness training as a clinical intervention: A conceptual and empirical review. *Clinical Psychology: Science and Practice, 10,* 125–140.

Baer, R. A., & Huss, D. B. (2008). Mindfulness- and acceptance-based therapy. In J. L. Lebow (Ed.), *Twenty-first century psychotherapies: Contemporary approaches to theory and practice* (pp. 123–166). Hoboken, NJ: John Wiley & Sons, Inc.

Baldwin, D. S., Waldman, S., & Allgulander, C. (2011). Evidence-based pharmacological treatment of generalized anxiety disorder. *International Journal of Neuropsychopharmacology, 14,* 697–710.

Bandelow, B., & Baldwin, D. S. (2010). Pharmacotherapy for panic disorder. In D. J. Stein, E. Hollander, & B. O. Rothbaum (Eds.), *Textbook of Anxiety Disorders* (2nd ed.; pp. 399–416). Washington, DC: American Psychiatric Publishing.

Bandelow, B., Behnke, K., Lenoir, S., Hendriks, G. J., Alkin, T., Goebel, C., & Clary, C. M. (2004). Sertraline versus paroxetine in the treatment of panic disorder: An acute, double-blind noninferiority comparison. *Journal of Clinical Psychiatry, 65,* 405–413.

Bandelow, B., Seidler-Brandler, U., Becker, A., Wedekind, D., & Ruther, E. (2007). Meta-analysis of randomized controlled comparisons of psychopharmacological and psychological treatments for anxiety disorders. *World Journal of Biological Psychiatry, 8,* 175–187.

Bandura, A. (1977). Self-efficacy: Toward a unifying theory of behavioral change. *Psychological Review, 84,* 191–215.

Barabasz, M. (2012). Cognitive hypnotherapy with bulimia. *American Journal of Clinical Hypnosis, 54,* 353–364.

Bargh, J. A., Gollwitzer, P. M., Lee-Chai, A., Barndollar, K., Trotschel, R. (2001). The automated will: nonconscious activation and pursuit of behavioral goals. *Journal of Personality and Social Psychology, 81,* 1014–27.

Barlow, D. H. (1988). *Anxiety and its disorders: The nature and treatment of anxiety and panic.* New York: Guilford Press.

Barlow, D. H. (2000). *Anxiety and its disorders: The nature and treatment of anxiety and panic* (2nd ed.). New York, NY: Guilford.

Barlow, D. H. (2002). *Anxiety and its disorders: The nature and treatment of anxiety and panic* (2nd ed.). New York: Guilford Press.

Barlow, D. H., Craske, M. G., Cerny, J. A., & Klosko, J. S. (1989). Behavioral treatment of Panic disorder. *Behavior Therapy, 20,* 261–282.

Barrett, P. M., Dadds, M. R., & Rapee, R. M. (1996). Family treatment of childhood anxiety: A controlled trial. *Journal of Counseling and Clinical Psychology, 64,* 333 – 342.

Barrows, K. A., & Jacobs, B. P. (2002). Mind-body medicine. An introduction and review of the literature. *Medical Clinics of North America, 86*(1), 11–31.

Basker, M. A. (1979). A hypnobehavioural method of treating agoraphobia by the clenched fist method of Calvert Stein. *Australian Journal of Clinical Hypnosis, 7,* 27–34.

Bateman, A., & Fonagy, P. (2004). *Psychotherapy for borderline personality disorder: Mentalization based treatment.* Oxford, UK: Oxford University Press.

Baumeister, R. F., Masicampo, E. J., Vohs, K. D. (2011). Do conscious thoughts cause behavior? *Annual Review of Psychology, 62,* 331–361.

Beck, A. T. (1976) *Cognitive therapy and emotional disorders.* New York: International University Press.

Beck, A. T. (2005). The current state of cognitive therapy: A 40-year retrospective. *Archives of General Psychiatry, 62,* 953–959.

Beck, A. T., & Clark, D. A. (1997). An information processing model of anxiety: Automatic and strategic processes. *Behaviour Research and Therapy, 35,* 49–58.

Beck, A. T., & Emery, G. (with Greenberg, R. L.). (1985). *Anxiety disorders and phobias: A cognitive perspective.* New York, NY: Basic Books.

Beck, A. T., & Emery, G. (with Greenberg, R. L.). (2005). *Anxiety disorders and phobias: A cognitive perspective* (rev. paperback ed.). New York, NY: Basic Books.

Beck, A. T., Rush, A. J., Shaw, B. F., & Emery, G. (1979). *Cognitive therapy of depression.* New York, NY: Guilford Press.

Beck, J. G., Stanley, M. A., Baldwin, L. E., Deagle, E. A., & Averill, P. M. (1994). Comparison of cognitive therapy and relaxation training for panic disorder. *Journal of Consulting and Clinical Psychology, 62*(4), 818–826.

Behar, E., DiMarco, I. D., Hekler, E. B., Mohlman, J., & Staples, A. M. (2009). Current theoretical models of generalized anxiety disorder (GAD): Conceptual review and treatment implications. *Journal of Anxiety Disorders, 23,* 1011–1023.

Bennett-Levy, J., Butler, G., Fennell, M., Hackman, A., Mueller, M., & Westbrook, D. (Eds.),. (2004). *Oxford guide to behavioural experiments in cognitive therapy.* Oxford, UK: Oxford University Press.

Bergman, R. L., Piacentini, J., & McCracken, J. T. (2002). Prevalence and description of selective mutism in a school-based sample. *Journal of the American Academy of Child and Adolescent Psychiatry, 41,* 938–946.

Bernstein, D. A., & Borkovec, T. D. (1973). *Progressive relaxation training: A manual for the helping professions.* Champaign, IL: Research Press.

Bernstein, D. A., Carlson, C. R., & Schmidt, J. E. (2007). Progressive relaxation: Abbreviated methods. In P. M. Lehrer, R. L. Woolfolk, & W. E. Sime (Eds.), *Principles and practice of stress management* (3rd ed.) (pp. 88–122). New York, NY: Guilford.

Beutler, L. E., Clarkin, J. F., & Bongar, B. (2000). *Guidelines for the systematic treatment of the depressed patient.* New York: Oxford University Press.

Bird, H. R., Gould, M. S., Yager, T., Staghezza, B., & Canino, G. (1989). Risk factors for maladjustment in Puerto Rican children. *Journal of the American Academy of Child and Adolescent Psychiatry, 28,* 847–850.

Black, B., & Uhde, T. W. (1994). Treatment of elective mutism with fluoxetine: A double-blind, placebo-controlled study. *Journal of the American Academy of Child and Adolescent Psychiatry, 33*(7), 1000–1006.

Black, D. W., Wesner, R., Bowers, W., & Gabel, J. (1993). A comparison of fluvoxamine, Cognitive therapy, and placebo in the treatment of panic disorder. *Archives of General Psychiatry, 50,* 44–50.

Blanco, C., Schneier, F. R., Vesga-Lopez, O., & Liebowitz, M. R. (2010). Pharmacotherapy for social anxiety disorder. In D. J. Stein, E. Hollander, & B. O. Rothbaum (Eds.), *Textbook of anxiety disorders* (2nd ed.) (pp. 471–500). Washington, DC: American Psychiatric Association.

Blazer, D. G., Hughes, D., George, L. K., Swartz, M., & Boyer, R. (1991). Generalized anxiety disorder. In L. N. Robins & D. A. Regier (Eds.), *Psychiatric disorders in America* (pp. 180–203). New York: Free Press.

Blum, N. J., Kell, R. S., Starr, H. L., Lender, W. L., Bradley-Klug, K. L., Osborne, M. L., & Dowrick, P. W. (1998). Case study: Audio feedforward treatment of selective mutism. *Journal of the American Academy of Child and Adolescent Psychiatry, 37,* 40–43.

Bond, A. J., Wingrove, J., Curran, H. V., & Lader, M. H. (2002). Treatment of generalised anxiety disorder with a short course of psychological therapy, combined with buspirone or placebo. *Journal of Affective Disorders, 72,* 267–271.

Borkovec, T. D. (1987). Commentary. *Integrative Psychiatry, 5,* 104–106.

Borkovec, T. D. (1994). The nature, functions and origins of worry. In G. C. Davey & F. Tallis (Eds.), *Worrying: Perspectives in theory, assessment, and treatment* (pp. 5–34). New York, NY: John Wiley & Sons, Inc.

Borkovec, T. D., Alcaine, O., & Behar, E. (2004). Avoidance theory of worry and generalized anxiety disorder. In R. G. Heimberg, C. L. Turk, & D. S. Mennin (Eds.), *Generalized anxiety disorder: Advances in research and practice* (pp. 77–108). New York: Guilford Press.

Borkovec, T. D., & Newman, M. G. (1998). Worry and generalized anxiety disorder. In A. S. Bellack & M. Hersen (Eds.), *Comprehensive clinical psychology: Vol. 6. Adults: Clinical formulation and treatment* (pp. 439–459). Oxford, England: Pergamon Press.

Borkovec, T. D., Robinson, E., Pruzinsky, T., & DePree, J. A. (1983). Preliminary exploration of worry: Some characteristics and processes. *Behavior Research and Therapy, 21,* 9–16.

Borkovec, T. D., & Ruscio, A. M. (2001). Psychotherapy for generalized anxiety disorder. *Journal of Clinical Psychiatry, 62,* 37–45.

Borkovec, T. D., & Weerts, T. C. (1976). Effects of progressive relaxation on sleep disturbance: An electroencephalographic evaluation. *Psychosomatic Medicine, 38,* 173–180.

Bourne, E. J. (2000). *The anxiety & phobia workbook* (3rd ed.). Oakland, CA: New Harbinger.

Bouton, M. E., Mineka, S., & Barlow, D. H. (2001). A modern learning theory perspective on the etiology of panic disorder. *Psychological Review, 108,* 4–32.

Bowlby, J. (1973). *Separation: Anxiety and anger, Vol. 2.* New York, NY: Basic Books.

Brown, D. P., & Fromm, E. (1986). *Hypnotherapy and hypnoanalysis.* Hillsdale, NJ: Lawrence Erlbaum Associates.

Brown, D. P., & Fromm, E. (1990). Enhancing affective experience and its expression. In D. C. Hammond (Ed.), *Hypnotic suggestions and metaphors* (pp. 322–324). New York, NY: W. W.

Brown, K. W., Ryan, R. M., & Creswell, J. D. (2007). Mindfulness: Theoretical foundations and evidence for its salutary effects. *Psychological Inquiry, 18,* 211–237.

Brown, M., Smits, J. A. J., Powers, M. B., & Telch, M. J. (2003). Differential sensitivity of the three ASI factors in predicting panic disorder patients' subjective and behavioral response to hyperventilation challenge. *Journal of Anxiety Disorders, 17,* 583–591.

Brown, T. A., O'Leary, T. A., and Barlow, D. H. (2001). Generalized anxiety disorder. In D. H. Barlow (Ed.), *Clinical handbook of psychological disorders: A step-by-step treatment manual* (3rd ed.) (pp. 154–208). New York, NY: Guilford.

Bruce, S. E., Machan, J. T., Dyck, I., & Keller, M. B. (2001). Infrequency of 'pure' GAD: Impact of psychiatric comorbidity on clinical course. *Depression and Anxiety, 14,* 219–225.

Bryant, R. A., Guthrie, R. M., & Moulds, M. L. (2001). Hypnotizability is acute stress disorder. *American Journal of Psychiatry, 158,* 600–604.

Bryant, R., Moulds, M., Gutherie, R., & Nixon, R. (2005). The additive benefit of hypnosis and cognitive-behavioral therapy in treating acute stress disorder. *Journal of Consulting and Clinical Psychology, 73,* 334–340.

Burns, D. D. (1999). Feeling good: *The new mood therapy (revised and updated).* New York, NY: Avon Books.

Busch, F. N., Milrod, B. L., & Shear, M. K. (2010). Psychodynamic concepts of anxiety. In D. J. Stein, E. Hollander, & B. O. Rothbaum (Eds.), *Textbook of anxiety disorders* (2nd ed, pp. 117–128). Washington, DC: American Psychiatric Publishing.

Busch, F. N., Milrod, B. L., & Singer, M. B. (1999). Theory and technique in psychodynamic treatment of panic disorder. *Journal of Psychotherapy Practice and Research, 8*, 234–242.

Butler, G., Fennell, M., & Hackman, A. (2008). *Cognitive-behavioral therapy for anxiety disorders: Mastering clinical challenges.* New York, NY: Guilford Press.

Campbell-Sills, L., Barlow, D. H., Brown, T. M., & Hoffman, S. G. (2006). Effects of suppression and acceptance on emotional responses of individuals with anxiety and mood disorders. *Behavior Research and Therapy, 44*, 1251–1263.

Cardena, E. (2000). Hypnosis in the treatment of trauma: A promising but not fully supported, efficacious intervention. *International Journal of Clinical and Experimental Hypnosis, 48*, 225–238.

Cardena, E., Maldonado, J., van der Hart, O., & Spiegel, D. (2000). Hypnosis. In E. B. Foa, T. M. Keane, & M. J. Friedman (eds.), *Effective treatment for PTSD* (pp. 247–279). New York, NY: Guilford.

Carrington, P. (1977). *Freedom in meditation.* Garden City, NY: Doubleday.

Castonguay, L. G., & Beutler, L. E. (2006). *Principles of therapeutic change that work.* New York, NY: Oxford University Press.

Chambless, D. L. (1982). Characteristics of agoraphobics. In D. L. Chambless & A. J. Goldstein (Eds.), *Agoraphobia: Multiple perspectives on theory and treatment* (pp. 1–18). New York, NY: John Wiley & Sons, Inc.

Chambless, D. L. (1985). Agoraphobia. In M. Hersen & A. S. Bellack (Eds.), *Handbook of clinical behavior therapy with adults* (pp. 49–87). New York, NY: Plenum Press.

Chambless, D. L., & Goldstein, A. J. (Eds.) (1982). *Agoraphobia: Multiple perspectives on theory and treatment.* New York, NY: Wiley.

Charney, M. E., Kredlow, M. A., Bui, E., & Simon, N. M. (2013). Panic disorder. In S. M. Stahl & B. A. Moore (Eds.), *Anxiety disorders: A guide for integrating psychopharmacology and psychotherapy* (pp. 201–220). New York, NY: Routledge.

Chiesa, A., & Serretti, A. (2009). Mindfulness-based stress reduction for stress management in healthy people: A review and meta-analysis. *Journal of Alternative Complementary Medicine, 15*, 593–600.

Choy, Y., Fyer, A. J., & Lipsitz, J. D. (2007). Treatment of specific phobia in adults. *Clinical Psychology Review, 27*(3), 266–286.

Cisler, J. M., & Koster, E. H. W. (2010). Mechanisms of attentional biases towards threat in anxiety disorders: An integrative review. *Clinical Psychology Review, 30*(2), 203–216.

Clark, D. A. (2004). *Cognitive behavior therapy for OCD.* New York, NY: Guilford Press.

Clark, D. A. (Ed.) (2005). *Intrusive thoughts in clinical disorders: Theory, research, and treatment.* New York, NY: Guilford.

Clark, D. A., & Beck, A. T. (2010). *Cognitive therapy of anxiety disorders: Science and practice.* New York, NY: Guilford Press.

Clark, D. M. (1986). A cognitive approach to panic. *Behaviour Research and Therapy, 24,* 461–470.

Clark, D. M. (1988). A cognitive model of panic attacks. In S. Rachman & J. D. Maser (Eds.), *Panic: Psychological perspectives* (pp. 71–89). Hillsdale, NJ: Erlbaum.

Clark, D. M. (1997). Panic disorder and social phobia. In D. M. Clark & C. G. Fairburn (Eds.), *Science and practice of cognitive behaviour therapy* (pp. 121–153). Oxford, UK: Oxford University Press.

Clark, D. M., Ehlers, A., McManus, F., Hackmann, A., Fennell, M., Campbell, H., et al. (2003). Cognitive therapy versus fluoxetine in generalized social phobia: A randomized placebo-controlled trial. *Journal of Consulting and Clinical Psychology, 71,* 1058–1067.

Clark, D. M., & Salkovskis, P. M. (1986). *Cognitive treatment for panic attacks: Therapist's manual.* Unpublished manuscript, Department of Psychiatry, Oxford University, Warneford Hospital, Oxford, UK.

Clark, D. M., Salkovskis, P. M., Hackman, A., Middleton, H., Anastasiades, P., & Gelder (1999). Brief cognitive therapy for panic disorder: A randomized controlled trial. *Journal of Consulting and Clinical Psychology, 67,* 583–589.

Clark, D. M., Salkovskis, P. M., Hackman, A., Middleton, H., Anastasiades, P., & Gelder, M. (1994). A comparison of cognitive therapy, applied relaxation, and imipramine in the treatment of panic disorder. *British Journal of Psychiatry, 164,* 759–769.

Clarke, J. C., & Jackson, J. A. (1983). *Hypnosis and behavior therapy: The treatment of anxiety and phobias.* New York, NY: Springer.

Clum, G. A. (1989). Psychological interventions vs drugs in the treatment of panic. *Behavior Therapy, 20,* 429–457.

Cohan, S. L., Chavira, D. A., & Stein, M. B. (2006). Practitioner review: Psychosocial interventions for children with selective mutism: A critical evaluation of the literature from 1990–2005. *Journal of Child Psychology and Psychiatry, 47*(11), 1085–1097.

Compton, S. N., Walkup, J. T., Albano, A. M., Piacentini, J. C., Birmaher, B., Sherrill, J. T., et al. (2010). Child/Adolescent Anxiety Multimodal Study (CAMS): Rationale, design, and methods. *Child and Adolescent Psychiatry and Mental Health, 4,* 1–15.

Conrad, A., & Roth, W. T. (2007). Muscle relaxation therapy for anxiety disorders: It works but how? *Journal of Anxiety Disorders, 21,* 243–264.

Coplan, J. D., Papp, L. A., Pine, D., Martinez, J., Cooper, T., Rosenblum, L. A., Klein, D. F., & Gorman, J. M. (1997). Clinical improvement with fluoxetine therapy and noradrenergic function in patients with panic disorder. *Archives of General Psychiatry, 54*(7), 643–648.

Cortright, B. (2007). *Integral psychology: Yoga, growth, and opening the heart.* Albany, NY: State University of New York Press.

Covin, R., Ouimet, A. J., Seeds, P. M., & Dozois, D. J. A. (2008). A meta-analysis of CBT for pathological worry among clients with GAD. *Journal of Anxiety Disorders,22*, 108–116.

Craigie, M. A., Rees, C. S., & Marsh, A. (2008). Mindfulness-based cognitive therapy for generalized anxiety disorder: A preliminary evaluation. *Behavioral and Cognitive Psychotherapy, 36*, 553–568. doi:10.1017/S135246580800458X

Craske, M. G. (1999). *Anxiety disorders: Psychological approaches to theory and treatment.* Boulder, CO: Westview Press.

Craske, M. G., & Barlow, D. H. (2001). Panic disorder and agoraphobia. In D. H. Barlow (Ed.), *Clinical handbook of psychological disorders* (3rd ed., pp. 1–59). New York: Guilford Press.

Craske, M. G., Antony, M. M., & Barlow, D. H. (2006). *Mastering your fears and phobias: Therapist guide* (2nd ed.). New York, NY: Oxford University Press.

Craske, M. G., & Barlow, D. H. (2007). *Mastery of your anxiety and panic: Therapist guide* (4th ed.). New York, NY: Oxford University Press.

Craske, M. G., & Barlow, D. H. (2014). Panic disorder and agoraphobia. In D. H. Barlow (ed.) *Clinical handbook of psychological disorders: A step-by-step treatment manual* (5th ed.) (pp. 1–61). New York, NY: The Guilford Press.

Craske, M. G., Rapee, R. M., Jackel, L. & Barlow, D. H. (1989). Qualitative dimensions of worry in DSM-III-R generalized anxiety disorder subjects and nonanxious controls. *Behaviour Research and Therapy, 27*, 397–402.

Craske, M. G., & Waters, A. M. (2005). Panic disorder, phobias, and generalized anxiety disorder. *Annual Review of Clinical Psychology, 1*, 197–226.

Creswell, J. D., Bursley, J. K., & Satpute, A. B. (2013). Neural reactivation links unconscious thought to decision making performance. *Social Cognitive and Affective Neuroscience, 8*(8), 863–869.

Crits-Christoph, P., Newman, M. G., Rickels, K., Gallop, R., Gibbons, M. B. C., et al. (2011). Combined medication and cognitive therapy for generalized anxiety disorder. *Journal of. Anxiety Disorders, 25*, 1087–1094

Cunningham, C. E., Cataldo, M. F., Mallion, C., & Keyes, J. B. (1984). A review and controlled single case evaluation of behavioral approaches to the management of elective mutism. *Child and Family Behavior Therapy, 5*(4), 25–49.

Cunningham, C. E., McHolm, A., & Boyle, M. H. (2006) Social phobia, anxiety, oppositional behaviour, social skills and self-concept in children with specific selective mutism, generalized selective mutism and community controls. *European Child and Adolescent Psychiatry, 15*, 245–255.

Cunningham, C. E., McHolm, A., Boyle, M. H., & Patel, S. (2004). Behavioral and emotional adjustment, family functioning, academic performance, and social relationships in children with selective mutism. *Journal of Child Psychology and Psychiatry, 45*(8), 1363–1372.

Daitch, C. (2007). *Affect regulation toolbox: Practical and effective hypnotic interventions for over-reactive client.* New York, NY: W.W. Norton & Company.

Daitch, C. (2011). *Anxiety disorders: The go-to guide for clients and therapists.* New York, NY: W.W. Norton & Company.

Dalrymple, K. L., & Herbert, J. D. (2007). Acceptance and commitment therapy for generalized social anxiety disorder: A pilot study. *Behavior Modification, 31*(5), 543–568.

Davey, G. C. L. (1994). Worrying, social problem-solving abilities, and social problem-solving confidence. *Behavior Research and Therapy, 32*, 327–330.

Davidson, J. R. T. (2006). Pharmacotherapy of social anxiety disorder: What does the evidence tell us? *Journal of Clinical Psychiatry, 67*, 20–26.

Davis, R. N., & Nolen-Hoeksema, S. (2000). Cognitive inflexibility among ruminators and nonruminators. *Cognitive Therapy and Research, 24*, 699–711.

Deiker, T., & Pollock. D. (1975). Integration of hypnotic and systematic desensitization techniques in the treatment of phobias: A case report. *American Journal of Clinical Hypnosis, 17*, 170–174.

Delmonte, M. M. (1995). The use of hypnotic regression with panic disorder: A case report. *Australian Journal of Clinical Hypnotherapy and Hypnosis, 16*, 69–73.

Dengrove, E. (1973). The use of hypnosis in behaviour therapy. *International Journal of Clinical and Experimental Hypnosis, 21*, 13–17.

DePiano, F. A., & Salzberg, H. C. (1981). Hypnosis as an aid to recall of meaningful information presented under three types of arousal. *International Journal of Clinical and Experimental Hypnosis, 29*, 283–400.

Dick-Niederhauser, A., & Silverman, W. K. (2006). Separation anxiety disorder. In J. E. Fisher & W. T. O'Donohue (Eds.), *Practitioner's guide to evidence-based psychotherapy* (pp. 627–633). New York, NY: Springer.

Dijksterhuis, A., & Aarts, H. (2010). Goals, attention, and (un)consciousness. *Annual Review of Psychology, 61*, 467–490.

Dijksterhuis, A., Bos, M. W., Nordgren, L. F., & van Baaren, R. B. (2006). On making the right choice: The deliberation-without-attention effect. *Science, 311*, 1005–1007.

Dijksterhuis, A., & Nordgren, L. F. (2006). A theory of unconscious thought. *Perspectives on Psychological Science, 1*, 95–109.

Di Nardo, P., Brown, T. A., & Barlow, D. H. (1994). *Anxiety Disorders Interview Schedule for DSM-IV.* New York, NY: Oxford University Press.

Dobin, A., Maxwell, M., & Elton, R. (2009). A benchmarked feasibility study of a self-hypnosis treatment for depression in primary care. *International Journal of Clinical and Experimental Hypnosis, 57*, 293–318.

Dobson, D., & Dobson, K. S. (2009). *Evidence-based practice of cognitive-behavioral therapy.* New York, NY: Guilford.

Doobay, A. F. (2008). School refusal behavior associated with separation anxiety disorder: A cognitive-behavioral approach to treatment. *Psychology in the Schools, 45*(4), 261–272. doi: 10.1002/pits.20299

Dow, S. P., Sonnies, B. C., Scheib, D., Moss, S. E., & Leonard, H. L. (1995). Practical guidelines for the assessment and treatment of selective mutism. *Journal of the American Academy of Child and Adolescent Psychiatry, 34*(7), 836–846.

Dudley, R., Kuyken, W., & Padesky, C. A. (2011). Disorder specific and trans-diagnostic case conceptualization. *Clinical Psychological Review*, *31*(2), 213–224.

Dugas, M. G., Brillon, P., Savard, P., Turcotte, J., Gaudet, A., Ladouceur, R., et al. (2010). A randomized clinical trial of cognitive-behavioral therapy and applied relaxation for adults with generalized anxiety disorder. *Behavior Therapy*, *41*, 46–58.

Dugas, M. J., Freeston, M. H., Ladouceur, R., Rhéaume, J., Provencher, M., & Boisvert, J.-M. (1998). Worry themes in primary GAD, secondary GAD, and other anxiety disorders. *Journal of Anxiety Disorders*, *12*, 253–261.

Dugas, M. J., Ladouceur, R., Léger, E., Freeston, M. H., Langlois, F., Provencher, M. D., et al. (2003). Group cognitive-behavioral therapy for generalized anxiety disorder: Treatment outcome and long-term follow-up. *Journal of Consulting and Clinical Psychology*, *71*, 821–825.

Dummit, E., Klein, R., Tancer, N., & Asche, B. (1996). Fluoxetine treatment of children with selective mutism: An open trial. *Journal of the American Academy of Child and Adolescent Psychiatry*, *35*(5), 615–621.

Dymond, S., & Roche, B. (2013). *Advances in relational frame theory: Research and applications*. Oakland, CA: New Harbinger.

D'Zurilla, T. J., & Goldfried, M. R. (1971). Problem solving and behavior modification. *Journal of Abnormal Psychology*, *78*, 107–126.

Eaton, W. W. (1995). Progress in the epidemiology of anxiety disorders. *Epidemiological Review*, *17*, 32–38.

Edinger, J. D., & Jacobsen, R. (1982). Incidence and significance of relaxation treatment side effects. *Behavior Therapist*, *5*, 137–138.

Eiffert, G. H., & Heffner, M. (2003). The effects of acceptance versus control contexts on avoidance of panic-related symptoms. *Journal of Behavior Therapy and Experimental Psychiatry*, *34*, 293–312.

Elkins, G., Johnson, A., & Fisher, W. (2012). Cognitive hypnotherapy for pain management. *American Journal of Clinical Hypnosis*, *54*, 294–310.

Ellis, A. (1962). *Reason and emotion in psychotherapy*. New York, NY: Carol Publishing Group.

Ellis, A. (1994). *Reason and emotion in psychotherapy: A comprehensive method of treating human disturbances* (Revised and updated). New York, NY: Carol Publishing Group.

Ellis, A. (2005). Why I (really) became a therapist. *Journal of Clinical Psychology*, *61*, 945–948.

Elizur, Y., & Perednik, R. (2003). Prevalence and description of selective mutism in immigrant and native families: A controlled study. *Journal of American Academy of Child and Adolescent Psychiatry*, *42*(12), 1451–1459.

Eppley. K. R., Abrams, A. I., & Shear, J. (1989). Differential effects of relaxation techniques on trait anxiety: A meta-analysis. *J ournal of Clinical Psychology*, *45*, 957–974.

Erickson, M., & Rossi, E. (1979). *Hypnotherapy: An exploratory casebook*. New York, NY: Irvington.

Emmons, R. A., & Crumpler, C. A. (2000). Gratitude as a human strength: Appraising the evidence. *Journal of Social and Clinical Psychology, 19,* 56–69.

Esch, T., Fricchione, G. L., & Stefano, G. B. (2003). The therapeutic use of the relaxation response in stress-related diseases. *Medical Science Monitor, 9*(2), RA23–RA34.

Ewin, D. M., & Eimer, B. N. (2006). *Ideomotor signals for rapid hypnoanalysis: A how-to manual.* Springfield, IL: Charles C. Thomas.

Faravelli, C., Webb, T., Ambonetti, A., Fonnesu, A. & Sessarego, A. (1985). Prevalence of traumatic early life events in 31 agoraphobic patients with panic attacks. *American Journal of Psychiatry, 142,* 1493–1494.

Farnsworth, J. K., & Sewell, K. W. (2011). Fear of emotion as a moderator between PTSD and firefighter social interactions. *Journal of Traumatic Stress, 24*(4), 444–450.

Farris, A. M., & Jouriles, E. N. (1993). Separation anxiety disorder. In A. S. Bellack & M. Hersen (Eds.), *Handbook of behavior therapy in the psychiatric setting* (pp. 407–426). New York, NY: Plenum Press.

Fava, G. A., Zielezny, M., & Savron, G. (1995). Long-term effects of behavioral treatment for panic disorder with agoraphobia. *British Journal of Psychiatry, 166,* 87–92.

Fennell, M. J. V. (1999). *Overcoming low self-esteem.* London, UK: Constable-Robinson.

Fennell, M. J. V. (2006). *Overcoming low self-esteem self-help course: A 3-part programme based on cognitive behavioural techniques.* London, UK: Constable-Robinson.

Field, E. S. (1990). Stress reduction trance: A naturalistic Ericksonian approach. In D. C.

Hammond (Ed.), *Hypnotic suggestions and metaphors* (pp. 170–172). New York, NY: W. W. Norton & Company.

Finkelstein, S. (1990). The private refuge. In D. C. Hammond (Ed.), *Hypnotic suggestions and metaphors* (p. 158). New York, NY: W. W. Norton & Company.

Foa, E., & Kozak, M. J. (1986). Treatment of anxiety disorders: Implications for psychopathology. In A. H. Tuma & J. D. Maser (Eds.), *Anxiety and the anxiety disorders* (pp. 421–452). Hillsdale, NJ: Erlbaum.

Foa, E. B., Riggs, D. S., Massie, E. D., & Yarczower, M. (1995). The impact of fear activation and anger on the efficacy of exposure treatment for posttraumatic stress disorder. *Behavior Therapy, 26,* 487–499.

Foley, D. L., Pickles, A., Maes, H. M., Silberg, J. L., & Eaves, L. J. (2004). Course and short-term outcomes of separation anxiety disorder in a community sample of twins. *Journal of the American Academy of Child and Adolescent Psychiatry, 43,* 1107–1114.

Follette, V. M., & Smith, A. A. A. (2005). Exposure therapy. In A. Freeman (Ed-in-Chief), *Encyclopedia of cognitive behavior therapy* (pp. 185–188). New York, NY: Springer.

Fonagy, P., Gergely, G., Jurist, E., & Target, M. (2002). *Affect regulation, mentalization and the development of the self.* New York, NY: Other Press.

Forsyth, J., & Eifert, G. (2008). *The mindfulness and acceptance workbook for anxiety: A guide to breaking free from anxiety, phobias, and worry using acceptance and commitment therapy*. Oakland, CA: New Harbinger.

Frederick, C. (2005). Selected topics in ego state therapy. *International Journal of Experimental and Clinical Hypnosis, 53*, 339–429.

Forman, M. D. (2010). *A guide to integral psychotherapy: Complexity, integration, and spirituality in practice*. Albany, NY: State University of New York Press.

Fredrickson, B. L. (2002). Positive emotions. In C. R. Snyder & S. J. Lopez (Eds.), *Handbook of positive psychology* (pp. 120–134). New York, NY: Oxford University Press.

Fresco, D. M., Frankel, A. N., Mennin, D. S., Turk, C. & Heimberg, R. G. (2002). Distinct and overlapping features of rumination and worry: The relationship of cognitive production to negative affective states. *Cognitive Therapy and Research, 26*, 197–188.

Freud, S. (1909). *Analysis of a phobia of a five-year-old boy* (Vol. *III*). New York, NY: Basic Books.

Fyer, A. J. (1987). Simple phobia. *Modern Problems in Pharmacotherapy, 22*, 174–192.

Gabbard, G. O., & Bennett, T. J. (2006). Psychoanalytic and psychodynamic psychotherapy for depression and dysthymia. In D. J. Stein, D. J. Kupfer, & A. F. Schatzberg (Eds.), *Textbook of Mood Disorders* (pp. 389–405). Washington, DC: American Psychiatric Publishing.

Gabbay, F. H. (1992). Behavior genetic strategies in the study of emotion. *Psychological Science, 3*, 50–55.

Garcia, A. M., Freeman, J. B., Francis, G., Miller, L. M., & Leonard, H. L. (2004). Selective mutism. In T. H. Ollendick & J. S. March (Eds.), *Phobic and anxiety disorders in children and adolescents: A clinician's guide to effective psychosocial and pharmacological interventions* (pp. 433–455). New York, NY: Oxford.

Germer, C. K. (2005). Mindfulness: What is it? What does it matter? In C. K. Germer, R. D. Siegel, & P. R. Fulton (Eds.), *Mindfulness and psychotherapy* (pp. 3–27). New York, NY: Guilford Press.

Germer, C. K., Siegel, R. D., & Fulton, P. R. (Eds.). (2013). *Mindfulness and psychotherapy* (2nd ed.). New York, NY: Guilford.

Gibbons, D. E. (1979). *Applied hypnosis and hyperempiria*. New York, NY: Plenum.

Glick, B. (1970). Conditioning therapy with phobic patients: Success and failure. *American Journal of Psychotherapy, 24*, 92–101.

Gold, J. R., & Stricker, G. (2006). Introduction: An overview of psychotherapy integration. In G. Stricker & J. Gold (Eds.), *A casebook of psychotherapy integration* (pp. 3–16). Washington, DC: American Psychological Association.

Golden, W. L. (1994). Cognitive-behavioral hypnotherapy for anxiety disorders. *Journal of Cognitive Psychotherapy: An International Quarterly, 8*, 265–274.

Golden, W. L. (2012). Cognitive hypnotherapy for anxiety disorders. *American Journal of Clinical Hypnosis, 54*, 263–274.

Golden, W. L., Dowd, E. T., & Friedberg, F. (1987). *Hypnotherapy: A modern approach*. New York, NY: Pergamon Press.

Goldfried, M. R. (1971). Systematic desensitization as training in self-control. *Journal of Consulting and Clinical Psychology, 37*, 228–234.

Goldstein, A. J., & Chambless, D. L. (1978). A re-analysis of agoraphobia. *Behavior Therapy, 9*, 47–59.

Gortmaker, V., Warnes, E. D., & Sheridan, S. M. (2004). Conjoint behavioral consultation: Involving parents and teachers in the treatment of a child with selective mutism. *Proven Practice, 5*, 66–72.

Gosch, E., Flannery-Schroeder, E., Mauro, C., & Compton, S. (2006). Principals of cognitive-behavioral therapy for anxiety disorders in children. *Journal of Cognitive Psychotherapy, 20*, 247 – 262.

Gould, R. A., Safren, S. A., Washington, D. O., & Otto, M. W. (2004). A meta-analytic review of cognitive-behavioral treatments. In R. G. Heimberg, C. L. Turk, & D. S. Mennin (Eds.), *Generalized anxiety disorder: Advances in research and practice* (pp. 248–264). New York, NY: Guilford.

Gournay, K. (1989). *Agoraphobia: Current perspectives on theory and treatment.* London, UK: Routledge.

Gray, J. A. (1987). *The psychology of fear and stress* (2nd ed.). Cambridge, UK: Cambridge University Press.

Greenberg, L. Rice, L. & Elliott, R. (1993). *Facilitating emotional change: The moment-by-moment process.* New York, NY: Guilford Press.

Greeson, J., & Brantley, J. (2009). Mindfulness and anxiety disorders: Developing a wise relationship with the inner experience of fear. In F. Didonna (ed.), *Clinical handbook of mindfulness* (pp. 171–188).New York, NY: Springer.

Gros, D. F., & Anthony, M. M. (2006). The assessment and treatment of specific phobias: A review. *Current Psychiatry Reports, 8*(4), 298–303.

Grossman, P., Niemann, L., Schmidt, S., & Walach, H. (2004). Mindfulness-based stress reduction and health benefits: A metaanalysis. *Journal of Psychosomatic Research, 57*, 35–43.

Harrington, J. A., & Blankenship, V. (2002). Ruminative thoughts and their relation to depression and anxiety. *Journal of Applied Social Psychology, 32*, 465–485.

Hartland, J. (1971). *Medical and dental hypnosis and its clinical applications* (2nd ed.). London, UK: Bailliere Tindall.

Hasler, G., Fromm, S., Carlson, P. J., et al. (2008). Neural response to catecholamine depletion in unmedicated subjects with major depressive disorder in remission and healthy subjects. *Archives of General Psychiatry, 65*, 521–531.

Hayden, T. L. (1980). The classification of elective mutism. *Journal of American Academy of Child and Adolescent Psychiatry, 19*, 118–133.

Hayes, S. C. (2004). Acceptance and commitment therapy, relational frame theory, and the third wave of behavioral and cognitive therapies. *Behavior Therapy, 35*, 639–665.

Hayes, S. C., Barnes-Holmes, D., & Roche, B. (Eds.) (2001). *Relational frame theory: A post-Skinnerian account of human language and cognition.* New York: NY: Plenum.

Hayes, S. C., Levin, M. E., Plumb-Vilardaga, J., Villatte, J. L., & Pistorello, J. (2013). Acceptance and commitment therapy and contextual behavioral science: Exploring the progress of a distinctive model of behavioral and cognitive therapy. *Behavior Therapy*, *44*(2), 180–198.

Hayes, S. C., Luoma, J., Bond, F., Masuda, A., & Lillis, J. (2006). Acceptance and commitment therapy: Model, processes, and outcomes. *Behavior Research and Therapy*, *44*, 1–25.

Hayes, S. A., Orsillo, S. M., Roemer, L. (2010). Changes in proposed mechanisms of action during an acceptance-based behavior therapy for generalized anxiety disorder. *Behavior Research & Therapy*, *48*(3), 238–245.

Hayes, S. C., Strosahl, K. D., & Wilson, K. G. (1999). *Acceptance and commitment therapy: An experiential approach to behavior change*. New York, NY: Guilford Press.

Hayes, S. C., Strosahl, K. D., & Wilson, K. G. (2011). *Acceptance and commitment therapy: An experiential approach to behavior change* (2nd ed.). New York, NY: Guilford Press.

Hayes-Selton, S. A., Roemer, L., & Orsillo, S. M. (2013). A randomized clinical trial comparing an acceptance-based behavior therapy to applied relaxation for generalized anxiety disorder. *Journal of Consulting and Clinical Psychology*, *81*(5), 761–773.

Hayward, A. R., Killen, J. D., Kraemer, H. C., & Taylor, C. B. (2000). Predictors of panic attacks in adolescents. *Journal of American Academy of Child and Adolescent Psychiatry*, *39*, 207–214.

Hazlett-Stevens, H. (2006). Agoraphobia. In J. E. Fisher & T. O'Donohue (Eds.), *Practitioner's guide to evidence-based psychotherapy* (pp. 24–34). New York, NY: Springer.

Hazlett-Stevens, H., & Borkovec, T. D. (2001). Effects of worry and progressive relaxation on the reduction of fear in speech phobia: An investigation of situational exposure. *Behavior Therapy*, *32*, 503–517.

Hazlett-Stevens, H., Pruit, L. D., & Collins, A. (2009). Phenomenology of generalized anxiety disorder. In D. J. Stein, E. Hollander, & B. O. Rothbaum (Eds.), *Textbook of anxiety disorders* (2nd ed., pp. 47–55). Washington, DC: American Psychiatric Publishing.

Heap, M., & Aravind, K. K. (2002). *Hartland's Medical and Dental Hypnosis* (4th ed.). London, UK: Churchill Livingstone.

Hechtman, L. (1993). Aims and methodological problems in multimodal treatment studies. *Canadian Journal of Psychiatry*, *38*, 458–464.

Heide, F. J., & Borkovec, T. D. (1983). Relaxation-induced anxiety: Paradoxical anxiety enhancement due to relaxation training. *Journal of Consulting and Clinical Psychology*, *51*, 171–182.

Heimberg, R. G. (2002). Cognitive-behavioral therapy for social anxiety disorder: Current status and future directions. *Society of Biological Psychiatry*, *51*, 101–108.

Herbert, J. D., & Forman, E. M. (2014). Mindfulness and acceptance techniques. In S. G. Hofmann & D. J. A. Dozois (Eds.), *The Wiley-Blackwell Handbook of Cognitive Behavioral Therapy* (pp. 131–156). Hoboken, NJ: Wiley-Blackwell.

Hettema, J. M., Neale, M. C., & Kendler, K. S. (2001). A review and meta-analysis of the genetic epidemiology of anxiety disorders. *American Journal of Psychiatry, 158*, 1568–1578.

Hoffman, D. L., Dukes, E. M., & Wittchen, H.-U (2008). Human and economic burden of generalized anxiety disorder. *Depression and Anxiety, 25*, 72–90.

Hoffmann, S. G. (2004). Cognitive mediation of treatment change in social phobia. *Journal of Consulting and Clinical Psychology, 72*, 392–399.

Hoffmann, S. G., Rief, W., & Spiegel, D. A. (2010). Psychotherapy for panic disorder. In D. J. Stein, E. Hollander, & B. O. Rothbaum (Eds.), *Textbook of anxiety disorders* (2nd ed., pp. 417–433). Washington, DC: American Psychiatric Publishing.

Hofmann, S. G, Sawyer, A. T., Witt, A. A., & Oh, D. (2010). The effect of mindfulness-based therapy on anxiety and depression: A meta-analytic review. *Journal of Consulting and Clinical Psychology, 78*, 169–183. doi:10.1037/a0018555

Hofmann, S. G., & Smits, J. A. (2008). Cognitive-behavioral therapy for adult anxiety disorders:A meta-analysis of randomized placebo-controlled trials. *Journal of Clinical Psychiatry, 69*, 621–632.

Hofmann, S. G., & Smits, J. A. J. (2009). Cognitive behavioral therapy for adult anxiety disorders: A meta-analysis of randomized placebo-controlled trials. *Journal of Clinical Psychiatry, 43*, 634–641.

Hawton, K., Salkovskis, P. M., Kirk, J., & Clark, D. M. (1989). *Cognitive behavior therapy for psychiatric problems*. Oxford, UK: Oxford University Press.

Hellstrøm, K., Fellenius, J., & Öst, L. G. (1996). One versus five sessions of applied tension in the treatment of blood phobia. *Behavior Research and Therapy, 34*, 101–112.

Hellstrøm, K., & Öst, L. G. (1996). Prediction of outcome in the treatment of specific phobia: A cross-validation study. *Behavior Research and Therapy, 34*, 403–411.

Herbert, J. D., & Forman, E. M. (2014). Mindfulness and acceptance techniques. In S. G. Hofmann & D. J. A. Dozois (Eds.), *The Wiley-Blackwell Handbook of Cognitive Behavioral Therapy* (pp. 131–156). Hoboken, NJ: Wiley-Blackwell.

Hoffart, A., & Matinsen, E. (1993). The effects of personality disorders and anxious-depressive comorbidity on outcome of patients with unipolar depression and with panic disorder and agoraphobia. *Journal of Personality Disorders, 7*, 304–311.

Holmbeck, G., & Lavigne, J. (1992). Combining self-model and stimulus fading in the treatment of an electively mute child. *Psychotherapy, 29*(4), 661–667.

Hubble, M. A., Duncan, B. L., & Miller, S. D. (1999). *The heart and soul of change: What works in therapy*. Washington, DC: American Psychological Association.

Hung, S. L., Spencer, M. S., & Dronamraju, R. (2012). Selective mutism: Practice and intervention strategies for children. *Children & Schools, 34*(4), 222–230.

Hunter, C. R., & Eimer, B. N. (2012). *The art of hypnotic regression therapy: A clinical guide*. Bethel, CT: Crown House.

Huppert, J. D., & Sanderson, W. C. (2010). Psychotherapy for generalized anxiety disorder. In D. J. S. Stein, E. Hollander, & B. O. Rothbaum (Eds.), *Textbook of anxiety disorders* (2nd ed., pp. 219–238). Washington, DC: American Psychiatric Publishing.

Iglesias, A., & Iglesias, A. (2014). I-95 Phobia treated with hypnotic systematic desensitization: A case report. *American Journal of Clinical Hypnosis*, *56*(2), 143–151.

Imel, Z. E., & Wampold, B. E. (2008). The common factors of psychotherapy. In S. D. Brown & R. W. Lent (Eds.), *Handbook of counseling psychology* (4th ed.). New York, NY: Wiley.

Isen, A. M. (1998). On the relationship between affect and creative problem solving. In S. W. Russ (Ed.), *Affect, creative experience, and psychological adjustment* (pp. 3–17). Philadelphia, PA: Brunner/Mazel.

Issakidis, C., Sanderson, K., Corry, J., G. Andrews, & Lapsley, Y. (2004). Modelling the population cost-effectiveness of current and evidence-based optimal treatment for anxiety disorders. *Psychological Medicine*, *34*(1), 19–35.

Johnson, L., & Öst, L. G. (1982). Behavioral treatments for agoraphobia: An evaluative review. *Clinical Psychology Review*, *2*, 311–336.

Jurbergs, N., & Ledley, D. R. (2005). Separation Anxiety. *Psychiatric Annals*, *35*, 728–735.

Kabat-Zinn, J. (1990). *Full catastrophe living: Using the wisdom of your body and mind to face stress, pain, and illness*. New York, NY: Dell.

Kabat-Zinn, J. (2013). *Full catastrophe living: Using the wisdom of your body and mind to face stress, pain, and illness* (revised and updated ed.). New York, NY: Bantham.

Kanji N., & Ernst, E. (2000). Autogenic training for stress and anxiety: A systematic review. *Complementary Therapy Medicine*, *8*, 106–110.

Kapalka, G. M., & Peters, C. (2013). Separation anxiety disorder. In S. M. Stahl & B. A. Moore (Eds.) *Anxiety disorders: A guide for integrating psychopharmacology and psychotherapy* (pp. 260–284). New York, NY: Routledge.

Kariuki, C. M., & Stein, D. J. (2013). Social anxiety disorder. In S. M. Stahl & B. A. Moore (Eds.), *Anxiety disorders: A guide for integrating psychopharmacology and psychotherapy* (pp. 221–239). New York, NY: Routledge.

Kashdan, T. B., Uswatte, G., & Julian, T. (2006). Gratitude and hedonic and eudaimonic well-being in Vietnam War veterans. *Behavior Research and Therapy*, *44*, 177–199.

Katzman, M. A. (2009). Current considerations in the treatment of generalized anxiety disorder. *CNS Drugs*, *13*, 103–120.

Kenardy, J. A., Dow, M. G. T., Johnston, D. W., Newman, M. G., Thomson, A., & Taylor, C. B. (2003). A comparison of delivery methods of cognitive-behavioral therapy for panic disorder: An international multicenter trial. *Journal of Consulting and Clinical Psychology*, *71*, 1068–1075.

Kendall, P. C. (1990). *Coping Cat Workbook*. Ardmore, PA: Workbook Publishing.

Kendall, P. C. (1994). Treating anxiety disorders in children: Results of a randomized clinical trial. *Journal of Consulting and Clinical Psychology*, 62(1), 100–110.

Kendall, P. C. (2000). *Cognitive-behavioral therapy for anxious children: Therapist manual* (2nd ed.). Ardmore, PA: Workbook Publishing.

Kendall, P. C., Flannery-Schroeder, E., Panicelli-Mindel, S. M., Southam-Gerow, M. A., Henin, A., & Warman, M. (1997). Therapy for youths with anxiety disorders: A second randomized clinical trial. *Journal of Consulting and Clinical Psychology*, 65, 366–380.

Kendall, P. C., & Hollon, S. D. (1989). Anxious self-talk: Development of the Anxious Self-Statements Questionnaire (ASSQ). *Cognitive Therapy and Research*, 13, 81–93.

Kendall, P. C., Hudson, J. L., Gosch, E., Flannery-Schroeder, E. F., & Suveg, C. (2008). Cognitive-behavioral therapy for anxiety disordered youth: A randomized trial evaluating child and family modalities. *Journal of Consulting and Clinical Psychology*, 76, 282–297.

Kessler, R. C., Chiu, W. T., Demler, O., & Walters, E. E. (2005). Prevalence, severity, and comorbidity of twelve-month DSM-IV disorders in the National Comorbidity Survey Replication (NCS-R). *Archives of General Psychiatry*, 62(6), 617–627.

Kessler, R. C., Chiu, W. T., Jin, R., Ruscio, A. M., Shear, K., & Walters, E. E. (2006). The epidemiology of panic attacks, panic disorder, and agoraphobia in the National Comorbidity Survey Replication. *Archives of General Psychiatry*, 63(4), 415–424. doi:10.1001/archpsyc.63.4.415.

Kessler, R. C., McGonagle, K. A., Zhao, S., Nelson, C. B., et al. (1994). Lifetime and 12-month prevalence of DSM-III-R psychiatric disorders in the United States: Results from the National Comorbidity Survey. *Archives of General Psychiatry*, 51, 8–19.

Kim, Y. W., Lee, S-H., Choi, T. K., Suh, S. Y., Kim, B., Kim, C. M., Cho, S. J., Kim, M. J., Yook, K., Ryu, M., Song, S. K., & Yook, K. H. (2009). Effectiveness of mindfulness- based cognitive therapy as an adjunct to pharmacotherapy in patients with panic disorder or generalized anxiety disorder. *Depression and Anxiety*, 26(7), 601–606.

King, N. J., Tonge, B. J., Heyne, B. J., et al. (1998). Cognitive-behavioral treatment of school-refusing children: A controlled evaluation. *Journal of American Academy of Child and Adolescent Psychiatry*, 37(4), 395–403.

King, N., Tonge, B., Heyne, D., Turner, S., Pritchard, M., Young, D., et al. (2001). Cognitive-behavioral treatments of school-refusing children: Maintenance of improvement at 3- to 5-year follow-up. *Scandinavian Journal of Behavior Therapy*, 30, 85 – 89.

Kipper, L., Blaya, C., Teruchkin, B., Heldt, E., Isolan, L., Mezzomo, K., Bond, M., & Manfro, G. G. (2005). Evaluation of defense mechanisms in adult patients with panic disorder: Before and after treatment. *Journal of Nervous and Mental Disease*, 193, 619–624.

Kirsch, I., Capafons, A., Cardena, E., & Amigo, S. (Eds.) (1999). *Clinical and self-regulation therapy*. Washington, DC: American Psychological Association.

Kirsch, I., Montgomery, G., & Sapirstein, G. (1995). Hypnosis as an adjunct to cognitive-behavioral psychotherapy: A meta-analysis. *Journal of Consulting and Clinical Psychology, 63,* 214–220.

Kocovski, N. L., Endler, N. S., Rector, N. A., & Flett, G. L. (2005). Ruminative coping and post-event processing in social anxiety. *Behaviour Research and Therapy, 43,* 971–984.

Kocovski, N. L., Fleming, J. E., & Rector, N. A. (2009). Mindfulness and acceptance based group therapy for social anxiety disorder: An open trial. *Cognitive Behavioral Practice, 16* 276–289.

Kolvin, I., & Fundudis, T. (1981). Electively mute children: Psychological development and background factors. *Journal of Clinical Psychology and Psychiatry, 22,* 219–232.

Kocovski, N. L., Fleming, J. E., & Rector, N. A. (2009). Mindfulness and acceptance-based group therapy for social anxiety disorder: An open trial. *Cognitive and Behavioral Practice, 16,* 276–289. doi:10.1016/j.cbpra.2008.12.004

Kraft, D. (2011a). Countering resistance in agoraphobia using hypnosis. *Contemporary Hypnosis and Integrative Therapy, 28*(3), 235–248.

Kraft, D. (2011b). The place of hypnosis in psychiatry, Part 4: Its application to the treatment of agoraphobia and social phobia. *Australian Journal of Clinical and Experimental Hypnosis, 38*(2), 91–110.

Krijn, M., Emmelkamp, P. M. G., Olafsson, R. P., & Biemond, R. (2004). Virtual reality exposure therapy of anxiety disorder: A review. *Clinical Psychology Review, 24*(3), 259–281.

Kristensen, H. (2000). Selective mutism and comorbidity with developmental disorder/delay, anxiety disorder, and elimination disorder. *Journal of American Academy of Child and Adolescent Psychiatry, 39*(2), 249–256.

Krohn, D. D., Weckstein, S. M., & Wright, H. L. (1992) A study of the effectiveness of a specific treatment for elective mutism. *Journal of American Academy of Child and Adolescent Psychiatry, 31,* 711–718.

Labbe, E. E., & Williamson, D. A. (1984). Behavioral treatment of elective mutism: A review of the literature. *Clinical Psychology Review, 4,* 273–292.

Ladouceur, R., Dugas, M. J., Freeston, M. H., Léger, E., Gagnon, F., & Thibodeau, N. (2000). Efficacy of a cognitive-behavioral Treatment for generalized anxiety disorder: Evaluation in a controlled clinical trial. *Journal of Consulting and Clinical Psychology, 68,* 957–964.

Lankton, S. (1980). *Practical magic.* Cupertino, CA: Meta Publications.

Lankton, S. R. (2008). *Tools of intention: Strategies that inspire change.* Phoenix, AZ: Stephen R. Lankton.

Last, C. G., Hansen, M. S., & Franco, N. (1998). Cognitive-behavioral treatment of school phobia. *Journal of American Academy of Child and Adolescent Psychiatry, 37*(4), 404–411.

Leahy, R. L. (2003). *Cognitive therapy techniques: A practitioner's guide.* New York, NY: Guilford Press.

Leahy, R. L., & Hollon, S. J. (2000). *Treatment plans and interventions for depression and anxiety disorders.* New York, NY: Guilford Press.

Lease, C. A., & Strauss, C. C. (1993). Separation anxiety disorder. In R. T. Ammerman & M. Hersen (Eds.), *Handbook of behavior therapy with children and adults: A developmental and longitudinal perspective* (pp. 93 – 107). Needham Heights, MA: Allyn & Bacon.

LeBeau, R. T., Glen, D., Liao, B., Wittchen, H., -U., Beesdo-Baum, K., Ollendick, T., & Craske, M. G. (2010). Specific phobia: A review of DSM-IV specific phobia and preliminary recommendations for DSM-V. *Depression and Anxiety, 27*(2), 148–167.

Ledley, D. R., Marx, B. P. & Heimberg, R. G. (2005). *Making Cognitive-Behavioral Therapy Work: Clinical Process for New Practitioners.* New York, NY: Guilford Press.

Lee, J. K., Orsillo, S. M., Roemer, L., & Allen, L. B. (2010). Distress and avoidance in generalized anxiety disorder: Exploring the relationships with intolerance of uncertainty and worry. *Cognitive Behavior Therapy. 39*,126–136.

Leibowitz, M. R., Gelenberg, A. J., & Munjack, D. (2005). Venlafaxine extended release vs. placebo and paroxetine in social anxiety disorder. *Archives of General Psychiatry, 62*, 190–198.

Leichsenring, F. (2005). Are psychodynamic and psychoanalytic therapies effective? *International Journal of Psychoanalysis, 86*, 841–868.

Lesch, K. P., Weismann, M., Hoh, A., Müller, T., Disselkamp-Tietze, J., Osterheider, M., & Schulte, H. M. (1992). 5-HT1A receptor-effector system responsivity in panic disorder. *Psychopharmacology, 106*, 111–117.

Leichsenring, F. (2005). Are psychodynamic and psychoanalytic therapies effective? *International Journal of Psychoanalysis, 86*, 841–868.

Llera, S. J., Newman, M. G. (2011). An experimental examination of emotional avoidance in generalized anxiety disorder: Data supporting a new theory of emotional contrast avoidance. Paper presented at *119th Annual Convention of. American. Psychological. Association*, Washington, DC.

Levitt, J. T., Brown, T. A., Orsillo, S. M., & Barlow, D. H. (2004). The effects of acceptance versus suppression of emotion on subjective and psychophysiological response to carbon dioxide challenge in patients with panic disorder. *Behavior Therapy, 35*, 747–766.

Lewis-Fernandez, R., Hinton, D. E., Laria, A. J., Patterson, E. H., Hofmann, S. G., Craske, M. G., et al. (2009). Culture and the anxiety disorders: Recommendations for DSM-V. *Depression and Anxiety, 27*(2), 212–229. doi:10.1002/da.20647.

Ley, R. (1988). Panic attacks during relaxation and relaxation-induced anxiety: A hyperventilation interpretation. *Journal of Behavior Therapy and Experimental Psychiatry, 19*, 253–259.

Liber, J. M., Van Widenfelt, B. M., Utens, E. M. W. J., Ferdinand, R. F., Van der Leeden, A. J., Van Gastel, W., & Treffers, P. D. A. (2008). No differences between group versus individual treatment of childhood anxiety disorders in a randomized clinical trial. *Journal of Child Psychology and Psychiatry, 49*, 886–893.

Linehan, M. M. (1993a). *Cognitive behavioral treatment of borderline personality disorder*. New York, NY: Guilford Press.

Linehan, M. M. (1993b). *Skills training manual for treating borderline personality disorder*. New, NY: Guilford Press.

Lynn, S. J., & Cardena, E. (2007). Hypnosis and the treatment of posttraumatic conditions: An evidence-based approach. *International Journal of Clinical and Experimental Hypnosis, 55*, 167–188.

Lynn, S. J., & Kirsch, I. (2006). *Essentials of clinical hypnosis: An evidence-based approach*. Washington, DC: American Psychological Association.

Lynn, S., Kirsch, I., & Rhue, J. (1996). Maximizing treatment gains: Recommendations for the practice of clinical hypnosis. In S. Lynn, I. Kirsch, & J. Rhue (Eds.), *Casebook of clinical hypnosis* (pp. 395–406). Washington, DC: American Psychological Association.

Lyubomirsky, S., & Nolen-Hoeksema, S. (1995). Effects of self-focused rumination on negative thinking and interpersonal problem solving. *Journal of Personality and Social Psychology, 69*, 176–190.

Lyubomirsky, S., Tucker, K. L., Caldwell, N. D., & Berg, K. (1999). Why ruminators are poor problem solvers: Clues and phenomenology of dysphoric rumination. *Journal of Personality and Social Psychology, 77*, 1041–1060.

Ma, H., & Teasdale, J. D. (2004). Mindfulness-based cognitive therapy for depression: Replication and exploration of differential relapse prevention effects. *Journal of Consulting and Clinical Psychology, 72*, 31–40.

Macleod, C., & Rutherford, E. M. (2004). Anxiety and the selective processing of emotional information: Mediating roles of awareness, trait and state variables, and personal relevance of stimulus materials. *Behavior Research and Therapy, 30*, 479–491.

MacLeod, C. (1999). Anxiety and anxiety disorders. In T. Dagleish & M. J. Power (Eds.), *Handbook of cognitive emotion* (pp. 447–477). New York, NY: Wiley.

McHugh, R. R., Smits, J. A., & Otto, M. W. (2009). Empirically supported treatments for panic disorder. *Psychiatric Clinics of North America, 32*, 593–610.

Magee, L., Erwin, B. A., & Heimberg, R. G. (2009). Psychological treatment of social anxiety disorder and specific phobia. In M. Antony & M. B. Stein (Eds.), *Oxford handbook of anxiety and related disorders* (pp. 334–349). New York, NY: Oxford University Press.

Mahoney, M. J. (1991). *Human change processes: The scientific foundations of psychotherapy*. New York, NY: Basic Books.

Manicavasagar, V., Silove, D., Curtis, J., & Wagner, R. (2000). Continuities of separation anxiety from early life into adulthood. *Journal of Anxiety Disorders, 14*, 1–8.

Manzoni, G. M., Pagnini, F., Castelnuovo, G., & Molinari, E. (2008). Relaxation training for anxiety: A ten-years systematic review with meta-analysis. doi:10.1186/1471-244x-8-41

Marks, I. M. (1978). *Living with fear: Understanding and coping with anxiety*. New York, NY: McGraw-Hill.

Martin, L. L., & Tesser, A. (1989). Toward a motivational and structural theory of ruminative thought. In J. S. Uleman & J. A. Bargh (eds.), *Unintended thought*. New York, NY: Guilford.

Martin, L. L., & Tesser, A. (1996). Some ruminative thoughts. In R. S. Wyer (ed.), *Advances in social cognition*. Mahwah, NJ: Lawrence Erlbaum.

Masi, G., Mucci, M., & Millepiedi, S. (2001). Separation anxiety disorder in children and adolescents: Epidemiology, diagnosis, and management. *CNS Drugs, 15*, 93–104.

Masuda, A., & Wilson, K. (2009). Mindfulness: Being mindful in psychotherapy. In W. O'Donohue & S. R. Graybar (Eds.), *Handbook of contemporary psychotherapy: Toward an improved understanding of effective psychotherapy* (pp. 249–268). Los Angeles, CA: Sage.

Mathews, A. M., Gelder, M. G., & Johnson, D. W. (1981). *Agoraphobia: Nature and treatment*. New York, NY: Guilford.

Mathews, A. M., & MacLeod, C. (1994). Cognitive approaches to emotion and emotional disorders. In L. W. Porter & M. R. Rosenzweig (Eds.), *Annual Review of Psychology* (pp. 25–50). Stanford, CA: Stanford University Press.

McCabe, R. E., & Gifford, S. (2009). Psychological treatment of panic disorder and agoraphobia. In M. Antony & M. B. Stein (Eds.), *Oxford handbook of anxiety and related disorders* (pp. 308–320). New York, NY: Oxford University Press.

McCraty, R., Atkinson, M., Tomasino, D., & Bradley, R. T. (2009). The coherent heart: Heart–brain interactions, psychophysiological coherence, and the emergence of system-wide order. *Integral Review, 5*, 10–114.

McCraty, R., & Tomasino, D. (2006). Emotional stress, positive emotions, and psychophysiological coherence. In B. B. Arnetz, & R. Ekman (Eds.), *Stress in health and disease* (pp. 360–383). Weinheim, Germany: Wiley VCH.

McHolm, A. E., Cunningham, C. E., & Vanier, M. K. (2005). *Helping your child with selective mutism: Practical steps to overcome a fear of speaking*. Oakland, CA: New Harbinger.

McKay, Davis, & Fanning (2007). *Thoughts & feelings: Taking control of your moods & your life* (3rd ed.). Oakland, CA: New Harbinger.

McLaughlin, K., Sibrava, N., Behar, E., & Borkovec, T. D. (2006). Recurrent negative thinking in emotional disorders: Worry, depressive rumination, and trauma recall. In S. Sassaroli, G. Ruggerio, & R. Lorenzini (Eds.), *Worry, need of control, and other core cognitive constructs in anxiety and eating disorders* (pp. 37–67). Milan: Raphael Cortina Publisher.

McNally, R. J. (1999). Theoretical approaches to the fear of anxiety. In S. Taylor (ed.), *Anxiety sensitivity: Theory, research, and treatment of the fear of anxiety* (pp. 3–16). Mahwah, NJ: Lawrence Erlbaum.

Meichenbaum, D. (1974). *Cognitive behavior modification*. Morristown, NJ: General Learning Press.

Mellings, T. M. B., & Alden, L. E. (2000). Cognitive processes in social anxiety: The effects of selffocus, rumination and anticipatory processing. *Behaviour Research and Therapy, 38*, 243–257.

Mennin, D. S., Heimberg, R. G., & Turk, C. L. (2004). Clinical presentation and diagnostic features. In R. G. Heimberg, C. L. Turk, & D. S. Mennin (Eds.), *Generalized anxiety disorder: Advances in research and practice.* New York: The Guilford Press.

Mennin, D. S., Heimberg, R. G., Turk, C. L., & Fresco, D. M. (2005). Preliminary evidence for an emotion dysregulation model of generalized anxiety disorder. *Behavior Research and Therapy, 43,* 1281–1310.

Mennin, D. S., Holaway, R. M., Fresco, D. M., et al. (2007). Delineating components of emotion and its dysregulation in anxiety and mood psychopathology. *Behavior Therapy, 38*(3), 284–302.

Merckelbach, H., de Ruiter, C., van den Hout, M. A., & Hoekstra, R. (1989). Conditioning experiences and phobias. *Behavior Research and Therapy, 27,* 657–662.

Meyer, V., & Crisp, A. (1970). *Phobias.* In C. G. Costello (Ed.), *Symptoms of psychopathology: A handbook.* New York, NY: John Wiley and Sons.

Michelson, S. E., Lee, J. K., Orsillo, S. M., & Roemer, l. (2011). The role of value-consistent behavior in generalized anxiety disorder. *Depression and Anxiety, 28,* 358–366.

Milrod, B., Busch, F. N., Leon, A. C., Aronson, A., Roiphe, J., Rudden, M., Singer, M., Shapiro, T., Goldman, H., Richter. D., & Shear, M. K. (2001). A pilot open trial of brief psychodynamic psychotherapy for panic disorder. *Journal of Psychotherapy Practice & Research, 10,* 1–7.

Milrod, B., Leon, A. C., Busch, F., Rudden, M., Schwalberg. M., Clarkin, J., Aronson, A., Singer, M., Turchin, W., Klass, E. T., Graf, E., Teres, J. J., & Shear, M. K. (2007). A randomized controlled clinical trial of psychoanalytic psychotherapy for panic disorder. *American Journal of Psychiatry, 164,* 265–272.

Moncrieff, J., & Cohen, D. (2009). *British Medical Journal, 338,* 1535–1537.

Morita, S. (1998). *Morita therapy and the true nature of anxiety-based disorders (shinkeishitsu).* Albany, NY: State University of New York Press.

Moore, M., & Tasso, A. F. (2008). Clinical hypnosis: An empirical evidence. In M. R. Nash & A. J. Barnier (eds.), *The Oxford Handbook of Hypnosis: Theory, Research and Practice* (pp. 697–725). New York, NY: Oxford University Press.

Moore, R. (1990). Dental fear: Relevant clinical methods of treatment. *Tandlaegebladet, 94,* 58–60.

Morissette, S. B., Spiegel, D. A., & Heinrichs, N. (2005). Sensation-focused intensive treatment for panic disorder with moderate to severe agoraphobia. *Cognitive and Behavioral Practice, 12,* 17–29.

Morreale, M., Tancer, M. E., & Uhde, T. W. (2010). Pathogenesis of social anxiety disorder. In D. J. Stein, E. Hollander, & B. O. Rothbaum (Eds.), *Textbook of anxiety disorders* (2nd ed., pp. 453–469). Washington, DC: American Psychiatric Publishing, Inc.

Morrison, N., & Westbrrok, D. (2004). Obsessive compulsive disorder. In J. Bennett- Levy, G. Butler, M. J. V. Fennell, A. Hackman, M. Mueller,

& D. Westbrook (Eds.), *Oxford guide to behavioral experiments in cognitive therapy* (pp. 101–118). Oxford, UK: Oxford University Press.

Mowrer, O. H. (1960). *Learning theory and behavior*. New York, NY: Wiley.

Muris, P., Roelofs, J., Meesters, C., & Boomsma, P. (2004). Rumination and worry in nonclinical adolescents. *Cognitive Therapy and Research, 28*, 539–554.

Muris, P., Roelofs, J., Rassin, E., Franken, I., & Mayer, B. (2005). Mediating effects of rumination and worry on the links between neuroticism, anxiety, and depression. *Personality and Individual Differences, 39*, 1105–1111.

National Centre for Health Statistics (1994). *Advance report of final mortality statistics, 1991 (Monthly Vital Statistics Report, 42)*. Washington, DC: U. S. Government Printing Office.

Newman, M. G., & Llera, S. J. (2011). A novel theory of experiential avoidance in generalized anxiety disorder: A review and synthesis of research supporting a Contrast Avoidance Model of worry. *Clinical Psychology Review, 31*, 371–382.

Newman, M. G., Llera, S. J., Erickson, T. M., Przeworski, A., & Castonguay, L. G. (2013). Worry and generalized anxiety disorder: A review and theoretical synthesis of evidence on nature, etiology, mechanisms, and treatment. *Annual Review of Clinical Psychology, 9*, 275–297.

Newman, M. G., &, Fisher, A. J. (2013). Mediated moderation in combined cognitive behavioral therapy versus component treatments for generalized anxiety disorder. *Journal of. Consulting and Clinical Psychology. 81*, 405–414.

Newman, M. G., Przeworski, A., Fisher, A.J,, Borkovec, T. D. (2010). Diagnostic comorbidity in adults with generalized anxiety disorder: impact of comorbidity on psychotherapy outcome and impact of psychotherapy on comorbid diagnoses. *Behavior Therapy. 41*, 59–72

Nichol, M. P. & Schwartz, R. C. (2008). *Family therapy: Concepts and methods* (8th ed.). New York, NY: Pearson Education.

Nolen-Hoeksema, S. (1991) Responses to depression and their effects on the duration of depressive episodes, *Journal of Abnormal Psychology, 100*, 569–582.

Nolen-Hoeksema, S. (2000). The role of rumination in depressive disorders and mixed anxiety/depressive symptoms. *Journal of Abnormal Psychology, 9*, 504–511.

Nolen-Hoeksema, S., & Morrow, J. (1991). A prospective study of depression and posttraumatic stress symptoms after a natural disaster: The 1989 Loma Prieta earthquake. *Journal of Personality and Social Psychology, 61*, 115–121.

Nolen-Hoeksema, S., Wisco, B. E., & Lyubomirsky, S. (2008). Rethinking rumination. *Perspectives on Psychological Science, 3*, 400–424.

Norcross, J. C. (2002). *Psychotherapy relationships that work: Therapist contributions and responsiveness to patient needs*. New York, NY: Oxford University Press.

Norton, P., & Price, E. (2007). A meta-analytic review of of adult cognitive behavioral treatment outcome across the anxiety disorders. *Journal of Nervous and Mental Disease, 195*, 521–531.

Nutt, D. J., Glue, P., Lawson, C., & Wilson, S. (1990). Flumazenil provocation of panic attacks: Evidence for altered benzodiazepine receptor sensitivity in panic disorder. *Archives of General Psychiatry, 47*, 917–925.

Oon, P. P. (2010). Playing with Gladys: A case study integrating drama therapy behavioural interventions for the treatment of selective mutism. *Clinical Child Psychology and Psychiatry, 15,* 215–230.

Orsillo, S. M., & Roemer, L. (2011). *The mindful way through anxiety: Break free from chronic worry and reclaim your life.* New York, NY: Guilford.

Orvaschel, H. (1988). Structured and semistructured interviews for children. In C. J. Kestenbaum & D. T. Williams (Eds.), *Handbook of clinical assessment of children and adolescents* (Vol. *1*, pp. 31–42). New York, NY: New York University Press.

Ossman, W. A., Wilson, K. G., Storaasli, R. D., McNeill, J. W. (2006). A preliminary investigation of the use of Acceptance and Commitment Therapy in a group treatment for social phobia. *International Journal of Psychology & Psychological Therapy, 6*(3), 397–416.

Öst, L. G. (1987a). Applied relaxation: Description of a coping technique and review of controlled studies. *Behaviour Research and Therapy, 25,* 397–409.

Öst, L. G. (1987b). Applied relaxation vs. progressive relaxation in the treatment of panic disorder. Behaviour Research and Therapy, *26,* 13–22.

Öst, L. G. (1988). Applied relaxation vs. Progressive relaxation in the treatment of panic disorder. Behavior Research and Therapy, *26,* 13–22.

Öst, L. G. (1992). Blood and injection phobia: Background and cognitive, physiological, and behavioral correlates. *Journal of Abnormal Psychology, 101,* 68–74.

Öst L. G., & Breitholtz, E. (2000). Applied relaxation vs. cognitive therapy in the treatment of generalized anxiety disorder. *Behaviour Research and Therapy, 38,* 777–790.

Öst, L. G., Fellenius, J., & Sterner, U. (1991). Applied tension, exposure in vivo, and tension-only in the treatment of blood phobia. *Behavioral Research and Therapy, 29,* 561–574.

Öst, L. G., & Hughdahl, K. (1983). Acquisition of agoraphobia, mode of onset, and anxiety response patterns. *Behavior Research and Therapy, 21,* 623–631.

Öst, L. G., Johansson, J., & Jerremalm, A. (1982). Individual response patterns and the effects of different behavioral methods in the treatment of claustrophobia. *Behavior Research and Therapy, 20,* 445–460.

Öst, L. G., Sterner, U., & Fellenius, J. (1989). Applied tension, applied relaxation, and the combination in the treatment of blood phobia. *Behavior Research and Therapy, 27,* 109–121.

Öst, L.-G.,Thulin,U., & Ramnerö, J. (2004). Cognitive behavior therapy vs. exposure in vivo in the treatment of panic disorder with agoraphobia. *Behaviour Research and Therapy, 42,* 1105–1127.

Öst, L.-G., & Westling, B. E. (1995). Applied relaxation vs. Cognitive behavior therapy in the treatment of panic disorder. *Behaviour Research and Therapy, 33,* 145–158.

Öst, L. G., Westling, B. E., & Hellstrom, K. (1993). Applied relaxation, exposure in vivo and cognitive methods in the treatment of panic disorder with agoraphobia. *Behavior Research and Therapy, 31,* 383–394.

Olatunji, B. O., & Wolitzky-Taylor, K. B. (2009). Anxiety sensitivity and the anxiety disorders: A meta-analytic review and synthesis. *Psychological Bulletin, 135*(6), 974–999.

Padesky, C. A. (1993). Schema change as self-prejudice. *International Cognitive Therapy Newsletter, 5/6,* 16–17.

Papageorgiou, C. & Wells, A. (2004) *Depressive rumination: Nature, theory and treatment.* Chichester, UK: John Wiley & Sons, Ltd.

Papageorgiou, C., & Siegle, G. J. (2003). Rumination and depression: Advances in theory and research. *Cognitive Therapy and Research, 27,* 243–245.

Papp, L. A. (2010). Phenomenology of generalized anxiety disorder. In D. J. Stein, Hollander, E. & B. O. Rothbaum (Eds.), *Textbook of anxiety disorders* (2nd ed., pp. 159–171). Washington, DC: American Psychiatric Publishing, Inc.

Perls, F. S., Hefferline, R., & Goodman, P. (1951). *Gestalt therapy.* New York, NY: Dell.

Perna, G., Daccò, S., Menotti, R., & Caldirola, D. (2011). Antianxiety medications for the treatment of complex agoraphobia: Pharmacological interventions for a behavioral condition. *Neuropsychiatric Disease and Treatment, 7,* 621–637. http://dx.doi.org/10.2147/NDT.S12979

Persons, J. B. (1989). *Cognitive Therapy in Practice: A Case Formulation Approach.* New York, NY: Norton.

Persons, J. B., Davidson, J., & Tompkins, M. A. (2001). *Essential components of cognitive-behavior therapy for depression.* Washington, DC: American Psychological Association.

Perwien, A. R., & Bernstein, G. A. (2004). Separation anxiety disorder. In T. H. Ollendick & J. S. March (Eds.), *Phobic and anxiety disorders in children and adolescents: A clinician's guide to effective psychosocial and pharmacological interventions* (pp. 272–305). New York, NY: Oxford University Press.

Rachman, S. J., & Bichard, S. (1988). The overprediction of fear. *Clinical Psychological Review, 8,* 303–312.

Rapee, R. M. (1991). Generalized anxiety disorder: A review of clinical features and theoretical concepts. *Clinical Psychology Review, 11,* 419–440.

Rees, C. S., Richards, J. C., & Smith, L. M. (1999). The efficacy of information giving in cognitive-behavioral treatment for panic disorder. *Behavior Change, 16,* 175–181.

Reinblatt, S. P., & Walkup, J. T. (2005). Psychopharmacologic treatment of pediatric anxiety disorders. *Child and Adolescent Psychiatric Clinics of North America, 14,* 877–908.

Resick, P. A., & Schnicke, M. K. (1992). Cognitive processing therapy for sexual assault victims. *Journal of Consulting and Clinical Psychology, 60,* 748–756.

Roemer, L., & Borkovec, T. D. (1994). Effects of suppressing thoughts about emotional material. *Journal of Abnormal Psychology, 103*(3), 467–474.

Roemer, L., Erisman, S. M., & Orsillo, S. M. (2008). Mindfulness and acceptance-based treatments for anxiety disorders. In M. M. Antony & M. B. Stein (Eds.), *Oxford handbook of anxiety and related disorders* (pp. 476–487). Oxford: Oxford University Press.

Roemer, L., & Orsillo, S. M. (2007). An open trial of an acceptance-based behaviour therapy for generalized anxiety disorder. *Behavior Therapy, 38,* 72–85.

Roemer, L., & Orsillo, S. M. (2009). *Mindfulness and Acceptance-Based Behavioral Therapies in Practice.* New York: Guilford Press.

Roemer, L. & Orsillo, S. M. (2013). Mindfulness and acceptance-based behavioral treatment of anxiety. In C. K. Germer, R. D. Siegel, & P. R. Fulton (Eds). *Mindfulness and psychotherapy* (2nd ed.) (pp. 167–183). New York, NY: Guilford Press.

Roemer, L., & Orsillo, S. M. (2014). An acceptance-based behavioral therapy for generalized anxiety disorder. In D. H. Barlow (ed.), *Clinical handbook of psychological disorders: A step-by-step treatment manual* (pp. 206–236). New York, NY: Guilford.

Roemer, L., Orsillo, S. M., & Salters-Pedneault, K. (2008). Efficacy of an acceptance-based behavior therapy for generalized anxiety disorder: Evaluation in a randomized controlled trial. *Journal of Consuling and Clinical Psychology, 76,* 1083–1089.

Roemer, L., Williston, S. K., Eustis, E. H. & Orsillo, S. M. (2013). Mindfulness and acceptance-based behavioral therapies for anxiety disorders. *Current Psychiatry Reports, 15,* 1-10. DOI 10.1007/s11920-013-0410-3.

Rossi, E., & Cheek, D. (1988). *Mind-body therapy: Methods of ideodynamic healing in hypnosis.* NewYork, NY: Norton.

Ryan, W. (2011). *Working from the heart: A therapist's guide to heart-centered psychotherapy.* Lanham, MD: Jason Aronson.

Rye, M. S., & Ullman, D. (1999). The successful treatment of long-term selective mutism: A case study. *Journal of Behavior Therapy and Experimental Psychiatry, 30,* 313–323.

Rygh, J. L., & Sanderson, W. C. (2004). *Treating Generalized Anxiety Disorder: Evidence- Based Strategies, Tools, and Techniques.* New York, NY: Guilford.

Sacks, H., Comer, J. S., Pincus, D. B., Camacho, M., & Hunter-Ronnanelli, L. (2013). Effective interventions for students with separation anxiety disorder. In C. Franklin, M. B. Harris, & P. Allen-Meares (Eds.), *The school services source book* (2nd ed.) (pp. 105–124). New York, NY: Oxford University Press.

Sadock, B. J., & Sadock, V. A. (2003). *Kaplan and Sadock's synopsis of psychiatry: Behavioral sciences/clinical psychiatry* (9th ed.). Philadelphia, PA: Lippincott Williams & Wilkins.

Safer, M. A., & Leventhal, H. (1977). Ear differences in evaluating emotional tone of voice and rverbal content. *Journal of Experimental Psychology: Human Perception and Performance, 3,* 75–82.

Shedler, J. (2010). The efficacy of psychodynamic psychotherapy. *American Psychologist, 65*(2), 98–109.

Salkovskis, P. M. (1991). The importance of behavior in maintenance of anxiety and panic: A cognitive account. *Behavioral and Cognitive Psychotherapy, 19,* 6–19.

Salkovskis, P. M. (1996). The cognitive approach to anxiety: Threat beliefs, safety-seeking behaviour, and the special case of health anxiety obsessions. In P. M. Salkovskis (Ed.), *Frontiers of cognitive therapy* (pp. 48–74). New York, NY: Guilford Press.

Salkovskis, P. M. (1999). Understanding and treating obsessive–compulsive disorder. *Behaviour Research and Therapy, 37,* S29–S52.

Sauer-Zavala, S., Boswell, J. F., Gallagher, M. W., Bentley, K. H., Ametaj, A., & Barlow, D. H. (2012). The role of negative affectivity and negative reactivity to emotions in predicting outcomes in the unified protocol for the transdiagnostic treatment of emotional disorders. *Behavior Research and Therapy, 50*(9), 551–557.

Schneier, F. R., Johnson, J., Hornig, C. D., Leibowitz, M. R., & Weissman, M. M. (1992). Social phobia: Comorbidity and morbidity in an epidemiologic sample. *Archives of General Psychiatry, 49,* 282–288.

Schoenberger, N. E. (2000). Research on hypnosis as an adjunct to cognitive-behavioral psychotherapy. *International Journal of Clinical and Experimental Hypnosis, 48,* 154–169.

Schoenberger, N. E., Kirsch, I.,, Gearan, P., Montgomery, G., & Pastyrnak, S. L. (1997). Hypnotic enhancement of a cognitive-behavioral treatment for public speaking anxiety. *Behavior Therapy 28,* 127–140.

Schwartz, J. A. J., & Koenig, L. J. (1996). Response styles and negative affect among adolescents. *Cognitive Therapy and Research, 20,* 13–36.

Segal, Z. V., Williams, J. M. G., & Teasdale, J. D. (2002). *Mindfulness-based cognitive therapy for depression: A new approach to preventing relapse.* New York, NY: Guilford Press.

Segal, Z. V., Williams, J. M. G., & Teasdale, J. D. (2012). *Mindfulness-based cognitive therapy for depression: A new approach for preventing relapse* (2nd ed.). New York, NY: Guilford Press.

Segerstrom, S. C., Tsao, J. C. I., Alden, L. E., & Craske, M. G. (2000). Worry and rumination: Repetitive thought as a concomitant and predictor of negative mood. *Cognitive Therapy and Research, 24,* 671–688.

Shapiro, F. (1995). *Eye movement desensitization and reprocessing: Basic principles, protocols, and procedures.* New York, NY: Guilford.

Sharkey, L., & McNicholas, F. (2008). 'More than 100 years of silence', elective mutism: A review of the literature. *European Child and Adolescent Psychiatry, 17,* 255–263.

Shear, M. K., Cooper, A. M., Klerman, G. L., Busch, F. N., & Shapiro, T. (1993). A psychodynamic model of panic disorder. *American Journal of Psychiatry, 150,* 859–866.

Shearer, D. S., Harmon, S. C., Younger, R. D., & Brown, C. S. (2013). Specific phobia. In S. M. Stahl & B. A. Moore (Eds.) *Anxiety disorders: A guide for integrating psychopharmacology and psychotherapy* (pp. 240–259). New York, NY: Routledge.

Shedler, J. (2010). The efficacy of psychodynamic psychotherapy. *American Psychologist, 65,* 98–109.

Shih, M., Yang, Y.-H., & Koo, M. (2009). A meta-analysis of hypnosis in the treatment of depressive symptoms: A brief communication. *International Journal of Clinical and Experimental Hypnosis, 57*(4), 431–442.

Shipherd, J. C., Beck, J. G., & Ohtake, P. J. (2001). Relationships between the anxiety sensitivity index, the suffocation fear scale, and responses to CO_2 inhalation. *Journal of Anxiety Disorders, 15*(3), 247–258.

Siev, J., & Chambless, D. L. (2007). Specificity of treatment effects: Cognitive therapy and relaxation for generalized anxiety and panic disorders. *Journal of Consulting and Clinical Psychology, 75*, 513–522.

Silove, D., Marnane, C., Wagner, R., Manicavasagar, V., & Rees, S. (2010). The prevalence and correlates of adult separation anxiety disorder in an anxiety clinic. *BMC Psychiatry, 10*, 21, doi:10.1186/1471-244X-10-21

Simos, G. (2002). *Cognitive behavior therapy: A guide for the practicing clinician.* Sussex, UK: Brunner-Routledge.

Sluckin, A., Foreman, N., & Herbert, M. (1991). Behavioral treatment programmes and selectivity of speaking at followup in a sample of 25 selective mutes. *Australian Psychology, 26*, 132–137.

Smith, A. (1790/1976). *The theory of moral sentiments* (6th ed.). Indianapolis, IN: Liberty Classics.

Smith, W. (1990). Hypnosis in the treatment of anxiety. *Bulletin of the Menninger Clinic, 54*, 209–216.

Soon, C. S., Brass, M., Heinze, H. J., Haynes, J. D. (2008). Unconscious determinants of free decisions in the human brain. *Nature Neuroscience, 11*, 543–545.

Spiegel, D. (1981). Vietnam grief work using hypnosis. *American Journal of Clinical Hypnosis, 24*, 33–40.

Spiegel, D., Hunt, T., & Dondershine, H. E. (1988). Dissociation and hypnotisability in post-traumatic stress disorder. *American Journal of Psychiatry, 145*, 301–305.

Spiegel, D., & Spiegel, H. (1990). Hypnotic treatment techniques with anxiety. In Corydon D. Hammond (Ed.), *Handbook of hypnotic suggestions and metaphors* (pp. 157–158). New York, NY: W. W. Norton.

Stahl, S. M., & Moore, B. A. (2013). *Anxiety disorders: A guide for integrating psychopharmacology and psychotherapy.* New York, NY: Routledge.

Starcevic, V. (2010). *Anxiety disorders in adults: A clinical guide* (2nd ed.). New York, NY: Oxford University Press.

Stafrace, S. (1994). Hypnosis in the treatment of panic disorder with agoraphobia. *Australian Journal of Clinical Hypnosis, 22*, 73–86.

Stefano, G. B., Fricchione, G. L., Slingsby, B. T., & Benson, H. (2001). The placebo effect and relaxation response: Neural processes and their couplong to constitutive nitric oxide. *Brain Research and Brain Research Review, 35*, 1–19.

Stein, C. (1963). Clenched-fist as a hypnobehavioral procedure. *American Journal of Clinical Hypnosis, 2*, 113–119.

Stein, D. J., Ipser, J. C., & van Balkom, A. J. (2009). *Pharmacotherapy for social anxiety disorder (review)*. The Cochrane Library.

Steinhausen, H. C., & Juzi, C. (1996). Elective mutism: An analysis of 100 cases. *Journal of the American Academy of Child and Adolescent Psychiatry, 35*(5), 606–614.

Standart S., Le Couteur A (2003) The quiet child: A literature review of selective mutism. *Child Adolescent Mental Health, 8*, 154–160.

Stanton, H. E. (1997). Adoring the clenched fist technique. *Contemporary Hypnosis, 14*, 189–194.

Stickney, E. L. (1990). Island of serenity. In Corydon D. Hammond (Ed.), *Handbook of hypnotic suggestions and metaphors* (pp. 159–160). New York, NY: W. W. Norton.

Stone, B. P., Kratochwül, T. R., Sladezcek, I., & Serlin, R. C. (2002). Treatment of selective mutism: A best-evidence synthesis. *School Psychology Quarterly, 17*, 168–190.

Strick, M., Dijksterhuis, A., Bos, M. W., Sjoersma, A., van Baaren, R. B., Nordgren, L. F. (2011). A meta-analysis on unconscious thought effects. *Social Cognition, 29*, 738–762.

Stuntman, R. K., & Bliss, E. L. (1985). Posttraumatic stress disorder, hypnotisability and imagery. *American Journal of Psychiatry, 142*, 741–743.

Surman, O. (1979). Postnoxious desensitization: Some clinical notes on the combined use of hypnosis and systematic desensitization. *American Journal of Clinical Hypnosis, 22*, 54–60.

Suzuki, D. T. (1997). *Touyouteki ma mikata* (Eastern way of thinking). Tokyo: Iwanami Shoten.

Tallman, K., & Bohart, A. C. (1999). The client as a common factor: Clients as self-healers. In M. A. Hubble, B. L. Duncan, & S. D. Miller (Eds.), *The heart and soul of change: What works in therapy* (pp. 91–132). Washington, DC: American Psychological Association.

Tamminen, J., Payne, J. D., Stickgold, R., Wamsley, E. J., & Gaskell, M. G. (2010). Sleep spindle activity is associated with the integration of new memories and existing knowledge. *Journal of Neuroscience, 30*, 14356–14360.

Tatem, D. W., & Delcampo, R. L. (1995). Selective mutism in children—A structural family-therapy approach to treatment. *Contemporary Family Therapy, 17*, 177–194.

Taylor, S. (Ed.). (1999). *Anxiety sensitivity: Theory, research, and treatment of the fear of anxiety*. Mahwah, NJ: Lawrence Erlbaum.

Taylor, S. (2000). *Understanding and treating panic disorder: Cognitive-behavioral approaches*. Chichester: John Wiley & Sons, Inc.

Taylor, S. (2006). *Clinician's guide to PTSD: A cognitive-behavioral approach*. New York: Guilford Press.

Taylor, S., & Rachman, S. (1994). Stimulus estimation and overprediction of fear. *British Journal of Clinical Psychology, 33*, 173–181.

Teachman, B. A., & Woody, S. R. (2003). Automatic processing in spider phobia: Implicit fear association over the course of treatment. *Journal of Abnormal Psychology, 112*, 100–109.

Teasdale, J. D. (2004). Mindfulness-based cognitive therapy: In J. Yiend (Ed.), *Cognition, emotion and psychopathology* (pp. 270–289). Cambridge, UK: Cambridge University Press.

Teasdale, J. D., Segal, Z. V., Williams, J. M. G., Ridgeway, V., Soulsby, J., & Lau, M. (2000). Reducing risk recurrence of major depression using mindfulness-based cognitive therapy. *Journal of Consulting and Clinical Psychology, 68,* 615–623.

Telch, M. J., Cobb, A. R., & Lancaster, C. L. (2014). Agoraphobia. In J. A. J. Smits (Ed.), *The Wiley handbook of cognitive behavioral therapy volume 111.* New York, NY: John Wiley & Sons, Ltd.

Telch, M. J., Lucas, J. A., Schmidt, N. B., Hanna, H. H., LaNae, Jaimez, T., et al. (1993). Group cognitive-behavioral treatment of panic disorder. *Behavior Research and Therapy, 31,* 279–287.

Thackery, E., & Harris, M. S. (2003). *The Gale encyclopedia of mental disorders, Vol. 2.* Detroit, MI: Thomson Gale.

Treanor, M., Erisman, S. M., Salters-Pedneault., K., Roemer, L., & Orsillo, S. M. (2011). Acceptance based behavioral therapy for GAD: Effects on outcomes from three theoretical models. *Depression & Anxiety, 28*(2), 127–136.

Turner, S. M., Beidel, D. C., & Wolff, P. L. (1996). Is behavioral inhibition related to the anxiety disorders? *Clinical Psychology Review, 16,* 157–172.

Twenge, J. M., & Campbell, W. K. (2009). *The narcissism epidemic: Living in the age of entitlement.* New York, NY: Free Press.

Van Ameringen, M. A., Lane, R. M., Walker, J. R., Bowen, R. C., Chokka, P. R., Goldner, E., & Swinson, R. P. (2001). Sertraline treatment of generalized social phobia: A 20-week, double-blind, placebo-controlled study. *American Journal of Psychiatry, 158,* 275–281.

Van Apeldoorn, F. J., van Hout, W. J. P. J., Mersch, P. P., Huisman, M., & Slaap, B. R. (2008). Is a combined therapy more effective than either CBT or SSRI alone? Results of a multicenter trial on panic disorder with or without agoraphobia. *Acta Psychiatrica Scandinavica, 117,* 260–270.

Van Gaal, S., de Lange, F., & Cohen, M. X. (2012). The role consciousness in cognitive control and decision making. *Frontiers in Human Neuroscience, 6,* 1–15.

Vasey, M. W., & Dadds, M. R. (2001). An introduction to the developmental psychopathology of anxiety. In M. W. Vasey & M. R. Dadds (Eds.), *The developmental psychopathology of anxiety* (pp. 3–36). Oxford, UK: Oxford University Press.

Veale, D. (2003). Treatment of social phobia. *Advances in Psychiatric Treatment, 9,* 258–264.

Vecchio, J. L., & Kearney, C. A. (2005) Selective mutism in children: Comparison to youths with and without anxiety disorders. *Journal of Psychopathology and Behavioral Assessment, 27,* 21–37.

Velting, O. N., Setzer, N. J., & Albano, A.m. (2004). Update on and advances in assessment and cognitive-behavior treatment of anxiety disorders in children and adolescents. *Professional Psychology: Research and Practice, 35,* 42–54.

Vøllestad, J., Nielsen, M. B., & Nielsen, G. H. (2012). Mindfulness- and acceptance-based interventions for anxiety disorders: A systematic review and meta-analysis. *British Journal of Clinical Psychology, 51*, 239–260.

Wagner, U., Gais, S., Haider, H., Verleger, R., & Born, J. (2004). Sleep inspires insight. *Nature, 427*, 352–355.

Wancata, J., Fridl, M., & Friedrich, F. (2009). Social phobia: Epidemiology and health care. *Psychiatria Danubina, 21*, 520–524.

Walsh, R. (2011). Lifestyle and mental health. *American Psychologist, 66*, 579–592.

Ward, A. H., Lyubomirsky, S., Sousa, L., & Nolen-Hoeksema, S. (2003). Can't quite commit: Rumination and uncertainty. *Personality and Social Psychology Bulletin, 29*, 96–107.

Watkins, E., & Baracaia, S. (2001). Why do people ruminate in dysphoric moods? *Personality and Individual Differences, 30*, 723–734.

Watkins, E., Moulds, M., & Mackintosh, B. (2005). Comparisons between rumination and worry in a non-clinical population. *Behaviour Research and Therapy, 43*, 1577–1585.

Watkins, E. R., Teasdale, J. D., & Williams, R. M. (2000). Decentring and distraction reduce overgeneral autobiographical memory in depression. *Psychological Medicine, 30*, 911–920.

Watkins, J. G. (1971). The affect bridge: A hypnoanalytic technique. *The International Journal of Clinical and Experimental Hypnosis, XIX*, 21–27.

Watkins, J. G., & Barabasz, A. F. (2008). *Advanced hypnotherapy: Hypnodynamic techniques*. New York, NY: Routledge.

Watson, D., & Clark, L. A. (1984). Negative affectivity: The disposition to experience aversive emotional states. *Psychological Bulletin, 96*, 465–490.

Wegner, D. M. (2011). Setting free the bears: Escape from thought suppression. *American Psychologist, 66*(8), 671–680.

Weiller, E., Bisserbe, J. C., Boyer, P., Lepine, J. P., & Lecrubier, Y. (1996). Social phobia in general health care: An unrecognized undertreated disabling disorder. *British Journal of Psychiatry, 168*, 169–174.

Weissman, M. M., Bland, R. C., Canino, G. J., et al. (1997). The cross-national epidemiology of panic disorder. *Archives of General Psychiatry, 54*, 305–309.

Wells, A. (1995). Meta-cognition and worry: A cognitive model of generalized anxiety disorder. *Behavioral and Cognitive Psychotherapy, 23*, 301–320.

Wells, A. (1997). Cognitive therapy of anxiety disorders: *A practical manual and conceptual guide*. Chichester, UK: John Wiley & Sons, Ltd.

Wells, A., & Matthews, G. (1994). *Attention and emotion: A clinical perspective*. Hove, UK: Erlbaum.

Weels, A. (2000). *Emotional disorders and metacognition: Innovative cognitive therapy*. Chichester, UK: John Wiley & Sons, Ltd.

Wells, A. (1997). *Cognitive therapy for anxiety disorders: A practical manual and conceptual guide*. Chichester, UK: John Wiley & Sons, Ltd.

Wells, A., & Matthews, G. (1994). *Attention and emotion: A clinical perspective*. Hove, UK: Erlbaum.

Wells, A. & Matthews, G. (1996). Modeling cognition in emotional disorder: The S-REF model. *Behavior Research and Therapy, 32*, 867–880.

Welwood, J. (1983). *Awakening the heart: East/West approaches to psychotherapy and the healing relationship.* Boulder, CO: Shambhala.

Wenger, D. M. (1994). Ironic processes of mental control. *Psychological Review, 101*, 34–52.

Wenzlaff, R. M. (2005). Seeking solace but finding despair: The persistence of intrusive thoughts in depression. In D. A. Clark (Eds.), *Intrusive thoughts in clinical disorders: Theory, research, and treatment* (pp. 54–85). New York, NY: Guilford.

Whisman, M. A., & Beach, S. R. H. (2010). Models for understanding interpersonal processes and relationships in anxiety disorders. In J. G. Beck (Ed.), *Interpersonal processes in the anxiety disorders: Implications for understanding psychopathology and treatment* (pp. 9–35). Washington, DC: American Psychological Association.

White, K., & Barlow, D. H. (2002). Panic disorder and agoraphobia. In D. H. Barlow (Ed.), *Anxiety and its disorders: The nature and treatment of anxiety and panic* (2nd ed., pp. 328–379). New York, NY: Guilford Press.

Wiederhold, B. K., & Wiederhold, M. D. (2005). *Virtual reality therapy for anxiety disorders: Advances in evaluation and treatment.* Washington, DC: American Psychological Association.

Wilber, K. (2000). *Integral psychotherapy: Consciousness, spirit, psychology, therapy.* Boston, MA: Shambhala.

Williams, J. M. G., Watts, F. N., MacLeod, C., & Mathews, A. (1997). *Cognitive psychology and emotional disorders* (2nd ed.). Chichester, UK: Wiley.

Wilson. R. (2009). *Don't panic: Taking control of anxiety attacks* (3rd ed.). New York, NY: Harper.

Wilson, T. D., Lindsey, S., & Schooler, T. Y. (2000). A model of dual attitudes. *Psychological Review, 107*, 101–126.

Woldt, A. L., & Toman, S. M. (Eds.) (2005). *Gestalt therapy: History, theory, and practice.* Thousand Oaks, CA: Sage.

Wolfe, B. E. (2005). *Understanding and treating anxiety disorders: An integrative approach to healing the wounded self.* Washington, DC: American Psychological Association.

Wolfe, B. E. (2006). An integrative perspective on the anxiety disorders. In G. Stricker & J. Gold (Ed.), *A casebook of psychotherapy integration* (pp. 65–77). Washington, DC: American Psychological Association.

Wolfe, B. E., & Sigl, P. (1998). Experiential psychotherapy of the anxiety disorders. In L. S. Greenberg, J. C. Watson, & G. Lietaer (Eds.), *Handbook of experiential psychotherapy* (pp. 272–294). New York, NY: Guilford Press.

Wolgast, M., Lundh, L., & Viborg, G. (2011). Cognitive reappraisal and acceptance: An experimental comparison of two emotion regulation strategies. *Behavior Research & Therapy, 49*, 858–866.

Wolitzky-Taylor, K. B., Horowitz, J. D., Powers, M. B., & Telch, M. J. (2008). Psycholgical approaches in the treatment of specific phobias: A meta-analysis. *Clinical Psychology Review, 28,* 1021–1037.

Wolpe, J. (1958). *Psychotherapy by reciprocal inhibition.* Stanford, CA: Stanford University Press.

Wolpe, J. (1990). *The practice of behavior therapy* (4th ed.). New York, NY: Pergamon Press.

Wolpe, J., & Lazarus, A. A. (1966). *Behavior therapy techniques.* New York, NY: Pergamon Press.

Wolitzky-Taylor, K. B., Horowitz, J. D., Powers, M. B., & Telch, M. J. (2008). Psychological approaches in the treatment of specific phobias: A meta-analysis. *Clinical Psychology Review, 28*(6), 1021–1037.

Wood, A. M., Joseph, S., & Linley, P. A. (2007). Coping style as a psychological resource of grateful people. *Journal of Social and Clinical Psychology, 26,* 1108–1125.

Wood, A. M., Joseph, S., Lloyd, J., & Atkins, S. (2009). Gratitude influence sleep through the mechanism of pre-sleep cognitions. *Journal of Psychosomatic Research, 66,* 43–48.

Wood, A. M., Joseph, S., & Maltby (2009). Gratitude predicts psychological well-being above the Big Five facets. *Personality and Individual Differences, 45,* 655–660.

Woodman, C. L., Noyes, R., Black, D. W., Schlosser, S., & Yagla, S. J. (1999). A 5-year follow-up study of generalized anxiety disorder and panic disorder. *Journal of Nervous and Mental Disease, 187,* 3–9.

Wright, H. H., Miller, M. D., Cook, & Littmann, J. R. (1985). Early identification and intervention with children who refuse to speak. *Journal of American Academy of Child and Adolescent Psychiatry, 24,* 739–746.

Yapko, M. D. (1992). *Hypnosis and the treatment of depressions: Strategies for change.* New York, NY: Brunner/Mazel.

Yapko, M. D. (2003). *Trancework: An introduction to the practice of clinical hypnosis* (3rd ed.). New York, NY: Brunner/Routledge.

Yapko, M. A. (2012). *Trancework: An introduction to the practice of clinical hypnosis* (4th ed.). New York, NY: Routledge.

Young, J. (1990). Cognitive therapy for personality disorders: A schema-focused approach. Sarasota, FL: Professional Resource Exchange, Inc.

Zinbarg, R. R., Craske, M. G., & Barlow, D. H. (2006). *Mastery of your anxiety and worry (therapist guide)* (2nd ed.). New York, NY: Oxford University Press.

Index